Finding God in the Dark

**John J. Pungente, SJ
and Monty Williams, SJ**

Finding God in the Dark

Taking the Spiritual Exercises of
St. Ignatius to the Movies

Foreword by John English, SJ

NOVALIS   Pauline
               BOOKS & MEDIA

© 2004 Novalis, Saint Paul University, Ottawa, Canada
"P" and PAULINE are registered trademarks of the Daughters of St. Paul

Cover design: Richard Proulx
Cover image: Jupiter Images
Layout: Christiane Lemire and Francine Petitclerc

Business Office:
Novalis
49 Front Street East, 2nd Floor
Toronto, Ontario, Canada
M5E 1B3

Phone: 1-877-702-7773 or (416) 363-3303
Fax: 1-877-702-7775 or (416) 363-9409
E-mail: cservice@novalis.ca
www.novalis.ca

Library and Archives of Canada Cataloguing in Publication

Pungente, John J.
        Finding God in the dark: the spiritual exercices of St. Ignatius
go to the movies/John J. Pungente and Monty Williams; foreword by
John English.

ISBN: 2-89507-519-0

1. Ignatius, of Loyola, Saint, 1491–1556.   Exercitia spiritualia.
2. Spiritual exercices. 3. Motion pictures–Miscellanea.   I. Williams,
Monty. II. Title.

BX2179.L8P85 2004   242   C2004-904286-6

Published in the United States by:
Pauline Books & Media
50 St. Pauls Avenue
Boston, Massachusetts, U.S.A. 02130-3491

Phone: 617-522-8911
Fax: 617-541-9805
E-mail: customerservice@pauline.org
www.pauline.org

ISBN: 0-8198-2680-4 (U.S.A.)

Library of Congress Cataloging-in-Publication Data is on file at the Library of Congress, U.S.A.

Printed in Canada.

Scripture quotations are from the Revised Standard Version of the Bible, Oxford: Oxford University Press. Translations of the Spiritual Exercises are from the following works: George E. Ganss SJ, *The Spiritual Exercises of St. Ignatius: A Translation and Commentary* (St. Louis: The Institute of Jesuit Sources, 1992); Louis E. Puhl SJ, *The Spiritual Exercises of St. Ignatius: Based on Studies in the Language of the Autograph* (Chicago: Loyola Press, 1997); other translations by Monty Williams SJ.

We acknowledge the financial support of the Government of Canada through the Book Publishing Industry Development Program (BPIDP) for our publishing activities.

5 4 3 2 1   08 07 06 05 04

For our mothers and fathers, in thanksgiving:
Mary Pungente, John A. Pungente
Lyma Dorothy Williams, Joseph Lewis Williams

Thanks to:
Barry Alford; Neil Anderson; Kevin Burns; Sasha and Elijah Craig; Sarah Crawford;
Elaine Frigo; John Gahan, SJ; Paul Gratton; Ron Mercier, SJ; Gail Noble;
Mike Rosinski, SJ; Joe Schner, SJ; Phil Shano, SJ

In memory of John English, SJ
1924–2004

The day will come when,
after harnessing space, the winds, the tides, and gravitation,
we shall harness for God the energies of love.
And on that day, for the second time in the history of the world,
we shall have discovered fire.

Pierre Teilhard de Chardin, SJ

Contents

Foreword

It is an honour to write the Foreword to this book. That privilege has nothing to do with self-esteem – that prime disorder of human nature noted in the Spiritual Exercises of St. Ignatius. Rather, it has to do with tradition. Tradition is a handing on and a handing over of the gift of the Spirit, a gift that was handed over to the giver by one who came before, and so on back through the ages.

I was given the gift of the Exercises of St. Ignatius when I entered the Society of Jesus in the Upper Canada Province in 1949. Those Exercises have shaped my life. As a Novice Master I gave them to one generation of young Jesuits in the turbulent years of the late 1960s and early 1970s. Since then I have given them to a now large but forgotten number of other Jesuits, religious men and women, and lay people. In giving them I have made them my own. I have prayed them, prayed about them, taught them, written about them and presented them in ways that I have always considered essential for our times.

In the beginning I was convinced that these Exercises were more effective if they were given individually rather than preached to groups, which was the custom that was passed down to me. The individually directed retreat was, to my way of thinking, more personal. It allowed for the adaptation that St. Ignatius encouraged; the retreatant was seen as one of a kind, and discovered in a unique way God's personal love for him or her.

That new way of presenting the Exercises took off and became, for most of the Christian world, the norm for the latter part of the 20th century. But the Spirit was not satisfied with only that. Even though we are individuals and each of us has a unique relationship with God, we are communal beings. We live in community – in communities – and these communities mediate God's presence to us. So the next big question for me was how to give the Exercises in a way that would foster that integral communal dimension of our lives. Creating small communities whose individual and communal lives were shaped by communal discernment became my next project. My creative energies over the last quarter century were spent promoting and fostering Christian life communities rooted in Ignatian spirituality.

In praying and discerning with these communities, the broader dimension of community – the relationship with all of creation, and specifically with the ecological dimension of our human existence – began to impress itself on me. To be human is to realize that we, all of us together, are in a dynamic, fluid relationship with each other and with all of creation. The spiritual implications of this relationship have shaped my life.

These three areas of my work have, thanks be to God, been sown in good soil. They have taken root and have thrived, and I feel that I have handed on the gift of the Spirit – in all of its creative energies – that has been given to me.

But it has grieved me that the gift of the Exercises has been restricted to those who have been fortunate to have good spiritual directors and good spiritual direction. I have always been conscious of the evangelical passion of St. Ignatius. He preached the good news to all he met – the poor, the rich, the learned and the simple – on street corners, in classes, around the dinner table, at the pulpit. My concern has always been finding ways to emulate that high ideal in our contemporary world, with its distrust of religion, its growing secularism, and its equally strong cry for spiritual sustenance in a world overwhelmed by destructive forces.

It is out of this concern that I welcome this present work by my fellow Canadian Jesuits John Pungente and Monty Williams. They belong to the generation after me. Both were my tertians (tertianship is the final intensive year of Jesuit training) and Monty Williams was also my novice from 1967 to 1969. In tertianship and novitiate, Jesuits are in formation. They do the full exercises and also have classes on them.

Since those days of formation, John has distinguished himself throughout the world in media literacy; Monty has been giving retreats and conferences in spiritual direction as well as writing about it for about 25 years. They both bring to their work a passion for contemporary culture and analysis.

What they have done in this book is remarkable. They have had the insight that cinema today is the form of contemporary church that is attentive to the concerns of a postmodern world, and they have laid out the way church – as a community seeking, embracing and living out of the creative Spirit of God – functions in the world today.

In this new but obvious paradigm, when you think about it, they find the language of the Exercises today, which presents the way God communicates a merciful love that can heal and transform each of us. Since the Exercises also offer us a mode of discerning how to live most humanely and lovingly in the world, it is no surprise that we find in this book that same Ignatian mode of discernment.

The heart of Ignatian spirituality is the overwhelming, compassionate mercy of God for us and for all of creation: it heals us and invites us to labour with those other creative forces and energies and people throughout history. It creates community that extends beyond the personal to the social, communal, ecological – even, dare I say, cosmic – where life is more valued than death, love overcomes hatred, and alienation is no more. Even though that process will not be completed in our lifetimes, still we acknowledge our common heritage and our common goal.

I have passed on to many what was given to me. I am grateful to John and Monty for accepting what was given to them, and for giving it over – transformed but yet the same – to others. This is the gift of life. I hope that whoever reads this book receives this gift. A blessing on you, and on that journey.

John English, SJ
May 2004

10

Introduction

A Jesuit Dinner Party

This book was first conceived, in typical Jesuit fashion, at a dinner party one night. A group of English-Canadian Jesuits meets several times a year, over drinks and a meal, to discuss the state of Jesuits today and to support each other without falling into that trendy title of a support group. Conversation is frank, funny, and wide-ranging. One night in September 2002, the conversation got around to the failure of traditional retreat houses to attract the growing population of the spiritually hungry. It was not as if those retreat houses did not have some of the expertise of contemporary spiritual practitioners, as well as those normally associated with traditional Christian spiritual direction. They could not be accused of irrelevance. In fact, on the contrary, they might be accused of selling out those ways of becoming spiritually literate that have been around for hundreds of years. The question was how to make that form of literacy available today. Retreats are quite expensive things, and subsidies from religious orders are no longer a viable option to support institutions with diminishing sources of income. A second concern was the inability to find good spiritual directors. The third was that even if it was possible to contact a spiritual director, committing the time in today's busy world was often a very real problem. The hunger for direction was there: what was not there was a simple, inexpensive way of presenting valid spirituality and grounded spiritual practice in an accessible way to those who, because of constraints of time and economy, as well as a suspicion of the complicit use of spirituality by religious institutions, were unable to understand and develop their spiritual life.

We were two of the Jesuits at that dinner party. John Pungente is a world-famous authority on media literacy; Monty Williams, besides being interested in contemporary culture and critical analysis, is on staff at Regis College, University of Toronto, and at Loyola Retreat House in Guelph – a place that has an established reputation for solid, creative work on spirituality and, in particular, on the Spiritual Exercises of St. Ignatius of Loyola. Why not, we wondered, combine our two interests? To be sure, work had already been done on religious themes and images in film. Studies are available on the spirituality of such classic and somewhat esoteric European directors as Bergman, Bresson, Olmo and Kieslowski. But what about popular films? As this Introduction will show, film is profoundly spiritual. And so, from these two Jesuits comes this book. It uses popular films to engage the reader on a significantly personal and transformative journey through the Spiritual Exercises of St. Ignatius. The Exercises, since their establishment in the first half of the sixteenth century, have formed the spiritual fabric of the Society of Jesus. They have influenced founders of other religious orders, statesmen, artists, writers, educators, philosophers, not a few saints, and countless millions of women and men, all of whom have discovered in them a personal, passionate, and intimate spirituality that transformed their lives and their culture.

Who Is Ignatius?

To understand the Exercises, it is helpful to know something of the man who created them and something about the spirituality of the Jesuit tradition, which has kept alive those Exercises for the last 450 years. Ignatius of Loyola was born of minor Basque aristocracy in about 1492. Like the nobility of his time, he was interested in maintaining his position in the world by promoting himself through honour and glory. He was vain, venal, and charismatically aggressive, obsessed with the secular ideals of courtly love and chivalry. The world he sought to promote came crashing down at Pampalona, Spain (now famous for the running of the bulls) in 1521, when he was badly wounded and had to return to Loyola for a long period of enforced recuperation. There he distracted himself by reading both the lives of the saints and the worldly romances of chivalric exploits and love. He discovered that both stirred his heart to perform deeds of dramatic action. But he also noticed that the excitement he felt while reflecting on the lives of the saints remained with him, while the pleasure he felt reading the romances soon went away, leaving him desolate. He decided to follow the path of the saints rather than seek earthly glory.

There began a long period of the purification of his desires. In 1522, he found himself in a cave at Manresa, where he spent the next several months in a regime of extreme asceticism, alternating between severe depression, scruples, thoughts of suicide, and amazing mystical experiences. He decided to use his religious experience there – upon which the Spiritual Exercises as we know them today are based – to help

others. Indeed, Ignatius used these Exercises to direct others, and in 1540, with some of these people formed the Society of Jesus, or as we know them today, the Jesuits. The Jesuits have their charism from that direct encounter with God that Ignatius discovered is possible for all. For St. Ignatius and in Jesuit spirituality, God is in constant and intimate dialogue with us; we experience this in our daily lives as feelings of union with or disconnection from God. It is only when we reflect on these movements within ourselves that we discover, for each one of us, that language of love.

The Exercises and Film

The Spiritual Exercises that you are holding in your hands right now, which have been tested for over 400 years, are a way to discover God's unique love for each of us and to learn that language of love with which God speaks to us. We learn this language by looking at our own lives and at the forces that shape them.

These Exercises are divided into what has traditionally been called Four Weeks. But Ignatius did not expect the person making the Exercises to complete them in a calendar month. They are meant to be adapted, as we have done here, to accommodate your personal situation. Ignatius writes, "It is not meant that each week should necessarily consist of seven or eight days…. It may be necessary…at times to shorten the Week, and at others to lengthen it" (#4). What is crucial is not fitting into a specific time frame, but having enough time to get "the fruit that is proper to the matter assigned" (#4). For Ignatius, the matter assigned in these Exercises is divided into four parts. The first part invites us to discover God's love for each one of us by looking at those areas of our lives where we have not experienced love. That week ends when we experience a personal liberation from the forces that make us see ourselves as unlovable and unloving. The second part channels those liberated energies into a personal relationship with Christ, who manifests the Compassionate Mercy of God. The third part invites us to accompany that love in the face of suffering and death; the fourth part celebrates the triumph of God's love over the forces of destruction in the world and invites us to share in that triumph by working together to transform the world through acts of love.

You need to work through the weeks in order, since one week builds on the next, and within each week, one Exercise builds on the one preceding it. At the beginning of each week, material is given to prepare you to enter the Week; at the end, material is again given to help you see what has happened to you during that Week. At the end of the Four Weeks in this book, a final chapter ties together the whole journey. By that time you will have experienced the complete Spiritual Exercises of St. Ignatius using the contemplative vehicle of film.

Underlying each section is the constant mercy of God. The weeks elaborate on this basic attitude of God to us. The First Week contains the theme of us as loved sinners. The Exercises here help us get in touch with the fact that God loves us even as we sin and desires to free us from the entrapment and illusions of sin. Within the material of the First Week is an eight-day retreat on the Beatitudes, which carries us through a process of liberation to joyful service. The theme in the Second Week is one of growing intimacy with Christ as the embodiment of the Father's mercy. The Third Week deals with the passion Christ has for his God, which allows Christ, and us, to endure the passion and destruction common to all humankind without falling into despair. In the Fourth Week we experience the joy of Christ's resurrection and our entry into it, which allows us to become manifestations of God's mercy to all.

Because this book presents the Spiritual Exercises of St. Ignatius of Loyola using the medium of film, it is almost impossible to do the full exercises in 30 days. They can be done over three months, or six months, or a year. It is a wonderful way to integrate spiritual growth into your daily life, at home or in a place where you gather with others. It presents the significance of the Exercises using contemporary popular film, where watching the film becomes the act of contemplative prayer.

The book is designed to be used by individuals or groups, at home or in retreat, pastoral, academic or parish settings. Such a broad range of applications is possible because the Exercises of Ignatius focus on the imagination as embodying spirituality. Imagination does not exist in particular contexts. It is the context out of which we live our lives and the context in which the Incarnation occurs – that is, where God encounters us, communicates with us, and transforms us.

Our Imagined Worlds

St. Ignatius had the insight that we all live in imagined worlds, and that our imagination constructs the worlds in which we live using our experiences, our lived contexts, our hopes, our pains, and our joys. In effect, we live in a highly selective world, and this world defines what is possible for us. It also defines how we see ourselves, how we interact with others and the contexts in which we find ourselves.

It is now a postmodern cliché that we are shaped by the media. But humans have always been shaped by the media of their day: the preachers in a predominantly oral culture; the frescos and paintings of religious themes in a visual culture; the spiritual dramas and novels of a literate culture. Each of these media interacted with the imaginations of their times to create a living faith, effect a conversion, or deepen people's relationship with God.

Today, the media that shape us are film and television. Television uses the sensibilities of a culture formed by film. Film proposes to us forms of the world and ethical ways of living in the world it creates. When we watch a film, we are not just being entertained; we are being formed and shaped. We are exposing ourselves to narratives that shape what is possible, and we live out of those possibilities.

Ignatian prayer uses the imagination to present to us our world, and allows us to open ourselves to the dynamic presence of God in the world. For St. Ignatius, God desires to be fully present to us and in us, and the interface between us and God occurs in the imagination during prayer. In this personal and sacred space of encounter, the energies of our lives are integrated with the divine energies of God. It is not that we are doing all the creating, or that God is doing all the creating. The creation of the world we contemplate is done by God and us working together. Later on in this book you will find the ground rules for that mutual co-operation: self-revelation, self-understanding, and communication. How they work becomes clear as you enter into the Exercises. Film is the contemporary way of entering into this mutual self-revelation of us and God; using film merely brings Ignatius' basic insight of the power of the imagination to our present world.

This book presents the basic insight that God's own medium is the Christ, and the Christ incarnates the divine mercy of God in the world. The medium is not only the message and the massage; here it becomes, even more radically, the dynamics of the

... We become the living word
...templa-

...ook, we
...d in the
...ging we
... by con-
...the spiri-
... love, to

...ant to be
...rmed, we
...the genre,
...act us, we
are curious. But when we look more closely at our reasons, we see that they are rooted in the basic experiences of being human and that those basic experiences are themselves expressions of the human desire for self-transcendence. The desire to be entertained and distracted comes from the attempt to escape boredom, that entrapment within oneself. To be informed comes from the quest for knowledge and truth. To be a fan of a star is to engage in a form of identification through idealization that ritualizes our own religious longings for self-awareness. Genre movies appeal to basic drives within us. Detective flicks call upon our innate desire for order; horror movies allow us to face the fears of unknown powers that can destroy us; love stories affirm the power of relationships to maintain and foster identity. And if we go to the movies to be with friends, then we see the cinema as a place for celebrating community. Finally, those who go to the cinema because of work are asked, if they are critics, to be creative; if ushers,

to be welcoming; if projectionists, to be attentive and responsible. If we fill such roles in some way when we go to the movies, we are exercising, whether consciously or not, a religious sensibility, which engages us in the rituals of self-transcendence.

Cinema is contemporary church. Beyond the postmodern axiom that image is reality – that what we see on the screen is God inasmuch as it creates and defines what is real for us – the cinema has taken on for most of our culture the effects and resources of religious worship. This is not surprising. The earliest forms of drama were religious in nature; reading originated in spirituality; visual representation was, and is (considering censorship) conscribed by the politics of the holy; and the imagination, as Samuel Coleridge defined it and as William Blake has etched on our awareness, is the divine in human form. The films we see, from the most elevated and profound to the most exploitative and banal, all share those manifestations of the divine.

Sacred Space

Picture yourself in a movie theatre. Literally, spiritually, and metaphorically. The architecture of the theatre is ecclesial in nature. It is designed for a religious ceremony so that we can be both individual and yet community. We sit in a sacred space differentiated from our everyday world by its manipulation of space and time. At the movies, it is neither day nor night. The attendant darkness is divorced from time of day or season of the year. It is its own time. What time occurs is determined by what is enacted in front of our eyes. Both the context and what we are there to see are technically designed to engage and focus all our senses in a deliberately selective manner. That engagement is not passive.

A bright light shines through a moving strip of celluloid, projecting onto a screen a series of static images which, in their superimposition, give the illusion of movement. The mind creatively transforms that illusion into a semblance of reality, and the individual takes on the critical task of evaluating the commitment he or she will make in accepting what is imagined as real. Realism is not reality. It is a cultural convention. Thus the audience spontaneously determines the level of allegorical meaning to be attached to what is being presented. Indeed, political censorship often revolves around the question of allegory, where one thing is taken to represent something else. But beyond that issue of interpretation is the broader question of how what is seen to be presented is created: production values, plot, characters, techniques used to depict the conventions of reality that are acceptable to an audience. The process by which the industry presents a product is the same as the process by which the audience translates into a product the raw data it is given.

Only then do questions of engagement and alienation occupy the audience. Both the process and the questions are profoundly spiritual in nature. The process is one of creativity; the questions of engagement are about the nature of contemplation and, in uniquely Ignatian terms, about contemplation in action. What we are looking at here is the broader notion of media literacy. Media literacy is expertise in reading and understanding media – which today includes television, cinema, and the Internet – based on the premise that the media are not transparent instruments that transmit objective messages from sender to receiver. Rather, each instrument is shaped by both sender and receiver, and manipulates the data it processes. Thus the evening TV news has been carefully tailored for its audience – including

15

attention span and demographics –according to the ideologies of the networks that broadcast it. The technology of television determines what is shown and how it is shown. Media literacy teaches that what is presented is not objectively and immediately real. What is shown, how it is shown, what is received and how it is received are all products of the creative imagination.

Spiritual Literacy

When God communicates with us, the same dynamics of the imagination are employed. Rawly put, media literacy is spiritual literacy; this book contains a series of exercises to make people spiritually literate by developing their media literacy. The medium in question is God's self-communication to us, in what the theology of St. John calls "the Word-made-Flesh," through the workings of the imagination. God is creative; the imagination is creative; and we are creative. In spiritual literacy, these creativities fuse in the act of contemplation.

Illiteracy, on the other hand, has a linear concept of time and a sense of inevitability. The sequence of the celluloid images admits no deviation. Its inevitability leads to a tragic view of life. What is recorded cannot be changed. This is a monolithic reading of film, of narrative, and of life. Film, though it advances, simply does not operate in this way. Flashback, simultaneity, cross-cutting, reversals, overlays, changes in perspective, tempo, lighting, tone – all create a sense of multiplicity that allows for an understanding and imagining of a God who is not caught up by a Greek chronos, by inevitability, and by tragedy, but rather allows for variation, change, the carnavalesque, all that seems to some like chaos. To read the pattern in chaos, to see chaos as part of a bigger pattern, is spiritual literacy. The journey

from a monolithic view of life – regarded as natural and then, by extension, divinely ordered – requires exposure to polyvalent forms of difference. The dialogue with "otherness" requires not just a suspension of disbelief in the realism of what is other, it presupposes an ability to be present to the other in a common ground that extends beyond what has been accepted as normal. We begin to discover that we are more than who or what we think we are. That pilgrim journey into the unknown is facilitated by the films we see. We observe and reflect upon the actions and choices of the characters that attract our attention, and on the worlds in which they find themselves. We also reflect upon the way those characters and worlds are presented to us. Out of the encounter with what we contemplate, we fashion our lives and their contexts. Such contemplation is spiritual literacy.

This literacy is not a spectator sport, but a commitment. It is engaged with and defined by what it sees. Even without conscious acknowledgment, that awareness is changed by what it sees. The exposure to different films – with their different plots, techniques, rhythms, forms of narrativity and cultural sensitivities – frees an audience's perspective and imagination. This literacy is an engagement with the world common to those on a spiritual path.

What Is Contemplation?

But how does this work? Watching a film is an act of contemplation. In contemplation, you open yourself to what you contemplate, just as what you contemplate opens itself to you. In that encounter, both are changed. In Ignatian contemplation, you take a scripture passage and enter into the action. There are levels of involvement here as there are in watching a film. You can be a spectator – an enormous involvement because you attribute unity and coherence to what you are watching. A deeper level is possible when you get emotionally involved and become part of the action. At an even deeper level, you can be so moved that the experience is visceral and transformative. In all of these levels, the creative energies of the imagination are engaging the whole person, which is different from fantasy or daydreaming, where there is limited or superficial involvement. In contemplative prayer, intentionality is important. We desire to make contact with God; in prayer, God also desires to make contact with us. In that prayer, human creativity meets divine creativity through the imagination. When one uses film as prayer, the same thing happens.

In that act of mutual presence, the viewer experiences a story that explores possibilities within a defined context and embodies values in actions and choices. This occurs in the content of the film and in the way that content has been formulated technically. Editing, camera angle, lighting, sound, even the stock used all contribute to an overall sensation which, though spontaneous, has been mediated by a creative process. A person watching has instinctive reactions to what is being presented, which are experienced as feelings. In watching a film, we are present to a depiction of certain values that reinforce, erode or challenge our value systems. In contemplation, we are attuned to our imagination; we resonate with or come into conflict with what we value. As a result, we enter a state of either consolation or desolation.

Consolation and Desolation

These Ignatian terms need explanation. In the Spiritual Exercises of St. Ignatius, the terms are used in a nuanced way. Those who delight in selfishness experience consolation when they get the opportunity to live selfishly. But those who are trying to be free from their selfishness experience desolation as they struggle against those habits that give pleasure but are not liberating. The terms are used in this way for people oriented towards their own interests. They are used differently, however, for those people whose orientation is away from selfishness and towards any form of self-transcendence, such as care for others and the betterment of the community. One experiences consolation when one moves to the good and to the greater good, but desolation when one rejects the greater good. Consolation and desolation are not feelings. They are indicators of the direction in which we are pointed based on our underlying attitude. If we are basically selfish, looking at the greater good causes desolation; if we are basically caring, then looking at the greater good causes consolation. In spiritual direction, a good director will first allow us to find out who we are, and then to help us see which direction we are going in, and help us figure out the next step to take on the path.

A Liturgical Act

So when we watch a film, what we feel depends on our basic commitment. The film shows us who we are. This is a profoundly spiritual act, but going to a movie is also a liturgical act. Going to the cinema is public prayer; watching a DVD or a video with friends or alone can be communal or private prayer. That prayer is an encounter with an "otherness" that helps us define ourselves. We define ourselves through acts of the imagination. Film is a product of that imagination. Today, life is often mistakenly separated from the imagination. Some authorities denigrate imagination by defining it in culturally aesthetic terms. What they are doing is setting "life" as an absolute value, knowing that in controlling the experiences of life, they restrict what is "real" to what happens. But the contemplative act – whether watching a film or praying – fuses imagination and life. What happens is only one version of what is real, of what is possible. Film explores those possibilities and allows us to explore imaginatively our possibilities in the world. As in prayer, that engagement occurs in a context that is secure enough for us to become vulnerable so that we may engage with imagination. We do not just hand ourselves over to the film to imprint itself upon our awareness, just as we do not simply hand ourselves over to prayer. Both are relationships, and the communication is mediated by our imagination.

For Ignatius, God is not separate from us. A constant dialogue has been going on between God and us all through our lives and all through creation and human history. For God, and for us, creation is not a fixed, self-enclosed entity. What we experience as creation is the ongoing process of God creating. Creation is not complete; for the Christian, creation is open and incomplete and finds its integrity beyond itself in God. Sin, in whatever form it takes, is alienation from God. Sin seeks to find its integrity without God. Transcendence is going beyond self-enclosure, not into nothingness but into dialogue with God that results in an ever-more inclusive relationship with God. Within human history, that dialogue is symbolized in the holy people of the times, then through the Christ and through the gift of his Spirit in each of our lives and in our world.

When we enter into contemplative prayer and find our imaginations enacting the drama of a scriptural passage, is this just a willed projection of our desires and fears? Sometimes it can be that. But in moments of true prayer, we find ourselves carried out of ourselves into places of surprise or to insights that we could not have imagined or created by ourselves.

What happens then is that the history, the concerns, and the energies of our lives become the material and the media God uses for self-expression.

But just as there is within each of us that basic desire to be one with God and within God to be one with us, there is within us a selfishness that does not desire self-transcendence. Each of us, without exception, is trapped in encompassing forms of destruction that distort human freedom and seek to frustrate the human desire to love and be creative and to create community. Often, knowingly or unknowingly, we participate in them. Sometimes our institutions – religious, cultural, or juridical – destroy the innocent, the marginalized, or those without power or voice.

In those contexts we are asked to align ourselves with the good, to overcome our selfishness, and to be creative in transforming the world. But before we can do that, we need to understand who we are and what is possible for us. Otherwise we contribute to the patterns of destruction out of ignorance or a self-will that deludes itself that it is working for the good.

Seeing Ourselves

We cannot step out of ourselves or out of the creation to make some sort of objective judgment about the situations in which we find ourselves. What we can do is enter into the dialogue with the One who makes creation. That dialogue occurs in the contemplative mode, which is where film becomes significant. With film we get the opportunity to see ourselves in two basic ways.

First, in film we are shown representations of life that interact with our horizons of consciousness. We begin with what we know; then there is what we know we do not know; next is what we do not want to know; and beyond that is what we do not know we do not know.

In film, more than any other medium, we are in touch with that diversity; through that contact we discover that our world extends beyond our immediate concerns and interests.

Second, the films we watch stir up in us the basic opposition of consolation and desolation. These two modes of relationship reveal to us where, and how, we are situated in our path to self-transcendence when we approach film as a contemplative act. For example, the film *Apocalypse Now* can bring us face to face with the levels of self-deception – personal, political, military, religious, and cultural – endemic in our society. Even the exuberant self-conscious indulgence of the film's production values reveal a fascinated disgust with evil that indicates a complicit entrapment with its subject. The film displays a clarity of reality that is both thrilling and sobering. It challenges us to examine the ways in which each of us copes with the chaos of a postmodern world. It shows us the broken myths by which we might try to make sense of, or control, that world. It brings us to a felt experience of entrapment in that world. How we spontaneously respond to that felt sense reveals to us where we are in regards to that entrapment. There may be the consolation that the truth of the world is revealed, that its lies have been exposed. There may be desolation if one sees the human effort as all that is possible in such a world.

Here it might be helpful to look at one of the reasons that St. Ignatius says we experience desolation. He holds that "God wishes to give us a true knowledge and understanding of ourselves so that we may have an intimate perception of the fact that it is not within our power to acquire or attain great devotion, intense love…or any other spiritual consolation" (#322). A film such as *Apocalypse Now* forces us to examine the limitations of trying to transform the world by purely human means.

The risk that God takes with us is to allow us to experience starkly the destructive consequences of the disorder of creation. Our response can be despair if we lose our sense of that larger context in which we live. God is merciful. God knows and loves us better than we know or love ourselves. God knows our basic nature is for union with God, and in that union for a life-giving mutual relationship. When we come to the limits of human possibility we discover the compassionate presence of a God who, in and through creation, maintains and supports our basic sense of life without denying us our freedom to try to destroy ourselves. If we can enter into our unredeemed history and face the disorder in our personal lives, the disorder in our family history, those in our societies and cultures, we discover the abiding presence of a divine Mystery whose creativity is to maintain our life and to transform the disorder of history into a new creation. It is in and through creation that creation is transformed. In the mysticism of St. Ignatius, which we share as we do the Spiritual Exercises, God enters creation and we discover God by our full participation in creation.

Participating in Creation

There are levels to this participation. Although we are part of creation, we can live as if we were separate from creation, or we can dominate creation, or we can live our lives as a purely unspiritual manifestation in creation. But we can go beyond these three levels. We can acknowledge the conflicting forces of good and evil in creation, and enter into the critical task of discerning good from evil and into the creative task of transforming evil into good. To perform these last three works we need to discover how we are individually structured: that is, how God communicates with us and the ways in which we personally need God's help to become truly creative. We also need to know the traps we are prone to fall into that reinforce our narcissism and how to get the help we need to avoid those traps.

This is where film is invaluable. God communicates through our imagination, and in the exercise of our imagination we learn the language and the grammar of that communication. Coleridge says in his *Biographia Literaria* that human imagination incarnates the Divine creativity. Moreover, he would claim that as we perceive from our imaginations – or, as William Blake would put it, "I see through my eye, not with my eye" – the act of perception is essentially creative. Everything that is a human construct is a product of the imagination, and so manifests some trace of the divine creativity. Art raises that level of creative awareness to a self-conscious activity, and film combines the diverse manifestations of human creativity in sound, image, drama, and community in the most flexible and fluid ways to offer the most comprehensive shapings of space and time available to human consciousness. When we watch a film attentively, we participate in a form of contemplation that allows us to experience the imagination fully engaged in creating. We are not accustomed to thinking about it this way, but it is prayer.

There is a sentimental way of thinking about prayer: as an escape from the world or as a way of attaining God's unquestioning acceptance through affirming our own sense of self-identity. In effect, prayer gives us an entry into God's love. That love seeks out the damaged in creation – including us – to repair, console, and transform. Inasmuch as we participate in that love, we too are carried into the pain of the world and past the illusions of ourselves that

contribute to the pain of the world. We become present to the source of creativity. By bringing our own creativity into a mutual engagement, we co-operate with God in showing compassionate mercy to the people and situations in our lives.

That engagement manifests itself in the act of contemplation. We contemplate God contemplating us. We can use Scripture or we can use film. In our culture today, the Scriptures of the Old and New Testament are venerated as classic documents that have helped shape our institutions. But they no longer give access to our spiritual myths and identity as they once did. It is not just the secularism of the times that has devalued them, or the ways that they have been used to justify destructive religious perspectives that have rendered their import suspect. The easy and present accessibility of multicultural spiritual traditions has relativized their importance. What has replaced them in the postmodern imagination is film.

Film represents the collective cultural unconscious of our time, and offers us a creative product that enters into a self-conscious dialogue with our personal stories and interests. That cultural unconscious, as a manifestation of creation – or, rather, of God's ongoing creativity with the productions of human longing and effort – is not a closed myth that we quarry for stories, form, and content, nor is it a broken myth of master narratives that we pillage for pragmatic ends. Rather, it is an open dynamic that holds the repositories of the creative effort, both positive and negative, to be one with God that has existed since the birth of time. The energies of that dynamic are not exhausted by human limitation, because it is the presence of the Spirit of God, restless and unquenchable until it transforms all into the creative image of God. Film shows us the spiritual questing of humanity in our time in ways that are symbolic of, and appropriate for, the postmodern consciousness. We contemplate them, as the icons of our time, because they provide us with the language of our communication with God.

Contemplation and Spirituality

Contemplation is a spiritual exercise. Ignatian contemplation is structured to a particular end, which is to be disposed to receive the grace that we seek in a given prayer period. That grace is a particular response to our deepest desire, an ever-growing intimacy with God. At one time it may be a profound awareness of God's mercy holding us even when we, blinded by our disorders, sinned to find what we thought was love. At another time it may be such a personal bonding with Christ, the human manifestation of God, that we desire fully to be with him as he reveals to the world God's unceasing and compassionate mercy for creation. At still another time, it may be to follow the path of that divine love through the misery and destructiveness of this world. At the end of the Ignatian Exercises, we pray for the grace to be a part of that joyful labour that transforms our world.

We ask for these graces with the expectation that we will receive them in our prayer. At the end of that prayer we look back over what we have experienced to see where and how we have received them. Our understanding is that God desires to communicate with us and that by disposing ourselves to receive that communication, we signal to God our desire to accept this free and loving gift.

There are, as we well know, levels of gift. A gift can be offered and not received; a gift can be received and not accepted; that gift can be accepted but not opened; opened but not used; used but not shared; shared but not celebrated. The journey through the Exercises, using the world of contemporary popular film, carries us through the levels of gift to the place where we become one with the giver, one with what is given, and one with the creation to whom that gift is always offered.

(2) How to Use This Book

This book is a manual. Like all manuals, it will yield limited results if you read it without taking the time to engage in the process it lays out. Yet you can reap some benefits by simply reading a section when the spirit moves you and reflecting on it. More good will be achieved if you commit to preparing yourself to enter into the process. To that end you will need to set aside some time to read each section and reflect on the questions at the end of that section. This will prepare you to watch the film in question with a certain intention and focus; this controlled disposition results in viewing of the film becoming a contemplative act. There are more questions to reflect on after you have watched the film. Do not move to the next section until you have exhausted the riches contained in the present section. In Ignatian terms this is called "repetition." Repetition is not just repeating an exercise, but focusing on the points of the exercise that were significant in your prayer and reflection. You could think of this as a "zoom in," in which you pray and ponder over important aspects of a general view to reveal important insights and connections in your life. We recommend that you keep a journal of the significant moments you experience.

How to Prepare to Watch

Each section in this book is an exercise in prayer. Just as you prepare for physical exercise, you dispose

[handwritten margin notes: "prepare", "watch", "reflect", "journal"]

21

yourself for prayer. Find a time and a space where you can pray without being disturbed. Start by being intentional about what you want. This is called asking for the grace; each section presents the grace to be prayed for. Asking for a grace focuses your awareness. Then ask for the Spirit to help you receive the grace. Read the text slowly and reflectively, pausing where you feel moved. At the end of the reading, return to those points that moved you and allow them to be the entry into prayer. At the end of that prayer, go through the questions that follow the text, paying special attention to those questions that stir up something in you. Write in your journal what moved you in the prayer and the reflections.

All of this disposes you to the contemplative act of watching the film. The films we suggest are not intended to provide moral examples of the insights of the prayer; rather, they manifest those energies – both positive and negative – that you will experience as you enter into those meditations and contemplations set out by Ignatius in the Exercises. You enter the film as a contemplative act: you are to notice its effect on you – what it evokes in terms of consolation and desolation, the significant movements of the spirits within you.

You will not have time to do a whole section of reflection and film at one sitting. It is better to proceed at a slower pace, and watch the film only after you have absorbed the material for reflection. This disposition will allow you to encounter the full power of the film as a contemplative moment.

After Watching

After watching the film, it will be helpful to have a conversation with the Father, or with Jesus, or with a significant spiritual figure in your life about what occurred in the prayer period. You might wish to discuss something that moved you, or something that came up during the prayer, such as a memory, an association or a question. St. Ignatius, following Christ, addresses God as "Father." God, of course, is neither masculine nor feminine, but has qualities of a Father, a Mother, and much more than we can ever imagine. We are aware of the bias today of calling God "Father," but also of the intimate personal relationship that Christ has with the Mystery he calls Father; Ignatius has a similar relationship to this identification of God. It was on a pilgrimage to Rome that Ignatius had a vision at La Sorta where he beheld the Father telling the Son about Christ," I want you to put this man under your standard." For these reasons this book has used "Father" to maintain that relationship between that identification of God and the person doing the Exercises. If another term is more appropriate for you, feel free to use it.

Journalling this prayer helps you focus on the significant moments in the experience and on why they are significant. For the Ignatian method of discernment, it is important to pay attention to the times where you were moved either to consolation or desolation. (Consolation refers to those times when you are encouraged or feel alive and connected to God, to others and to yourself. Desolation is the opposite; it describes times when you are feeling apathetic, disinterested in what is good and life-giving, trapped and despairing.) For St. Ignatius, such moments reveal something significant about ourselves: through them God speaks to us, and so we need to return to them to discover what is being said. They reveal whether we are turned to God or away from God.

Discernment

Discernment is not that simple, however. When we are turned away from God, we might get feelings of pleasure from doing what is wrong. That is not consolation. Moreover, even if we are on the right path and are doing what is pleasing to God, we can still be given a false consolation: what we think and feel may be good, but it leads us away from the true good. We only know that it is a false consolation when we see the effects and discover that entering into that "good" feeling leads us to disturbed and ego-centred states. When you note in your journal your consolations and desolations, you also need to note where they lead you.

Consolations and desolations reveal to us "like bearings on a compass" where to go and how to behave if we truly are seeking to know God. If on our path to God we experience desolations, we know that we are encountering forces that seek to block our progress. It helps to examine what might be causing that disturbance. Does it come from an inappropriate attitude or understanding of our relationship to ourselves, to others or to God? Bringing that blockage to consciousness allows us to bring it to prayer. Then God's mercy can deal with whatever is hindering us from loving freely and joyfully. It might be a hurt in our past or an undeveloped aspect of ourselves that has become so much a part of our personality that we are unconscious of it, but that influences the way we see and feel and behave.

Consolations also help carry us closer to God. Ignatius defines consolation as being so inflamed with the love of God that we love in an ordered manner and so "can love no creature on the face of the earth for its own sake, but only in the Creator of them all" (#316). That love can move us to tears for our sins, and sorrow for the sufferings of any member of the community that is the Body of Christ. It is present when we relish things properly, when we grow in faith, hope and love and are attracted to all that leads to God filling our soul with peace and quiet. Consolation is not just feeling good. Sorrow and pain can also be signs of consolation. What is significant, for our spiritual awareness, is what the feelings mean and whether they orient us to seeking God.

So the first step in discernment is being able to identify the feeling. The second step is to become aware of what those feelings mean. As you gain more experience, you will find it easier to catch yourself more quickly. The third stage in discernment is seeing in which direction the state that manifests itself in a particular feeling is tending. This discernment is extremely personal. These are your feelings and no one else's. They indicate your particular language with God and God's own language with you. You might think of your feelings in prayer as the language lovers use with each other.

Journalling these states of consolation and desolation, together with what aroused them, allows you to come to a better understanding of yourself and of how you operate in the world. God's communication with you is always about how to live your life in a way that is more focused and more rooted in love. Journalling also allows you to see the patterns in your life; you will soon discover that the consolations, like desolations, are interconnected. They reveal to us our redeemed history and God's care for us even in those times when we might have felt far from God, or not even particularly concerned with spiritual things. Bringing this to our awareness enables us to appropriate more deeply God's constant mercy for us and communication with us.

The First Week: The Mercy of God

Ignatius' missionary thrust is to make all become aware that God loves us, and that God always and at every moment communicates with us. Ignatius even devised an examination of consciousness whereby at the end of every day we reflect on where we found consolation and desolation. He asks us to be grateful for moments of consolation and to reflect on moments of desolation to see why they happened and how we can prevent their occurrence. Ignatius believes that God wants us to be happy, and that God works in the world to bring us to our true self and to our true happiness.

To achieve that happiness we sometimes find ourselves having to make important decisions. The Exercises give us a process through which to make correct discernments. The Exercises are not techniques for discovering God's will, however. Rather, they dispose us to a true relationship with God and offer us a language by which God communicates with us. We can love someone and talk meaningfully with them but still make bad decisions. This is an existential truth. But that love and communication limit the possibility of making bad decisions. The Exercises make us prone to making good and life-giving decisions through the personal language of consolation and desolation.

The Second Week: Walking with God

Ignatius places decision-making in the Second Week of the Exercises, because people first need to experience radically that God loves them even though they have been and remain sinners. The First Week establishes a foundational openness to God; unless that happens, the decisions you make will be skewered by blindness to your true identity and to your true relationships with others and with God. By the end of the First Week, you will have come to an overwhelming sense of God's mercy in all aspects of your life – personal, communal, social and cultural – as well as a deep sense of how disorder on all levels of your existence corrupts your true awareness of your life. The liberation experienced in the First Week is a liberation to love, to be loving and to accept love. It is felt as a deep desire to live that love out in the world.

But how are we to do this? The Second Week of the Exercises introduces us to God's way of operating in the world as manifest in the presence and actions of Jesus Christ.

In that Second Week we are invited to journey with Christ and to pray for the grace of such an intimate knowledge of him that we desire only to love and to follow him. In the contemplations of that Week we can bring the decision we wish to make to the prayer and to discussions we have with God following the prayer. We check to see if in those moments of dialogue we are filled with consolation or desolation as we ponder our decision. Consolation means that we have made the right decision; desolation tells us that we are on the wrong track. But even in the contemplations themselves we can learn something useful. If we find God distant or uninvolved with us in those contemplations, we know something is wrong. Or if we find that we are acting, in those contemplations, in ways not consonant with Jesus' own activity, then we know we are on the wrong path. The liberated energies of our life are embodied in the decision we are trying to make; these shape the way we relate to the Christ as he journeys through his own earthly life. If those energies are consonant with the energies of the Christ, then we have consolation and the felt assurance that we are one with the Christ on mission. If there is dissonance, we have desolation and the signs of a bad decision.

The Third Week: A Passionate Love

In the decision-making process, that consonance and dissonance continue throughout the rest of the Weeks of the Exercises. If we are making the right decision we find that we can journey in union with Christ through his passion and death and resurrection. We suffer and are sad with Christ suffering. Indeed, at times we might even feel nothing, that same nothing we feel when we are at the last days of someone we love and the emotion that dominates our life is too deep even for feeling. With the wrong decision we find ourselves distant from the suffering, or we want to stop the suffering, or we are distracted from the main event by our own preoccupations and impose our own attitudes and perspectives on what is going on in the drama we are contemplating.

We are not to be masochistic or sadistic here. We do not delight in suffering for its own sake, nor do we take on that suffering to show just how good and holy we are. Christ did not choose his suffering. He chooses, as always, the Father and his path to the Father. The disorders of the world and of evil resist his manifestation of the Father as Compassionate Mercy by imposing a suffering designed to break his relationship or to eliminate him altogether. Similarly, the suffering we experience in the Third Week is one of identification with someone whom we love and follow, and with whom we now have the same path, the same spirit and the same passion.

The Fourth Week: A Transforming Life

That passion for the Father leads us to the Fourth Week. In this week we experience Christ's resurrection from the dead. The Christ does not raise himself from the dead; the Father manifests his love for him and reaches into the ultimate power of sin – death – and brings Christ, not back to life, but to a new level of creation, uncorrupted by evil: resurrection. Ignatius asks us, at this point in our spiritual journey, "to ask for the grace to be glad and rejoice intensely because of the great joy and the glory of Christ our Lord" (#221). We are not asked to experience joy because of what we have done, but rather to share Christ's joy and glory in his return to the Father. This is crucial for our discernment process, because here we can see if our decision has united us with the Christ. If it has, then we can experience the pure gift of Christ's joy; if it hasn't, then we will not.

The awareness of consolation and desolation can attune us more closely to the creative presence of God in our world and give us a personal language for listening to God. For Ignatius, God is never silent in the world, but manifests in every one of us no matter who or what or where we are. Ignatius would go even further and say that God uses everything to communicate with us. This book uses film because it is contemporary contemplation, and in contemplation one enters into communion with God. But this communication is not restricted exclusively to periods of prayer.

Ignatius, in the manual called the Spiritual Exercises, introduces the exercises themselves in the context of a daily examination of consciousness. In this examination he asks us to look at our day prayerfully at the end of it and see where we were consoled and where we experienced desolation. Even in the ordinariness of our day, God speaks. Ignatius suggests that we give praise for where, in the ordinary, we were consoled, and that we examine the moments of desolation to see what God is telling us. Ignatius' emphasis on the ordinary is echoed in the films we have chosen. We could have chosen art films, or foreign films with a certain aesthetic sensibility, but instead we chose films that are available at the major commercial cinemas and video and DVD rental stores throughout the country.

The Key Concepts of Media Literacy

Reading these popular films using the techniques of spiritual literacy given in this chapter is not just a professional, academic or religious task. Such reading is based on the techniques of media literacy that we absorb by reflecting on what we see in the media culture we live in today. The following eight key concepts provide a theoretical base for all media literacy, and give a common language and framework for media discussion.

1. *All media are constructions.* This is arguably the most important concept. Media do not simply reflect external reality. Rather, they present carefully crafted constructions that reflect many decisions and are the result of many determining factors. Media literacy works towards deconstructing these constructions (i.e., taking them apart to show how they are made so that we do not take them literally). Our imaginative projects and our perceptions occur in the same way; the spiritual discipline of contemplation and reflection frees a person from being trapped by forces that determine what we see and imagine and spontaneously evaluate those seemingly natural acts.

2. *The media construct aspects of reality.* The media are responsible for the majority of the observations and experiences we use to build our personal understandings of the world and how it works. Much of our view of reality is based on preconstructed media messages with built-in attitudes, interpretations and conclusions. Thus the media, to a great extent, give us our sense of reality. In fact, the media also give us

our sense of spirituality, but it is the dynamic nature of spirituality to refuse to be constrained by such constructions, just as it is the very nature of God to refuse to be constrained by creation.

3. *Audiences negotiate meaning in media.* If the media provide us with much of the material we use to build our picture of reality, each of us finds or "negotiates" meaning according to individual factors: personal needs and anxieties, the pleasures or troubles of the day, racial and sexual attitudes, family and cultural background, moral standpoint, and so on. Spiritual literacy examines the dynamics of that mediation in the light of our own consolations and desolations, which reveal in an intimate manner our relationship with the mystery we call God.

4. *Media messages have commercial implications.* Media literacy aims to encourage awareness of how the media are influenced by commercial considerations, and how these impinge on content, technique and distribution. Most media production is a business, and so must make a profit. Questions of ownership and control are central: a relatively small number of individuals control what we watch, read and hear in the media. This may seem Marxist, in that it suggests the economic basis for all media messages and for all cultural artifacts. Marxism is useful in unveiling the mystification of motives by using a hermeneutic of suspicion. But Marxism contains the drive to self-transcendence that underpins all human activity, including Marxist analysis itself. Spiritual literacy focuses on that basic drive to self-transcendence and on its satisfaction in the free gift of love by a creative and compassionate God.

5. *Media messages contain ideological and value messages.* All media products are advertising in some sense values and ways of life. The mainstream media convey, explicitly or implicitly, ideological messages about such issues as the nature of the good life and the virtue of consumerism, the role of women, the acceptance of authority, and unquestioning patriotism. Our perceptions and imagination are shaped by these values. We can never be value free, and we can never escape the ideologies that can underpin those values. But we do not have to be imprisoned by those ideologies and values if we experience them as always inadequate manifestations of our true nature, which is to be in conscious union with the divine. Spiritual literacy builds on media literacy, for while media literacy can examine from a certain point of view the messages that are the media, it cannot examine itself. Spiritual literacy allows that examination and promotes the freedom that such an examination raises.

6. *Media messages contain social and political implications.* The media have great influence in politics and in forming social change. For example, television can greatly influence the election of a national leader on the basis of image. The media involve us in concerns such as civil rights, famines in Africa, and HIV/AIDS. They give us an intimate sense of certain national and global concerns so that we can imagine we have become Marshall McLuhan's global village. We should be hesitant about such a quick generalization, however. We all know that what we are being given is not all there is; we also know that we are unable to assimilate even that much. Similarly, we know that the media that is our imagination and our perception is also limited. Who we are is a mystery, and the implications of our actions in the world we live in are beyond our control. Inasmuch as our presence in the world is also media, we embody and represent social and political values. We are not just receptors of media messages, we are transmitters. Consider the enormous significance of designer labels and ideograms attached to our clothes, our food, our living styles. We embody mystery, but within the operative freedoms of our culture. How we choose to appropriate that freedom and manifest it in our lives becomes a matter of spiritual literacy. How others read that is media literacy.

7. *Form and content are closely related in media message.* As McLuhan noted, each medium has its own grammar and codifies reality in its own way. Different media will report the same event but create different impressions and messages. When we contemplate a gospel passage, our personality and the energies that compose our life shape the way that passage and encounter with Christ come alive. Even the representation of Christ is shaped by those energies. But it would be a serious mistake to think that such contemplations are just projections from our own personality. The contemplations are also the product of God's activity within the very intimacy of our psyche. In fact, God uses those images and energies to create a media message appropriate to our personal path. The form and content of what we experience in a contemplation reveals the unique communication and language that God has with us. The ability to read that communication is spiritual literacy

8. *Each medium has a unique aesthetic form.* Just as we notice the pleasing rhythms of certain pieces of poetry or prose, so we ought to be able to enjoy the pleasing forms and effects of the different media. You will notice in prayer that if it goes well, you have a sense of time passing without notice. If it does not go well, time drags; you are distracted, bored, irritable or wishing you could do something else. Personal prayer has an aesthetic in what is represented, in its modes of representation, in its narrative flow and editing. When we pay attention to our contemplations, we must look not only at the insight we think

27

is given, but at all the factors that compose that contemplation.

Clearly, contemplation is like film; film, viewed as a spiritual discipline, and contemplation are identical. Media literacy, at the level of spirituality, becomes the reflection tool for what occurs in our prayer. This book suggests using film, not to reinforce the particular insights of the Spiritual Exercises but as manifestations of the Exercises themselves. It sees media literacy as spiritual literacy, film as contemplation, and cinema as making available to a mass audience contemporary forms of prayer that discuss relevant issues and the quest for transcendence.

You can see, then, how what appears to be just a film becomes an instrument for a dialogue with God. The consolations and desolations we experience in that context alert us to the ways we are oriented, or not oriented, to God. Using a journal to note the different movements of the spirits within us, and the contexts in which those spirits are moved, sharpens our skills at learning our personal language with God. This makes us more flexible in walking through the currents of our world with freedom and integrity and a certain joy this world cannot give.

We invite you now to that freedom and that joy.

An Outline to Follow in Using This Book

Below we give an outline of the process we describe in this chapter. It will provide a handy guide until you become familiar with the structure of the prayer.

1. Make sure you have enough time for the exercise.

2. Find a quiet space and ask for the Spirit to help you make a good prayer.

3. Ask for the specific grace that is suggested in the introductory reflection.

4. Read the reflection slowly and carefully. Dwell on those sections, one at a time, that have moved you the most, either to a sense of well-being or to a sense of discomfort.

5. Invite God to enter into your prayerful journey through those sections.

6. Discuss with God what emerges in that journey and in those deliberations.

7. Use the questions provided at the end of the reflection to appropriate your experience or to enter further into prayer.

8. Journal the significant moments of this prayer experience.

    Note: In your journal you will want to write

    • the questions that moved you in each exercise and your response to them, in terms of both the introduction to the Exercises and the film,

    • what took place in prayer (the significant consolations and desolations), and

    • how you received the grace you requested.

When you feel you have appropriated the reflection, you are ready to watch the film.

A. Make sure you have enough time to watch the whole film at one sitting.

B. Make sure that you will not be disturbed or distracted.

C. Ask for the same grace as suggested in the introductory reflection.

D. Watch the film.

E. Examine yourself: Where in the film were you especially moved?

F. Use the questions provided for each film to appropriate better that contemplative experience.

Note 1: Each of the three sections of reflections that follow the movie contains a number of questions for reflection. You do not need to deal with all of these questions. Read the questions and respond to those that move you —in terms of attraction or repulsion.

Note 2: The questions are not intended to deal with every aspect of the film. There is just not enough space to do so. For example, a number of the movies are adaptations of short stories or novels. We have chosen not to deal with the issues of expectations about the story and/or the characters in such films.

G. Have a discussion with God about what moved you in the film and your reflections on the film.

H. Write in your journal what has been significant in this prayer period and reflection. It is helpful every so often to review all your journal entries to see if you can discern a pattern or a path.

I. At the end of every Week of the Exercises, reread carefully the journal entries for that Week. Try to summarize the overall movement of that Week. At the end of the Four Weeks, take time to reread all your journal entries. Summarize what has been given to you in your experience of journeying through the Exercises of St. Ignatius in this way.

John Pungente, SJ
Monty Williams, SJ
April 2004

Part I

The First Week: The Mercy of God

Theme

The Sense of Being a Loved Sinner

Most of us live in the world unreflectively. At best, we are concerned only with our own interests and projects, which reveal the sense we have of ourselves. Indeed, the only times we question that sense of self is when something happens to disturb our carefully controlled universe: the death of someone significant to us, an accident, the loss of a job, bad news from a routine medical check-up…or even misplacing our car keys, being stood up for an appointment, or losing a night's sleep. Interestingly enough, when good things happen to us, they confirm our sense of self, but bad things force us to question ourselves. Most of us react against that move to reflectivity.

Ignatius, in the First Week of his Spiritual Exercises, sets up a program that allows us to do precisely that radical self-examination. Its aim is not to destroy us, but rather to help us abandon the false self-images we have of ourselves and the false stories we maintain about ourselves. At the same time, it permits us to see, understand and experience the deeper truth of ourselves: that we are always and everywhere loved by God, who seeks us out as a lover searches for a lost beloved. That lover will not rest until the beloved knows at a profound level the personal and intimate love that constantly creates, supports, and transforms him or her.

The encounter between the beloved and the lover, between us and God, occurs in the context of examining not only our personal history, but also our social and cultural history – indeed, all human history – within the cosmic history of creation. Considering ourselves in this vast context helps diminish the value we place upon our ego, which is a tiny, fragile thing in the vast tides of human and cosmic history.

Creation of the earth began 15 billion years ago. The forces and energies that shape this ongoing process also feature significantly in our own moments of self-consciousness

If we think about it, we did not create our sense of self. We are shaped not only by our parents' genes, and they by their parents', back to the dawning of humanity, but also by the historical forces surrounding us. Those forces are in turn subject to the environmental and ecological dimensions that mitigate against, or promote, our well-being.

So who are we? This is not a question we can answer for ourselves; the answer lies before and beyond ourselves. Maybe it is even the wrong question to ask. Maybe a better question to ask is this: What do we think or believe or understand of ourselves? Closely tied into that question are two others: What makes us think of ourselves that way? How does this perception shape the way we see and relate to ourselves, to others and to that mystery we call God? When we fall in love, we discover that we change, the world changes, possibilities open, and we become focused and creative.

The First Week of the Spiritual Exercises of St. Ignatius of Loyola invites us to walk this path of love.

Questions for Reflection to Prepare for the First Week

1. Who are you?
2. Why do you say you are this person?
3. Where does this self-understanding come from?
4. Are you content with this self-understanding?
5. What do you think is missing?
6. How do you experience that missing self?
7. How did your family shape that self-understanding? Your relationships with your parents? With your siblings? With the other members of your family? With your spouse or partner?
8. How is your self-image shaped by the culture(s) you grew up in and the one you live in now? List the ways in which you are shaped by your social background, your class, your ethnicity, your economic status, your sexuality, the part of the world you come from or now live in.
9. How does the environment shape my self-awareness? Which season resonates most with you? Are you a day person or a night person? Why do you say this?
10. What is your image of God? Of religion? Of spirituality? How does your relational life (friends, mate, children) reveal to you who you are?
11. What are the questions that haunt your life? How do you deal with them? How do they deal with you?

The Movie
2001: A Space Odyssey

Directed by Stanley Kubrick (1968 –139 mins.)
Starring: Keir Dullea, Gary Lockwood, Douglas Rain

1. Summary

When a four-million-year-old black monolith is discovered on the moon, the government sends a team of scientists on a fact-finding mission while hiding the truth from the public. Later, another team is sent to Jupiter in a ship controlled by the perfect HAL 9000 computer to investigate further the giant object. On the journey, the astronauts come into conflict with HAL. Only one survives, undergoing a unique rebirth.

2. Questions about the Movie

1. Kubrick took his title from Homer's *Odyssey*, only here the heroes – and the viewer – embark on a journey across the galaxy.

    Both Kubrick and Director John Boorman spoke of the importance of the concept of myth in this movie. What is there in us that looks for myths? What are the elements of myth? How does 2001 transcend the usual sci-fi movie to become myth?

2. Kubrick wanted 2001 to be a movie that relied on picture and sound more than on word. There are only 46 minutes of dialogue in the 139 minutes of running time in the film. At times, the visual says more to advance the theme than language does.

    Music is the basic sound in this movie. Throughout these exercises, you will find a number of questions about the use of music dealing with either the film score or songs chosen for use in the movie. Music is an important element in any movie. It is a way into the emotional content of scenes and the life of the characters. It can be used to advance the theme of the movie as well as to create mood. What happens in 2001: *A Space Odyssey* when music combines with image – without dialogue?

3. *Catholic Film Newsletter*, April 18, 1968: "Knowledge, information, and the life principle itself…cannot be destroyed, but rather will be sought and regenerated over and over…. Kubrick's art, like the poet Yeats', is intensified by the mystery of his metaphysics as well as by the vigor of his imagination." Does the writer mean simply that someone (God?) ensures that what has been created will remain alive in some form? What role does art like Kubrick's play in this process?

4. C.S. Lewis' science fiction trilogy – The Ransom Trilogy – was about God's relationship to

humankind in all its contemporary aspects. In Kubrick's 2001, with its analogies in Lewis' trilogy and the Christian myth, we can't get to God; God gets to us. How does God get to us in 2001? What does God offer us?

3. The Relationship of the Movie to the Theme of the Exercise

Kubrick told *Rolling Stone* (quoted in Vincent LoBrutto, *Stanley Kubrick* [New York: Donald I. Fine Books, 1997], p. 313): "On the deepest psychological level, the film's plot symbolized the search for God, and it finally postulates what is little less than a scientific definition of God."

Bowman meets God. It is that simple and that complicated. Passing through the Star Gate he is plunged into a voyage of inward discovery much like the one St. Ignatius plans for those involved in the First Week of the Exercises. He witnesses the creation of all matter, the stars, the universe, galaxies and life. All consciousness is his, all knowledge is his. Bowman "dies" and is reborn to a new consciousness.

So who are we? Perhaps the last shots from the movie will help us to find an answer. The astronaut becomes — or does he? — an intellect beyond human and machine. He becomes perhaps even beyond death. What has caused the man to become the child? What possibilities are now open to him?

4. The Relationship of the Movie to One's Self in the Exercise

Vincent LoBrutto wrote in *Stanley Kubrick* (New York: Donald I. Fine Books, 1997, p. 312): "2001 had a spiritual and religious power to the children of McLuhan who stared at the screen and remained staring as the curtain closed after witnessing Bowman's spectacular rebirth."

It is the level of subjective response — when the movie leaves the screen and enters into your experience — that matters most. The search for the meaning of this movie involves, as St. Ignatius would tell us, a turning inward.

1. Who is the HAL in your life? How do you respond to it? Can you shut it down? Do you even want to, though it has "killed" much that is dear to you?

2. Are you, like Bowman, changed by your response to God's call? If so, in what ways have you become like the image of the child? What lies beyond the Star Gate for you after you respond to this call?

3. Kubrick wanted to make a movie about our place in the universe — something that had never before been attempted in the movies — and he wanted that movie to inspire wonder, awe and terror. What does it inspire in you? Why?

1st Exercise
(1) Cosmic Disorder

Then I saw a new heaven and a new earth; for the first heaven and the first earth passed away, and the sea was no more. And I saw the holy city, a new Jerusalem, coming down out of heaven from God, prepared as a bride adorned for her husband; and I heard a loud voice from the throne saying, "Behold, the dwelling of God is with mortals. He will dwell with them and they shall be his people, and God himself will be with them; he will wipe away every tear from their eyes, and death shall be no more, neither shall there be mourning nor crying nor pain no more, for the former things have passed away.

(Revelation 21:1-4)

We should apply memory to the sin of the angels, that is recalling they were created in the state of grace, that they did not want to make use of the freedom God gave them to reverence and obey their Creator and God, and so falling into pride, were changed from grace to hatred of God, and cast out of heaven into hell.

(Sp. Ex. #50)

Grace: To ask for a sense of how I, and all humanity, am implicated in a disorder larger than ourselves and how I, consciously, or unconsciously, participate in and contribute to that disorder.

Ignatius sees all of creation intrinsically finding its meaning and fulfillment in responding lovingly and freely to God, who creates in love and with love and by love. This love makes all free, and in that freedom all have the choice of how to find meaning and fulfillment. The mystery of evil is that one can choose not to love, or not to respond to love. One can set oneself up as knowing better than God how to be or how to manifest one's identity.

In the mythology that Ignatius uses, the most radical level of created spirituality to misuse its free choice was certain cosmic powers called angels. It is hard to imagine that extremely spiritual beings could opt to be evil, yet we can see even in the human realm extremely gifted people spiritually who become cult leaders or religious fanatics or who abuse their gifts for selfish or misconceived ends. Some angels, in their freedom, behaved in such a way. Their disorder contaminated all of creation, our human history and even our very selves.

Ignatius does not try to understand the mystery of evil and sin. For him these are existential realities. It is possible to turn away from love. It is possible to become destructive because of that turning away. Sin entered creation because of that one act, and it is unimaginable to hold in one's awareness the damage that that one act has created. When we are asked to meditate on that one single act and on its consequences, we find ourselves in a state of confusion and horror. This state of confusion is the grace Ignatius asks us to pray for as we allow ourselves to become aware of the depths of that absurdity of the angels and of the implications on every single created being.

Often – almost as if to protect our sanity – we refuse to dwell on that disorder, yet popular films are filled with explorations of the evil that exists beyond human creation and human control. These films might give us some indication of the malign forces that are unleashed against the innocent and the unwitting.

Ignatius does not ask us to enter into this meditation to depress us, or to titillate us with some Gothic darkness that excites our fantasies and casts us in the role of victims. Indeed, we are warned against those ways of maintaining our egos. Rather, Ignatius asks us to enter into that dimension of the reality of our lives so we will realize that, in spite of our own vulnerability, we have not been overwhelmed, subjugated and destroyed by such powers. How is this possible? It is simple: God chooses in a loving freedom to protect and maintain us without taking away from us whatever freedom we still have under these circumstances.

Second, Ignatius wants us to realize that just as that single act of the dark angels created a world of destruction, any one of our many destructive acts also create and contribute to that unleashing of chaos and suffering. He asks us to enter into that profound feeling of shame for our own rejection of love, for times when our acts that lack mercy or compassion create a domino effect of pain, hurt and alienation beyond our control. Each selfish act opens a Pandora's box of evils. And yet, we discover that we are still loved by God and by those who align themselves to goodness.

We need to become aware of that love that sustains and forgives and re-creates us, but we can do so only when we realize how strong the opposition is to our living good and creative lives.

What usually happens on a retreat at this time is denial of the dreadful and profound facts of evil and sin and the ways each of us is contaminated and implicated. This can be as simple as a refusal to believe that what Ignatius proposes we examine prayerfully is true. Or it can be a little more nuanced and we can consider this from a detached point of view. We can say to ourselves: Yes, I suppose it is true – if you believe in that sort of thing – but it really has nothing to do with me. We can even go further and think about the mystery of evil as an intellectual problem, considering why the angels did what they did, why God permits evil, and how there can be evil and God. We can enter into these meditations emotionally and feel overwhelmed by what is presented. Often at this level incidents from our own past – whether we were the aggressor or the victim – emerge.

In all of these responses we see the ego struggling to maintain itself as the centre of its universe. But what Ignatius wants us to realize is that in the midst of being dreadfully implicated in cosmic spiritual disorder, we are held by a compassionate God who cherishes us even as we act out of our blindness and disorder.

Questions for Prayer and Reflection

1. How do you feel when you watch the daily news? How does that feeling contribute to the disorder you see around you? How are you made to feel what you see is all of reality, or the most significant parts of it?

2. As you contemplate the above reflection, what aspects move you the most? Why? What do they trigger in you?

3. In what ways do you see yourself as a victim of the larger forces around you? How do you respond to that sense of victimhood and entrapment?

4. Within that larger context of disorder, in what ways do you feel truly empowered? Where does that sense of empowerment come from? How does it sustain you?

5. What questions about the nature of God as good or compassionate does the reality of evil raise in your life?

6. In your spiritual life, how do you reconcile a good God with the suffering of the powerless and the innocent?

7. How do you think evil operates? How does it operate in you and on you?

8. How are you protected and defended from having that evil destroy you?

9. In your daily life and your life as a whole, how are the forces of life and creativity at work in you and around you?

10. How are you conscious of these forces? What response do you offer to them?

The Movie
Koyaanisqatsi

Director: Godfrey Reggio (1983 – 87 mins.)

1. Summary

Koyaanisqatsi is both a documentary and a visual concert of images set to the music of Philip Glass. The title is a Hopi term meaning "life out of balance." Using both slow motion and sped-up motion, the film speaks of the world around us – from natural environment to manmade environment. In doing so, the film conveys the message that life is out of balance, in turmoil, disintegrating. It makes clear that we must look towards another way of living.

2. Questions about the Movie

1. Translation of the Hopi Prophecies sung in *Koyaanisqatsi*:

   "If we dig precious things from the land, we will invite disaster."

   "Near the Day of Purification, there will be cobwebs spun back and forth in the sky."

   "A container of ashes might one day be thrown from the sky which could burn the land and boil the oceans."

   As we look at the chaos that is our modern world, how might we see the prophecies fulfilled not only in the world but in our own lives?

2. "We usually perceive our world, our way of living as beautiful because there is nothing else to perceive.... We have encased ourselves in an artificial environment that has remarkably replaced the original, nature itself. We do not live with nature any longer; we live above it, off of it as it were. Nature has become the resource to keep this artificial or new nature alive." (*Koyaanisqatsi* Web site)

   Why are we unable to understand that it is we who have made vanish the beauty that was once all around us? What has replaced that beauty?

3. "It is a deliriously beautiful vision of America and a cautionary tale of what technology is doing to the earth and us.... It is both funny and depressing." (Joseph Gelmis, *Newsday*, September 25, 1983)

   Technology is a great gift, but one that we have misused. Recall the images of nature and the music that foretell the misuse that is to come:

   - tumbledown sky-scrapers of mountains
   - emptiness of the Badlands
   - foothills like rotten teeth
   - wormy rivers eating away soft stone.

Why has our struggle to subdue nature had such terrible results?

3. The Relationship of the Movie to the Theme of the Exercise

1. "The absence of voice-over or other overt messages causes us to concentrate on the visual patterns and become, perhaps, absorbed by them.... It is easy to imagine *Koyaanisqatsi* as one long, unbroken meditation on the modern world." (*DVD Savant*, September 14, 2002)

   Contrast the sweeping and soothing unviolated landscapes that open the film with the time lapse and fast-motion photography that turns everyday sights – freeway traffic, pedestrians, assembly lines – into a mesmerizing roller coaster of patterns.

   How does the film show you what was, what is, and what should be? How are you implicated in all of this?

2. "There is a hint of the horror movie as we ride the speeded-up storms in the stratosphere, with clouds like boiling milk in which strange heats pulse." (Alan Brien, *New Statesman*, September 2, 1983)

   How are these and other such images signs of the chaos you are about to see? Why would you not want to dwell on such images?

3. Philip Glass's music is the perfect counterpart: not only for scenes where natural forces are perverted – mammoth strip-mining operations and outdoor nuclear detonations – but also when the film turns to alienation and rapidation of life as a further perversion of nature.

How does the music, like St. Ignatius' words, force you to focus your attention on what is happening not only in your world but in you?

4. The Relationship of the Movie to One's Self in the Exercise

1. "Any meaning or value *Koyaanisqatsi* might have comes exclusively from the beholder. The film's role is to provoke, to raise questions that only the audience can answer. This is the highest value of any work of art, not predetermined meaning, but meaning gleaned from the experience of the encounter." (*Koyaanisqatsi* Web site)

   The viewer becomes a participant by having to work through what is heard and seen to the final meaning. What questions does the film raise about the spiritual disorder within your life and the ways you handle it?

2. Many people have seen the film as a type of "drugless high." If that drugless high only presents us with the spectacle of the United States in all its ugliness, what can we do? What prevents despair from taking over your life as the awareness of the chaos within yourself becomes clearer?

40

(2) The Disorder of Adam and Eve: The Sin of Humanity

God said, "Let us make mortals in our image, after our likeness...." So God created mortals in his own image, in the image of God he created them; male and female he created them. And God blessed them.... (Genesis 1:26-31). Now the serpent was more subtle than any other wild creature that the Lord God had made.

(Genesis 3:1)

Recall to memory how on account of [the sin of Adam and Eve] they did penance for so long a time, and the great corruption which came upon the human race that caused so many to be lost in hell.

(Sp. Ex. #51)

Grace: To experience how I am trapped in the fallen human condition and how I contribute to it.

There was a time when the concept of original sin did not need any explanation. One forgets that the term came from St. Augustine, who used it to counter the Pelagian heresy that free will alone was sufficient to live a full Christian life and obtain full salvation. The Genesis story exposes the lie of that heresy. Even in Paradise, Adam's and Eve's essential freedom cannot sustain the way of their continual relationship with God.

Once again Ignatius uses the mythology of the Genesis story to allow us to see that we are born into a context that is further disordered by human interaction. He asks us to examine in a prayerful context how that story plays out several important manifestations of the nature of evil in which we are implicated.

In the protected context of the mythical garden of Eden, humans are created by God. But because of the malice of the sin of the fallen angels, that context is already threatened; it is insecure and unstable. Nevertheless, it is the place where humans can still communicate intimately and unselfconsciously with God. Against the simplicity of that relationship comes the temptation of the evil one. It creates suspicion against God's love for us. It rouses irritation over the boundaries defined by God's demands by suggesting the possibility of unlimited freedom and creativity – without indicating the costs and implications of that suggested possibility. It leaves unsaid the rationale – malice – for broaching the subject, raising instead the desire for an immediate good promised by the performance of one sinful act.

That one sinful act has harmful consequences for the sinners themselves. It damages their relationships with each other and forces them self-consciously to isolate themselves from God. When their broken trust is brought to their attention they defend themselves by rationalizing it and by blaming others, but they still suffer the consequences of their action.

While the sinners hide from God, God seeks them out and has them face the reality of their choices.

Once again Ignatius asks us to reflect prayerfully on this. He asks us to consider how temptation causes mistrust of God, offering a way for immediate gratification and exalting the ego to equality with God. Sin offers the illusion of creation taking on the role of Creator. Through this sin of pride, we feel separated from God and thrust into a heightened and alienating self-consciousness. This affects not only the sinners but their offspring.

The object of this meditation is to become vividly aware of the human cost of choice, especially choice that is made without taking into account its implications and consequences. Moreover, this meditation works against the ego's defence of believing that it knows best, and so does not need God; or that it knows better than God how things should operate; or of the radically opposite position of giving up because it does not know all that is going on. When the ego's defences are broached in this way, there arises in the self a sense of confusion and shame.

Confusion occurs when the tidy systems we live by are discovered to be inadequate; shame arises when we are compelled to enter into the taboo areas of our psyche in discovering exactly that we operate very much like Adam and Eve did.

Of importance in this meditation is our growing discovery of the constructions of our ego. We see that we are shaped by our parents – by their genetic makeup, their attitudes and values, their experiences in the world, and their own parents' struggles in raising them. In an almost infinite regress, we discover that our identity has been shaped by the prison of DNA, of family histories, of social and economic class, of cultural and ethnic background, of an intricate weave of multi-layered histories in which we find that our self-identity is not as free as we thought. We discover that our way of relating to ourselves, to others and even to God has been determined in ways that are closed and broken. As Ignatius puts it, it is "to see in imagination…my whole composite being as an exile here on earth" (#47). If these reflections at this time produce a growing sense of entrapment, we are bringing to light the real situation of our lives, with the illusions we seduce ourselves with, or are seduced by, removed. This may be painful. We can only endure that pain when we realize that we are held by God even as we break out of the cocooned comfort of our deceptions. While we might think and feel we are far from God, God is not at all far from us. Indeed, that God who loves us is closer to us than we are to ourselves.

Questions for Prayer and Reflection

1. How do you see yourself as trapped?

2. What do you do to escape from these traps?

3. In what ways can you not escape from these traps?

4. How does that make you feel?

5. How can you live with the notion of "no escape"?

6. In what ways do those traps define who you are?

7. In what ways do those traps define how you relate to others?

8. In what ways do your image of religion and of God entrap you?

9. How do you feel when someone says to you in your traps, "God loves you"?

The Movie
Requiem for a Dream

Director: Darren Aronofsky (2000 – 102 mins.)
(Note: The film contains violence, sex, nudity, profanity.)
Stars: Ellen Burstyn, Jared Leto

1. Summary

Four people live out their dreams through their addictions to drugs and pills: Sara Goldfarb, a lonely, TV-obsessed widow; her son Harry; his girlfriend, Marion; and their drug dealer, Tyrone. Trapped in their addictions, their attempts to attain their dreams become yet another addiction, and they are caught in a downward spiral that will destroy them.

2. Questions about the Movie

1. "They held each other and kissed and pushed each other's darkness into a corner, believing in each other's light, each other's dream." (from the novel *Requiem for a Dream* by Herbert Selby Jr.)

   To whom does this statement refer? What are their dreams? What is their darkness?

2. In the film, the ideals of the human spirit are threatened by addictions. What are the addictions that face Sara, Harry, Marion and Tyrone?

3. The ending of this movie is almost impossible to watch. Why? Because we do not want to watch the revolting scenes that portray an obvious redemptive moral message? Or because we want to avoid such scenes, which make us aware of the consequences of our choices? Why do we want to avoid watching the manifestations of the nature of evil in which we are all implicated?

3. The Relationship of the Movie to the Theme of the Exercise

1. The main characters want to change in order to show the world that they are somebody. Yet in doing so they seek unlimited freedom, without realizing what this will cost them. What does this cost each of the four main characters? Do any of them actually fulfill their dreams?

2. The search for immediate gratification – in return for which they have only to perform one act, over and over – overwhelms these four people. Why can't they stop?

3. "Evil and horror are not explained: they are just placed before us with sphinx-like calm. Somehow, a spore or germ of evil has entered their universe, and fatally infected everything and everyone, like the needle in Harry's arm." (Peter Bradshaw, *The Guardian*, January 19, 2001)

   This is the ultimate horror of this film. We can see the confusion that occurs when the characters move out of their ordinary lives. All that they are, all that they have inherited from their families and backgrounds, has left them open to this evil. We see them, as Ignatius did, as being "an exile here on earth." Is there any chance for them to come out of this exile?

4. The Relationship of the Movie to One's Self in the Exercise

1. "Sara is just a lonely vulnerable person, a decent person who only wants to go on a TV show. And yet Aronofsky, with relentless, almost aesthetic cruelty, shows her fate as exactly equivalent to her son's." (Peter Bradshaw, *The Guardian*, January 19, 2001)

   It is far too easy to come away from this movie thinking that none of this applies to us. Yet in your own life there are many "addictions" available to you that have nothing to do with what we might call criminal behaviour. Such addictions can lead you to make choices without being aware of their implications and consequences. What are the possible "addictions" in your life?

2. Harry tries to warn his mother off the diet pills, but she tells him: "I'm somebody now, Harry! Everybody likes me! It's a reason to get up in the morning. It's a reason to smile." How carefully we are entrapped – piece by piece and step by step until we find ourselves able to justify just about anything. How does this apply to your own addiction/entrapment?

1st Exercise
(3) The Sin of One

Have mercy on me, O God,
According to your steadfast love;
According to your abundant mercy
Blot out my transgressions.
Wash me thoroughly from my iniquity,
And cleanse me from my sin!

For I know my transgressions,
And my sin is ever before me.
Against you, you only have I sinned,
And done what is evil in your sight .

(Psalm 51:1-4)

Imagine Christ Our Lord present before you upon the cross and begin to speak with him asking how it is that though he is the Creator, He has stooped to become human, and to pass from eternal life to death here in time, that thus he might die for my sins.

(Sp. Ex. #53)

This conversation is made by speaking exactly as one friend speaks to another, or as a servant speaks to a master, now asking for a favour, now blaming himself for some misdeed, now making known his affairs to him, and seeking advice in them.

(Sp. Ex. #54)

Grace: To be open to what Christ offers me.

Here Ignatius asks us to consider the personal destructiveness of one deadly sin. In the scriptures, the most common understanding of sin is (a) the willful rejection of the known will of God, (b) rebellion against God and God's love, and (c) guilt, as the way sin twists and distorts a person's integrity. The example of David's manipulations for Bathsheba reveals these three aspects. In committing adultery he has rebelled against God's commandment, placed greater value in his lust than in God's love, and sacrificed his conscience by his abuse of power in taking what he desires. In none of this is God essentially harmed. Those harmed are the sinner, those connected to the sinner, and ultimately humanity and all of creation.

The New Testament deepens and transforms those themes because it depicts a more intimate relationship between us and God, who becomes human to be with us. He becomes mortally vulnerable to the ravages of sin. The blind malice of evil as manifested by Judas's betrayal, by the conspiracy to silence him by the Jewish priesthood in Jerusalem, and by the Roman bureaucracy in maintaining a status quo, results in the death of Jesus – whose sole mission was to reveal the depth of his Father's love for a creation turned against God.

Ignatius asks us to consider how one radical sin can destroy a person spiritually, just as a single foolish or impassioned or negligent act can destroy a person physically. A tainted needle, a moment of blind anger, an unbuckled seatbelt, and a life is lost. Ignatius asks us further to consider just how many such acts have actually killed real people, and how many times we have or may have committed even more such acts without having been destroyed.

The point is not to drive us to a position of hyper-attention, as if we can be in total control of all aspects of every situation of our lives all the time. That would just be to submit further to the tyranny of the ego trying to maintain control. Rather, the point is to admit and feel and experience what it is not to be in control – that sense of confusion, of vertigo almost, as the illusions we build our lives on are seen to be without substance. It is also to experience that profound sense of shame as we realize the many times and the many ways we have tried to maintain control at the cost of losing our integrity and our soul. As Jesus asks, "What does it profit us to gain the whole world and to suffer the loss of our own soul?"

Moreover, the point is to experience the amazing and unacknowledged mercy of God when we realize that we have not destroyed ourselves, but have been rescued time and again from that self-destruction, or from the destruction of others. This is not to deny that we have been wounded or have wounded others. It is to admit that we have not been destroyed, and have been given the time and the opportunity to return to God not only those who have wounded us, but also those whom we have wounded.

Questions for Prayer and Reflection

1. Do you experience God as forgiving?

2. Do you experience God as creatively building new life out of the ruins of your life?

3. And out of the ruins of those whose lives you have ruined?

4. Can you bring to mind the situations and moments when you have been destructive? Self-destructive?

5. Why were you not destroyed?

6. How did your destructiveness affect you? How did it affect others? What were the consequences?

7. How do you live with those consequences?

8. Can you allow God to enter into those areas? How does it feel when you let that happen?

The Movie

Insomnia

Director: Christopher Nolan (2002 – 118 mins.)
Starring: Al Pacino, Robin Williams

1. Summary

A psychological thriller set in contemporary Alaska, *Insomnia* tells of a Los Angeles police detective, Will Dormer, who is sent to investigate the murder of a teenage girl in an Alaskan town. Once there he is involved in a fatal incident. Instead of admitting fault, he's offered an alibi that multiplies the emotional complexity and guilt he feels over the death. Now he not only has the murder to solve but also finds himself being investigated by a local detective and watched and manipulated by a mysterious antagonist.

2. Questions about the Movie

1. Here in Nightmute, unable to sleep under a sun that never sets, Dormer becomes fatigued physically and mentally. But he also has something else weighing on his conscience. Dormer's room at the lodge is the place where he attempts literally to shut out the daylight and hide from the truth about himself. It's almost as if the use of light represents the truth Dormer fears.

   How is this mood created in the film? How is light – which we associate with good – used to portray the darkness of sin?

2. As unlikely allies, Dormer and Finch present the audience with a moral challenge. We're faced with two apparent bad guys seeking justice in a murder they are both, in their own way, involved with. Are we faced with – finally – trying to come up with an answer to that moral question of whether the end ever justifies the means? Certainly Dormer believes this. Faced with a choice, he chose what he believed to be the greater good. But was it? Finch even tells Dormer: "You made your own choices." Does the end justify the means? Is a "white" lie in the aid of "goodness" acceptable? Does the fact that one supposed bad guy becomes a moral example for the rookie Ellie Burr make him more honourable than the other bad guy?

3. Appearances are deceiving. What seems real may be only a version of reality. At one point Dormer threatens to kill Finch telling him that he can make it appear to be an accident. Finch replies, "You can if you want it to." Even Dormer's name – which is a play on the French *dormir* – to sleep – is an appearance, for he cannot sleep. Appearance and reality is a prominent theme in *Insomnia*.

   Although much is deliberately left unclear, what is certain is that within the first 20 minutes we have left the conventional cop-chases-killer film. We have entered a world that is at once more interesting and more compelling – the world of a movie that is all about choices, the right ones and the wrong ones, and how they haunt us.

How did Dormer find himself in this situation? What choices and actions brought him to a point where the only solution seems to be one more sinful act?

3. The Relationship of the Movie to the Theme of the Exercise

1. The director has filmed the movie in such a way that we often see things from Dormer's point of view. As we watch him, we find ourselves not only drawn to him but somehow becoming part of him, getting inside his head. We're led to become complicit in everything he does and – in some very real way – to experience his doubts and anxieties. Because of this do you begin to feel more strongly what sin has done to Dormer?

2. "A good cop can't sleep because he's missing a piece of the puzzle. A bad cop can't sleep because his conscience won't let him." So said Dormer once, and now he is reminded of his words by a rookie cop.

   Both Dormer and Finch have made single mistakes that destroy them on many levels. As Ignatius asks, how many times have you committed such acts? Why then are you not destroyed? What do you see that you have that neither Dormer nor Finch appear to know or care about?

3. How does Insomnia show us that one moment, one act, can change our lives, our circumstances, our entire future, and that once we blur those lines of truth, everything becomes relative? Where does this apply to this Exercise?

4. The Relationship of the Movie to One's Self in the Exercise

1. "Dormer is a fidgeting, tormented man made all the more restless by the lack of sleep.... Dormer hunts evil, yet he can't deny its appeal." (Rick Groen, *The Globe and Mail*, May 24, 2002) There is often something seductive about sin that comes from our desires. Yet by giving in to them, we hurt ourselves and often others. How is this evident in your own life?

2. Though we tend to think of Ignatius' "radical sin" as some horrific act, is this true in Dormer's case? His sin is not that he killed his partner (that act was almost certainly an accident) but that he covered it up, and then made a deal with the enemy to keep the truth buried. He cannot admit to what has happened. How often have you done the same thing in your life? What is it like not to be in control?

3. Dormer appears to have sacrificed his conscience by abusing his power and killing his partner to prevent the end of his career. In your own sinfulness, what have you been willing to sacrifice?

2nd Exercise
Repetition

Create a clean heart in me, O God,
And put a new and right spirit within me.
Cast me not away from your presence,
And take not your holy Spirit from me.
Restore to me the joy of your salvation,
And uphold me with a willing spirit.

(Psalm 51:10-12)

I shall reflect upon my self and ask:
"What have I done for Christ?"
"What am I doing for Christ?"
"What ought I to do for Christ?"

(Sp. Ex. #53)

Grace: To experience my whole being as an exile here on earth.

(Sp. Ex. #47)

Carrying Our Past

Most of us live our lives focused on our immediate needs and our immediate problems. If we think beyond these, it is usually in terms of our immediate relationships. We figure, pragmatically, that the past is the past and cannot be changed, and so much of the future is beyond our control that it is no use worrying about it. We see ourselves as tiny, insignificant people caught in a world too large and complex and powerful for us. We consider such a perspective mature; it certainly helps us avoid lots of anxiety and insecurity.

But such an approach to life is not real, not true, and it carries with it the not quite hidden burdens of repression, blindness and despair. It is only during moments of quiet reflection, or during a sudden interruption of our daily habits, that we are forced to reconsider who we are and what we are doing. These are the cracks that let in the light.

Our lives are shaped by our past. Often we carry that past around with us, as if we were houses haunted by ghosts that refuse to leave. These are the traumatic moments that have stunted our healthy growth and made us cautious, closed off, insecure, pained and wounded. Unless those moments are brought to light and transformed by love, they fester and pervert us. They can even kill us spiritually. They are the sorts of things that make us think we must look after ourselves. No one else will.

This brokenness renders us immobile in the larger sphere of world action. It is also the nature of the world to create passive citizens who maintain the status quo. One way we do this is by denying our responsibility towards creation. That responsibility goes beyond social justice and ecological wholeness. It goes beyond us seeing our evolving creation on a purely natural level. We are not asked to be involved in the social and political and cultural dimensions of our world; we are involved. We need to become aware that we are involved, that each of us matters, and that any one of us can be an instrument for change – for good or for evil. If we understand that, then we can look at how we, personally, have been involved and complicit with the world.

Living with Disorder

We also have relationships with the natural world through the ways our innate urges for territory, dominance, survival, food, sex, transcendence and bonding are caught up in moral systems and behaviours that aim either towards good or away from it. Spiritualizing the natural merely creates ideologies of Romanticism. But we want to assert that basic spiritual insight that the natural finds its fulfillment in the spiritual, just as the spiritual finds its expression through the natural. To live in the natural as just natural is ultimately frustrating and subversive.

Yet we often and unconsciously do just that. Most of us would like to believe that in becoming civilized we have achieved some form of transcendence from the natural. That is good. It is when that transcendence is short-circuited that we also fall into more civilized forms of disorder. Then the natural is subjected to forms of ideology. We enter the world of privilege. Technology seeks to dominate or reconfigure the natural. Cosmetics abort the aging process; commercial forms of energy pollute the environment.

We are a part of those institutions, and participate consciously or unconsciously in them. Our personal disorder is a part of and contributes towards social disorder. Social disorder is part of and contributes to cultural disorder. Cultural disorder is a part of and contributes to the disorder of the human race. The human race is contextualized in the natural and the cosmic. We are all part of creation. We act on it and it acts on us. But we can only find out how it does so if God, who is beyond creation, can show us. This exercise is to ask for and to seek such a showing.

We usually receive this showing when we enter into all the dimensions of our lives. This inner journey of self-discovery leads to an outer journey where we find our place in the universe and in God's love.

These are things we have to learn from our own lives. No one else can teach us. Let us try to enter these places now.

In this prayer period we enter into the finding of ourselves in our relationships with others, with creation, and with God. We ask for the grace to see how we affect others and are affected by them. At the end of the prayer period have a conversation with Christ, as the Word through whom the Father creates the universe, about whatever arises from the prayer or your concerns.

Questions for prayer and reflection

1. How was this prayer different from the previous three prayer periods?

2. Did anything come together in this prayer period – in terms of insight or emotion or your relationship with God?

3. What was the most consoling moment in this prayer? What did it mean for you?

4. What was the most desolate moment in this prayer period? What does that mean for you?

5. What is happening to the ways in which you understand yourself?

6. What is happening to the ways in which you understand the relationships and moments in those relationships that have come up in your prayer?

7. How do you experience the world in this prayer period?

8. Is there any healing you would like to see happen to you now? In your own life? In relationships that have shaped you? In the way you deal with the world and the world deals with you?

The Movie
Stand by Me

Director: Rob Reiner (1986 – 89 mins.)
Starring: Wil Wheaton, River Phoenix, Corey Feldman, Jerry O'Connell

1. Summary

The death of a friend causes a writer to recall a boyhood journey he took with three friends to find the dead body of a missing teenager.

2. Questions about the Movie

1. In many ways this is a "road picture" – a movie where the main characters take a trip that changes their lives. As they sit in the junkyard, Teddy says: "This is really a good time." And the grown-up Gordie says that there was more to this than just them being together. Each of them knew that everything was right, and they knew "exactly who we were and where we going." Things won't remain this way. How are each of the boys – Gordie, Chris, Teddy and Vern – changed by their time together?

2. The music of the period plays an important role in this movie – not only to set mood but to express theme. How does the title song do this?

3. "*Stand by Me* is a vision of childhood's magic and childhood's end, and how the two interlock. It's the underside of the childhood pastoral that a kid doesn't fully understand but an adult, looking back, does." (David Edlestein, *Village Voice*, August 19, 1986) How do the events of the movie form both the end and the beginning of something for the four boys?

3. The Relationship of the Movie to the Theme of the Exercise

1. The Exercise tells us that a sudden interruption of our daily habits helps us to see beyond our immediate relationship. How does the announcement of a death affect not only the older Gordie but also his younger counterpart (and his three friends)?

2. Each of the boys carries the past with him: Gordie, the death of his brother; Chris, his reputation; Teddy, his abusive father; and Vern, his image as a fat kid. They are all wounded, cautious and insecure. How does their trip change this for each of them?

3. As the boys return to town, the grown-up Gordie says: "We'd only been gone two days but somehow the town seemed different, smaller." This trip lets light into their lives and makes them realize a lot about themselves. Where in their lives – as the Exercise puts it – are the cracks that let in the light?

4. The Relationship of the Movie to One's Self in the Exercise

1. "Why did Danny have to die?" is Gordie's reaction on first seeing the dead boy. He has come face to face with his past, and his actions after that show how he has changed and how he becomes involved. When you have come face to face with your past, have you reacted like Gordie? If not, what prevented you?

2. Chris tells Gordie not to give up being a writer, a gift that God gave him. Chris feels he has to say this – in place of it being said by Gordie's father – because: "Kids lose everything unless someone is there to make sure they don't." What is the moment in your life where someone faced you and made you aware that hiding the gifts God gave you will only leave you wounded?

3. Early in the morning, Gordie sees a deer beside the tracks but he tells no one. The grown-up Gordie says: "I have never written or told anyone about this till now." Why did Gordie keep this to himself? Should he have shared it with the other three? What things in your life do you keep to yourself that you ought to share?

3rd Exercise
Destruction

Out of the depths I cry to you, O Lord!
Lord, hear my voice!
Let your ears be attentive
To the voice of my supplications!

If you, O Lord, should mark iniquities,
Lord, who could stand?
But there is forgiveness with you.

(Psalm 130:1-4)

I will conclude with a colloquy, extolling the mercy of
God, our Lord, pouring out my thoughts to Him, and
giving thanks to Him that up to this very moment He has
granted me life.

(Sp. Ex.#61)

Grace: This is to ask for what I desire. Here it will be to ask
for a growing and intense sorrow and tears for my sins.

The third exercise asks to us to examine thoroughly the ways we have been actively or passively involved in, or have contributed to, the destructiveness of sin. Ignatius asks us now to pray for "a growing and intense sorrow and tears for my sins" (#55:2). The thrust of this exercise is to break down the defenses of the ego so that it becomes aware of its limitations and defects in contrast to the goodness, mercy, wisdom, and life-giving creativity and generosity of God. We realize here that we are not God; we are not the centre and the meaning of the universe. God, the centre and meaning, cares for our true selves, and sustains, maintains, and cherishes them. The focus of this exercise is on the mercy of God as realized by our new and growing understanding of our sinful nature.

People falling in love usually share their deepest and darkest secrets with the other, almost to test if the beloved could bear to love them in that darkness. In this Exercise we are encouraged to share those secrets: not to debase ourselves but to confirm to ourselves that we are loved to the core of our being, and that we can be held even as we admit those moments when we were unloving, unlovable, and unloved.

Because this is a difficult Exercise to do, it is worthwhile to break it up into separate parts. We will use the path through the Beatitudes in Matthew's Gospel to discover our poverty of spirit and God's overwhelming love for us in this state. We will look at the ways we destructively compensate for that poverty of spirit. To experience God's love we are called to enter into those tragic dimensions of our lives. When we do this prayerfully and patiently we discover the transforming power of God's love. The Beatitudes, which embody the Christian vision, are a powerful way of opening ourselves to conversion. Most of us see and live out of our hurts. Praying the Beatitudes transforms those hurts into encounters with God's compassionate mercy. At this time, using just one film, *Magnolia*, we will spend several prayer periods slowly going through the Beatitudes step by step. This journey will carry us to experience passionately a love that embraces us into the fullness of life. This journey is the essence of the First Week of the Exercises. The personal dimensions we encounter here embody the very brokenness of our lives and God's invitation to hold them up to the power of resurrection.

In Matthew's Gospel, Jesus Christ is presented as the new Moses leading his people out of slavery through the desert into the promised land. Praying the Beatitudes leads us from the bondage of whatever stops us from being free, and its illusions of what freedom is, to a life that rejoices in a personal intimacy with God.

To enter the Beatitudes and be carried by them we must start by sitting with the first one, which allows us to experience at the same time just how much our lives are beyond our control and just how much we are held and cherished by God. The unfinished business that arises in our prayer from each Beatitude carries us in an intensely personal way to the next one. That path we journey on leads to an ever-deeper awareness of God's presence in our lives. Give yourself enough time to enter into each beatitude. Each is a blessing that reveals its depths only in patience and prayerful reflection. It is helpful to watch *Magnolia* after reading the reflection on the first beatitude and again when the reflection on a particular prayer leads you back to it. It is a film that rewards repeated viewing as you journey through the Beatitudes.

The first beatitude describes the human condition and God's gift to us as we truly are.

1. Blessed are the poor in spirit: theirs is the kingdom of God

To be a follower of Jesus is to follow the path of Christ. It is to realize in our daily lives that our lives are handed over to the mystery we call God – not in some abstract way, but here and now, concretely – with who we are, who we are with, and in the situations within ourselves, within our immediate communities, our families and friends, and within the manifestations of the Church today. To realize this is to realize our poverty.

We have little control over these areas of our lives. Often we prefer to hide from this poverty and from the fact that we are truly broken people. We are broken intellectually, physically, emotionally, spiritually, communally. Today we are asked to take time to acknowledge the brokenness in our lives – the brokenness that is our life. We are asked to put aside, gently but firmly, the illusions we have of being otherwise. To be otherwise is to pretend that we are God, but truly, we are the emptiness that only God can fill.

Before we can be filled we need to admit our poverty. It is only then that we can open ourselves to the path leading to the kingdom of God. Instead of seeing our poverty as a horror and a burden, we can see it as a door through which we need to walk. We need to be led and carried by our poverty to the wounded places where we are raw and vulnerable and naked. If we can go there and stay there, we get in touch with not only our own poverty, but that of other people and of the world. Poverty allows us to discover community, which is the kingdom of God in our midst.

Poverty of spirit is the radical sense of our nothingness, and our awareness of our dependence on

Divine Providence for health, approval, image, identity, friendship, even life itself. To enter into poverty of spirit is to enter the realm where we are stripped of illusions – even the illusions of our illusions. Poverty of spirit sentences us to death, beyond the awareness of our mortality. When we live out of that poverty, things happen to us. We start seeing every moment as a gift, as a wonderful luxury. Every moment is pure wonder. Such poverty cuts out a lot of nonsense from our lives. Because we cannot compromise that poverty, we do not need to defend ourselves or sacrifice ourselves to maintain false images. We can be simple and tolerant in our suffering towards the suffering of others.

The discipline of poverty is to remain empty. Into that emptiness comes the presence of God. It is there that we realize the scandal of the cross being transformed into the awe of the resurrection. To live in that emptiness is to change our self-image, our expectations of others and the way we imagine the world. It is to be so open that the energies of God can flow through us into the world.

Poverty of spirit is liberation. It is the liberation from illusion, the place where we can be simply and shamelessly passionate with God and where God is simply and shamelessly passionate with us. Even here and now.

Questions for prayer and reflection

1. What are your gifts? How do you use them? How are you trapped by them?

2. What are your poverties? How do you hide from them? What happens to you when you enter into those areas?

3. In what areas do you not believe in yourself? In what areas do you not believe in others, or in God?

4. Where do you feel threatened? Where does your body tell you that you are threatened?

5. How are you threatened by God? By your community? By yourself? By your prayer? How do you experience that threat in your body?

6. What are the areas of vulnerability in your life?

7. What areas can humiliate you?

8. In what areas are you humbled?

9. Poverty is to take only what you need from this world, nothing more. Can you distinguish between what you want and what you need? To know what that is requires discipline, spirit, wisdom. Can you pray for that grace – generally and in specific instances?

Scripture suggestions for prayer

Matthew 5:3
Psalm 136; 34
Isaiah 41:17-20; 55:1–56: 9
Luke 1:5-38
Philippians 2:1-11
Revelation 3:14-22

2. Blessed are the gentle; they shall inherit the earth

We are all vulnerable. If we were to meditate on our vulnerability we can discover in ourselves opposing tensions in our living out of our vulnerability. Such vulnerability can breed fear when we internalize the forces that threaten us. This fear creates alienation when we understand the "other" to be inimical to our well-being, and the alienation manifests itself in violence as we try to defend that space in which we find our identity. Then "the kingdom of heaven is taken by violence and the violent destroy it" (Matthew 11:12).

But there is another approach to being vulnerable. Vulnerability can open us up to the dimensions of Divine Providence in our lives when we realize, in examining our histories, that we are not destroyed but instead are saved in spite of ourselves. The awareness of our lives being held in God's care moves us to gratitude, especially when we see just how easily we can be destroyed. The spirit of gratitude manifests itself in the gentleness with which we deal with ourselves, others and the world. We do not have to be violent to maintain ourselves. God's power comes "to save all the meek of the earth" (Ps 76:10).

To be gentle is, first of all, to face not only our vulnerability but also the horror, the abject nakedness and the blind misery that masquerade as the powers of this world, without freezing or being trapped by fear – our own or others'. To be gentle calls us to be attentive (as opposed to being blind) to the forces that make up our world; to be discerning, insightful, political and flexible in dealing with these forces; and to be responsible, rather than reactive, for transforming the oppressor and the oppressed. To be gentle calls us to dance in the flames, and the ashes, and the hard places of this life. The witness of this gentleness lies neither in our devotion to an ideology of a social justice nor in a withdrawal from the arenas of social change. It lies in the manifest joy of knowing the presence of the powers of good that hold, protect, affirm and guide us along the path that is salvation.

That joy allows us to see in the cracks and the terrors of this world the promise of paradise. It invites us to co-operate with the powers of good by being present, humbly and gratefully, at precisely those places so that through our simple presence God can enter the world.

Questions for prayer and reflection

1. What are the areas of violence in your personal life? In your community?

2. In what ways does your lifestyle create violence to your integrity, your family, the larger community?

3. How do you feed and communicate your violence – in your silence, apathy, speech, narcissism – in your daily life?

4. What difficulties do you have in reconciling your notions of gentleness with your idea of what it means to inherit the earth?

5. What possibilities of transformation open up when you do not assert your self-righteousness?

6. What comes to you when you pray for the grace to be gentle?

7. How can you affirm others in being a person for/with others despite your limited resources? How can others affirm you?

Scripture Passages for Prayer

Matthew 27:15-23
Matthew 11:25-30
Matthew 7:7-12
Isaiah 29:13-21
Isaiah 61:1-4
Psalms 37; 75; 131; 138

3. Blessed are those who mourn, for they shall be comforted

To mourn is to acknowledge death, and the call to a life beyond death. Mourning is the movement to resurrection where we are saved – not by anything we have done or can do, not even by hope, but by the generosity of God. In mourning we let go of our dead into the shaping spirit of the One who forms us all. Mourning is the responsibility we have to the dead. In mourning them we are present to them; we allow God to reach through us to touch them.

To mourn, then, we first must acknowledge the presence and effect of the dead in our lives. To remember them as they were is to become a tomb, for it means that this life is all that they are. Sometimes we hold on to a rotting corpse; we are disgusted by the corruption and fear of the stink. Something in us wants to flee. Our fear is a form of despair that death is the end. We repress death and enter into a false freedom where the dead possess us unconsciously and shape the path we walk. We believe that because we no longer think or brood about the dead, they are gone. This illusion of clarity is, in effect, the fear of being haunted and devoured by the dead. Such a fear denies that God is stronger than death and more compassionate than us.

Second, we must make room for the dead in our lives, becoming conscious of the ways they influence our perceptions and our ways of thinking and acting. If we do this, we become aware what our tradition – the handing on of our particular spirit – is. This is not to enter into a passionate love of death, but to see death as a part of life. It is only when we acknowledge the presence of the dead in our lives that we become responsible for passing on the spirit transformed by our creativity.

Finally, we can walk with the dead on our mutual path to the fullness of life of the resurrection only when they and we and all of creation come together as one in joy and in the shared gratitude of being redeemed into a common life. For to mourn is to enter into community; the comfort offered to those who mourn is the growing realization that in the act of mourning, resurrection happens. Mourning creates joy. Mourning transforms grief into hope. To grieve is to be aware of loss, of the fragility of the world in which we live and find our meaning. It is to admit our inability to maintain that world, to live with the fragments of that world and with the empty spaces between those fragments that nothing can fill. Grief can kill. Mourning offers life. When we mourn we bring all that to God. We wait, in prayer and in the lived consolation of being companions together in this dreadful adventure, for the tombs to open and the new life we call resurrection to occur.

Questions for prayer and reflection

1. What are the dead of your life? What are the things you despair over, believe are unchangeable, in your own life, in the life of your family and the larger community?

2. What dangers do you encounter in your mourning? For example, how do you distinguish between mourning and being critical? Can you distinguish between "coming back for the dead" and "resurrection"?

3. Who, or what, have you found personally helpful in your own process of mourning?

4. Do you have any instances of resurrection in your life? How were you surprised? How have you shared the resurrection you received?

5. What are the things, places, works, and/or people in your life that you would like to experience resurrection? What ways have you tried, or do you try, to promote resurrection to these? In other words, how do you comfort others?

Scripture Passages for Prayer

John 11:1-45
Luke 7:11-17
Matthew 9:1-7
Matthew 17:1-13
Luke 4:14-30
Luke 23:50–24:11
John 20:11-18

4. Blessed are those who hunger and thirst for justice; they shall be satisfied

The practice of freedom lies in evil, not beyond it. If our choices enslave anyone we are not free. True freedom is generated through God's saving activity and the intimate relationship God establishes and maintains with us here and now, in the midst of suffering. True justice comes from justification. It is only when we accept that we, and all, are loved – even when and as we sin – that we can begin to understand what it means to be justified. Otherwise, our understanding of justice remains fallen. We see it merely in terms of recompense, of contract, and our commitment to justice – on the personal, communal, social or cultural level – stays within the boundaries of self-knowledge and self-interest, like the Pharisees and the Zealots did.

That position denies the depths of what it means to be human. It denies the pervasiveness of sin in our lives, and our constant hunger for God that underlies that sin. Moreover, it manipulates the hunger others have for God into an acceptance of cult and ritual through guilt and repression. We are not saved by the word of the law, but only by the Giver of the spirit that is expressed in the law. Our hunger is not satisfied by the law but by our relationship with the living Word, under whose cross we find our life. To hunger and thirst for salvation is to commit ourselves to that life – not only for ourselves, but for all. It is to experience the agony of the passion as we use all our energies to ensure that the fullness of life may be tangibly present to all in the sacrament of daily life.

On the cross, Christ is at his most creative. In that act he overcomes those powers that, in their blindness, self-service and malice, attempt to block that life from being given to all who desire it. When we hunger and thirst for God in this world, we hunger and thirst for relationships for all in which the only criterion is mutual love. In John's Gospel Jesus prays to the Father for his companions, "that they may be one even as we are one, I in them and thou in me, that they may become perfectly one" (17:22-23).

How we treat ourselves and others shows not only what and whom we love but how we love. That love is where we put our lives. Ignatius says that "love ought to manifest itself in deeds rather than in words"; he continues, "the lover gives and shares with the beloved what he possesses" (Sp. Ex: 230:1, 231:2). When we hunger and thirst for justice, we place ourselves in our poverty in such a way in the world that the passion of the Father makes us also his living words in the circumstances in which we find (and lose) ourselves.

We desire to be saved because we cannot save ourselves. When we follow the path of that desire we allow God to come to us. The joy and gratitude we experience when that happens emboldens us to continue His mission in the world because we discover we are all one.

Questions for prayer and reflection

1. Can you accept that you are loved? If not, what stops you from accepting that?

2. What areas in your life are silenced, not believed, oppressed, marginalized, colonized?

3. What are you passionate about?

4. What is the connection between the way you see social justice and the way you experience God?

5. How do you inflict alienation on others? Do others experience you as an open door to the mystery we call God?

6. In what ways do you need to be more joyful?

7. What subverts your creativity into anger? Into apathy?

8. What excites your creativity? What affirms your creativity right now? In what ways can you commit yourself to your creativity?

Scripture Passages for Prayer

Psalm 130
Matthew 5:20-28
Luke 18:1-14
Romans 8:1-39
Romans 12:9-21
Exodus 3:1-18

5. Blessed are the Merciful, for they shall obtain mercy

Mercy is absurd. It is neither prudent nor politic. It has no aims, expects no rewards and is not self-congratulatory. It strives to love its enemies, expecting nothing in return. In this it imitates God, who is "kind to the ungrateful and the selfish" (Luke 6:36). The merciful are always aware that God is good to us even as we sin; they come to the realization that God's justice is his mercy, his constancy of help and his patience. That mercy is not a kind of pity that sees the suffering of the other and is only interiorly moved by it. Human mercy, like divine mercy, goes out of itself to transform the suffering of the sinner. Human mercy flows as an act of gratitude for having experienced divine mercy; that gratitude covenants God and humanity. That spirit of gratitude does not abet sin but strives to bring those trapped in sin to the truth of their lives — to accept that they are loved and can be loving towards others.

The merciful are not judgmental. They know what it is to be trapped and then freed from those traps, and how easy it is, but for the constant support of God, to be trapped again. That personal history makes them attentive to the broken of the world, be they rich or poor, powerful or weak, the shamed or the shameless. It gives them the lived experience that helps them distinguish between want and need, and allows them to respond to other people's needs, for they recognize that because all life is interconnected, everything concerns us and evokes our compassion.

But we cannot do everything. Trying to do everything denies mercy to ourselves. We can only do what we have been gifted to do. Our gifts are at the service of those we meet. We are to be open doors through which the world's needs meet God.

The preferential option for the poor sees and addresses the poverty in everyone, as Jesus did, to the outrage of the self-righteous – those who were blind to their own needs and so blind to the needs of others (Matt 25:34-40).

We can never be as merciful as we would wish, but we can be merciful as we are, with the little we have. In sharing our poverty, we discover what it means to be human. The hard heart that cannot be hurt cannot love, either. To be merciful is risky: we may be taken advantage of, be made a fool of. Indeed, this is often the case if we are concerned with ourselves. But if we are giving what we have been given, this is never the case. It is easy to abuse God's gifts. Our human history is filled with such abuse, but God keeps giving and therefore our history is one of salvation. The mercy we are enjoined to offer is rooted in the absurdity of love – of being loved and of being given the opportunity to love. It is expressed as gratitude for that felt knowledge.

Questions for prayer and reflection

1. Have you ever received mercy? Have you ever offered mercy? When?

2. What are you truly grateful for? What do you accept as your right? What do you reject?

3. What gifts can you offer others now? What gifts can you accept from others?

4. What gifts can you offer your community? What do you do if the community rejects your gifts?

5. How do you deal with rejection?

6. What can you risk to create community? What do you risk to create community?

7. Have you ever been trapped? How did you become free?

Scripture Passages for Prayer

Psalms 22 and 23; 86; 88 and 118
Luke 6:27-38
Luke 18:9-14
John 8:2-11
Luke 23:32-46

6. Blessed are the Pure in Heart, for they shall see God.

Our deepest desire is from God. Our deepest desire seeks God in all things. Our spiritual path is to be led by that desire. In living our lives we discover that we are shaped by many desires. We find ourselves asking: Which desires lead to the building up of the kingdom of God? Which of the desires do not? The desires that are the manifestations of our deepest desire move us to be companions of Christ. Those other desires are energies, or patterns of energy, that have somehow become detached from our deepest desire and lead a separate existence. They can be identified by that separation. Consolation occurs when our desires harmonize with the energies of the Spirit; joy occurs when our energies harmonize with those of those around us; happiness occurs when the energies surrounding us harmonize with ours; pleasure occurs when those energies submit to us. The range from consolation to desolation is from community to narcissistic pleasure.

To be pure in heart is to be on the path to integration where all the energies of our life – spiritual, social, communal, personal, emotional, intellectual, sexual – are woven together by our deepest desire. The focus of that path is on relationship rather than ritual, prophecy rather than professionalism. The integrity of the weave of those energies makes no distinction between private and public, between self and other. To be pure in heart is to realize the unity of all that exists and to value all that exists. This unity includes the energies that make up ourselves, and manifest singleness of purpose. As we move on the path of purity of heart, we discover in ourselves a singleness of purpose that makes us flexible to the Spirit. That union of spirit carries us to places where displaced energies come to light. Like people possessed, we endure the exorcisms of encountering love that reweaves those straying energies.

The trials of living life this way embody the struggle between narcissism and community. As we walk the path and struggle for that more total integration we discover that nothing human is foreign to us. Such self-awareness makes us humble. In that humility we become more and more disposed to the dance of the energies, more open to the darkness in which God dwells, where we see first not with the eyes but with the heart.

What the heart sees is that everything that exists is holy. To be pure in heart is to enter into the struggle of creation, in which everything is involved, to realize that holiness in all the circumstances of life. Evil is fragmented holiness. The task of the pure in heart is to carefully gather up those fragments into unity, to unknot the tangled energies that bind us in the bondage of compulsion and oppression. The pure of heart, by the simple act of being present, heal the afflicted, bind up the broken-hearted, give sight to the blind, set free the enslaved, and announce to the world the presence of God among us so that they can freely enter into the play and the delight of the life where God dwells.

Questions for prayer and reflection

1. What are the divisions in your personal life? In the life of your community?

2. How do those divisions affect you? What are you doing about them concretely?

3. What difficulties do you encounter as you strive to witness not to your own integrity but to the integrity of God?

4. Can you discern between passion and compulsion? Between indifference and apathy? Between pilgrimage and forced marches?

5. Where are the freedoms in your life? How do those freedoms come together? What aspects of your life are in pilgrimage, as opposed to bondage and its forced marches? Where do you celebrate? How? With whom?

6. What is the witness of your life? Who witnesses God to you?

Scripture Passages for Prayer

Genesis 22:1-19
Psalm 116
Romans 8:1-39
Matthew 4:1-11
Mark 5:1-20
Revelation 19: 9-11

7. Blessed are the peacemakers; they shall be called the children of God

Hatred destroys not only the other, but also us. In maintaining hate we sacrifice ourselves to the lie that the enemy deserves to die. That war breeding more war "is only a cowardly escape from the problems of peace," as Thomas Mann once said. The only way to overcome an enemy is to make the enemy a friend. The problem of peace is how to make an enemy a friend. To make peace is to move beyond apathy or tolerance. To make peace is to create community. In community, the energies of all are allowed positive expression. It is a question of imagination. Because we live in imagined worlds, what we imagine as real defines how we relate with others. When we indulge ourselves to imagine the world, instead of allowing ourselves to live as God imagines us, we follow the path of fantasy. As Yeats observed of those fighting against each other in the civil war in Ireland:

Their hearts are fed by fantasies
Their hearts have grown brutal from the fare.

Before we can create community, we need to ask what fantasies shape our lives and, further, what forces in our lives come together to maintain those fantasies. If we see only out of our hurts – rather than the call that gives us our vision – we project onto those we hate those forces that have hurt us. We deny that these forces are in our own lives, but we know they are there because they trap us.

We become peacemakers only when we make peace with ourselves, only as we acknowledge the hurt in our lives, through a healing of memories and sensibilities within the vision that gives our life meaning. This meaning is not accessible in terms of satisfaction but through the modes of consolation. In consolation we are redefined not according to fantasy but through an open metaphor. We move beyond the boundaries of reality so that what we thought was impossible becomes possible. In this way, the enemy can become the friend – not by our manipulation, but by the other's freedom of choice. Even self-sacrificing love – radical openness – does not

make the other free. But it is the most we can do. It is our vocation.

Christ comes to reconcile us to God, to each other, to ourselves, and to all the forces of creation. Reconciling the estranged is the mission of the peacemaker, the Son of God. According to today's beatitude, his companions inherit that same mission from God. Community can be built only if people share a common vision, if everyone maintains a common good. That common good is manifested differently according to different gifts, but underlying the differences is the same spirit and a common vocation. The dynamic of integration that we need to be persons of peace is also necessary to be a community. Prayer, dialogue, openness, intimacy and celebration create life. The path of the peacemaker leads to the broken and hard places of our own lives, our own community, and our own world. It takes up the standard and cross of Christ, our brother.

Questions for prayer and reflection

1. How do you find your community? Does it support your integrity? Are you inspired by the community, the society, the culture you live in?

2. How do you celebrate life in your community? Do you pray for each other regularly in community? Do you have adequate structures to promote spiritual conversation, formally and spontaneously? Who in your community knows about your spiritual life? What can you do to promote life in your community?

3. What ideals of community life do you hold that alienate you from the people you live with? Do you know the estranged parts of your life? Do you know the integrated parts of your life? Do you live out of alienation or integration with

yourself and your community? How do we realize, individually and collectively, our call to be peacemakers?

4. What healing do you need now? What reconciliations dare you ask God to effect?

5. What happens when you pray for the grace to imitate Christ in his task of forgiveness and reconciliation?

6. What happens when you pray for the grace of abandonment to Divine Providence?

Scripture Passages for Prayer

John 14:15–15:17
Galatians 5:13–6:2
Ephesians 2:8-22, 4:1-16
Romans 5:1-11
Daniel 10:15-19
Isaiah 11:1-11

Futher questions for prayer and reflection

1. Who is your community – the ones you share your life with? Why do you say that? How did you come to that relationship?

2. Who is not your community? Why do you say that? How do you treat those others?

3. What boundaries do you impose upon imagining yourself? Are those boundaries open or closed? How do you experience yourself, and others, as mystery?

4. With whom are you intimate? How are you intimate with yourself – in terms of self-awareness, self-knowledge, being comfortable with yourself, loving yourself into transcendence? How are you intimate with others? How are you intimate with

God, so that God can be fully present, through you, in the world?

5. What difficulties do you have with intimacy? What stops you from trusting? What concrete elements stop you from risking – moving beyond trust into the darkness? What forms of fear, of established positions, of power, of disillusionment, possess you?

6. Where do you find life? Where do you give life? Where do you take life?

7. To whom, with whom and for whom do you feel responsible?

Scripture Suggestions for Prayer

Matthew 5:9
John 17:6-26; 1 John 1:5–2:17
1 Corinthians 12:1-14
Genesis 22:1-14
Genesis 32:24-31
Song of Songs 3:1-5; 8:6-7
Revelation 21:1-8

8. Blessed are those who are persecuted for righteousness' sake

When our hearts are so filled with longing for the kingdom that that longing shapes everything we do, we hold different values from the world. We trust what the world neither sees nor believes in and then, because we are judged as "other," we may become objects of derision, or fear, or hatred. Once, in a house, there was a wedding festival. The musicians sat in a corner and played their instruments, the guests danced to the music and were merry, and the house was filled with joy. A deaf man passing by the house looked in through the window and saw the people whirling about the room, leaping and throwing about their arms. "See how they fling themselves about!" he cried. "It is a house filled with madmen!" For he could not hear the music to which they danced.

To be possessed of the desire only for God is to be judged crazy or eccentric like Francis of Assisi stripping naked in the public square of his father's town. It is to be seen as dangerous by the Inquisition, like Ignatius asserting how God could be found in this world. That hunger makes us fools for Christ's sake and lets us share in the passion the Father has for his Son and in the passion the Son has for the Father. That passion is to say yes to life, to make the leap of faith in every moment of life, and to return to the marketplace bearing gifts is the Spirit.

The path of the Beatitudes returns always to a world to be transformed. We leave that world because it does not satisfy our needs; in that journey we discover the dead we carry with us and experience the humility of the powerless saved. The zeal our transformation engenders is tempered into a mercy that makes us one with God in compassion for the world. Living compassionately in this world, we manifest the prophetic presence of being living words of God, companions of Jesus. In each stage of the path there are trials to be endured. Each stage brings a death and a resurrection. Then, like Paul, "We rejoice in our hope of sharing the glory of God. More than that we rejoice in our suffering, knowing that suffering produces endurance and endurance produces character, and character produces hope, and hope does not disappoint us, because God's love has been poured into our hearts through the Holy Spirit that has been given to us" (Romans 5:3-5).

Through the Beatitudes our devotion becomes the sacrifice making the world holy and uniting us in God's embrace. In living that embrace we live not for or through ourselves. Rather, Revelation lives us through our commitment. "You are the salt of the earth; but if salt has lost its taste, how shall it be restored? It is no longer good for anything except to be thrown out and trodden under foot. You are the light of the world. A city set on a hill cannot be hid. Nor does anyone light a lamp and put it under a bushel, but on a stand, and it gives light to all in the house. Let your light shine before all, that they may see your good works and give glory to your Father who is in heaven" (Matt 5:13-16).

Questions for prayer and reflection

1. How are you to live your life here and now?

2. What do you need to live that life?

3. Which beatitude gave you the greatest consolation? Which beatitude challenges you the most? What does this tell you about your path and about your shadow?

4. How do the people you admire live the Beatitudes? How do you live the Beatitudes?

5. What is the concrete relationship between the Beatitudes and your daily life, the way you see yourself and others, the ways you share life and make decisions?

6. Where are you now?

7. What work do you need to do to continue the experience of being loved into life by God?

Scripture Suggestions for Prayer

Psalm 42 and 24
John 21
John 1:13-23
Luke 21:1-4
Acts 2:1-28
Mark 3:13–35

The Movie
Magnolia

Director: Paul Thomas Anderson (1999 – 188 mins.)
Starring: Jason Robards, Julianne Moore, Tom Cruise, William H. Macy

1. Summary

On one random day in the San Fernando Valley, a dying father, a young wife, a male caregiver, a famous lost son, a police officer in love, a boy genius, an ex-boy genius, a game show host and an estranged daughter will each become part of a dazzling multiplicity of plots, but one story.

Through a collusion of coincidence, chance, human action, shared media, past history and divine intervention they will weave and warp through each other's lives on a day that builds to an unforgettable climax. Some will seek forgiveness, others escape. Some will mend frayed bonds, others will be exposed.

2. Questions about the Movie

1. "This imposing tapestry about the mysterious workings of fate and coincidence and the need for interconnection and love interweaves the story of a dozen characters as they embark on a moral odyssey during one intense day." (Emanuel Levy, *Variety*, December 13-19, 1999)

   The soundtrack music plays an important role in developing this tapestry, becoming almost another character. What do the opening song and the images that go with it tell you about each of the characters?

2. There are two sequences that people refer to with a degree of puzzlement:

   1) The Frog Scene: Throughout the movie signs appear referring specifically to the plague of frogs described in Exodus 8:2. Here the ferocious and surreal rain of frogs is a device that serves to bring the film's lonely characters together.

   2) In a type of climax, just before each character acts for the last time, they all – one by one (even two who are comatose) join in singing a song with songwriter Aimee Mann called "Wise Up." The director thought that such a moment flowed naturally from all that had gone before and that many people – when they are lonely or sad – sing along with a song on the radio.

   Which of these two scenes was the more difficult for you to accept? Why do you think the director uses such devices? Do they convey his theme successfully?

4. "Anderson does not know that he was making a movie about the absence of grace. He sets the stage for two ministers of grace – a melancholy Christian policeman and a compassionate male

nurse – and a spectacular act of God." (Steve Lansingh, *Christianity Today*, July 24, 1999)

Forgiveness is at the heart of *Magnolia* – but it is a forgiveness that gives life. LAPD Officer Jim Kurring is the embodiment of this – the Common Man, if you will. What he says at the end of the film – "Sometimes people need a little help, sometimes people need to be forgiven, and sometimes people need to go to jail. The hard part is to forgive." – expresses the fact that we as Christians are expected to give forgiveness to ourselves and to all. How effective are the two "ministers of grace" – one explicitly religious, one implicitly – in their role?

3. The Relationship of the Movie to the Theme of the Exercise

1. The Exercise encourages us to share our darkest secrets, not to debase ourselves but to confirm to ourselves that we are loved to the core of our being, and that we can be held even as we admit those moments when we were unloving, unlovable and unloved. What scene in the movie best exemplifies this statement?

2. The eight Beatitudes – the keys to the 2nd Exercise – are listed below, together with some statements you've been given about them. Which characters are examples of the particular beatitude or are still caught in the sin that prevents them from reaching a particular beatitude?

   A: The poor in spirit:

   "We are broken intellectually, physically, emotionally, spiritually, communally."

   "Poverty of spirit is liberation from illusion."

B: The gentle:

"Face our own vulnerability and the powers of this world, without freezing or being trapped by fear – our own or others'."

"To be gentle calls us to be attentive and to be responsible for transforming the oppressor and the oppressed."

C: Those who mourn:

"Acknowledge the presence of the dead in our lives."

"Become conscious of the ways the dead influence our ways of thinking and acting."

"To mourn is to enter into community."

D: Those who hunger and thirst for justice:

"Commit ourselves to life – not only for ourselves but for all."

"How we treat ourselves and others shows not only what and whom we love but how we love."

E: The merciful:

"Mercy strives to love its enemies, expecting nothing in return."

"To be merciful is risky: we may be taken advantage of."

F: The pure in heart:

"Our deepest desire is from God and is to be a companion of Christ."

"The pure of heart, by the simple act of being present, heal the afflicted."

G: The peacemakers:

"To make peace is to create community."

"The path of the peacemaker leads to the broken and hard places of our own lives, community and world."

H: The persecuted:

"When our hearts are so filled with longing for the kingdom that that longing shapes everything we do, we hold different values from the world."

"That passion to say yes to life is the Spirit."

4. The Relationship of the Movie to One's Self in the Exercise

1. Go back to the exercise above, where you looked at the individual beatitudes and how the characters in the movies related to them. Now, using the same format, look at the ways you have undergone similar experiences to those of the characters regarding the beatitudes. What has this done to your life?

2. Asking for and granting forgiveness in modern life is a risky business, but *Magnolia* shows us just how beautiful it can be. The path of the Beatitudes returns always to a world to be transformed.

    What needs to be sacrificed or transformed in your life – right here, right now – before you can embrace God?

68

4th Exercise
Repetition

O Lord, you have searched me and known me,
You know when I sit down and when I rise up;
You discern my thoughts from afar.
You search out my path and my lying down,
And are acquainted with all my ways.

(Psalm 139:1-3)

This exercise will consist in repeating the First and Second Exercise. In doing this we should pay attention to and dwell upon those points in which we have experienced greater consolation or desolation or greater spiritual appreciation.

(Sp. Ex. #62)

Grace: A deep knowledge of my sins and a feeling of abhorrence for them; an understanding of the disorder of my actions, that filled with horror of them, I may amend my life and put it in order; a knowledge of the world, that filled with horror I may put away from me all that is worldly and vain.

(Sp. Ex. #62)

The Three Goals of Repetition

Ignatius, as you will soon discover, uses repetitions of previous prayer materials to reinforce a point, or to achieve depth, or even to move the retreatant to a different place by exhausting his or her sense of curiosity and thus let the deeper elements of the prayer exercise emerge.

This exercise asks you to repeat the most significant points you have discovered in the previous exercises. You need to examine what you have found in yourself, and what you need to do with what you have found.

The easiest way of doing this is to ask what has been the most significant moment in the previous exercises and to stay with that significant moment in prayer. If there were several significant moments, you will need to spend prayer time with each of these before moving on.

The second way is to ask, in each prayer period that you have had so far, what has brought you closer to God (note that this does not necessarily mean pleasant) and what has taken you away from God (e.g., distractions, boredom, agitation, daydreaming, pleasant or not).

If we consider the movement of the Exercises so far, you might think of the Exercises as opening up with a wide-angle shot that slowly zooms in on you. In this exercise, we examine that self with increasing close-ups but to achieve a distance from that self. And so this repetition aims for three things.

First Goal

First, it aims to give you a deep experience of your own disorders, without actually having you re-enact or re-engage in them, and a feeling of abhorrence for them. If sin traumatizes you by defining you in an obsessive-compulsive way, you need to re-

69

enter those moments of trauma – this time from the context of being held in God's love – and walk through each trauma with God, Jesus or Mary as a companion. This will help you "re-educate" the self in a more loving way by responding spontaneously to those elements of your disordered self in history.

Second Goal

Second, this exercise aims to help you understand those disorders – how they arise, what triggers them, how you manifest them. Filled with a horror of them, you might amend your life and allow it to be ordered by God's love. It is one thing to re-experience those moments now in a self-conscious perspective as being loved by God, even as you sin and recall those sins, but there is the deeper level of integration. That level seeks to understand why you have done what you have done, and how.

Third Goal

Third, this exercise aims to give a true knowledge of the nature of the world and how it affects you, that you may be filled with a horror of it and put away from yourself all that tends to that destructive worldliness. Here we look at the context that traps you in sin, or into sinning, to find out how that world operates and how you are rendered complicit in its activities.

Breaking the Cycle

You are not doing this to save yourself, which you cannot do, or to save anyone else. What you can do is have a firm purpose of amendment. That purpose resolves itself in a hatred for what you have done; a desire to find out why you have done it so as not to do it again; and a resolution not to do it again. Even if we have been sinned against, we seek not to continue that cycle of sin and destruction but rather to ask God's grace to break that cycle, to hold it up to be redeemed, and to try to transform what is destructive into life. We also need to find out the nature of the world that drives us to such a condition and how it makes us complicit in its activities. These are the graces we pray for as we consider at a deeper level not our sinfulness in itself, but how we can co-operate with that merciful love of God in re-creating the world and the relationships we have damaged. What we are doing here is the first step in responding lovingly to the love that we have found so far in our lives.

Ignatius does something interesting in this exercise of repetition. He encourages us to call upon those forces of love that have rejected the sin of the cosmos and the sins of humanity to intercede for us. For Ignatius these are first Mary, the Mother of God; then Jesus Christ, the Messiah; and finally, the source of life itself, the Father. Our alignment with the forces of God and the good occurs when we seek their help to obtain the graces we pray for in this exercise.

Questions for prayer and reflection

1. What were the significant moments of the previous prayer periods for you?

2. Can you divide these moments into consolations and desolations?

3. What happened in these prayer periods when you prayed over each of those moments?

4. Did you find you were getting the three graces you asked for?

5. What are the sins of your life? How does sin operate in your life? How does the corruption in the world affect you?

6. What happens when you discuss the answers of these three questions with Mary, with Jesus, and with the Father?

The Movie
L.A. Confidential

Director: Curtis Hanson (1997 – 138 mins.)
Starring: Kevin Spacey, Russell Crowe, Guy Pearce, Kim Basinger

1. Summary

This is the story of three Los Angeles cops: Jack Vincennes, a technical adviser to a weekly TV police drama whose sidelines include setting up vice busts of show-business personalities for a tabloid magazine; Ed Exley, a highly ambitious police officer on the rise, who's despised by his fellow cops for his rampant self-interest and rigid principles; and Bud White, a hot-tempered cop in love with a high-class prostitute, who swears to uphold the law even if he has to break the law to do it.

A brutal murder brings the three detectives together. As they work to solve the crime, they are drawn into a tightening spiral of corruption, mystery and death. No one is beyond suspicion, no one is beyond elimination. And nothing is what it seems.

2. Questions about the Movie

1. *L.A. Confidential* presents the L.A. of the 1950s as a film noir. Film noir – literally "night film" or "dark film" – was a term coined by French movie critics to describe those Hollywood films of the '40s and '50s that portrayed the dark and gloomy underworld of crime and corruption. In these films, the heroes, as well as the villains, are cynical, disillusioned and often insecure, loners, inextricably bound to the past and unsure or apathetic about the future.

   In terms of style and technique, the film noir characteristically abounds with night scenes, both interior and exterior, with sets that suggest dingy realism, and with lighting that emphasizes deep shadows and accents the mood of fatalism. Its music emphasizes darkness and anxiety.

   How are the lighting, sets and music used to contribute to the seedy, diseased, polluted atmosphere of *L.A. Confidential*? How are they used to hide part of the truth?

2. Each of the three central characters is an insecure loner who grows more cynical, unsure, and disillusioned even as he tries desperately to find some meaning in his life, some sort of redemption. And each of them has a tragic flaw that is not unlike the tragic flaws found in Shakespeare's tragic heroes.

   What are the tragic flaws of each main character?

   How do they cause the characters to be careless or miss an important clue that will ultimately lead to their destruction or injury?

3. In film noir movies, the major female character is usually portrayed as a dark and somewhat myste-

rious person on the edge of the underworld. But she is also the person who will "save" the hero from himself, his cynicism and his loneliness. Lynn Bracken is the beautiful and alluring femme fatale who appears only as a minor character in the main events of the movie, but she is key to what happens to each of the three heroes.

How is her relationship different with each of the three men?

What influence does she have on what happens to them?

3. The Relationship of the Movie to the Theme of the Exercise

1. We are asked to have "a deep experience of our own disorders." This Exercise is a series of close-ups, and L.A. Confidential gives us a series of close-ups of the three major characters.

"A key struggle for film noir heroes is to discover the truth, even though they are cynical and pessimistic. Their heroism lies in their seeking truth and justice, even if it leads to their own death or destruction. The heroes are usually damaged people, struggling with violent or abusive past experiences in corrupt circumstances to find some honour, some redemption from their feelings of disgust with their lives and their deeds. In spite of, or maybe because of, their unworthiness and cynicism, they seek to redeem themselves and be worthy of a normal, moral life." (Neil Andersen, Scanning the Movies Study Guide, 1997)

What are the disorders of the three main characters? Do they manage to free themselves?

2. "At some points, the music becomes the major storytelling element, where it plays behind a string of events, commenting on their morality or inflecting their meaning." (Neil Andersen, Scanning the Movies Study Guide, 1997)

Consider the "Wheel of Fortune" sequence. How do each of the three main characters come to face their own problems and change their fortunes during this song?

3. In this Exercise we ask "to be given a true knowledge of the world and how it affects me, that I may be filled with a horror of it." Director Hanson concentrates on telling a story of characters in a past setting and time. Yet much of what is told is as relevant today as it was those 40 some years ago when the events took place. Their world reflects our own. The crime, corruption and destructive worldliness in the movie mirrors our own world. How is this true?

4. The Relationship of the Movie to One's Self in the Exercise

There is some aspect of Jack Vincennes, Bud White, Ed Exley, Lynn Bracken and Sid Hudgens in each of us. They can be seen to illuminate part of the darkness that is either in our lives or to which we are tempted. For example, all of them lead unfulfilled lives – a fear that many of us have.

As you work through experiencing and understanding your own disorders, look at the disorders in these characters and consider which of them might be something that you need to address. Below is a list of some of their disorders – more will be evident to you from thinking about the movie. How do they apply to you?

1. Jack Vincennes – prefers the spotlight to all else, selling people to ensure he remains in it; fearful of becoming an unknown; is a person who smiles easily but not openly.

2. Bud White – willing to break the rules to make sure things work out as he thinks they should; always willing to do the right deed for the wrong reason; led basically by his emotions.

3. Ed Exley – climbs over everyone in his path to become the top person in his field; a cold-hearted, manipulative careerist; represses all emotions.

4. Lynn Bracken – gives up her own life to become someone she is not in order to make money.

5. Sid Hudgens – through his tabloid, *Hush Hush*, feeds off the disorders of others, looking to make profit from the sins of those around him, not recognizing the sin in his own life.

5th Exercise
Repetition

"'You shall love the Lord your God with all your heart, and with all your soul, and with all your mind.' This is the greatest and first commandment. And the second is like it: 'You shall love your neighbour as yourself.'"

(Matthew 22:37-39)

We are created to praise, reverence, and serve God our Lord, and by this means to save our souls. The other things on the face of the earth are created for us to help us attain the end for which we are created.

(Sp. Ex. #23)

Grace: To see, know and love ourselves the way God sees, knows and loves us and to see, know and love all others the way God sees, knows, and loves all.

Being Named

Ignatius asks us to repeat the Third Exercise. This repetition is a distillation of what we obtained in the previous exercise. Since the previous exercise occurred over several prayer periods. Ignatius is looking for the essence of those prayer periods. Can we name ourselves from that essence? Maybe we need to ask in prayer for that gift of self-recognition. Such naming is not just applying a label onto someone, but is something that reaches up from the depths of our being as it encounters a love that has been searching for it since the beginning of time. We need to sit in that profoundly contemplative space and allow that connection to be made. The naming,

if it is done, is often beyond words or images. It just resonates with a felt intimacy.

We can abandon ourselves to that awe we experience of being fully and truly known. That is the naming on the level of experience.

We can find ourselves being called "loved sinners." That is the naming on the level of concept. This echoes the Easter Vigil liturgy, which sees the sin of humanity, rendered archetypically in Adam and Eve, as "O happy fault" because it brings into our lives the human embodiment of God in the form of Jesus Christ.

We can find our naming in the response we now offer to that love that has found us. This can be manifest in an attitude of humility and gratitude towards this awesome mystery, whose sole desire is that we come to life and to the fullness of life. The humility emerges from the profound awareness of our limitations, and blindness, and destructive actions; the gratitude comes from that profound awareness that we are always held and loved into being.

We may also find our naming in what we do. The life that names us also defines us by what we do. It is the choices we make that define our identity. As the famous prayer of Fr. Pedro Arrupe, the last Father General of the Jesuits, puts it:

Nothing is more practical than finding God,
that is, than falling in love
in a quite absolute, final way.
What you are in love with,

what seizes your imagination,
will affect everything.
It will decide what will get you
out of bed in the morning,
what you will do with your evenings,
how to spend your weekends,
what you read, who you know,
what breaks your heart,
and what amazes you with joy and gratitude.
Fall in love; stay in love,
and it will decide everything

Finally, we can live love, in all of its mysterious complexity and simplicity. We let love name us and guide us in the very depths of our being. Of particular use here is the eight-fold noble path of the Buddha. The Buddha, centuries before Jesus, after his enlightenment devoted his life to promoting the insights that enlightenment gave him into living correctly. We adapt the Buddha's insights here, for a Christian context, because those insights represent eight interrelated approaches that create a wholesome spiritual path. To live an integrated life there needs to be right view; right thinking; right action; right livelihood; right diligence; right mindfulness; and right concentration. We look at these here to clarify those aspects of our lives that are out of sync with who we are called to be. With that clarity we can see where we still need to pray to experience God's compassionate mercy.

The Eight Practices of Wisdom

• *"Right view"* reminds us that we are rooted in God's love, that we are all lovable and capable of loving, no matter what situation we find ourselves in. St. Paul puts it this way: "Nothing, neither death, nor life, nor angels, nor principalities, nor things present, nor things to come, nor powers, nor height, nor depth, nor anything else in all creation, will be able to separate us from the love of God in Christ Jesus our Lord" (Rom 8:38-9).

• *"Right thinking"* refers to the process of reflection that grounds the experience of God's love for us, rather than those negative tapes that debilitate us and alienate others. Right thinking does not ignore the real presence of evil but knows — as Julian of Norwich knows — that "all shall be well and all manners of things shall be well." It knows that good overcomes evil and transforms evil. It knows that basically we are aligned to good.

• *"Right mindfulness"* is being attentive to what is and so being able to discern truth from illusion. It seeks God in all situations and in living in the love the Christ has for the Father. It is to have that same focus and desire as the Christ and to live fully in the gift of the present.

• *"Right speech"* speaks the truth lovingly. Truth without love is a lie; and love without truth is sentimentality.

• *"Right action"* manifests itself in a reverence for life through generosity, responsible gestures — a gesture is an act of homage to God performed in this world — and the way we place our body as incarnate spirit.

• *"Right effort"* examines how we spend the energy we have: "To do the right deed for the wrong reason…the greatest treason" (T.S. Eliot). Why do we do what we do? Evil encloses us ever more tightly in the webs of narcissism; right effort struggles against those ego-limitations to ever more comprehensive relationships within the realities in which we find ourselves.

• *"Right concentration"* is a spiritual calm that acknowledges both the transitory and the Absolute at the same time.

• *"Right livelihood"* is having an occupation that fosters our vocation to be a witness to love.

Along with this is right community. We are not isolated individuals but need the support of others who share our vision. The above eight practices of wisdom allow for the creation of community, which is not a given, like an address, or a selection of cronies, but allows unity in diversity.

We can make a fundamental option to live that way, but how that is concretely and existentially realized is a matter for the following Weeks of the path we are walking. At the moment it is enough to acknowledge, joyfully and gratefully, that there is a way of living a redeemed life in this fallen world.

Once again, in this prayer period, we speak first to Mary, the Mother of God; then Jesus; and, finally, the Father about what has occurred in the prayer.

Questions for prayer and reflection

1. Where has your prayer led you?

2. Using each element of the eight-fold noble path, examine your life to see where you stand, where you are called to grow; where you are invited to be disciplined; where you need, because you may still be trapped, God's help and mercy.

3. What has been the consolation of this set of prayer periods? What does that tell you?

4. What have been the desolations? What does that tell you?

The Movie
Gossip

Director: David Guggenheim (2000 – 90 mins.)
Starring: James Marsden, Kate Hudson, Joshua Jackson

1. Summary

Three college students decide to do their class project on the way gossip grows. But the rumour they start spreading has terrible consequences. The person on the other side of the gossip must handle the embarrassing situation before it destroys her reputation and her relationship with her boyfriend.

2. Questions about the Movie

1. One of Marshall McLuhan's ideas is that we live in a global village – that modern communications mean that we can see, sometimes instantly, what is happening in almost any area of the world. McLuhan also believed that the major causes of change in cultures and civilizations are not ideologies, wars or religions, but rather new communications technologies. When a new communications technology is created, society finds itself restructured by it. Yesterday, it was the printing press; today it is electronics. Information technologies are responsible for drastically changing cultures and affecting every issue involving social values.

   What role does information technology play in the social values issues that are so evident in this movie?

2. When Derrick is asked by Professor Goodwin to explain gossip and news, he says: "People are people, we do what we do. And then we gossip about it. I wish we were more noble but we're not." How accurate a definition of "news" is this?

3. Derrick, Jones, Travis – three completely different people. Despite the ending, each of them is guilty of spreading gossip, but in different ways. What is the gossip that each of them spreads – other than the gossip about Naomi and Beau?

3. The Relationship of the Movie to the Theme of the Exercise

1. The Exercise speaks of "right community." There are at least three communities in the movie: the college, the members of Professor Goodwin's class, and the community of the three roommates. Which of the eight practices of wisdom quoted in the Exercise are found in these communities? Go through them and consider how different the three communities would be if even some of the "right" was in place.

2. The Exercise presents some five ways to find out "naming." Which of these ways applies best to the roommates whom you believe comes closest to "self-recognition"?

4. The Relationship of the Movie to One's Self in the Exercise

This Exercise is a repetition – a review – of what has gone before. Think back, for example, to the way that small acts can have huge effects.

1. Where have small acts you have done gone on to have huge effects, in your in own life or in the lives of the people around you?

2. Derrick likes the rumour they chose to spread because it is "simple," "close to the truth," and "has room to grow." Where have you gone after something that will lead you away from God thinking that it is just a small thing, simple and close to the truth?

3. Following Beau's arrest, Derrick admits that none of them intended for the gossip to go as far as it did. He says they made a mistake. And he excuses it by saying that they are young and need to use this time to make mistakes.

   How often have you refused to take that first step towards self-recognition by saying that you are still "young" and that there will be time to change?

6th Exercise
Hell

Whatever overcomes a person enslaves that person.

(2 Peter 2:19)

I shall also thank God for this, that up to this very moment He has shown Himself so loving and merciful to me.

(Sp. Ex. #71)

Grace: "I should ask for what I desire. Here it will be to beg for a deep sense of the pain which the lost suffer, that if because of my faults I forget the love of the eternal Lord, at least the fear of these punishments will keep me from falling into sin."

(Sp. Ex. #65)

Understanding Mysteries

This is a meditation on hell. We are asked to enter as fully as possible, imaginatively, into the realm of hell from our present perspective on life and to use our senses to become aware of the pain that the lost suffer. From medieval times to today, popular preaching uses graphic depictions of hell as a motivation for upright behaviour. In this context, Ignatius is no different. He notes that "if because of my faults I forget the love of the eternal Lord, at least the fear of these punishments will keep me from falling into sin." (Sp. Ex. #65) The question is this: How can a loving God allow hell to exist? The following question is similar: How can a God of love allow evil to exist and allow the effects of evil to

attack the innocent? These are big questions. They raise the very real issue of our image of God, or our understanding of love, and even more radically the limitations of our understanding to comprehend these mysteries.

Before we can enter into this meditation we need to examine the ways we experience hell on earth. There are wars and famine; there is oppression and the brutality of self-righteous power; people torture each other; there is disregard and prejudice; there are garbage dumps that people live off of; there is despair and self-pity; there is meaninglessness; there is anger and abuse and neglect; there is the idolatry of expecting the world to be God and of sacrificing oneself to that world; there is malice and confusion. We do not have to cast our awareness to some Gothic scenario to be present to this reality. It is part of our world, our culture, our lives, and, if we dare acknowledge it, even our own hearts.

This exercise attempts to bring to light those areas in our own lives, in our own hearts, in our pre-dispositions, that prefer to accept the disorder of a fallen world and its implications rather than accept and live out of the mercy of God. Inasmuch as we live in this world, and we accept this world as it is, we not only live in hell (and at times hell can be comfortable), but we also contribute to it. When we experience love and reject it, or manipulate its free gifts for our own ends, we are in hell. Hell is nothing but the rejection of love. The passion of God's love is everywhere. Hell is filled with the love of God, but the lost refuse to acknowledge that love and thus experience their rejection and the torments of that rejection. The mystery is not that hell exists, but that one can prefer to live out of such a rejection rather than acceptance. And that is the mystery of the freedom that God offers us in his love. In fact, on whatever level it happens, falling in love is the path to becoming free.

Those Without Love

In this Exercise Ignatius asks us to consider those who have never experienced love, those who have been offered love but chose otherwise, and those who have been offered, accepted and experienced love but later reject it. One might want to consider child soldiers whose only experience of life is brutality, or those in our culture who prefer success to relationships, or those who become afraid of intimacy and so retreat back into the self-destructive security of narcissism.

But, more importantly, we can consider how these three dynamics operate in our own lives and, by looking at those, the effects of living in those destructive ways. The prayer attempts to flush out any residual resistance we might have to accepting God's love. Of course there is resistance. If we are honest, we will realize that there will always be resistance and ways of living beyond our control. We can admit this. In the end we fall upon the mercy of God, who is always willing to embrace, support, encourage and purify us to an always deepening love.

In becoming aware of this mercy, of allowing ourselves to experience and accept it, and in opening ourselves up to it at deeper and more comprehensive levels of ourselves, we find ourselves more and more in the posture of gratitude and thanksgiving.

Ignatius suggests that we conclude this prayer period by allowing ourselves spontaneously to express that thanksgiving to the mystery of God we call "Abba" and to conclude with the recollected praying of the "Our Father," which expresses our relationship to the One who loves us.

Questions for prayer and reflection

1. Where is hell in your life?

2. How do you experience it?

3. How do you respond to it?

4. What happens when you find yourself in contact with it?

5. How does it affect you?

6. Are you helpless in those moments and situations?

7. What can you do?

8. Where is Christ in all of this? (Here you may want to recall that Elie Weisel story of the Jewish prisoner being beaten to death in one of the prison camps while the rest were lined up and forced to watch. In one of the lines a voice whispered: Where is God in all of this? Another voice answered: There he is, being beaten to death in front of us.)

9. Where is the Father in all of this? Why don't you ask him where he is?

10. Have you ever experienced the mercy of God? Where? How?

11. How do you experience the mercy of the Father now?

12. How does that mercy feel?

The Movie
The Thin Red Line

Director: Terence Malick (1998 – 170 mins.)
Starring: Sean Penn, George Clooney, John Cusack, Elias Koteas

I. Summary

Based on the novel by James Jones, *The Thin Red Line* tells the story of a group of men, an Army Rifle company called C-for-Charlie, who change, suffer and ultimately make essential discoveries about themselves during the fierce World War II battle of Guadalcanal. The story takes place as Army troops are moved in to relieve battle-weary Marine units. It follows their journey, from the surprise of an unopposed landing, through the bloody and exhausting battles that follow, to the ultimate departure of those who survived.

2. Questions about the Movie

1. War films have always been part of Hollywood history. Yet most of these films stress patriotism – think of the John Wayne movies about World War II. *The Thin Red Line* portrays the dark side of battle and its effects upon the human soul. How does this counterbalance earlier, more patriotic films?

2. A fascinating element of the movie is the voice-over monologues where the characters express their thoughts. Their words – and the images that go with them – create an impressionistic view of what brings meaning to the lives of these men.

    How is it possible for there to be more than one "reality" in the world of this movie? Or are these simply differing views of the real world made personal for each man?

3. "If there's an organizing principle to this haunting three hour meditation on the toll taken by organized conflict on the human spirit, it's the sheer wonder of war. Why do we do it? How can we do it? And having done it, how can we live with it? And this accounts for one of the movie's most haunting visual refrains, the close-up faces of soldiers dumb-struck with incomprehension, the human face of Conrad's 'the horror.'" (Geoff Pevere, *Toronto Star*, January 8, 1999) What answers does the movie offer you to those questions about war?

3. The Relationship of the Movie to the Theme of the Exercise

1. Through a voice-over we hear these words: "How did we lose the good that was given us or let it slip away? Scatter it carelessly? Trade it for what has no worth? Can I find it here even where

the world is darkest? Where evil surrounds us on all sides?" How does this quote sum up much of what is presented to you in this Exercise?

2. It is clear in the Exercise that hell involves alienation. In the movie, the characters are as alienated from each other as they are from the enemy. How is this so?

3. The Exercise ask us to consider the three dynamics of love in our lives. Which characters in the movie have never experienced love? Been offered love but chose otherwise? Been offered love, accepted it, and then rejected it? What do these people show us about out own acceptance of God's love?

4. The Relationship of the Movie to One's Self in the Exercise

1. Jean-Paul Sartre, in his play *No Exit*, says that hell is other people. This is, in the briefest form possible, Sartre's definition of humanity's fundamental sin. If, as in the play, you were to be confined for all eternity with two other people in one room, which two characters from *The Thin Red Line* would you least like to be with? Why? Which two people from your own life would you least like to be with? Why?

2. In some way, each of the characters in the movie contributes to the hell in which they live. Look at the way three of the characters do this. Reflect on how you may contribute to the hell in your own life.

3. What is your response to the question at the end of the movie: "Where does the love come from?"

7th Exercise
Death

God so loved the world that He gave his only Son that whoever believes in him should not perish but have eternal life. For God sent the Son into the world, not to condemn the world, but that the world might be saved through him.

(John 3:16-17)

This is to consider how God works and labours for me.
(Sp. Ex. #236)

Grace: To experience oneself deeply as a loved sinner

Death Is Our Friend

Ignatius suggests two other exercises to help us experience the loving mercy of God: one on death and one on judgment. These two exercises reinforce the graces of the First Week and so they are included here.

We will all die. In fact, we are dying at this very moment. Heidegger points out that we are beings thrown towards death, and nothing can stop that process. Often our life is an attempt to ignore or deny death. The exaltation of youth as the standard for beauty, the accruing of power as symbolic of life, and the refusal to face the depletion of resources in the effort to maintain an extravagant and vital lifestyle are just three ways that people, societies and cultures maintain a deliberate blindness to the life cycle in nature. Such blindness leads to aggression, then frustration, and then despair, and out of that despair comes the malice of self-hatred and of vindictiveness towards others.

But we do not have to regard death as an enemy. Constant awareness of death allows for a calm indifference to "the slings and arrows of outrageous fortune"; it allows us to examine our values and to commit ourselves to those that are most important; it helps us to relish the beauty in the transient; it encourages us to seek for what abides under the transient. Death shows us that, ultimately, we cannot hold onto life. In Western mythology, the vampire is the one who in trying to hold onto life becomes instead a living death, corrupting everything and everyone who crosses its path.

But if we enter into the mercy of God, we discover that death can be a friend. Rather than being the final destination of an inconstant life, death becomes a doorway towards a greater life, resurrection even. Moreover, as we relax more fully into the mercy of God, we start to discover the many smaller deaths that are stations in our life so far. For example, each stage of our development involves rites of passage; in each of these pivotal moments we leave behind the old, enter into the unknown and its uncertainties, become familiar with the new state of life and establish relationships according to that new state of life, and journey forward again into the darkness becoming light.

Transition Points

In this meditation, consider any one of those transition points in your life and the ways you have negotiated a significant moment. You may even want to re-enter prayerfully into that time, especially if it was a difficult one, or if it left you with scars that are not signs of the resurrection. When you re-enter these moments, do so conscious of the mercy of God present there. Ask to be held and transformed by that mercy as you allow those images, sensations and memories to emerge.

One significant way of entering this contemplation is to imagine our own death. We imagine our fading powers, our growing dependence upon others; imagine being surrounded by God's love, manifested in his tangible mercy, supported by the saints and angels and all the powers of good, by all those we know and love who have gone before us. They all encourage us to become one with that love and that sense of compassionate presence that desires only the fullness of life for us. In this prayer we can sink into that sense of presence that shows us that no one dies alone, and that this death is a time to lay down all our burdens. It is time to trust that the Divine Presence, who has cared for all from the beginning of creation, will kindly take care of all our unfinished business. We dwell in this warm, embracing sense of presence, with its sense of light entering into the depths of our being. We allow what emerges at this time of simple dwelling to be the matter for reflection and discussion with God, who desires only that we come to the fullness of life.

Questions for prayer and reflection

1. How do you deal with death?

2. What experiences of death have you had?

3. How do you experience death in your world?

4. How do you react to that experience?

5. In what ways has your denial of death shaped the way you live? How has it influenced your projects and plans?

6. How have you negotiated the significant transition points of your life?

7. Is there a common pattern of behaviour to those experiences?

8. Is this the way to deal with your death?

9. What would you wish to be different? What would you keep the same?

10. Is death a friend for you? Or an enemy?

11. How can you make death a friend?

12. What happens when you imagine yourself surrounded and penetrated by God's love and light as you lie on your deathbed? Is there any unfinished business that you want God to take care of for you? Is there anything you would like to tell God or the people in your life, past and present? Is there anything you wished you had done? Or left undone?

13. How do you experience God's mercy touching those areas in your prayer?

The Movie
Big Fish

Director: Tim Burton (2003 – 122 mins.)
Starring: Albert Finney, Ewan McGregor, Billy Crudup, Jessica Lange, Helena Bonham Carter, Alison Lohman, Steve Buscemi, and Danny DeVito

1. Summary

The movie tells of the final days of Edward Bloom and his strained relationship with his son, William. William had not spoken to him for three years as a result of growing animosity at the tales his father used to pass as truth to family and friends. But when Edward is dying of cancer, William comes to his father's bedside in Alabama and the stories of Edward's youth are told one more time.

2. Questions about the Movie

1. "Bloom is a mixture of Odysseus, Candide and your long-winded uncle, and just when the movie seems in danger of veering off into the sentimental, Burton pulls it back." (Lynn Hirschberg, *The New York Times Magazine*, November 9, 2003, p. 52) There are many examples of this happening in *Big Fish*. How does this take place during the extraordinary ending when William finally gets to tell his own story?

2. Director Tim Burton: "*Big Fish* is about what's real and what's fantastic, what's true and what's not true, what's partially true and how, in the end, it's all true. To show those contrasting elements was the challenge." (Quoted in Lynn Hirschberg, *The New York Times Magazine*, November 9, 2003, p. 52) How well do you think Burton succeeds in what he is trying to do? What got you involved with the movie? Or what stopped you from becoming involved in the movie?

3. "*Big Fish* argues that sometimes it's better to accept the truth you want to believe about yourself. In effect, you need to get in touch with your inner deceiver." (Peter Howell, *Toronto Star*, December 10, 2003) Why is it difficult for you to accept this interpretation of the movie?

4. "Will, a journalist who has made his career by serving facts straight, hates his father for constructing myths to hide behind. It's the myths, of course, that most reveal the real Edward. And Burton wisely builds his movie around them." (Peter Travers, *Rolling Stone*, December 11, 2003) What do the myths reveal about the real Edward?

5. How do William's final lines in the movie explain the theme of the movie?

3. The Relationship of the Movie to the Theme of the Exercise

1. The Exercises show us how the denial of death can turn us towards the malice of self-hatred and vindictiveness towards others. How does Edward react to his death? How do the stories he has told prepare him for death?

2. Perhaps it is William who regards death as an enemy. Death will rob him of the chance to find out just who his father is. William – a journalist – looks for the factual truth about his father: not the emotional truth, which is a very different thing. Do you think Edward ever said a single true thing? Perhaps he never did, but perhaps every story he told had a deeper level of truth behind it. What is one scene that shows this possibility to you?

3. Edward is well aware that he is dying – and he believes he knows just how he will die. He has no need to contemplate his own death, for he has often contemplated the ending to his life that he saw as a child. How does the story William tells to the dying Edward ensure that all this will come to pass?

4. The Relationship of the Movie to One's Self in the Exercise

1. The Exercise speaks of the many smaller deaths that are stations in our own life so far. It is obvious what these stations are in the lives of both Edward and William. But what are these smaller deaths – these significant moments – in your own life? What have you learned from them?

2. Towards the end of the Exercise is a list of the steps we can take in contemplating our own death. In prayer, you have tried to do this. In the movie we have seen how Edward handles these steps. What is the most difficult of the steps for you to accept?

3. No one dies alone. The movie shows us the many people from Edward's life who come to be with him as he dies. But the Exercise is not speaking of the presence of people around us as we die. It speaks to us of the comforting presence of God embracing us. What comes to your mind when you acknowledge and reflect on this simple but powerful fact of God's love for us?

8th Exercise

Judgment

Now the word of the Lord came to me saying:
Before I formed you in the womb I knew you,
And before you were born I consecrated you.

(Jeremiah 1:5)

The lover gives and shares with the beloved what he possesses, or something that he has or is able to give; and vice versa, the beloved shares with the lover.

(Sp. Ex. #231)

Grace: To experience God's healing love pouring into the broken and damaged places of our life transforming them and integrating them into the community that is the fullness of our life.

The Lies of Evil

God has an abiding judgment of us. God judges that we are lovable and capable of loving. In all of his dealings with us, God has never deviated from that judgment. God creates in love, with love, and through love. At our very essence we are love incarnate, for we are made in God's image and likeness.

It is evil that judges us as other than God's creation, God's creatures and God's delight. In the beginning of the book of Job, Satan is described as "the accuser." It is the evil one, or as Ignatius so aptly calls him, "the enemy of our human nature," who judges us negatively and asks us to judge ourselves as incapable and unworthy of love.

From the life we have lived on earth, the choices we make show whether we agree with God or with Satan. At the judgment we encounter after death, in Christian mythology, we find ourselves in the presence of God. There we experience the freedom and the self-image that we have shaped with our choices in this life. We may experience ourselves as a mass of obsessive-compulsive behaviours that manifest our narcissism, or we may find ourselves as acknowledging with our very lives that we are children of God, seeing God in everything and in each other and in ourselves. We may be astonished at this self-revelation and ask, "But Lord, when did we see you?" And he will reply, "When I was hungry and you fed my hunger; when I was lonely and you became community; when I was with the oppressed and you struggled to set them free; when I was with the joyful and you celebrated life with us; when I was with those creating and you did not abandon me." For truly God is in all places and all times and with all peoples. Nothing and no one is left out, for truly God chooses freely to be committed to us.

What we see now and at the judgment emerges from who we are. At that judgment we shall experience God as God, and we shall experience ourselves as we truly are. We can rejoice because we are finally found and are finally coming home; or we can be like Adam and Eve in the garden after they ate the forbidden fruit and hid from themselves and from

God. Even there we can trust either in our egos or in the mercy of God.

Surrounded by Saints

For this meditation, imagine that you are already dead and are surrounded by the dynamic, compassionate love of God, surrounded by all the saints and the powers of good who pour out their energy and love into us, surrounded by all those whom we love and who love us and desire only what is best for us. Allow yourself to enter into that embrace, and allow that embrace to enter into the very depth of yourself. Deeper and ever deeper. Just remain in that state of acceptance and see what happens, and how you respond. Allow whatever emerges to your awareness to come and offer it up, without holding onto it, to that mercy who transforms everything into life. Stay with that state of presence until it stops.

Have a conversation with the Father what happened in that prayer period. Allow yourself to express all the things that you experienced, and discuss what you experienced with the Father. Close with the "Our Father."

Questions for prayer and reflection

1. What self-image do you hold now?

2. Where does that self-image come from?

3. The medieval mystic Meister Eckhart says, "The eye by which I see God is the eye by which God sees me." What does he mean?

4. How do you experience God seeing you?

5. How do you experience God?

6. What was significant in the prayer?

7. Why was this significant?

8. What does it tell you about your relationship to God? Your relationship to yourself? God's relationship to you?

9. What are the crucial elements in a relationship for you?

10. Do you experience God trusting you? How do you experience that? How does it feel?

11. How do you respond?

12. How did the prayer experience reveal you to yourself?

The Movie

The Adventures of Priscilla, Queen of the Desert

Director: Stephen Elliott (1994 – 104 mins.)
Starring: Terrence Stamp, Hugo Weaving, Guy Pearce

1. Summary

Two drag queens and a transsexual are hired to perform a show at a resort in northern Australia. They travel from Sydney aboard their bus named Priscilla. A series of adventures gives them insight into their lives.

2. Questions about the Movie

1. This is a road movie with a difference. In most road movies, characters tend to travel west to the ocean and to a new life. Here, the three men start at the ocean and burrow inland to the centre of things. But in all road movies, the characters end up with a different understanding of themselves. What changes take place in the lives of Adam, Tick and Bernadette?

2. "Gradually the queens lose their strangeness, their 'abnormalcy.' Gradually they begin to appear as much a force of nature as the nature (both physical and human) around them – just as unique, just as inevitable and just as acceptable. Sure, we continue to laugh, but without the edge of embarrassment now, without any trace of accusation." (Rick Groen, *The Globe and Mail*, August 19, 1994)

How difficult was it for you to accept the three characters as real people and not as oddities? At what point in the movie did this happen for you? Or did it?

3. "We realize that the real subject of the movie is not homosexuality, not drag queens, not show-biz, but simply the life of a middle-aged person trapped in a job that has become tiresome." (Roger Ebert, *Chicago Sun-Times*, August 26, 1994)

What – for you – is the real subject of the movie?

3. The Relationship of the Movie to the Theme of the Exercise

1. The Exercise reminds us that it is the evil one who judges us negatively and who asks us to judge ourselves as incapable and unworthy of love. In the movie, why do each of the three main characters see themselves as incapable and unworthy of love?

What happens to change this in each of their lives so that they see themselves as lovable and capable of loving?

2. God's judgment on us is that we are lovable and capable of loving. How can we, therefore, judge others to be anything else? How is this shown in the scene where the three men, stranded in the desert, enter an Aboriginal camp?

3. The Exercise tells us that God has never deviated from his judgment that we are lovable and capable of love. How can this apply to these three men whose very lifestyle appears to stand in stark opposition to the Church's teaching?

4. The Relationship of the Movie to One's Self in the Exercise

1. Although we are not these three characters, there is something of each of them in us. What do each of them have that can help us find that we are both lovable and capable of loving?

2. The movie manages a impressive feat of offering a lesson of tolerance without preaching about it. We all believe in tolerance and in not judging others. How do you put this into practice in your own life?

9th Exercise
Summary of the First Week

"We know that all things work for the good of those who love the Lord".

(Romans 8:28)

The Spiritual Exercises have "as their purpose the conquest of self and the ordering of one's life in such a way that no decision is made under the influence of any inordinate attachment."

(Sp. Ex. #21)

Grace: To ask the Father to show you your life as He sees it, and to rejoice in the life and in the path that is one's life.

Finding the Pattern

You have just been through the rather intense experience of the First Week of the Spiritual Exercises of St. Ignatius of Loyola. Before we continue on this spiritual journey, it is helpful to reflect on what has happened and how it has affected you. A simple way of doing this is to ask yourself the following questions:

- What has changed in me because of this experience?

- How was I before entering this journey? How am I now?

- What accounts for the difference?

- What have I learned from this experience?

- What are the graces I was given by God by opening myself up to these exercises?

Take some time to reflect on these questions before you proceed to the outlook presented below. Write your responses in your journal.

The aim of the First Week is to experience the mercy of God and achieve some self-awareness of being a sinner and yet being loved.

This conversion pattern seeks to liberate the self from the constraints of the ego as defined by sin operating on cosmic, human, and personal levels. What is brought to light are the illusions of the illusion we hold to be the self. Those illusions encompass self-image and radical ways of seeing the world, relationships and even God. Some of the ways that false self is deconstructed include the self-questioning of every exercise, the imaginative reconstructions of self exposed to God's love, and by our growing self-acceptance as defined by God rather than by the traumas that create self-consciousness.

Different people experience this pattern differently. Some find the experience of facing up to themselves to be a source of desolation; others find it a relief finally to abandon the project of creating the self and to rest in God's creative mercy. Many move from desolation to consolation in this set of exercises. At first there tends to be both conscious and unconscious resistance. At this level, we experience the boundaries of the self and resist accepting the unredeemed areas of our lives. These challenge the sense of comfort and the habitual by which we maintain our sense of ego-worth.

When the prayer invites us past these boundaries, we often experience as threatening or overwhelming the fear of what is other to ourselves. At the same time, we have a profound sense of entrapment and bewilderment. We are asked to remain in that sense of the unknown until we start to realize that we are neither destroyed nor overwhelmed by it. We experience a liberation of energies and the consolation of being loved and accepted beyond ourselves. We then finally sink into God's love and discover a renewed sense of being alive and of being amazed at the life that is given to us.

But what does all of this mean in terms of grace? First, we discover the truth of our very self, and the dynamic context of love in which all of our lives are held. So we find ourselves falling in love with a God who has fallen in love with us even before we knew it. This awareness of being loved also makes us realize that we are not God, and so we become aware of our boundaries and limitations and of our constant need for God's mercy. Finally, as we sink into that love, we are invited to continue that journey: both inwardly, as we discover ourselves more and more, and outwardly, as we are invited to share in that creative love seeking to transform the world.

Questions for prayer and reflection

1. How helpful has the description of the First Week been for you?

2. How has it illuminated your experience and self-understanding?

3. What was different?

4. How do you explain this difference?

5. In what ways does the mystery of God remain a mystery?

6. How comfortable are you in living in such a mystery?

7. What do you feel called to do next?

The Movie
Romeo + Juliet

Director: Baz Luhrmann (1996 – 120 mins.)
Starring: Leonardo DiCaprio, Clare Danes

1. Summary

A contemporary retelling of the classic story of Romeo and Juliet, set in a modern-day city of Verona Beach. The Montagues and Capulets are two feuding families whose children meet and fall in love. Romeo and Juliet are Shakespeare's "star-crossed" lovers; the movie follows their tragic love affair.

2. Questions about the Movie

1. "Although Luhrmann courageously sticks with the prose, it's spoken as a language. It works, as there is the unwritten assumption that the audience are already familiar with the text and if not, will get the gist of it. This leaves Luhrmann free to stun his audience with the visuals." (Sandi Chaitram, *BBC1 Films on line*, updated May 4, 2001) Think back to the opening of the movie and the two versions of the prologue – one spoken by a TV newscaster and the other delivered like a music video. Why do you think the director repeats the chorus?

2. "To see the gang toughs in modern dress and then hear them spit out their threats and quarrels in Elizabethan English makes absolute sense. It plays a bit like *West Side Story* meets *Priscilla, Queen of the Desert*. The film has been organized visually to make the dialogue (and the action) clear to anyone not familiar with the play. *Romeo & Juliet* is jammed with little eye-catching jokes and plays-on-words. Throw in a soundtrack that includes such out-there choices as "Young Hearts Run Free" and "When Doves Cry" and you get a sort of gobsmacking sight and sound experience.... *Romeo & Juliet* is also very sexy and...surprisingly sorrowful. Golly – we laughed, we cried. That would seem to be exactly what Shakespeare intended." (Liz Braun, *Toronto Sun*, November 1, 1996) It has been said that if Shakespeare were writing today, he would be writing television dramas like *Six Feet Under* or *The Gilmore Girls* or *Joan of Arcadia* as well as sit-coms like *Will and Grace*. Why (or why not) does it make sense to say that Luhrmann's adaptation is something that a contemporary Shakespeare would have been happy to have written?

3. "No doubt the most aggressively modern, assertively trendy adaptations of Shakespeare ever filmed, this overwhelmingly of-the-moment version of one of literature's most enduring tragic love stories can serve as a litmus test for any viewer's willingness to accept extreme stylistic

attitudinizing as a substitute for the virtues of traditional storytelling." (Todd McCarthy, *Variety*, October 28–November 3, 1996) Is the critic praising or damning the movie? How far do you agree with him?

3. The Relationship of the Movie to the Theme of the Exercise

1. The First Week is not the easiest to get through – it is very intense and leads us down the path of self-awareness. How much self-awareness do Romeo and Juliet achieve in the course of the movie? Who is the more mature of the two – the more self-aware?

2. The First Week helps us see the illusions of the illusion we hold to be the self – as the exercise tells us. Where in the movie do any of the principal characters come to see the illusion they hold to be their selves?

3. Through the First Week we have learned to deconstruct our false selves by

   • self-questioning
   • imaginative reconstructing of ourselves as exposed to love
   • growing self-acceptance of ourselves.

   Which characters help Romeo and Juliet work through such a deconstruction until they come to true knowledge of themselves?

4. The Relationship of the Movie to One's Self in the Exercise

1. Some people find facing up to themselves to be sheer desolation; others find it to be a relief. In the movie, Romeo and Juliet – and their parents – each react in a different way to this process. How do you react – now, at the end of the First Week – to this facing up to yourself?

2. The Exercise reminds us that we often experience the fear of what is other to ourselves as threatening or overwhelming. We know that this happened to Romeo and Juliet – and the movie makes it clear just how this happens. What "other" is the most challenging for you as you come to the end of the First Week?

3. With acceptance of self comes a liberation of energies and the consolation of being loved and accepted beyond ourselves. Romeo and Juliet each have this need, and try as they might, their tragedy is not to reach that. At the end of this First Week, how have you found yourself being loved and accepted beyond yourself?

Part 2

The Second Week – Walking with God

1st Exercise
The Kingdom

Happy is the one whose help is the God of Jacob,
Whose hope is in the Lord, our God,
Who made heaven and earth,
The sea and all that is in them:
Who keeps faith forever;
Who executes justice for the oppressed:
Who gives food for the hungry.
The Lord sets the prisoners free;
The Lord opens the eyes of the blind.
The Lord lifts up those who are bowed down;
The Lord loves the righteous
The Lord watches over those who journey;
He upholds the widow and the orphan
But the ways of the wicked he brings to ruin.

(Psalm 146)

Eternal God of all things, in the presence of your infinite goodness, and of Your glorious mother, and of all the saints of Your heavenly court, this is the offering of myself which I make of with Your favour and help. I protest that it is my earnest desire and my deliberate choice, provided only it is for Your greater service and praise, to imitate You in bearing all wrongs and all abuse and all poverty, both actual and spiritual, should Your most holy majesty deign to choose and admit me to such a state and way of life.

(Sp. Ex. #98)

Grace: Here it will be to ask of our Lord the grace not to be deaf to His call, but prompt and diligent to accomplish his most holy will.

(Sp. Ex. #91)

Becoming Engaged

We are all called to love. It is our very nature. The First Week of the Exercises shows us our very nature – who we truly are – and how we are situated in relationship to God, to others, and to the rest of creation. It is only when that is radically settled and affirmed that the next step on our spiritual journey appears. How are we to manifest that love in our concrete situation?

At this point we may be tempted to think we can make that decision by ourselves. We figure: I have experienced the love that loves me no matter what, so whatever I do will be all right because I am doing it in love. This temptation is very subtle and insidious because there is a lot of truth and value in it.

But it is not the whole picture. Think of yourself as driving a car that is a wreck. You take it to a garage where it is fixed, serviced and filled up with gas. Now you are on the road again. "The open road…freedom…yes, this is the life!" you might say to yourself. This analogy might describe your situation at the end of the First Week. But just because the car is now roadworthy doesn't mean your worries are over. You can still have engine trouble. You can still hit potholes. You can still fall asleep at the wheel. The idea that whatever you do will be okay suffers from three problems. First, it presumes that you no longer need God's grace. Second, you do not know the route that will make more effective your new-found desire to be more loving. Third, you do not yet know how to communicate with the God you met in the First Week. Now that you are in relationship with God, you need to consult God on how to live the rest of your life. Think of the Second Week of the Exercises in terms of an engagement between a couple who have fallen in love in the First Week.

During the engagement period, each finds out more about the other, and accommodates plans and projects to include the other. In this stage of our journey we risk our new-found lives to God and God risks his fullest manifestation in creation to us. The grace we seek at this time is to enter into this developing relationship as deeply as possible. Ignatius puts it this way: "Here it will be to ask of God the grace not to be deaf to His call, but prompt and diligent to accomplish His most holy will" (#91). It is very much the stance of the lover asking the beloved: What do you want? What do you want of me? What do you want with me? What do you want for me? What do you want us to do in this world in which we find, and lose, ourselves? We desire to give of ourselves in any way that might help.

The Cost of Loving

To enter into this contemplation, Ignatius asks us to consider how we might respond to someone who is doing God's work. For Ignatius it is important that that person be "chosen by God Our Lord Himself" (#92). Many projects and enterprises claim to be from God; many leaders use spiritual, religious, moral and ethical arguments to validate their ways of proceeding. Ignatius, instead, insists that it is God who does the choosing, not humans who conscript God. Human choices around God – gender, religious tradition, political subscription, ethnic nationality, economic or social status – therefore do not matter. Indeed, the history of God's choices show a significant indifference to race, creed, colour, sexual orientation or economic status. What it does show is how the chosen people give witness to the same values as God's chosen, the Christ.

All of God's chosen leaders offer a sharing of the life of service to the Father. This life of service follows the same pattern as the life of Jesus Christ. It is a life of creativity that labours and suffers, as Christ did, to allow people to experience what you experienced in the First Week of the Exercises – the acceptance of your self as lovable and capable of loving. Ignatius knows that such a labour, while it gives a joy the world cannot offer, also involves suffering as we work against the forces of disorder present in ourselves, our circle of relationships, our culture and our world.

Indeed, Ignatius does not cover up the cost of engaging in such an enterprise. This kind of love in action is not sentimental or occasional. It is battered by forces within and without. It is hopeful without being naive, faithful without being self-serving, compassionate without being weak. It is human with all the flaws and glories of being human, when being human asks us always to go beyond ourselves, to move from sincerity to authenticity.

We cannot make such an offering to God of ourselves, by ourselves. We need God's constant presence, and the constant presence of the company of those who have committed their lives to God's service. We make that offering knowing deeply and passionately that we are never alone in the struggle to bring life to a disordered time.

Ignatius asks us to contemplate the life or lives of those who have witnessed to such a dedication. He asks us to consider how we feel when we examine such a life. He also asks us to experience the sense of a common mission and the resulting sense of community. He suggests that we conclude our reflection with a prayer of offering of ourselves to be part of that community:

"O most gracious God, source of all life, I can only make this offering with your grace and your help. I make it aware of your constant loving goodness and in the presence of all those who have dedicated their lives to you — all the forces of good in all times and in all places throughout creation, and all the saints of every tradition. My deepest wish and desire, only if it serves to build up the community of all creation infinitely open to your never-ceasing love, is to become an intimate companion of your Son, the Christ, and to be with him wherever he is and goes, and to share his life, his joys and sorrows, and like him to bear all injuries and wrongs, all abuse and poverty, actual as well as spiritual, if doing that helps build up your community of loving, and only if you desire to choose for me such a way of life, and to receive me into that life, and, because I am weak and fickle, if you be with me strongly in such a life."

Questions for prayer and reflection

1. How is your life of value now? What are those elements of value?

2. What elements in your life are in conflict with your deeper values?

3. How do you deal with those elements?

4. What happens when you let yourself experience the desire to do something of greater value with your life?

5. What stands in the way of your doing this?

6. When you contemplate the Christ speaking to you, what does he say and do?

7. How do you feel about that?

8. How do you see your life as a companion of Christ, as one who shares his vision and work of being the compassionate and creative presence of the Father in the world?

9. What would your prayer of self-dedication be? (Let this come out of your prayer, rather than out of some idealized way you might see yourself or want to see the world.)

10. What is possible given your real circumstances?

The Movie

The Lord of the Rings
The Fellowship of the Ring (2001 – 178 minutes)
The Two Towers (2002 – 179 minutes)
The Return of the King (2003 – 200 minutes)

Director: Peter Jackson
Starring: Elijah Wood, Ian McKellan, Sean Austin, Viggo Mortensen, Orlando Bloom
(Choose one of the three movies to watch – preferably the first if you have not seen any of the others)

1. Summary

An ancient ring, long thought lost, has been found, and through a strange twist of fate ends up in the possession of a Hobbit named Frodo. When the wizard Gandalf discovers that the ring is in fact the One Ring of the Dark Lord Sauron, he sends Frodo on an epic quest to return the ring to the Fire of Doom where it was forged in order to destroy it and the evil power it possesses. Both Gandolf and Frodo are aware of the power of the ring to change for the worse the person who holds it. Accompanying Frodo are three Hobbit friends, as well as five other men connected to the ring. This Fellowship of the Ring faces evil and danger in this first of three films based on J.R.R. Tolkien's classic trilogy, *The Lord of the Rings*.

2. Questions about the Movie

1. "The movie works. It has real passion, real emotion, real terror and a tactile sense of evil...we root for the survival of the heroes with a depth of feeling that may come as a surprise. The movie keeps drawing you in deeper." ("A Ring to Rule the Screen," David Ansen, *Newsweek*, December 10, 2001) How does the movie portray evil?

2. "Here is an epic with literature's depth and opera's splendor – and one that could only be achieved in the movies. What could be more terrific?" ("Seven Holiday Treats," Richard Corliss, *Time*, December 15, 2003) What gives these movies their "depth" and "splendor"?

3. "Like it or not, Tolkien's trilogy is the real thing, folk gruel as much as Holy Grail, set in a mythic distillation of north-western Europe by a man obsessed with ancient sagas, philology and the provision of legends for a Britain he regarded as lacking an inspiring culture." (Philip French, *The Observer*, December 16, 2001) What kind of film do such remarks lead you to expect? Were your expectations fulfilled?

4. "The Lord of the Rings in toto is one of the screen's most convincingly majestic epics. But it's also playful, a warm adventure, packed with emotion, tenderness and awe. I loved the first two episodes of the movie Ring cycle because they summoned up not just the literary traditions

Tolkien mines so brilliantly, but because they shine out like some great summation of all the movie adventure classics we treasure in youth. When I left *King* finally, it was with real regret, finally ejected from a world I was loathe to lose. Like all great fantasies and epics, this one leaves you with the sense that its wonders are real, its dreams are palpable." (Michael Willmington, *Chicago Tribune*, December 15, 2003) What makes such "wonders" seem "real" and "palpable"? What is it about the characters and the story that draws us into this world?

3. The Relationship of the Movie to the Theme of the Exercise

1. The fifth of the Key Concepts of media literacy indicates that all media contain, explicitly or implicitly, values messages. What human values – especially those given in this Exercise – are found in the *The Lord of the Rings*? Consider the symbolism of the ring and the idea that the Fellowship of the Ring itself is a ring that can be broken.

2. The Second Week of the Exercises deals with the next step of our spiritual journey – how we manifest God's love for us. While *The Lord of the Rings* is a mythical story about Frodo's attempt to save his world from evil, what are the parallels to the mission that Christ was born to accomplish?

3. In the Exercise we learn that it is important to see how even flawed characters can risk and, in so doing, change their world. What are Frodo's flaws?

4. "Ethically and philosophically, the story argues that evil lurks within us all and that the One Ring is designed to bring it to the surface. The Ring reveals our unworthy desires as it tempts us to fulfil them. Yet the heroes – characterised and individualised – are licensed to wreak whatever havoc they wish on the undifferentiated Orcs and other forces of evil." (Philip French, *The Observer*, December 16, 2001) How is the "love in action" that this Exercise calls us to able to respond to such a criticism?

4. The Relationship of the Movie to One's Self in the Exercise

1. The ring corrupts each side. What is the difference between those who want to use the ring to do what is right and those who want it to gain power and control? What is the "ring" in your own life? How does it hold you back as you continue your spiritual journey?

2. There are costs involved in continuing this journey. How does each one – as the Exercise lists them – apply to the members of the Fellowship? How does it apply to you?

    • love in action is not sentimental or occasional
    • love in action is battered by forces within and without
    • love in action is hopeful without being naive
    • love in action is faithful without being self-serving
    • love in action is compassionate without being weak.

3. Love in action, as we learn in this Exercise, is also "human with all the flaws and glories of being human." What "flaws and glories" that you see in Frodo are reflected in your life?

4. We need the help of others in this endeavour. As the Exercise puts it, we need "that constant presence of God, and that constant presence of the company of those who have committed their lives to God's service." How does the Fellowship serve as this force for Frodo? How is God coming to be constantly present in your life? Who are the "others" who help you so that you are never alone in your struggle and your journey?

2nd Exercise

This exercise has two parts: the Divine Presence's concern for the world
and their decision to do something at the right time;
and the human response of Mary at the Annunciation.

(1) The Incarnation

Who is like the Lord, our God,
Who is seated on high,
Who looks far down
Upon the heaven and the earth?
He raises the poor from the dust,
And lifts the needy from the ash heap,
To make them sit with the rulers,
With the rulers of his people.
He gives the barren woman a home,
Making her the joyous mother of children.
Praise the Lord!

(Psalm 113)

The Three Divine Persons look upon the whole expanse
or circuit of all the earth, filled with human beings. Since
they see that all are going down to hell, They decree in
Their eternity that the Second Person should become man
to save the human race.

(Sp. Ex. #102)

Grace: This is to ask for what I desire. Here it will be to
ask for an intimate knowledge of our Lord, who has
become man for me, that I may love Him more and fol-
low him more closely.

(Sp. Ex. #103)

Imagining the World

The Spiritual Exercises of St. Ignatius expand our understanding of how we are present to ourselves, to others and to the world. One of the most significant ways it does this is by expanding our imagination and allowing us to experience our imagination not just as the producer of fantasy and images, but as the producer of all that is. If we look around, even where we are now, there is nothing that we do not see or feel or hear that was not first a product of the imagination. The process of transforming that imagined entity to a sensible reality also requires an imaginative process. When our imaginations are frozen, we end up with the notion that reality cannot be changed; when our imaginations are subverted by evil, we end up creating distorted forms of reality; but when our imaginations are liberated by God, we end up imagining as God imagines and creating as God creates.

The First Week opens with our imaginations trapped in fallen creation. The work of that First Week is to liberate those trapped energies of the imagination so that we can see and experience ourselves as God sees and experiences us. That liberation is present in the first part of this second exercise, where we are asked to imagine being in the very presence of God as the three persons of the Trinity contemplate the disordered state of our world. The divine energies of love, manifest in the Father, the Son, and the Holy Spirit, are not detached, dispassionate omni-powers; they are the fullest manifestations of an involved and concerned Love that creates constantly, sustains without ceasing, and redeems always by entering into the traps of sin and death to bring all, in their patient wisdom, to the process of resurrection.

Seeing as God Sees

In the contemplation we are invited to enter, we are asked to share the perspective of the three Divine Persons of the Trinity as they look at the state of the world. They are not filled with moral disgust at the desperate state of humanity; rather, they determine that the best way for us to be saved is by one of them becoming one of us. In this way we can see that it is still possible – despite the terrible straits we find ourselves in, and the illusions we enslave ourselves to – to realize our union with God. The deceptions we are mired in either suggest to us that this is not possible, or offer erroneous ways to achieve that reality that only increase our frustration and despair. As we discovered in the Exercises of the First Week, we cannot do this for ourselves, but we must, or we lose our integrity as human beings created in the image and likeness of God. The question is this: How can we be both ourselves and yet beyond ourselves?

The Trinity's solution to this question is the Incarnation. God enters into the human condition, into created history, to show us that we can enter into God's condition, God's creativity, God's very life. They offer the gift of themselves, and they offer the way for us to receive and open and live and share that gift.

Because of this action of God, we are given the opportunity to become most truly ourselves by going beyond how we see ourselves. We start seeing ourselves with the possibilities God always sees in us and calls us to.

Questions for prayer and reflection

1. How do you receive gifts?

2. How do you open gifts?

3. How do you use gifts?

4. How do you share your gifts? Have you ever been given a gift that you did not know existed? That you did not know how to ask for? What was it?

5. Have you even been in love?

6. Have you ever loved anyone – not for yourself, but just for that other person?

7. What is/was it like?

8. How does it keep changing your life?

9. In this prayer period, what does it feel like to enter into the imagination of God?

10. How do you feel as you become a part of the Trinity's decision not to give up on us, humankind? What were these conversations and concerns about?

The Movie
Pleasantville

Director: Gary Ross (1998 – 123 mins.)
Starring: Tobey Maguire, Reese Witherspoon, Joan Allen, William H. Macy

1. Summary

The cheerful 1950s TV sitcom *Pleasantville* is revived in the '90s on cable. A shy teen, David Wagner, escapes from reality by watching the show. When he and his sister Jennifer can't agree on what to watch on TV, they fight over the remote control and it breaks. The new remote given them by a strange TV repairman zaps them inside Pleasantville, where their new sitcom parents are businessman George Parker and wife Betty. As "Bud" and "Mary Sue," the teens take up residence in a black-and-white suburbia where sex does not exist and the temperature is always 72 degrees. Life is always pleasant, books have no words, bathrooms have no toilets, married couples sleep in twin beds, and nobody ever questions "The Good Life." David fits right in, while Jennifer does what she likes. Suddenly there is a red rose growing in Pleasantville – and more wonderful and frightening changes start to take place.

2. Questions about the Movie

1. Three movies of the 1990s – *The Truman Show* (1998), *EDtv* (1999) and *Pleasantville* (1998) – specifically examined, in different ways, how television has made an impact on our world, our culture, and our values. What does *Pleasantville* say about television's impact on these three areas?

2. "In *Pleasantville*, Ross tackles his country's obsessive compulsion to indulge in intolerance, repression and racism in the name of false gods such as 'family values' and 'social stability'.... Hollywood satire is not usually this enjoyable. Both savage and silly." (Bruce Kirkland, *Toronto Sun*, October 23, 1998) What is the purpose of satire? Why is a satire like *Pleasantville* better able to deal with such issues than a more serious movie tackling the same issues?

3. "*Pleasantville* is a truly original film that soars with energy and beauty. It has deep meaning and relevance in today's society, and should serve as a reminder for most that the world is made up of how its residents think and act. 'You can't stop something that's inside you,' says David, and that could be a summation of all that *Pleasantville* stands for." (Luke Buckmaster, in *Film Australia*, February 1999). What does David's comment mean to you ? Does it sum up what the movie means for you?

3. The Relationship of the Movie to the Theme of the Exercise

1. In the Exercise we read: "When our imaginations are frozen, we end up with the notion that reality cannot be changed; when our imaginations are subverted by evil, we end up creating distorted forms of reality, but when our imaginations are liberated by God, we end up imagining as God imagines and creating as God creates." How does this apply to what David and Jennifer encounter as they slowly – sometimes painfully – bring colour (and all that comes with it) to the black-and-white world of Pleasantville?

2. The TV repairman tells David and Jennifer: "You don't deserve paradise." How might one see Pleasantville as "paradise"? What are David and Jennifer creating in this paradise? Could you say that they bring the tree of knowledge of good and evil to the people of Pleasantville? What happens after the people have knowledge of good and evil?

3. David and Jennifer bring light to Pleasantville, a light that transforms people. The Gospels remind us that it is the light of Christ that transforms our vision and allows us to see differently. Christ's entrance in the world, which comes about as a result of the Trinity's decision to intervene, also brings a light that transforms our vision if we only stop to look. What is the effect of the light that David and Jennifer bring to Pleasantville?

4. "What happens next, when the denizens of Pleasantville discover imagination and passion, is rather poignant and profound, on every level…the story of a whole community of people remaking the world, led by youth." (Judy Gerstel, *Toronto Star*, October 23, 1998) How do the citizens of Pleasantville do what the Exercise asks of us – use their imaginations to transform an imagined entity into a sensible reality?

4. The Relationship of the Movie to One's Self in the Exercise

1. We want to change to the "sensible reality" called for by the Exercises. What is subverting our imagination and not allowing us to "imagine as God imagines, create as God creates"?

2. The people of Pleasantville have to struggle to overcome the deceptions the Exercise speaks about – the deception that this new reality is not "our reality," the deception that causes people to attempt "erroneous ways" to achieve this reality. How do these two deceptions appear in your life as you try to manifest God's love for you in your spiritual journey?

3. This Exercise encourages us to expand our imagination, seeing it not only as the producer of fantasy and images but also as the "producer of all that actually is." *Pleasantville* shows us what such expansion can cause to happen. In your own life, on your own journey, what use do you make of the mass media – particularly TV and film? How do they help you to expand your imagination?

(2) The Annunciation

My soul magnifies the Lord,
And my spirit rejoices in God my Saviour,
For he has regarded the low estate of his handmaiden.
For behold, henceforth all generations will call me
blessed;
For he who is mighty has done great things for me,
And holy is his name.
And his mercy is on those who fear him from generation
to generation.
He has shown strength with his arm,
He has scattered the proud in the imagination of their
hearts,
He has put down the mighty from their thrones,
And exalted those of low degree;
He has filled the hungry with good things,
And the rich he has sent empty away.
He has helped his servant Israel,
In remembrance of his mercy,
As he spoke to our ancestors

(Luke 1:46-55)

This will be to consider what the persons on the face of
the earth do, for example, wound, kill and go down to
hell. Also what the Divine Persons do, namely, work the
most holy Incarnation, etc. Likewise, what the Angel and
our Lady do; how the Angel carries out his office as
ambassador; and how our Lady humbles herself, and
offers thanks to the Divine Majesty.

(Sp. Ex. #108)

Grace: Here it will be to ask for an intimate knowledge of
our Lord, who has become man for me, that I may love
Him more and follow Him more closely.

The Risks of God

In the narratives of the Bible, God constantly risks his plans and desires with his human collaborators. In the Old Testament it starts with Adam and Eve, then moves through Abraham and Sarah, Isaac, Jacob, Joseph, Moses, David, and the chosen people. They all agreed to the covenanted relationship but they all broke it. God chose in love and kept on risking his life with each of them. God is also constantly risking his plans and desires with each of us.

In the New Testament, God's risk-taking reaches new levels. The Three Persons of the Trinity commit all of their creative plan to the free response of a politically, socially and culturally insignificant young woman in a small village in a wartorn and occupied territory in the Middle East. They desire that she become the mother of the Word made Flesh. This has never happened before in human history. The God of all creation asks Mary, who is engaged but not yet married to Joseph, to break all the codes of orthodox religious behaviour and consent to a plan that challenges the boundaries of established sanity and conventional wisdom. The story is told in Luke 1:26-38.

In the contemplation today, you are asked to enter into the dynamics of this mystery.

The iconic depictions of Mary's response presented in Luke's Gospel have been refined in order to express post-resurrection theology. But imagine a young girl's crisis when she finds herself unmarried and pregnant. How can she explain the pregnancy to her betrothed? To her family? To his family? To the village? Historically, young girls have from time immemorial become suddenly pregnant. The excuses have varied but the reality has remained the same, and the punishments in the Middle East, as in many other cultures of the world, for bringing such shame upon one's clan, were brutal.

Even before Mary agrees to co-operate with God's plan, the implications of such an act weigh in. Mary has the freedom to accept or to decline. God neither seduces nor rapes. For Mary, this is not a moment of reckless romantic abandon that no after-life of prudent consideration will compensate for. She does not hurl herself into this act unthinkingly. Neither does she bargain. What shapes her answer is her own love story with God. Her love for God frees her to trust her entire being, and future, to that One from whom she has accepted the gift of being the beloved. She agrees to become the mother of the Messiah.

Opening to Love

In this contemplation we are asked to do two things: to be fully present as possible to God's incredible vulnerability and trust in offering the deepest mystery of his love to one of his creation, and to enter into Mary's profound sense of self-offering as she says yes to God's invitation. In doing so we may feel ourselves being opened by love to our very depths. We may choose in the prayer to behold Mary with God's eyes, and find ourselves profoundly grateful for that love that says yes to what it does not understand, yes to that intimacy that will carry it to places beyond its imaginings. We may even choose to enter into the role of the angel who mediates between God and Mary, and experience what it means to be missioned and to find one's life and joy and meaning in that service.

To facilitate this contemplation, you might want to read the passage in Luke's Gospel that describes this scene (Luke 1:26-38). What is important is that you spend time with the encounter. Allow the energies of the Annunciation to touch your own energies in their desire to be part of the ongoing incarnation that occurs when we open ourselves to God in love.

The love affair that we are invited to here is willing to risk itself for us and in us. It invites us to respond – not impetuously, but freely. Where we are free, we experience love. Where we are not free, we experience the tug of compulsion. We can offer only what we have. The love that has waited since the beginning of time for Mary to appear and to be ready now waits for us.

Questions for prayer and reflection

1. Have you ever felt called in love to do something?

2. How was this different from being compelled?

3. Do you know the difference between passion and intensity?

4. Have you ever waited on someone in love?

5. What is it like?

6. Have you ever experienced someone waiting on you in love? What was that like?

7. Our lives are filled with moments of annunciation. Identify some of these moments and enter into those experiences again.

8. What was the prayer you just experienced like?

9. What did it reveal to you about yourself? About God? About your path in the world?

10. If you were to have a conversation with Mary about her experience of annunciation what would you say? What do you think she would say to you?

The Movie
A.I.: Artificial Intelligence

Director: Steven Spielberg (2001 – 146 mins.)
Starring: Haley Joel Osment, Sam Robards, Jude Law, William Hurt, Frances O'Connor

1. Summary

The melting of the polar ice caps have forced humans to move inland and to become dependent on the robots (mechas) they create. David is the first mecha designed to experience love. He is meant to replace the comatose son of a middle-aged couple. But when the son recovers, David is abandoned and sets out to become a "real" boy so that his foster mother will come to love him again. His adventures take him through a strange world of mechas and humans to a submerged New York City, where his life changes dramatically.

2. Questions about the Movie

1. "*Artificial Intelligence* is based upon Pinocchio, a fairytale favourite of both Kubrick and Spielberg. In that story, a marionette becomes a real live boy. When Pinocchio asks his father/carver for an explanation for this miracle, Gepetto explains, "When bad boys become good and kind, they have the power of making their homes gay and new with happiness." In Pinocchio, the marionette becomes human by demonstrating human qualities, specifically courage and kindness. David is a machine questing for humanity, which he thinks can be grant- ed by The Blue Fairy.' (Neil Andersen, *Scanning the Movies Study Guide*, June 2001). Do you think David became a real live boy? If so, at what point in the movie?"

2. Gigolo Joe tells David: "They made us too smart, too quick, and too many." Among other things, the movie raises the whole question of the ethics involved: Do we have the right to give "life" to an inanimate object? And if we do so, does that object then become human? What are our obli- gations to this object? As the student says in the opening scene, "If a robot can truly love a per- son, what responsibility does that person have in return?"

Scientists are technically very close to creating such mechas and will do so probably within the lifetime of our children. As we create artificial life, we are ultimately defining what we mean by "alive" and "human." Previously, contemporary robots in movies and television – like *Star Trek's* Data or *Voyager's* The Doctor – attempted to answer these questions. Now we have a movie that takes us a step further. How do you respond to such questions? How does your faith enter into your response?

3. There are, arguably, two endings to the movie. Is what happens before the added-on Spielberg ending really best able to be described as Groen does here? "That ambivalence, that ambiguity, and the drama it inspires, crystallize in a thrilling final image — a tableau of eternal, romantic yearning that rivals Keats' Grecian urn. What a gorgeous ending, a moment as timeless as the struggle it depicts." (Rick Groen, "Artifical Sweetner," *The Globe and Mail*, June 29, 2001) Which of the two endings do you prefer? Why?

3. The Relationship of the Movie to the Theme of the Exercise

1. "Science fiction has often been called pop culture's answer to metaphysics, a secular way to explore the myth of transcendence. Spielberg believes this, and it is probably why *E.T.* is his most popular film. 'Science fiction does not have to go very far to connect with the spiritual,' he says. 'Science fiction is about pure imagination, about dreaming. And imagination and dreaming are as close to basic beliefs as anything we can cherish.' They're also the building blocks of art...." ("Regarding Stanley," Rachel Abramowitz, *Los Angeles Times*, May 6, 2001) Building on the notion of developing the imagination that you examined in the last Exercise, how does this film take you beyond mere fantasy to deal with issues of love and caring?

2. David knows only that he feels intense love for his foster mother. He was created to love and accepts this love that he cannot understand, knowing that, as the Exercise tells us, it will carry him "to places beyond imagining." Where does David's love take him? What happens to him as he travels to these places?

3. In the Exercise we see how what God asks of Mary challenged "the boundaries of established sanity and conventional wisdom." How does David's search also challenge everything that had been known up to that time about mechas? How does his search appear to be the act of someone who is not sane?

4. The Relationship of the Movie to One's Self in the Exercise

1. We can only imagine the loneliness Mary felt when she accepted God's call. No one would believe her if she were to tell them what had happened. When David sets out on his journey to become human — a first for any mecha — he also experiences extreme loneliness. In your own response to God's call, who do you turn to when you fall into loneliness? Who gives you the strength to continue? How do they do that?

2. This Exercise is an invitation to respond freely but not impetuously to the love that calls us. What is it in David's life and in your own life that causes you not to be able to respond in this way?

3. The love that is God asks only that we offer what we have. What does David have to offer on his journey to find love? What do you have to offer?

3rd Exercise
The Nativity

She gave birth to her first-born son and wrapped him in swaddling cloths, and laid him in a manger, because there was no place for them in the inn.

(Luke 1:7)

This will be to see and consider what [the Holy Family] are doing, for example, making the journey and labouring that our Lord may be born, in extreme poverty, and that after many labours, after hunger, thirst, heat, and cold, after insults and outrages, He might die on the cross, and all this for me.

(Sp. Ex. #116)

Grace: This is to ask for what I desire. Here it will be to ask for an intimate knowledge of our Lord, who has become man for me, that I may love Him more and follow Him more closely.

The Illusions of Christmas

We have sentimentalized Christmas. We have made it pretty and politically correct. We are trapped in the tug of unreality this creation imposes upon us with its saccharine depictions of peace, family harmony, Victorian cheer according to Charles Dickens, and nativity crèches of pious and frozen poses. Prayer does not support such illusion; instead, it puts us in touch with the truth, of which those illusions are fragmented distortions. The contemplation on the nativity of Christ allows us to experience the mystery of the divine love, and of various forms of human love being simply present to each other in mutual dependence in the most difficult of circumstances. It invites us to share in that reality as we now read and contemplate prayerfully Luke 2:1-14.

Between the Annunciation and Jesus' birth, Mary's life has not been settled. She has told Joseph of her condition. He decides to break their engagement quietly and is only dissuaded against doing that by a dream. He has not been involved in Mary's original decision, yet his life, too, is turned upside down by these unique events, about which he has to make choices and commitments. Then Mary leaves to visit Elizabeth, her kinswoman who has become pregnant in her old age. Mary cares for her and then returns home, only to have to set out for Bethlehem to register in the Roman census with her husband and his family. Her baby will be born soon. There, in spite of the cult of hospitality, her condition and the shame it brings upon them affords her and Joseph no space in his family homes. There is no mention of care or concern from those quarters. There is not even room in the inn. It is in the place where animals are stabled that the Christ is born.

Caring for God

Ignatius asks us to enter into that human drama of struggle and sacrifice so that love can be born. In our contemplations of the sequences leading up to and including the birth, he suggests that we make ourselves "poor, little, and unworthy servant[s] [of the holy family] gazing at them, contemplating them, and serving them in their needs…with all possible respect and reverence" (#114). In this poverty, we imitate the Divine Word, who "did not count equality with God as something to hold onto, but emptied himself, taking on the form of a servant" (1 Phil 2:7). That second person of the Trinity becomes poor and humble in the service of a love that desires to save us and all of creation. As we enter into that love, we find ourselves taking on its characteristics.

Mary and Joseph also take on those characteristics of self-emptying. One of the points of this contemplation, Ignatius tells us, "is to behold and consider what they are doing; for example, journeying and toiling that the Lord may be born in greatest poverty; and that after so many hardships of hunger, thirst, heat, cold, injuries, and insults, he may die on the cross! And all this for me!" (#116).

In this contemplation we witness that self-emptying love in Mary and Joseph and in their relationships with each other. Mary gives up her own personal interests and desires because of that love. God does not abandon her after the moment of annunciation. His love and loving remains active in her world. When Joseph wants to dismiss her, God intercedes with him in his dreams and he takes her as his wife. That same God protects Joseph and Mary and the child in their trials when the political forces of the day seek to destroy Jesus. But even with this help, their lives are not easy; rather, their lives are rooted in a love for God that goes beyond their self-interests. They respond to God's love, which, in its mysterious ways, chose them to be part of its merciful providence.

When we enter into this contemplation, we enter into all the aspects of that journey to birthing God in this world. We go with Mary and Joseph on their journey, and make it our own journey. We are present to the perils and the uncertainties of that journey, present to the care and concern they show to each other. We are present at the birth of Christ, the miracle of seeing God fully human and fully vulnerable, needing us. We can ask to hold that child and that love in our arms, in our hearts and with our lives.

We conclude this prayer period with a conversation to the Trinity, to the Christ, or to Mary about what stirs in us during the contemplation.

Questions for prayer and reflection

1. How did you find this contemplation?

2. What happened to you in this contemplation? Where did it take you?

3. What was deeply personal for you in this prayer?

4. How did it feel to hold the child Jesus?

5. What did the prayer confirm in you?

6. What was the conversation at the end of the contemplation like?

7. Is there any part of the prayer that you feel called to return to because you know there is more in it for you?

8. Did you find any part of the prayer difficult or dry? Why do you think that was so? What does it tell you about yourself?

The Movie
The Matrix

Director: Andy and Larry Wachowski (1999 – 136 mins.)
Starring: Keanu Reeves, Lawrence Fishburne, Carrie Anne Moss

1. Summary

In the near future, a computer hacker named Neo discovers that all life on Earth may be nothing more than an elaborate facade created by a malevolent cyber-intelligence to placate us while our life essence is "farmed" to fuel the Matrix's campaign of domination in the "real" world. Neo joins like-minded rebels Morpheus and Trinity in their struggle to overthrow the Matrix.

2. Questions about the Movie

1. From film critics to philosophers and theologians, from college students to pop culture writers, from skateboarders to lawyers, it seems everyone, of every age, has their own idea of what *The Matrix* is all about. While *The Matrix* can be viewed as a Christian parable with many parallels to the life of Christ, Eastern philosophy can also feel at home in it. The movie may not exactly be a study of society, but it does explore the theme of man versus technology, and even the theme of nihilism. Or maybe it's just a hi-tech twist of *Alice in Wonderland* or *The Wizard of Oz. The Matrix* is wide open for interpretation. What do you believe to be the theme of *The Matrix?*

2. Director Larry Wachowski: "We're interested in mythology, theology, and, to a certain extent, higher mathematics. All are ways human beings try to answer bigger questions, as well as The Big Question. If you're going to do epic stories, you should concern yourself with those issues. People might not understand all the allusions in the movie, but they understand the important ideas. We wanted to make people think, engage their minds a bit." (Quoted in "Popular Metaphysics," Richard Corliss, *Time*, April 19, 1999, p. 55.) Has the director succeeded in this goal with you? If he did, what in the movie made this happen? If he didn't succeed, what turned you off the movie?

3. "Through the symbol of the matrix, they (the directors) encourage us to question our beliefs and seek enlightenment in a world where too many are willing to accept the world as it seems. At the same time, they also seem to believe that the world as it seems is still very much worth saving." ("Speaking out: Looking for God in The Matrix," Greg Garrett, *Christianity Today*, May 16, 2003.) What is the sacred ground this movie covers for people of faith?

3. The Relationship of the Movie to the Theme of the Exercise

1. We've looked at the importance of the use of the imagination in the Exercises. *The Matrix* is a movie that uses imagination to interpret what might be called transcendental themes – life and death, alternate worlds, appearance and reality, love and betrayal. Which of these themes appeals to you? How does the movie reveal it to you?

2. The Exercise speaks to us about the human drama of struggle and sacrifice that must take place before love can be born. In *The Matrix*, where do we find such a struggle and sacrifice? What is waiting to be born?

3. Mary's and Joseph's lives are rooted – as the Exercise says – in a love that went beyond their self-interests. What parallels are apparent in the characters of *The Matrix*?

4. The Relationship of the Movie to One's Self in the Exercise

1. When we are present at the birth of Christ, we are asked to note the perils and uncertainties of the journey as well as the care and concern that those involved show to each other. How is this type of care and concern reflected in *The Matrix*? How is it reflected in your own journey of love? What are the perils and uncertainties of your journey?

2. Watching the movie, we each find our own way through the maze and exit with our own lesson learned. What is real? What is true? As Neo and Trinity must find their truth, so too can we…depending on what we are willing to see. What stops you from fully entering into the journey?

3. Neo must learn to overcome his doubts and understand that he is the One chosen to lead the human race to freedom. The Exercise refers to such a process as working towards "self-emptying." What prevents you from such an act? What is there still within you that must come out?

4. We learn in the Exercise that Mary must give up her own personal interests and desires and, as we've seen, Neo must do likewise. Now it is your turn. What personal interests and desires are you being asked to give up?

4th Exercise
The Early Life of Christ (I)

Jesus increased in wisdom and in stature, and in favour with God and man.

(Luke 2:52)

I will make myself a poor little unworthy slave, and as though present, look upon them, contemplate them, and serve them in their needs with all possible homage and reverence.

(Sp. Ex. #114)

Grace: This is to ask for what I desire. Here it will be to ask for an intimate knowledge of our Lord, who has become man for me, that I may love Him more and follow Him more closely.

(Sp. Ex. #104)

The First Ones to See Jesus

Ignatius divides the early incidents of the life of the Christ child in the following sequence: the angels' announcement of the birth of Christ to the shepherds (Luke 2:8-20); the circumcision of Christ (Luke 2:21); the visit of the three kings (Matthew 2:1-12); the purification of Our Lady and the presentation of the Infant Jesus (Luke 2:22-38). Normally, each one of these incidents would be a prayer period in itself. The intent of each section, and of the whole sequence, is to proclaim God's mercy to the human condition. In our contemplations we are asked to find ourselves in that mercy, and so we always pray during this Week of the Exercises for that grace of "an interior knowledge of Our Lord, who became human for me, that I may love him more and follow him more closely" (#104).

A Politically Incorrect God

The shepherds were the first to be shown the birth of Christ. Shepherds, in Christ's time, were regarded as corrupt and outside of the Law. They were social outcasts and considered to have less value than the animals they protected. When you are poor, no one believes in you; you do not even believe in yourself. Yet it is to these that the angels came with the news of Christ's birth, and they were the first outsiders to see him in the flesh. At this point it is helpful to remember the gift of the First Week, when the divine mercy came to those who were alienated from themselves and from others. The love we experience in this contemplation is the same love that goes out to the shepherds. It is the desire of the divine love that nothing and no one is left out of its embrace.

That divine mercy calls to all: poor and rich, wise and unlearned. It calls to the magi – those wise ones from a religious tradition other than the Jewish faith. Following their heart's desire and using the knowledge available to them, they too encounter the Christ child, they worship, and they offer their gifts to this tiny human manifestation of the Divine. On their journey to Bethlehem they also encounter Herod, the duplicitous, who seeks their knowledge for his own ends; because they are under the divine mercy, they escape his wiles. For Ignatius, God's love is not exclusivist or otherworldly. It concerns itself with everyone, no matter what their state of life. The nativity story shows a God who touches the lives of a variety of people to affirm, protect or rescue them or to answer their needs. Inasmuch as we, too, are touched by that divine mercy, we see, as the Trinity does, everyone in need of love. In our desire to be one with that love, we offer freely to all, here and now, what has been given to us freely and joyfully.

Circumcision is the sign of the covenant between the Jewish people and God. When Christ is circumcized, he witnesses to that covenanted love. In being named "Jesus," he becomes the embodiment of that naming that "God saves." Where we place our bodies witnesses to what we value, and how we place our bodies incarnates those values. Among the Christmas names of Jesus is "Emmanuel" – God is with us. In the Christ child we see a God who is one with humanity, who in human form is still the second person of the Trinity. We experience the value God places in us: he enters our human condition so that one day we can enter into God's own life. In these prayers we ask to experience ourselves as ones who are so valued. The contemplation asks us to enter into that experience of being so valued – not just intellectually, but intimately and with all of our senses and desires. It asks us to relish that intimacy and to rest in it.

The Patience of Hope

It is this intimacy that Simeon and Anna relish when they encounter Joseph and Mary as they bring Jesus to present him to the temple. Both Simeon and Anna were devout people. They had lived through the trials of a Roman occupation and through the corruptions of Herod's religious politics without abandoning hope that one day they would experience the deliverance of Israel. They always remained faithful to God's promise, not knowing when it would be given or what form it would take. God is gracious to them in their patience and humility and long-suffering. That day at the temple, God rewards their patience and fidelity. They know Jesus to be that lived answer to their hope and their faith. They feel, touch, see and hold their hearts' desire. Too often we give up our heart's desire. We accept what the world has to offer as the only reality. But our desire never gives up on us, for to do that is to die. If we can open ourselves to our deepest desires, to the pain and the longing, and to its promise, in this contemplation we discover, like Simeon and Anna, that we have been given a gift that answers that longing. It is the Christ. Let us relish that gift in this contemplation.

Questions for prayer and reflection

1. In the contemplation, which particular incident was particularly meaningful for you? Why?

2. How does it feel to enter into Christ's life in your contemplations?

3. How does it feel to have Christ enter into your life during these contemplations?

4. What does this tell you about your developing relationship with God?

5. What comes up as significant in your conversations with God, or with Mary, or with Jesus, at the end of the prayer period?

6. Does anything disturb you in the prayer? What? Why do you think that happens?

7. How is your prayer influencing the rest of your day or week?

8. How is the time out of prayer affecting your contemplations?

9. Do you think you are getting the grace of an intimate knowledge of the Christ from your prayer?

10. How does that grace affect you?

The Movie
O Brother, Where Art Thou?

Director: Joel Coen (2000 – 103 mins.)
Starring: George Clooney, John Turturro, Tim Blake Wilson, Charles Durning

1. Summary

Three 1920s convicts escape from jail intent on getting to the loot stashed away by one of them. They embark on a comedic journey that takes them through a rural Mississippi landscaped with characters based on Homer's Odyssey. They find themselves talking their way out of various jams and even form an impromptu musical band. Eventually their journey comes to a wet end and most of their troubles are washed away in a flood.

2. Questions about the Movie

1. "There would be no momentum to this story were it not for the sound of glorious noise made by simple peoples. Throughout this knockabout, backwoods odyssey, our heroes are constantly drawn from their path of self-interest by the joyful ringing in their ears." (Geoff Pevere, *Toronto Star*, December 29, 2000, p. D3) It is not possible to think about this movie without considering the role that the music plays – it is a living presence and at times the star of the movie. What are several examples where the music plays a part in either furthering the plot or setting the mood of a scene? Why does using old-time bluegrass, country and blues standards work so well here?

2. "Lack of irony and complexity in the wrap-up may be a shortcoming, but it also points up the welcome absence of condescension and ridicule in the film's portrait of dimwits, con men, rednecks and country folk. Most of the characters, including the three leads, may be dumb, misguided and delusional, but they are also engaging…." (Todd McCarthy, *Variety*, May 22-28, 2000, p. 21) Choose one of the major scenes in the movie. Is this statement true?

3. "*O Brother, Where Art Thou?* similarly offers a fairytale view of an America in which the real brutalities of poverty and racism are magically dissolved by the power of song. Because the Coens are smart enough to know that such a place has ever existed only in fable and song, their vision takes on an unexpected poignancy. Rather than wallow in nostalgia for the past, they dare to reinvent it, to make it something strange, beautiful and new. *O Brother, Where Art Thou?* is a tribute to, and example of, the persistent vitality of the American imagination. It's bona fide." (A.O. Scott, *The New York Times*, December 22, 2000)

Why is it important that imagination be used this way by filmmakers?

3. The Relationship of the Movie to the Theme of the Exercise

1. Like the shepherds in the Exercise, the three convicts are social outcasts and regarded as less than human. The Exercise tell us that we have to experience ourselves as valued. How does the movie show that the three men are valued by God?

2. The three convicts, despite occasional outbursts, get along well with each other – they declare themselves to be "true friends." Even more remarkably, they accept without judgment all the very strange people they encounter in their journey. The Exercise tells us that it is the desire of love that nothing and no one is left out. How do the three men show this love to the various people they meet?

3. The intent of this part of the Exercises is to manifest the witness of proclaiming God's mercy within the human condition. Certainly, throughout the movie, there seems to be someone guiding the three men on their journey. Ulysses tries to shrug off what appears to be a miraculous answer to his prayer. Do you believe that what happens is a proclaiming of God's mercy? Why? Why not?

4. We learn from the Exercise that when you are poor, no one believes in you; you do not even believe in yourself. The movie shows us people who are "poor" and people who are "rich" in many senses. Who are some of these people? Why are those who appear to be poor quite rich in reality? What makes them rich?

4. The Relationship of the Movie to One's Self in the Exercise

1. Ulysses Everett McGill does all that he does out of love for his wife and daughters and his desire to be reunited with them. What is there in your life that is motivated by love? What stops you from acting solely out of love in return for the love God gives you?

2. The three men clearly do what the Exercise tells us to do – offer to all, freely, here and now, what has been given to us freely and joyfully. Where in your life do you offer such love to those with whom you work and live and play?

3. Despite all odds, Ulysses refuses to give up on his heart's desire. He refuses to accept what the world has to offer as being the only reality. How willing are you to give your all for what God calls you to? What is the "reality" in your life that the world offers you in place of that love?

The Early Life of Christ (2)

An angel of the Lord appeared to Joseph in a dream and said, "Rise, take the child and his mother, and flee to Egypt, and remain there till I tell you; for Herod is about to search for the child, to destroy him.

(Matthew 2:13)

It is characteristic of God and His Angels, when they act upon the soul, to give true happiness and spiritual joy, and to banish all sadness and disturbances which are caused by the enemy.

It is characteristic of the evil one to fight against such happiness and consolation by proposing fallacious reasonings, subtleties, and continual deception

(Sp. Ex. #329)

Grace: This is to ask for what I desire. Here it will be to ask for an intimate knowledge of our Lord, who has become man for me, that I may love Him more and follow Him more closely.

(Sp. Ex. #104)

The Human Cost of Love

Until the beginning of Jesus' public life, the scriptures mention only three incidents after the presentation of Christ in the temple. Ignatius cites them as the flight into Egypt (Matthew 2:13-18), the return from Egypt (Matthew 2:19-23), and the finding in the temple at the age of twelve (Luke 2:41-50). All three show the human cost of love, the way those who commit themselves to the Divine Life are treated in the world. Innocents are slaughtered because they are suspected of being a political threat. Jesus and his family become refugees and lead lives abandoned to Divine Providence. The contemplations based on these scripture passages destroy the notion of a sentimental God as a divine Santa Claus. They show, instead, the power of love in hard times, in the face of absurdity and worldly malice. The focus of that love is always on the primary call of the Divine.

The Powers of the World

If we think only in secular terms and see reality only as a worldly construct, the idea of anything or anyone being a ruler becomes a challenge to the ruling powers of the time. That is the case with Herod when he heard the news of Christ's birth. He is dominated by his desire to eliminate what he sees as a challenge to his authority. As local king, he orders the death of any male child born in and around Bethlehem around the time of Christ's nativity. But Christ escapes that slaughter because Joseph is told in a dream to take his family and flee into Egypt. Matthew's story here echoes the story in Genesis of Joseph, the dreamer, who is sold by his brothers into slavery in Egypt, where he eventually rises to power and rescues the Israelites in a time of famine. Egypt, as we note in the book of Exodus, is place of exile and slavery. Matthew's Joseph and his family become refugees, aliens in an alien land. Their commitment to God, and God's commitment to them, prevents them from being destroyed, but it does not prevent them from suffering loss, hardship and exile. Moreover, the story also tells us the tragic cost to those families who had children about Jesus' age. The presence of God's mercy in this world provokes the powers of this world to acts of outrageous cruelty. No one, not even the innocent and the unwitting, are uninvolved in this cosmic human drama. All are involved, all are consumed. We, too, find ourselves in this sphere of action.

In this contemplation we encounter the forces of the divine and the energies of the despotic. We can ask in the midst of human suffering: Where is God in all of this? God can also ask: Where are you in all of this? God shows us where he is: he is the life in the midst of death. We are asked to follow the Christ.

The return from exile occurs when Herod dies. But the hope for homecoming is dashed when Herod's equally corrupt son assumes the throne. Instead of being able to return home Joseph, once again warned in a dream, withdraws with his family to Nazareth in Galilee, where Jesus grows up.

The Sacred Space in Every Exile

It is the dream of every exile to return home. Exiles define themselves by memory. They long for the place and the people they remember as their own. They suffer from a homesickness caused by too long an absence from all that roots them and gives them their identity. That dream and that desire become a passion, at times, even an obsession. This passion provokes a fanaticism for a homeland free of foreign influences. In Joseph's case, despite that dreadful and raw need, he remains faithful to the covenant promise of a Messiah to restore the fortunes of Israel. He waits, open to the mystery of God's provenance. His new home, he discovers, is within the relationships of Mary and Jesus, and not within the pre-established norms of clan, culture, and land.

When we enter into this contemplation, we enter into a sacred space where our own dreams and energies are realigned from clan and culture, ethnicity or ego-orientation, to our deepest passion: to be one with God. We acknowledge both what we desire from our human point of view and what God is giving us.

Even Mary and Joseph endure this human tension. They have sacrificed everything for the sake of the one they call Jesus. Yet, when the time for his ritual entrance into adulthood comes, at Passover, at the age of twelve, Jesus leaves them behind to stay in the temple. As he later tells them, "Did you not know I must be in my father's house?" (Luke 3:49). Jesus' passionate desire is always for the Father; everything else finds meaning only in that relationship. The story foretells another Passover, some 21 years later, when the Christ's passion for his Father, and the Father's passion for the Christ, reaches through the boundaries of human life and human relationships – death – to resurrection. The focus on Divine Providence that underlies the early life of Jesus, and his family, sets the stage for his public life and ministry.

If the earlier parts of this prayer period reveal the focus of love in a corrupt and cruel world, the prayer ends with that focus bearing in on the intimate relationships within a small family centred on the Christ. The pattern is the same: the relationship with God is of the utmost importance.

In this prayer you are asked to enter more and more deeply into that relationship by contemplating the early life of Christ in the world of his time.

Questions for prayer and reflection

1. In these prayer periods you have been asking for the grace of "an interior knowledge of Our Lord, who became human for me, that I may love him more and follow him more closely" (#104). How has this grace been given to you?

2. What has been revealed to you about the nature of the world? How do you react to that, spontaneously? How do you react to it when you travel with Christ?

3. What was the most consoling thing about this prayer? What does it tell you about yourself and about your relationship with God?

4. What has been the most negative thing about this prayer? When did it occur? What does it suggest about your values and relationships?

5. Have you ever had an experience of being alienated or separated from the people or the places you loved? How did you survive that separation?

6. Are any aspects of your life like being in exile, being a refugee or being the pawn of forces greater than you? What are they? What forces exile you?

7. How do you deal with those aspects and those forces?

8. Can you bring those forces and those aspects to your contemplation, or to your dialogues with God?

124

The Movie
The Hours

Director: Stephen Daldry (2002 – 114 mins.)
Starring: Nicole Kidman, Meryl Streep, Julianne Moore, Ed Harris

1. Summary

A day in the life of three women on the verge of a nervous breakdown. In the 1923 English countryside, Virginia Woolf battles insanity as she writes *Mrs. Dalloway*. In 1951, Laura Brown, a pregnant Los Angeles housewife who is planning a party for her husband, is reading the novel *Mrs. Dalloway* and becomes desperate to flee her family. In present-day New York, Clarissa Vaughn, a modern version of Mrs. Dalloway, is throwing a party for her friend Richard, a famous author dying of AIDS.

2. Questions about the Movie

1. "Virginia Woolf is somehow supposed to be the grandmotherly ancestor both of women's agony and the means to cure it. But by intercutting between them, Daldry more or less persuades us that the three women's stories are atemporal, that they exist alongside each other not in sequence but in parallel." (Peter Bradshaw, *The Guardian*, February 14, 2003) What difference would it make to the overall impact of the movie if the stories were told in sequence? Would anything be lost? Would anything be gained?

2. At the end of the movie, we see that "…lives without love are devastated. Virginia and Leonard Woolf loved each other, and Clarissa treasures both of her lovers. But for the two in the movie who do not or cannot love, the price is devastating." (Roger Ebert, *Chicago Sun-Times*, December 27, 2002) What price do these two characters pay? At what point did they find themselves unable to love?

3. "*The Hours* is a moving, somewhat depressing film that demands and rewards attention." (Philip French, *The Guardian*, February 16, 2003) What moved you in the film? How much "work" did you have to do to pay attention to the film? Was it worth the effort? Why? Why not?

4. "Some of the movie's most wrenching moments show Leonard Woolf (Stephen Dillane) frantically reaching out to his troubled wife and being rebuffed. It's not that the Woolfs don't love each other, but the agony Virginia is enduring can't be touched by love or reason. These moments bring home the film's deepest and most intimidating insight about the essential aloneness of the individual and its feminist corollary: that appearances to the contrary, women in their deepest selves do not and should not define themselves

in terms of men." (Stephen Holden, *The New York Times*, December 27, 2003) How much of this statement do you agree with? Some? All? None? Why?

3. The Relationship of the Movie to the Theme of the Exercise

1. The Exercise asks that we contemplate three episodes in the life of Christ – the flight into Egypt, the return from Egypt, and the finding in the temple – that show the cost of love. The movie also centres around three episodes, all of which are connected to the novel *Mrs. Dalloway*. How do each of these episodes show the cost of love?

2. "*The Hours* is not afraid to admit how terrifyingly alone we can be, how deep the chasms between individuals are, how little we care to or are even able to let others into our emotional lives. Yet it shows not only how critical but also how fragile are the attachments we do form." (Kenneth Turan, *The Los Angeles Times*, December 27, 2002) The Exercise speaks to us of the presence of God in the midst of human suffering. Where is God in the three stories presented in the movie?

3. The Exercise reminds us of the power of love in hard times, in the face of absurdity and worldly malice. Where is the power of love in the hard times that makes up the heart of each of the three stories in the movie?

4. The Relationship of the Movie to One's Self in the Exercise

1. All three stories in the movie centre around the fictional character of Mrs. Dalloway – a woman who, despite the face she puts on in public, is utterly alone, abandoned and unable to reach out to the romance she desires. What "face" do you present to the public? Does it show what you are really feeling? What stops you from reaching out to the love you know God offers you?

2. In the movie, the novelist, Richard Brown, is dying of AIDS. The Exercise tells us that God is life in the midst of death and suffering. All of us undergo a variety of suffering in our lives. Where is God in the midst of your own suffering? What keeps you from opening to God so he may show you his love?

3. As the Exercise tells us, Mary and Joseph endure this human tension. In the three stories that make up the movie, there is much human tension that each of the three women must endure in one way or the other. Where is your human tension? How do you "endure" it?

6th Exercise
The Hidden Life

In the beginning was the Word, and the Word was with God, and the Word was God. He was in the beginning with God; all things were made through him, and without him was not anything that was made. In him was life, and the life was the light of men. The light shone in the darkness, and the darkness has not overcome it.

(John 1:1-5)

In souls that are progressing to greater perfection the action of the good angel is delicate, gentle, delightful. It may be compared to a drop of water penetrating a sponge.

The action of the evil spirit upon such souls is violent, noisy, and disturbing. It may be compared to a drop of water falling upon a stone.

(Sp. Ex. #335)

Grace: This is to ask for what I desire. Here it will be to ask for an intimate knowledge of our Lord, who has become man for me, that I may love Him more and follow Him more closely.

Waiting for God

The following exercise may well be one of the most enigmatic of the prayer periods that St. Ignatius asks us to engage in. We are asked to contemplate the hidden life of Christ from age twelve to the beginning of his public ministry, when he sets off for the Jordan and is baptized by his cousin John. Nothing is written of these years except a general statement in Luke: "Jesus increased in wisdom and stature, in favour with God and man" (2:52).

Different people have different prayer experiences when they ask Jesus to reveal that hidden life. What is fairly common to all is that what is given deepens their personal relationship with Jesus. What is given is what each person needs to continue this spiritual journey to intimacy with God.

Up to now, the material of the Exercises has been contained in scripture or in a personal history. Now you are asked to enter the contemplation in the hope that something will be given to you. What is given has to come from God: it cannot be created by the one doing the Exercises, and yet it must completely involve that person's particular energies and concerns. It is just like someone falling in love saying to the beloved, "Tell me about yourself; tell me about yourself what you have never told anyone else." What is given is not conjecture to be verified against possible historical evidence. Its truth lies in the intimate weaving of the personal with the Divine within the depths of the psyche and is experienced through the contemplative imagination.

There is a level of intimacy in love that allows personal questions to be asked. The level of trust established allows those questions to be answered in such a way that the answer reveals both the lover and the beloved.

Here the unknown becomes known; here God makes the incarnation personal.

The relationship with God requires trust. This contemplation is about trust. From the time of the finding in the temple when Christ announces to his world that he is about his Father's business, Christ waits on the Father to reveal how that business is to take place. At a time when Jewish young men start to take on the responsibilities of their maturity, in having a job, a vocation, a family of their own, Jesus waits on the Father to reveal to him the next step. He waits 18 years. He learns to wait. This is an experiential learning that allows him to withstand the temptations in the desert and to wait on the Father's will; it is a learning that finds itself again on the cross, when Christ in his passion and death waits on the Father to reveal his love. That revelation is resurrection. But here, in the hidden life, we contemplate a young man's waiting. And we enter into our own waiting.

Learning to Be Ready

There are many ways to wait. We can "kill" time with distractions; we can freeze time in boredom; we can suffer time in anxiety as we search for meaning, purpose, fulfillment. We can slowly learn that the patience of God is time, and so become attentive to time, like Simeon and Anna, to what is daily given. We learn to cherish each moment without grasping it. In this we learn indifference, that basic stance of doing what we can to the best of our nature, and trusting that what we do reveals our acceptance of the constant mercy of God. Through this learning we become instruments of God, attuned to God's will. This is what it means to be contemplatives in action. It is not pious and sentimental, or intense and willful. It is being flexible and open so that we can delight in what is joyful, mourn with what is sorrow-ful, revere what is holy, shun what is destructive. It is learning to live fully in the world without becoming trapped by the world and its values and judgments.

In this contemplation we discover how Jesus learns and how he grows into that state of readiness that will allow him to hear and accept his call by the Father at his baptism in the Jordan.

What is happening to Jesus is also happening to us in this contemplation and in these Exercises. When we start becoming intimate with Christ, we share his relationship with the Father. Like him, we grow in our awareness of what that relationship is.

Questions for prayer and reflection

1. What happened when you entered into this contemplation? What surprised you about it?

2. What were the consolations and desolations of this contemplation?

3. How did the grace of intimacy with the Christ manifest itself to you?

4. How do you generally wait?

5. How do you view the future? With trepidation? With worry? With calm? With curiosity? With joy? How do you feel when you wake up in the morning?

6. How have you experienced time? Your history?

7. How do you find your relationships with people?

8. How do you find your relationship with that mystery we call Father?

9. How do you experience your sense of sinking into an intimacy with God?

10. How does that affect you?

The Movie
Hearts in Atlantis

Director: Scott Hicks (2001 – 101 mins.)
Starring: Anthony Hopkins, Anton Yelchin, Hope Davis, David Morse

1. Summary

In the summer of 1960, 11-year-old Bobby Garfield is sharing adventures with his best friends, Carol and Sully. Bobby lives with his self-absorbed mother, who looks for pleasures for herself without sharing much with her son. Into their lives comes a mysterious new boarder named Ted Brautigan, who befriends the boy but generates distrust from the mother. As time passes, the man and boy share confidences and special powers are revealed before something terrible happens.

2. Questions about the Movie

1. "*Hearts in Atlantis* weaves a strange spell, made of nostalgia and fear. Rarely does a movie make you feel so warm and so uneasy at the same time, as Stephen King's story evokes the mystery of adolescence, when everything seems to be happening for the very first time." (Roger Ebert, *Chicago Sun-Times*, September 28, 2001) How true was this for you?

2. "Movies have had a difficult time justifying their own existence, never mind their own publicity, but here may be what the commonweal is craving: a gentle, Stephen-King penned pulperatta that bleeds openly for suffering, lost innocence, and the American childhood." ("Children's Crusades," Michael Atkinson, *Village Voice*, October 3-9, 2001) When have you been disappointed with a well-publicized, hyped film that didn't deliver what it promised? Why is this movie neither more nor less than what it says it is – a story about a young boy growing up one summer?

3. "We're drawn in by the strangeness of the Hopkins character, the otherworldly elements of the story, the truth of the individual characters. The elegiac, reflective mood is treated almost incidentally, letting it earn a reaction naturally. The director, Scott Hicks, does a good job of capturing the point of view of a child – look at the scene where Hopkins and Yelchin venture into a bar, and reflect that while the camerawork seems to be plain, steady and unobtrusive, the framing is subtly highlighting the largesse of the place, evoking that feeling of awe and curiosity that you get as a kid when you're first allowed to enter a saloon." (Ian Waldron-Mantgani, *The UK Critic*, March 8, 2002) What other scene captures the child's point of view? What is your reaction to the "elegiac, reflective mood" of the movie?

4. "Hearts in Atlantis is an affective mood piece about youth, friendship and memories. But what's special about this memoir is the manner in which William Goldman's astute screenplay mirrors the way youthful recollections work. Memory is never reliable. Events get mixed up; people say things to you as a child that don't, in retrospect, always make sense; and the impact of small moments loom large in years to come." (Kirk Honeycutt, *The Hollywood Reporter*, September 10, 2001) What are some of the "small moments" that are recalled by the grown up Bobby? How do these moments affect this summer of his life?

3. The Relationship of the Movie to the Theme of the Exercise

1. Ted tells Bobby: "Sometimes when you are young, you have moments of such happiness, you think you're in some place magical, like Atlantis must have been. Then we grow up and our hearts break in two." The innocence that we have as children disappears when we become adults. How does this Exercise help us to preserve some of that innocence?

2. The Exercise defines contemplation in action as learning to live fully in the world without becoming trapped by the world and its values and judgments. Which scenes show us how Ted is a contemplative in action? What does Ted do to avoid being trapped by the world of the "Low Men"?

3. Ted's touch has given Bobby some power of his own, and he uses it in a very simple way. There's no slaying of a dragon, or vanquishing of a vampire, or closing down a hellmouth. It's something much simpler – against a monster with a small "m." Watch as the changes in Bobby's face, the music, and the camera combine to show us Bobby's power and his new ability to make magic happen. As the Exercise says, Bobby has trusted the unknown to become known. Is this only on a human level or is there something spiritual about it?

4. The Relationship of the Movie to One's Self in the Exercise

1. This contemplation is about trust. Bobby and Ted learn to trust each other – Bobby's need for a father and Ted's need for someone to understand him are part of the reasons for this trust. Whom do you trust? Trust completely? What might be preventing you from having such trust in God's love for you and all that follows from that?

2. Ted is relatively calm about what the future holds for him even though he knows it will not be pleasant. He draws this calm from deep within himself, from a knowledge of himself. What is it that you most fear about the future? Where will you go to try and relieve this fear?

3. The Exercise asks us to imagine that we are in love and that we say to the person we love: "Tell me about yourself; tell me about yourself something that you have never told anyone else." In the movie, Bobby and Ted do tell each other such things, and from that openness comes trust and all else that follows in the movie. Have you ever asked anyone such a question? If so, what changed in your life as a result? What stops you from asking such questions of Christ? What are you doing to make it possible for you to ask Christ such a question?

7th Exercise
The Two Standards

Beloved, do not imitate evil but imitate good.

(3 John 1:11)

An address should be made to our Lady asking her to obtain for me from her Son and Lord the grace to be received under His standard.
A second one should be to ask her Son to obtain the same favour for me from the Father
A third will be to beg the Father to grant me the same graces.

(Sp. Ex. #147)

Grace: This is to ask for what I desire. Here it will be to ask for a knowledge of the deceits of the rebel chief and help to guard myself against them; and also to ask for a knowledge of the true life exemplified in the sovereign and true Commander, and the grace to imitate Him.

(Sp. Ex. #139)

The Human Struggle

In the middle of the contemplations on Jesus' life and how he operates in his world, Ignatius has a break where he asks us to consider how we operate. He states, "While continuing to contemplate His life, let us begin to investigate and ask in what kind of life or in what state the Divine Majesty wishes to make use of us" (#135). He suggests that we do this by first looking at the ways Christ operates and the ways "the enemy of our human nature" operates. To this end he proposes a meditation on "Two Standards" (#136). In it he looks at the way we are seduced and trapped by evil. Then he looks at the way Jesus operates and asks us to follow. When we do evil, we operate under the Standard of Satan; when we do good we operate under the Standard of Christ. Ignatius adapts this military image from his years in the army, where soldiers declared their allegiance to a particular cause by serving under its flag or standard.

This is not an abstract process of reflection. Ignatius realizes that we need help in discovering these things. We cannot abstract ourselves either from our good or our bad to achieve these insights. And so he names four graces in this prayer period that he would like us to repeat four times to hammer home the individual patterns of our personality dynamics: 1) a knowledge of the deceits of the evil leader; 2) help to guard myself against them; 3) a knowledge of what gives genuine life as shown in Jesus and 4) the grace to imitate him.

People of the Lie

The simplest way of getting these insights is to consider how you behave when you feel vulnerable. We have two opposing ways of being in those situations: the way of the evil one and the way of Christ. The way of the evil one appeals to our strengths, so that we achieve the prestige and honour that our strength gives us and reinforce the pride of our egos. For example, when I enter a social situation where I feel uncomfortable, I can withdraw into a posture of witty cynicism that comes easily to me. People react to my comments and I become the centre of attention. This justifies my belief that I need only depend on myself.

Ignatius says that we are tempted first to covet riches, so that we might more easily attain the empty honours of this world, and from that come to overweening pride. This may happen literally. But riches are any talent or gift, or any other created thing, that we have or want to have and that we can use for our own ends so that we can live in a way that maintains our ego. For Ignatius, the movement to narcissism is what keeps us from being fully human. No one is ever free from this temptation. Ignatius does not claim that riches in themselves are bad. It is grasping at riches to live in unspiritual ways that boost our egos that is dangerous. It is the movement and direction we find in ourselves, and find ourselves in, that carries us to a self-enclosed ego-maintenance that is destructive. For Ignatius, there is no such thing as a static state of being; we are all moving either to transcendence or to more and more radical forms of self-enclosure and fragmentation.

In the meditation on the Two Standards, evil operates by terrorizing us and then offering us a way of coping with our fear in the face of such terror by seductive techniques of ego-maintenance. This meditation offers us a way of discovering how our own personality dynamics respond to being presented with situations that elicit our fear.

It is very useful here to examine our personal histories to see the pattern of our basic disorder at work, to discover how we become complicit in destruction. Awareness of this dynamic can help us overcome it. But we also need to learn other techniques to counteract these spontaneous tendencies. Ultimately, we realize that we cannot do this by ourselves; we need God's constant help and mercy. As we discovered in our prayer of the First Week, that help and mercy is constantly and freely given through the mediation of Christ and of those who bond with him.

The Hard Road

Opposed to the seductions, manipulations and entrapments of evil is the hard road to freedom offered by Christ. Ignatius' Christ and his followers "spread His sacred doctrine" to all, "no matter what their state or condition" (#145). That sacred doctrine is God's incarnate mercy. There is a pattern to embodying this mercy, and it all depends on God's own desire. For Ignatius, nothing should be done unless God desires it; the principle of all human action, in freedom, is God's desiring. Within that context, the pattern Christ offers is spiritual poverty, which leads, in this world, to desire exactly what this world does not desire, that is, insults and contempt, for from these spring humility (#146).

These are hard things to desire. We are so caught up in this world that even asking for them seems masochistic, inhuman and unnatural. The truth of the matter is we are totally and utterly dependent on God. But as our time in the First Week showed we generally live our lives away from this basic truth. We come to that truth when we realize our radical spiritual poverty. Too often we are so caught up with running from that understanding of ourselves that we also forget the God who creates, sustains, and redeems us. That Love does not desire our harm, but only that we be happy and become fuller and yet fuller manifestations of that love. The way we can witness to that love, and to our loving that love and trusting that love, is by living out of the poverty in our lives, should God so desire it. As Ignatius puts it, the call Christ makes to those who love him is that they "seek to help all, first by attracting them to the highest spiritual poverty, and should it please the Divine Majesty, and should it please Him to choose them for it, even to actual poverty" (#146).

Living Our Poverty

We do not offer to God the gift of our poverty, spiritual or material. The reality of our spiritual poverty is the human condition; the gift of actual poverty is what God also offers to some. This gift is not the imposition of poverty through personal misfortune, social injustice, economic imbalance of nations, or the results of global imperialism. Those are evils. Actual poverty is the choice of a lifestyle we make freely, desiring only God's love and to live out of God's loving providence in this world. We choose this only if we are confirmed that God desires this for us. Anything else is spiritual pride masquerading as poverty.

When we live out of the very poverty that is the centre of our being, we quickly discover that we do not live out of the values of this world. In fact, our path becomes offensive to the world, which responds with contempt, insults, mockery, abandonment. So, instead of the trappings of honour and prestige that the world delights in, some wear the tatters of humiliation. In this they identify with Jesus, who was also insulted, treated with contempt, humiliated. This identification with the beloved is important. We do not choose insults and reproaches, we choose Christ; we choose to be as Christ was and is in this world. To look for insults and injury while we have purely worldly values is to be sick and self-destructive. That is not what God desires. God desires that we be holy.

That holiness comes when, instead of fleeing from the full awareness of our poverty, we embrace it, and through it see our path to God with new eyes. We have in the examples of saints and holy people of all spiritual traditions this rejection of the values of the world while living in the world, and we have the long tradition of their ill-treatment in the hands of the world throughout human history in different cultures and religions.

What that ill-treatment from the world engenders is a profound humility. In humility, the ego does not have to defend itself; in humility we live, in our daily life, totally and intentionally dependent on God and on the manifestions of goodness in the world. We see everything given as a gift to be opened to discover the presence of God: every moment as offering an entry into the divine, our lives as an open space where God can enter into the world, and the pain of the world can encounter the compassionate mercy of God. In humility, we accept that we are God's beloved.

The Pattern of Our Choices

The meditation on the Two Standards allows us to see graphically in our own lives the choice that opens to us at every moment of our life, whether we are conscious of it or not. In our vulnerability, we can take up either the standard of evil or the standard of Christ. If we take up the standard of evil, we are led through coveting riches to honour and pride. If we accept the standard of Christ, we are offered poverty and through that the displeasure of the world and so reach humility. The choice is ours.

Ignatius realizes that this is a difficult and subtle meditation. He suggests that we do it four times so we can realize the graces we are asking for in this prayer. Those graces are to truly understand how we get trapped, to receive help to escape those traps, to understand how Christ behaves, and to receive the grace to follow him.

This prayer is not a pious exercise. It seeks to reveal the dynamic core of our being and our behaviour patterns. The resistance to that revelation is strong; God's love for us, however, is stronger.

We need to draw on all the help we can to achieve the graces we seek in this prayer. The Spiritual Exercises suggests that we seek the help of Mary, the mother of Jesus, then Jesus, and finally the Father, by discussing with them what we need and what arises when we enter fully into this prayer.

Questions for prayer and reflection

1. How do you spontaneously react when you are vulnerable?

2. What are your "riches," "honour," "pride"? How do they manifest themselves?

3. What is your "poverty"? How do you deal with your poverty? Have you ever found God in your poverty?

4. What happens when you pray to be identified with Jesus as he is insulted and held in contempt?

5. How do you live your humility? How does it shape the way you see and deal with others?

6. How does it affect your relationship with the things you possess?

7. What happened in your prayer that was consoling? What does this tell you?

8. What happened in your prayer that was negative? What does this tell you?

9. What happened in your conversations at the end of the prayer with Mary, Jesus and the Father?

10. As you prepare to repeat this prayer, what areas do you feel the need to focus on?

11. Were the graces you prayed for given? How? How did you receive them?

12. How does this prayer relate back to your earlier prayers of this Second Week?

The Movie

Harry Potter
and the Chamber of Secrets

Director: Chris Columbus (2002 – 161 mins.)
Starring: Daniel Radcliffe, Rupert Grint, Emma Watson, Kenneth Branagh, Maggie Smith, Robbie Coltrane, Richard Harris, Alan Rickman

1. Summary

Twelve-year-old Harry Potter, ignoring warnings, returns for his second year to Hogwarts School of Witchcraft and Wizardry. His friends Hermione and Ron join him in trying to discover the truth behind strange happenings at the school as students are becoming – literally – petrified. They learn of the Chamber of Secrets, which can be opened only by Salazar Slytherin's true heir. Because Harry is a Parsel-tongue – able to speak to and understand snakes – people fear he is that heir. Harry is faced with some terrible choices as he battles not only the evil Lord Voldemort but also the accusations of both his friends and his enemies.

2. Questions about the Movie

1. The movie contains a number of important themes. That there are so many themes reminds us of one of the key concept of media literacy, which talks about how audiences negotiate meaning – how each of us bring everything that makes up who we are to our viewing or hearing or reading of any media text. Each of us will find that one of these themes in Harry Potter will resonate with us. These themes are universal – they're for all of us because they are about all of us, not just about children.

    Which of the following themes appeal most to you? Which scenes best exemplify those themes?

    a) The theme of "the quest": Harry is on a journey of discovery to find out where he came from, who his parents were and where he belongs. Writer Joseph Campbell refers to such a journey as a heroic journey, one in which the hero – in this case, Harry – will face temptation to quit the quest, overcome obstacles, find the help of a wise guide, achieve his goal and return home to seek an end to his internal journey. Many heroic tales and legends as well as movies follow Campbell's ideas – *The Lord of the Rings* and the *Star Wars* movies are good examples.

    b) The theme of good versus evil: Lord Voldemort is the enemy – a powerful wizard who chose the standard of evil. The redeeming sacrifice of Harry's dead mother almost defeated him, but it is the loyalty and courage of Harry's own generation that must continue the battle with Voldemort. It is important to remember through all of this that Harry is fighting Voldemort not for personal revenge of his parents' murders, but because Voldemort is still a danger – to Harry and his friends, to the worlds of wizard and muggle (non-magic people) alike. Harry must face not only Voldemort but also those wizards who follow the evil Lord – such as Lucius Malfoy, father of Harry's enemy Draco.

c) Themes of Christianity: While there have been objections from right-wing evangelical groups, the Roman Catholic Church and the Protestant churches in the United Kingdom and Ireland have come out strongly in favour of the Harry Potter novels and movies, believing that the books illuminate the theme of the battle between good and evil. The books and the movies ask people to look again at the selfish material world and the presence within it of Christian values – truth, love and, supremely, self-giving and sacrifice. Harry Potter begins as one of the powerless and the voiceless, ignored and enslaved, but he has a destiny that he will use to help free himself and others. Harry is tempted to use his talents for evil, but he learns that a good person is defined not by abilities, but by choices.

d) The theme of social justice: freedom for those held captive or enslaved (the house elves).

e) The theme of equality: the rejection of prejudice and hatred on the basis of bloodline.

f) The theme of loneliness: In her novels, Rowling wanted to express just how defenseless even brave children can feel sometimes. All of her books have an undercurrent of sadness and loss. In creating Harry as a bright, inquisitive orphan and allowing him to discover the power of magic in the mysterious world of Hogwarts, she combines perfectly a character and setting to illustrate her theme. Even the teachers who are meant to help – such as Gilderoy Lockhart, the Professor of Defense against the Dark Arts – cannot.

g) The theme of belonging: For audiences around the world, the theme may be this simple. The books are about belonging. The first book is, in part, about Harry's discovering at Hogwarts the family and home he's never had. At the start of *The Chamber of Secrets* Harry is visiting Ron's house, where he is accepted as one of them – they are his new family. But still Harry searches for connections to his own family.

h) The theme of loss and grief: Rowling has admitted that much of the feeling of loss that Harry experiences derives from her own grief over her mother's death. Death is a central theme in all the Harry Potter books and movies –what it is and what it means to the bereaved.

3. The Relationship of the Movie to the Theme of the Exercise

1. As a former soldier, Ignatius visualizes us choosing the standard – the flag – of one of two kings: one good, one evil. The choice is always ours, and we will have to make such choices often. When Harry is in the Chamber of Secrets he understands the words of Dumbledore, a good wizard and the head of Hogwarts: "It is our choices, Harry, that show what we truly are, far more than our abilities." Dumbledore also warns

Harry that he is going to have to make choices because what is easy is not always right. This frightens Harry a great deal. While Rowling tells us that we will fully understand the implications of this for Harry only in the last two books of the seven-book series, we see enough now to know that Harry has good reason to be frightened. Which scenes best exemplify this in *Harry Potter and the Chamber of Secrets*?

2. As the Exercise tells us, evil operates by terrorizing us and then offering us a way to cope with our fear through seductive techniques of ego-maintenance. What is it about the situation at Hogwarts that terrorizes Harry? Is it the physical fear of what could be set free from the Chamber of Secrets, or the way the students and staff see him as the possible heir to evil? How does Harry overcome this evil?

3. *Harry Potter and the Chamber of Secrets* is filled with examples of Harry's lashing out at people he considered friends. He is almost consumed by anger and hatred for what he sees as unjustified accusations. Yet he also fears that he is responsible for the evil. The Exercise tells us that discovering for ourselves how we become complicit in destruction is a step towards overcoming the problem. How does Harry become aware of this – through something that happens or through Dumbledore's advice at the end of the movie?

4. The Exercise tells us that ultimately we cannot learn to counteract the complicity within ourselves on our own. How does this apply to the following statement? "It's the story of Harry fighting a serpent and overcoming it with the sword of Gryffindor. He is unable to accomplish this by himself and must call for help which comes from above.... It's not just a snake he must overcome but a snake summoned by Voldemort's memory.... The phoenix – a classic symbol of Christ, who dies and rises again – comes to help him. He kills the serpent, then in a moment quite shocking – I'm surprised Hollywood left it in – the phoenix weeps in his wound to heal him. That's a classic symbol of Christ's passion. It's Christ's tears that make us whole." (Scott Moore quoted in "The Real Magic of Harry Potter," Nancy Gibbs, *Time*, June 23, 2003, p. 56)

4. The Relationship of the Movie to One's Self in the Exercise

1. The Two Standards looks at the ways we are seduced by evil and the ways Jesus asks us to follow. Harry is tempted by Lord Voldemort to let loose evil upon the world, but chooses the way of good that Dumbledore has shown him. You, too, must choose between the standard of good and the standard of evil – as must we all. What tempts you to evil in your life? What or who is the Dumbledore who shows you the way of the good – the way of Christ?

2. Harry's ability to speak Parsel-tongue is one of his many gifts – one of his riches. He must overcome the temptation to use this gift for his own ends, despite being accused by students who are both his friends and his enemies. What gift do you have (or wish to have) that could tempt you to live in a way that maintains and boosts your ego and shuts out the good that is God?

3. Although Harry fears that he may be the heir of Salazar Slytherin, he tries to hide it by attempting to solve the various mysteries at Hogwarts.

Harry is, as the Exercise tells us, caught up in running from that understanding of himself that he needs. How often do you do this? What are you afraid to face? What are you running from that will not allow you to remember the God that creates, sustains and redeems us?

4. With help, Harry chooses to follow the good and manages to overcome the temptations of "riches," "honour" and "pride" in his battle with Voldemort, and emerges a stronger and more confident person. Which of your "riches," "honour" or "pride" is the most difficult for you to overcome? Why?

8th Exercise
The Three Classes of People

Behold, I have set before you an open door, which no one is able to shut; I know you have but little power, and yet you have kept my word and have not denied my name.

(Revelation 3:8)

Here it will be to behold myself standing in the presence of God our Lord and of all His saints that I may know and desire what is more pleasing to His Divine Goodness.

(Sp. Ex. #151)

Grace: Here it will be to beg for the grace to choose what is more for the glory of His Divine Majesty and the salvation of my soul.

(Sp. Ex.#152)

Our Choices Define Who We Are

In spiritual terms, people can be divided into three groups: a) those who do not care one way or the other about God, b) those who want God to support them in their schemes, and c) those who desire to follow God. No doubt each of us combines elements of all three types, but we each must decide on our basic orientation for how we will relate to God. It is a question of how we embody our deepest desire in our daily lives.

Let's look a little more closely at these three different types of people. The first group does not pursue a relationship with God, for a variety of reasons, some of which are valid ones. So the relationship never gets expressed. It is rather like being in love with someone and not admitting it to yourself, not declaring your love to that person, or not doing anything about it. The relationship remains, on your part, on the level of friendship. It is comfortable and safe and easy. Without entering into the risk of mature relationships, one remains a child, refusing to grow up. This is what the first type of person does.

The second type of person admits to being in love, but that love is defined only by personal needs. The beloved has to do and live only as the person in love wants. This type of love manifests itself in jealousy, or narcissism. The beloved has no individual life but instead must live as the lover's idealized projection. Abusive relationships often arise from such selfishness. That second type of person treats others, and God, as objects to be manipulated for immediate satisfaction.

The third type of person is committed to the beloved and lives out of that commitment in a responsible way. People of this type "seek to will or not will as God our Lord inspires them, and as seems better for the service and praise of the Divine Majesty" (#155). They enter the process of discernment by asking themselves how to love responsibly in the concrete circumstances of their lives so that neither they, nor anyone else, nor the witness to God's love gets destroyed as a result of their choices.

Of course, all of us would claim that we want to love in a way that brings life to those involved with us. It is difficult to achieve the level of true self-awareness of what we mean when we say we love. Ignatius suggests that instead of looking at love, we look at how we would use some riches – money or talent – that we have received. We know we should use it for good, because we do not want to be selfish. Having been through the First Week of the Exercises, we know that selfishness traps and destroys us, and we want to avoid that trap.

Facing Selfishness

The first type of person, unable to decide how to avoid being selfish, does nothing and so remains selfish. The second type of person makes a decision to be selfish and seeks to have God justify that selfishness. The third type of person is concerned only with making the best use of the gift. If the best use is seen as selfish by others, that is not their concern; if that best use is seen as wonderfully philanthropic by others, that is also not their concern. That person wants only to better serve and praise God. This exercise is not about making a decision, therefore; it is about the correct attitude needed in order to make a decision. St. Augustine sums up this attitude: "Love and do what you will." St. Ignatius asks: But what do you love? What you love is what you will. Your will-ing is your love in action. When you see where your will has led you, then you will see who and what you love.

Who you love and what you love may not love you. In fact, the expression of your desires may even destroy you. This is what happened to Christ. So it is not just a question of loving, but of loving properly.

If we are passionate for God and allow God to be passionate for us – as Christ is passionate for the Father, and the Father is passionate for Christ – then we become indifferent to all created things. We desire only what God desires. This does not mean being passive or wishy-washy. It means seeing and holding all things within the dynamism of that love that loves us back.

While we may agree wholeheartedly with this approach and find it very moving, it is very difficult to give up our self-will and to value things and other people only within the mutual love between God and us. St. Ignatius suggests that when we find it difficult, we should beg God to give us the freedom and the grace to work against our disordered desires and to come to the position of loving as God loves.

Questions for prayer and reflection

1. When have you been simply unable to make a decision? Why did that happen? How did it affect you?

2. When have you spontaneously expected the world, others, and even God to agree with your plans and desires? How did you try to manipulate those situations to meet your own needs?

3. When have you given yourself over unreflectively to a mood, a situation, another person, a political position, or social or cultural values because you felt it was the right thing to do?

4. In what ways have you loved? In what ways have what you loved not been in your best interests?

5. Have you ever loved in a way that you found life and brought life to one or more others?

6. Did that loving involve any sacrifice? How did you deal with that sacrifice?

The Movie
Mystic River

Director: Clint Eastwood (2003 – 137 mins.)
Starring: Sean Penn, Tim Robbins, Kevin Bacon, Laurence Fishburn, Marcia Gay Harden, Laura Linney

1. Summary

In a Boston working-class Irish neighbourhood, the lives of three children – Jimmy, Sean and David – are forever changed when David is abducted and molested. Twenty-five years later, ex-con Jimmy's daughter is murdered and police trooper Sean's investigation leads to David.

2. Questions about the Movie

1. "Casting is immaculate. Penn is in top form as the reformed hood whose basic instincts overtake him. Robbins surprises with his vulnerability as an unusually inward character still bleeding from old wounds that never heal. Bacon plays Sean rather like Eastwood himself might have done 30 years back...." (Todd McCarthy, *Variety*, May 26–June 1, 2003) What do these men do to create the characters? How do they "inhabit" these people so that we come to believe in what we see? Think of how they might prepare: the words they speak and how they speak them; their gestures and what they represent; their reaction to what is going on around them (often the hardest thing in acting is to react). How do all of these (and more) add up to make a character come to life on the screen?

2. *Mystic River* has been called a triumph for Eastwood and been compared to his masterpiece, *Unforgiven*. *Mystic River* digs deep into the dark side of human nature. But there is no getting around it. The movie is bleak and uncompromising, which does not always make for a "popular" movie. Eastwood has said that he believes there is an audience for serious adult movies. What do you look for when you go to a movie? Is it just entertainment? Would you have chosen to see *Mystic River*? What would attract you to such a movie? What would keep you from going?

3. *Mystic River* is very much a character-driven drama. All the psychological insights we get come from how the characters have or have not changed since childhood. How are the three main characters – Jimmy, Sean and Dave – changed by what happens when Dave gets into the strangers' car at age 11?

4. At the end of the movie, Annabeth, Jimmy's wife, tells him that "love is never wrong." What does she mean? Do you think she is right? What kind of a person does this final scene show her to be?

3. The Relationship of the Movie to the Theme of the Exercise

1. The Exercise speaks of three classes of people – those who do not care one way or another about God, those who want God to support their schemes, and those who desire to follow God. While it is true that we all carry elements of each of the three classes, the three men in the movie each belong in one class more than another. Which type is Jimmy? Sean? Dave? Why?

2. Near the end of the movie Jimmy says, "We bury our sins here, we wash them clean." Consider this remark in the light of the class of people where you think Jimmy belongs. What additional meaning does that insight give to his words?

4. The Relationship of the Movie to One's Self in the Exercise

1. Look at the three main characters in the movie. In which of them can you find parts of yourself? Why? Would you want to change what you see? How?

2. As the Exercise tells us, the perspectives of the three classes of people boil down to how we embody our deepest desires in our daily life. It is clear in the movie that each of the three major characters not only does this but has someone who helps them do it. How do you try to live your daily life based on your deepest desire? Who do you turn to for help? How do these people help you?

3. The Exercise points out how difficult it is to give up our self-will, to value things and other people only within the mutual love between God and us. In the movie, each of the three characters cannot give up some strong part of their self-will: Jimmy cannot give up seeking revenge for his daughter's death. What part of your self-will do you find most difficult to give up? Where do you turn for help? Do you see this as an ongoing process or will you be able to give up that part of you in time? Why? Why not?

143

9th Exercise
The Three Degrees of Humility

Have this mind among yourselves, which you have in Christ Jesus, who, though he was in the form of God, did not count equality with God a thing to be grasped, but emptied himself, taking the form of a servant, being born in the likeness of men. And being found in human form he humbled himself and became obedient unto death, even death on the cross.

(Philippians 2:5-8)

I desire and choose poverty with Christ poor, rather than riches; insults with Christ loaded with them, rather than honours; I desire to be accounted as worthless and a fool for Christ, rather than be esteemed as wise and prudent in this world. So Christ was treated before me.

(Sp. Ex. #167)

Grace: They should beg our Lord to deign to choose them for this third kind of humility, which is higher and better, that they might the more imitate and serve Him, provided equal or greater praise and service be given to the Divine Majesty.

(Sp. Ex. #168)

Being Human

The word "human" comes from the Latin word *humus*, meaning earth or soil. The word "humility" comes from that same root. To be human is to be humble. To be demonic is not to be humble, for then one is filled with pride and sets oneself up as a god. To be humble is to understand ourselves profoundly as a creature, born of the soil but loved by God. How we live as humans depends both on our awareness of our creaturehood and on how deeply we love.

Ignatius asks us in this Exercise to consider a development of the previous one, where he asked us to pray for the grace to love. In this Exercise he asks us to pray for the grace to love as deeply and passionately as Christ loves. He sees this approach, which he calls the Third Degree of Humility, as the most perfect way of being human.

Love and Goodness

The first degree of humility is to love as a good person. That person lives with integrity, is respectful of other people and creation, and loves God; is ethical, moral and upright; does not do wrong but lives life in a way that maintains essential relationships; admits limitations and boundaries and lives within them. This, admittedly, is a very high standard of morality, and most of us, if we are honest with ourselves, reach this level of commitment only in certain areas of our lives and at certain times. For the rest, we find ourselves caught in ambiguity and compromise. We acknowledge that we are sinners and that, in spite of our occasional best efforts, we get trapped by our own disorders and by the disorders of the world. We can even acknowledge that we are so trapped as to be blind, for the most part, to the ways we destroy ourselves, others or the world. For example, we can maintain a standard of living that does violence to the resources of the planet or live a stressful life style that damages our bodies and our spirits, and think that this is normal or mature or acceptable. This is not to say that we are not good people. We are. We are good people living at the first level of humility.

Love and Detachment

The second degree of humility moves from unconsciousness to an attitude of mind that seeks to become aware of what blinds us at the first level and to be indifferent to those things that we would normally take for granted. Ignatius gives us some examples of these. He says, "As far as we are concerned, we should not prefer health to sickness, riches to poverty, honour to dishonour, a long life to a short life" (#23).

Now this is quite radical. No one wants to be sick or poor or be despised or die without having lived enough. What Ignatius knows, from his own life, and what we know from examining the lives of the saints, is that illness can be a blessing. It was only when Ignatius fell ill that he started his quest for God; indeed, illness shows us the radical limitations of the self to control and maintain life. Similarly, we can learn that riches cannot buy happiness, and that in poverty we may discover a freedom to use our energies in more life-giving ways. We will also find, as we mature spiritually, that loving relationships, not the prestige of the world, establishes our identity, and a loving relationship with God takes away our fear of death.

Here Ignatius is not asking us to choose poverty, or sickness, or dishonour, or a short life. He is merely asking us to be indifferent to these things. To be indifferent is to be so passionate only for God that we desire only those things that will maintain that loving relationship. We value whatever we have only inasmuch as it helps that relationship deepen. It might well be that riches or health foster a vital relationship with God. In that case, we should actively cultivate them. All the second degree of humility describes is the attitude of mind that seeks only God, and seeks everything else only as it can help that relationship with God. This sensitivity is not just theoretical: it manifests itself actively in what we do and how we live.

Love and Passion

The third degree of humility is grounded on the first and second. It asks us not to be indifferent to poverty or dishonour, but to choose them: not for themselves (since they are just "creatures"), but in solidarity with Christ's poor and suffering and in a lover's identification with the condition of the beloved, the Christ, in this world. Moreover, that choice is made only if it gives greater praise and service to God.

This third way of loving is more than just a witness for God in a socially conventional manner. It means showing with our very life that abiding trust in Divine Providence that the love we give ourselves over to will not abandon or destroy us. It means putting our lives where the beloved has put his life.

In the great hymn in Philippians 2:1-11, we are told that the Christ did not count equality with God as something to be held onto but rather emptied himself, "taking on the form of a servant" and became one like us. He went even further, because as a human he "humbled himself and became obedient even unto death" – that shameful death on a cross.

Ignatius does not present an incarnate Christ who is a triumphalistic or autocratic human being. Rather, he presents a Christ who manifests himself in humble service to the mystery we call Father. He suggests that the highest form of human love is in identifying with the beloved. He offers to us the possibility of praying for that identification in the third level of humility, which says, "I want to be so like you that I am willing to live as you lived, love as you loved, suffer as you suffered." It says, "I am willing to share your life with those who are poor and suffering and dishonoured, neglected, mocked, ignored." It says, "I am willing, if you want me to, to become one of them and to live the fate of one of them because you loved me that much and because I too love you as you have loved me." This is not the path of the hero or the masochist; this is the path of the saint and the mystic. We are all called, every one of us, to be saints and mystics, for they express most fully our humanity and our response to being loved totally.

Questions for prayer and reflection

1. Have you reached even that first level of humility?

2. How do you respond to God's love knowing that you are a sinner?

3. Does an awareness of your sinfulness stop you from loving as fully as you dare?

4. How do you experience the urges to love more? How do you embody them without being imprudent or naive?

5. How does your culture condition you to accept yourself as it defines you? How do you break out of that conditioning? What helps you move beyond those definitions of yourself? How does it feel to live in those spaces beyond cultural definition?

6. Who are the saints that inspire you? How do they do that?

7. Who is someone for you who lives (or tries to live) that third level of humility today?

8. What happens to you when you consider living radically out of God's love?

9. What happens to you when you ask someone like Mary, the mother of Jesus, then Jesus himself, then the mystery Jesus calls his "Father" for the love to live and love as fully as they love you?

10. What do Mary, Jesus and the Father say to you in that prayer? How do you experience that prayer?

The Movie
Punch-Drunk Love

Director: Paul Thomas Anderson (2002 – 95 mins.)
Starring: Adam Sandler, Emily Watson, Philip Seymour Hoffman

1. Summary

In this comedy, Barry Egan, a small-business owner with seven overbearing sisters and a small violent streak, finds a harmonium in front of his business one morning. When a beautiful young woman asks him to help her with her car and then returns to see him a few days later, a rather odd romantic journey begins.

2. Questions about the Movie

1. Paul Thomas Anderson is one of the most interesting filmmakers of his generation. One of his basic themes is that of family and how a family can affect a person. *Hard Eight* is about a man creating a new family in order to overcome the guilt he feels for destroying his own; *Boogie Nights* is about creating a family to escape the dysfunction of one's own biological family; and *Magnolia* is about confronting and making peace with family members. How does Anderson present this theme of family in *Punch-Drunk Love*?

2. *Punch-Drunk Love* is "an antimovie that consistently rejects even the most minimal obligations to character and plot that commercial films are supposed to have. Stuff happens to Anderson's peo-

ple. They just keep soldiering on. Yet there is something arresting about it too. The damned thing keeps gnawing at your mind – if only for its almost perfect lack of conventional sentiment. Or movieness." ("Love is Strange, So is He," Richard Schickel, *Time*, October 21, 2002, p. 65) Is *Punch-Drunk Love* just a strange comedy to you? Or does something in it gnaw at your mind? If so, what is it that gets to you?

3. "At its heart the story is boy-meets-girl simple, but the movie is so full of lurches and discordances and flabbergasting non sequiturs that at times it's like an avant-garde dance-theater piece with injections of *Saturday Night Live*. I imagine that many will find it arch, and, on a narrative level, as bumptiously withholding as its protagonist. I found it exquisite…. I've never seen anything like the sequences in which Sandler, in his boxy, sea-blue suit, charges around his warehouse to the rhythm of Brion's harsh drums. The banging and binging and bumping suggests someone pounding on a door that won't yield; it could herald the start of an angry tap dance." (*Slate.msn.com* by David Edelstein, posted Friday, October 11, 2002) It is not often that a critic uses a word like "exquisite" to describe a movie.

Go back and look at the scene he describes. What one word would you use to describe this scene? The whole movie?

3. The Relationship of the Movie to the Theme of the Exercise

1. In wondrous ways, this movie charts the progression of Barry Egan from the first degree of humility through to the second degree and on to an attempt at the third. He is not aware of this progression, though the entry into his life of a harmonium and a beautiful woman will start the move upward. Which scenes show this progression? Which scenes clearly show the transition from one degree of humility to another?

2. The Exercise tells us that to be human is to be humble. How we live as humans depends on our awareness of our creaturehood and on how deeply we love. What is it about Barry's ordinary daily life – before the advent of the harmonium and the woman – that tells us just how human he is? Is he humble? Or is he just plain crazy?

3. Does the culture Barry lives in condition him to accept himself as it defines him? If this is true, what does Barry have to do to break out of this conditioning and learn to accept himself exactly for what he is, and not for what the culture says he is?

4. Looking at what Barry does – out of love – do you believe he is following the path of the hero or the masochist, of the saint or the mystic? Why?

4. The Relationship of the Movie to One's Self in the Exercise

1. Barry has many obstacles to overcome – not the least of which is himself (though his sisters are pretty formidable, too!) – before he can move forward. In many ways, he does come to understand what he has to do and then finds the motivation to do it. What motivates you as you attempt to move from one degree of humility to another? What stops you from moving from one degree to another? What can you do to overcome this obstacle?

2. Barry will do almost anything – sane or crazy – to win the woman he loves. This is a human love. How far are you willing to go to love God as God loves you? What will you do to achieve this love?

3. Once stirred out of his everyday life, Barry is not satisfied to be the person (basically a good person) that he was. He must change because he is drawn to something more than himself – something higher. What draws you to live a higher standard of morality than that of the world? What are some examples in your own life of areas and times when you have reached the high level of commitment that the Exercise talks about?

4. What do you think Barry thinks of himself? Does he see himself as a "good" person? Why? What about you? What stops you from seeing the goodness that is in you and that calls you to something more?

10th Exercise
Discernment

None of us lives to ourself, and none of us dies to ourself. If we live we live to the Lord, and if we die, we die to the Lord; so then, whether we live or whether we die, we are the Lord's.

(Romans 14:7-9)

In every good choice, as far as depends on us, our intentions must be simple. I must consider only the end for which I am created, that is, for the praise of God our Lord and for the salvation of my soul. Hence, whatever I choose must help me to this end for which I am created.

(Sp. Ex. #169)

Grace: To seek to find and serve God in all things.

(Sp. Ex. #233)

Seeking a Heart to Understand

We all want to love passionately and choose rightly. But we realize that not only do we not have all the facts necessary for the perfect choice, our perceptions of the facts can be biased by our disorders. But we still have to choose. Every day we make myriad decisions – major and minor – that determine the shape of our lives. With major ones, we become a little more conscious of the decision-making process. Each of us has our own way of making a decision. We collect facts, get insights, have intuitions, weigh the pros and cons, look for signs of rightness, ask friends for advice, or pray for God's help. We try to get into the right "space" to make a correct choice.

Sometimes the right thing to do comes clearly. Other times we have to find a quiet place and settle down to see what emerges from our deliberations. Sometimes we have to project ourselves imaginatively into living that decision and seeing what happens. Sometimes we ask God to show us the way.

Whatever we do, every decision is a risk and a creative moment where we set out on a path we have not walked before. But what is discernment? There is a difference between the two, even though the result might look the same. A decision is not necessarily a deliberate, self-conscious choice and it does not necessarily occur in the context of prayer. Discernment does both. With a discernment, we enter into a dialogue with God after establishing a right relationship. In that mutual sharing and trust, an answer emerges.

So far in these Exercises you have been establishing that right relationship with God, discovering how God communicates with you personally through your feelings and your history, and becoming aware of how you operate so that you know when you are being tempted to narcissism or being invited to self-transcendence. Now Ignatius is asking you to discern your life.

Making Correct Decisions

For St. Ignatius, correct decisions always move us towards God, community and each other, as well as integrating the different aspects of ourselves. But, like any other decision, we need to check them out to see if they are valid or illusory. This takes time. The time given to us is the time of the retreat. If you have a decision you want to discern, you can take it with you as you journey through the rest of these Exercises. You can bring that decision into your prayer and the reflection questions. You can see if that decision holds up to the relationship you form with Christ as you continue your journey. If it is a good decision, you will find that you are drawn closer to Christ and identify with him in your life. If it a bad decision, you will find yourself alienated from the Christ, at odds with yourself, and not rooted in the community.

If you are called to make a decision at this moment, you might want to use some of the ways suggested at the beginning of this Exercise. If you have made a decision and want to have it verified, you can bring it along as you journey through the rest of the Exercises. This will transform your decisions into discernments. If you do not have a decision to make or verify, you can still deepen your intimacy with God as you continue. What you need to remember is that as you are searching for God, God is searching for you. You will experience God's search for you in terms of that mercy and concern you can acknowledge in your path. Whatever decisions you make, you are always held in God's loving mercy.

Questions for prayer and reflection

1. How do you generally make decisions? How have they differed from the discernments you have made? Has involving God made a difference?

2. How have you made significant decisions in your life so far?

3. Of those significant decisions, how have you made the ones that have brought you life? Those that have been destructive?

4. What does this tell you about the way to make good decisions?

5. Is there any discernment that you need to make with God now? How will you two go about it?

6. Where does God feature in that process? How has God featured in your good decision-making process? Can you approach God in the same way this time?

7. When you pray about your life, what is God telling you about it?

The Movie
Bowling for Columbine

Director: Michael Moore (2002 – 119 mins.)
Starring: Michael Moore, Charlton Heston, Dick Clark, Marilyn Manson, et al.

1. Summary

With angry humour, filmmaker Michael Moore sets out in this award-winning documentary to explore the roots of firearm violence in the United States. His investigation shows how the most commonly heard answers – ready availability of guns, the violence inherent in US history, the amount of violence in television, film and video games, even national poverty – do not give the correct answer, since many other cultures share these same factors but do not have the same level of gun violence. And so Moore digs deeper for an answer – into the US's "culture of fear" and bigotry and the political and corporate interests that fan such a culture – for their own gains.

2. Questions about the Movie

1. *Bowling for Columbine* "condemns American culture as paranoid, gun-crazy at home and militaristic abroad." ("Moore likely to win Oscar," Liam Lacey, *The Globe and Mail*, March 13, 2003) The movie did win an Oscar as best feature-length documentary. It also became the highest selling non-concert documentary in history, won the Césare (the French Oscar), finished on the top-ten best film lists of mainstream publications such as *Time*, *USA Today* and *Entertainment Weekly*, was the first documentary in 46 years to be selected for competition at Cannes, and was voted "the greatest documentary of all times" by a poll of 2,000 documentary filmmakers. Yet not only does the movie make the United States – after 9/11 and in the midst of the war in Iraq – look bad, it attacks Charlton Heston, a highly respected Hollywood icon, and makes him look foolish. Why, then, was the movie so successful? What made so many people of so many different ages and political persuasions not only see it but go back to see it two or three times? It has been called "the right film at the right time." Why?

2. When Moore interviews *South Park* co-creator Matt Stone, who was raised in Littleton, Colorado, and who attended Columbine, Stone tells him that "the teachers were destructive in pounding home the message that any kid who wasn't overachieving in sixth grade 'would die poor and lonely.' He maintains many a troubled teen can't see past the crucible of high school to the future that nearly always vindicates the social misfits and punishes popular kids. Getting that message out might be more effective than gun control." (Lisa Nesselson, *Variety*,

May 27–June 2, 2002) Why does it make more sense to follow this route to an answer to violence in schools rather than look at the "usual suspects" of violent music and movies?

3. "In a breath-taking but sure-footed leap – and one that will draw criticism from some quarters – Moore identifies America's culture of fear as originating in the common link between its domestic gun murders, and the government-sanctioned murder that marks the history of American foreign policy. The attitude that sees the paranoid home-owner armed to the teeth and shooting at shadows is a microcosm of the same attitude on a world scale: the nation carrying out pre-emptive strikes on a neighbour in a bid to quash any possible future attacks against itself." ("Bowling for Columbine," Meg Mundell, *Metro Magazine* #135 [Australia]) Why would such a conclusion draw the ire of the United States government? How much truth do you think there is in Moore's thesis about the cause of so much gun violence in the US?

3. The Relationship of the Movie to the Theme of the Exercise

1. A documentary film has been defined as "the creative treatment of actuality." Michael Moore is very concerned about gun violence in the US. He wants to present "the facts," but our perception of facts can be biased by our disorders. Yet – as the Exercise tells us – we cannot do nothing, frozen by our limitations. We have to act. Moore acted by making this documentary. How does his bias show? Is his emphasis on "creative treatment" rather than on "actuality"? What are some examples of this?

2. The Exercise offers a number of means we use to discern. Which of the following does Moore use? How?

   a) collect facts

   b) get insights

   c) have intuitions

   d) weigh the pros and cons

   e) try to get into the "right" space to make a correct choice

   f) pray for God's help.

3. The Exercise mentions two ways for discernment to happen: suddenly and with clarity, or only after some quiet deliberation. Despite the frenetic pace of this film, how is it possible to see that Moore does make use of quiet deliberation?

152

4. The Relationship of the Movie to One's Self in the Exercise

1. In the Old Testament, the young king Solomon is devastated by the death of his father, David. Not knowing how to proceed, he calls on God. He does not ask for riches or a long life, but only for the heart to understand how to discern the difference between good and evil (1 Kings 3:9). What is the "good and evil" in your life that you are asking God to help you discern?

2. Moore does not hesitate in his search for an answer, and he does so knowing that every judgment is a risk and a creative moment. He chooses a path that has not been walked before. He makes blunders – such as the interview with Dick Clark, where Moore does not know how to handle Clark's reaction to his questions; he does outrageous things, such as opening a bank account just to get a gun; and he does wondrous things, such as working with a victim of the Columbine shootings to get a Kmart to phase out sales of handguns. How much risk are you willing to take in your discernment? What are these risks? What do you fear most about them?

3. For St. Ignatius, correct judgment always moves us towards God, community and each other. We can see this in the moment at the end of the movie outside the Kmart when Moore speaks with the Columbine survivor and, in a very haunting way, at the end of his interview with Charlton Heston. How have the discernments you have made moved you towards God, community and other people?

11th Exercise
The Baptism of Jesus

This is my beloved Son with whom I am well pleased.

(Matthew 3:17)

It is more suitable and much better that the Creator and Lord in person communicate Himself to the devout soul in quest of the divine will, that He may inflame it with His love and praise, and dispose it for the way in which it could better serve God in the future.

(Sp. Ex. #15)

Grace: This is to ask for what I desire. Here it will be to ask for an intimate knowledge of our Lord, who has become man for me, that I may love Him more and follow Him more closely.

(Sp. Ex. #104)

Living out of a Love that Trusts

All any spiritual discipline does is dispose us to God. It signals to God that we are willing to enter into a relationship with the Divine. It cannot compel that relationship to happen. Similarly, spiritual techniques and rituals can facilitate the relationship with the holy, but they can never substitute for the holy. They cannot compel the holy to be present to us in ways we find useful. The same thing can be said about the Spiritual Exercises. They do not make God present; they are just a way of presenting ourselves to God. This is what happens to Christ. He loves the Father and disposes himself to the Father, but he cannot compel the Father to act before his time or in ways that are opposed to his mystery. Love does not force love; love trusts love and expects love to be loving. Christ lives out of that trust and that love.

After his presentation in the temple at age 12, when he declares he must be about his Father's business, Christ gets no confirmation about what he is to do for the next 18 years. He waits on God for the next step. He waits for God. We do not know just how that waiting shapes him. We can imagine him learning patience, putting up with the growing concern of his relatives that "he has not found himself," and even working away at and studying what it means to be a just person in his religious context without ever having affirmed in the roots of his being what he intuits about himself. Because he is human, we can relate to his wondering who he is: his brooding about what others have told him about himself; his self-doubts; his sense of being special.

And then, one day, something happens. Jesus goes down to the river Jordan where his cousin John, an itinerant preacher, is preaching and baptizing. Jesus is baptized and has an epiphany. He receives his call when the Father says, "This is my beloved Son with whom I am well pleased" (Matthew 3:13-17). The call is given not in terms of a plan of action, but as a relationship of love, of generation. Jesus is acknowledged as the Father's son, and as the beloved who pleases his Father well.

When we are called to love, we are called to relationship. Each of us is loved for who we are, and not for what we do. It is the Other in the relationship that acknowledges us. This is pure gift. We can dispose ourselves to the possibility of its happening, but how it happens, and when and where and why and how, is beyond our control. We fall in love with someone and discover we are loved in return. We discover that we are in love with God and experience God loving us.

What's in a Name?

Only after we have received that gift and accepted it can we name it, for it occurs at the core of our being. It takes time before we even realize what has happened. It takes more time to accept it and to live out of that wonder. It takes even more time to let that love name us and to discover our own name for that love, which now nourishes and enlightens us and affirms that the core of our being is united to the source of all life, the Mystery Jesus calls "Father." That Mystery roots us. We know that we are created by God, sustained by God, and transformed by God. But to be rooted is to be carried to deeper levels of relationship that struggle for words to express them. This is what Christ experienced at his baptism at the Jordan; God declares Jesus to be "my beloved Son." It is what we experience when God calls us by name. This naming does more than the names our parents and our families bestow on us – it establishes our place in the structures and dynamics of creation. For this reason, names are sacred in spirituality: they tell us how we are holy.

In our lives, various incidents name us. When we are born we receive not only our family name but "given" names – the names of ancestors, saints or other significant people. We may choose a confirmation name; friends may give us nicknames. Society names us with professional titles. The ones we love have pet names for us, intimate endearments that have secret codes of meaning. God also names us, and in that naming is our call. Thus, in Genesis, "Abram" is named "Abraham" by God; that naming publicly establishes their relationship (Gen 17:1-14). A call is a vocation. Our naming shows us how we are to act in the world. Abraham's naming, for example, makes him the father of the Jewish people.

In Christ's baptism, he is named not only "Son" but also "Beloved." In the Second Week of the Exercises, the grace we pray for is a growing intimacy with Christ. As we are given that grace we discover that we, too, are called "Beloved," are named as God's living Word in the world.

Rite of Passage

That naming is a transitional point in our lives. In biblical topography the Jordan was the river that the Israelites crossed to the Promised Land, the place where they could live out their covenanted relationship with God in community and in a land they could finally call their own. When we hear our call, we reach a transition point in our lives. At times that transition is difficult, as the Jordan was difficult to cross and treacherous in places. Often when we hear our call, when we experience our baptism, we find ourselves in a difficult place. We must give up the comfort of an old way of life. We must risk and set off on a new path that was not open to us before. If we do it, though, we find ourselves.

As you enter this contemplation of Christ's baptism, remember the times and places when you were named and were given an identity. Recall from the work you did in the First Week the times when you were misnamed, given a false identity, and so lived in servitude. True naming emerges only in love and out of love. As you immerse yourself in the dangerous waters of transition, immerse yourself also in that love that surrounds you, cherishes you and calls you "Beloved," in the passionate intimacy that each of us uniquely shares with the one we call "God." Ask for the grace to hear your naming.

Questions for prayer and reflection

1. What happened in this contemplation as you asked to share Christ's baptismal experience?

2. What has named and shaped you? How did these manifest themselves in your life?

3. What are your experiences of being known truly and lovingly?

4. Whom do you love so much that they learned to accept themselves, which changed their relationships with others?

5. What risks do you take in loving, in giving love, and in sharing that love with others? Why do you take those risks?

6. What is the life you find as you risk in love? Does it sustain you? How?

7. When Jesus goes to the Jordan, he leaves home in such a way that he can never go back again. Have you ever left home that way? How did you deal with the resulting emotions? How can you bring those emotions to the prayer you are entering into?

8. How do you live out your being named "Beloved"?

The Movie
Almost Famous

Director: Cameron Crowe (2000 – 122 mins.)
Starring: Billy Crudup, Kate Hudson, Patrick Fugit, Frances McDormand

1. Summary

The year is 1973, and 15-year-old William Miller is hired by *Rolling Stone* – who has no idea of his real age – to tour with and write about a new rock band, Stillwater. During the trip, he becomes infatuated with groupie Penny Lane, who is herself infatuated with Russell Hammond, Stillwater's charismatic lead guitarist.

2. Questions about the Movie

1. "*Almost Famous* is about the world of rock, but it's not a rock film, it's a coming-of-age film, about an idealistic kid who sees the real world, witnesses its cruelties and heartbreaks, and yet finds much room for hope…. William Miller is not an alienated bore, but a kid who had the good fortune to have a wonderful mother and great sister, to meet the right rock star in Russell (there would have been wrong ones), and to have the kind of love for Penny Lane that will arm him for the future and give him a deeper understanding of the mysteries of women." (Roger Ebert, *Chicago Sun-Times*, September 15, 2000) How has William changed at the end of his stay with Stillwater? What role do the values given him by his mother and his sister play in the way he grows over this short period of time?

2. "The power of popular music – its ability to give shape, meaning and intensity to the inexpressible emotions of daily life – is something of a motif in Cameron Crowe's career as a director…. Mr. Crowe has always used rock not merely as soundtrack decoration but also as a window into the souls of his characters." (A.O. Scott, *The New York Times*, September 13, 2000) How does Crowe use the music of the 1970s to get into the souls of the main characters? Give some examples from specific scenes, telling which songs are used and what they tell you about the main character in that scene.

3. "Does each generation of kids get the music it deserves? No, but it gets the music that defines it. It's in the generational blood. Every joy or pang of growing up has an accompanying sound track. And decades later, car-radios playings of specific songs, good or bad, can be as acute a prod to sweet or rueful memory as Proust's tea cake. " (Richard Corliss, *Time*, September 18, 2000) For director Crowe it was the music of the 1970s that defined his generation, and that is the music that defines this movie. Based on what you

see in the movie, what impact did the music of the '70s have on that generation of kids? What was the music of your generation? Name one or two songs from your generation of growing-up years that still affect you when you hear them. What kind of memories do they raise for you? How to do they identify you as a child of that generation?

3. The Relationship of the Movie to the Theme of the Exercise

1. Both William's mother and his sister would say about William – as the Exercise says of the young Jesus – that "he has not found himself." William works hard at being the writer he wants to be. Yet, at the same time, he wonders about himself, about how others see him, and about his relationships with Penny Lane and Russell Hammond. Then something happens to him one day. Which scene in the movie would you say causes William to realize that he has a call – to what he sees as love and to what he sees as a relationship?

2. At first, the people around Stillwater do not know what to make of William. But then they start to give him an identity, which may or may not be a false one. What sort of identity do the following people give him?

   • the editors of *Rolling Stone*
   • his mother and sister
   • Penny Lane
   • Russell Hammond
   • the other members of Stillwater
   • Lester Bangs

3. In this Exercise we are immersed in the dangerous waters of transition, helped along mostly by the love that surrounds us, cherishes us and calls us. By the end of the movie, William has grown and changed. He has undergone a transition almost from boy to man – a turbulent and sometimes terrifying transition. What sustains William during this time? Does any one scene bring this out fully for you?

4. The Relationship of the Movie to One's Self in the Exercise

1. One of the key concepts of media education tells us that the audience negotiates meaning. This means that everything that makes us who we are – that names us – plays a role in how we look at media. What have you brought to the movie – what is it about you – that "names" you? What role does this "negotiation" play in causing you to be open to understanding the movie? What does it have to say to you? What role does it play in making you closed to what the movie has to say to you?

2. According to the Exercise, enlightenment is an accident; all the Exercises do is to make us accident-prone. William set out on the road trip with Stillwater only to write a story about the band for *Rolling Stone*, but his whole life changes as a result. What incidents from your life have led to enlightenment about you? How did you react to these situations?

158

12th Exercise
The Temptations in the Desert

Blessed be the God and Father of our Lord Jesus Christ, who has blessed us in Christ with every spiritual blessing in the heavenly places, even as he chose us in him before the foundation of the world that we should be holy and blameless before him. He destined us in love to be his own through Jesus Christ, according to the purpose of his will, to the praise of his glorious grace which he freely bestowed on us in the Beloved.

(Ephesians 1:3-6)

It is the mark of the evil spirit to assume the appearance of an angel of light. He begins by suggesting thoughts that are suited to a devout soul, and ends by suggesting his own. For example, he will suggest holy and pious thoughts that are wholly in conformity with the sanctity of the soul. Afterwards, he will endeavor little by little to end by drawing the soul into his hidden snares and evil designs.

(Sp. Ex. #332)

Grace: This is to ask for what I desire. Here it will be to ask for an intimate knowledge of our Lord, who has become man for me, that I may love Him more and follow Him more closely.

(Sp. Ex. #104)

Living Vulnerably

Something dramatic happens right after Jesus' baptism: "The Spirit immediately drove him out into the wilderness. And he was in the wilderness forty days, tempted by Satan; and he was with the wild beasts; and the angels ministered to him" (Mark 1:12-13). It is easy to think that when we are called and are filled with the Spirit and have a profound confirmation of our identity, things will become easy and we will be spared the terrors of this life. But that is simply not true. Rather, we immediately come in contact with malign forces – within us or outside of us – that try to make life unbearable and we are vulnerable. Just as it is human nature to help someone who is in need or in trouble, it is God's nature to go to the endangered aspects of creation.

In the wilderness, Jesus is tempted to use his newfound identity to satisfy his ego. What the wilderness does for Jesus – as it does for each of us – is make us conscious of our vulnerability. In that vulnerability we have choices. We can rely on ourselves; or we can rely on God. The evil spirit suggests to us that we rely on ourselves. God asks us to trust in that Divine Mercy that we have experienced constantly loving us.

More than an Animal

Thus, when Jesus is hungry he is tempted to turn the stones into bread. But he responds by saying that we do not live on bread alone but by every word that proceeds from the mouth of God. That all-creating word of the Father makes both stone and bread, but even more important, it manifests itself in the mercy of Divine Providence. Jesus is willing in his hunger to trust that Divine Providence rather than his own gifts. He chooses, in terms of the Two Standards, poverty rather than riches.

More than a Social Creation

Next he is offered the honour of the world (Luke 4:5-7). This he rejects by remembering that his basic identity comes from a relationship with God rather than with any aspect of creation. He affirms his basic stance of "praise, reverence, and service" to God rather than accepting the "authority" and "glory" of all the kingdoms of the world.

More than Self-determined

In the final temptation, Satan wants Jesus to throw himself from a high place, the pinnacle of the temple in Jerusalem. He reasons that if Jesus is the Son of God, God will save him. But Jesus knows that he cannot flaunt the Father's gift to him as his right. He can only operate out of it as a merciful dispensation from the Father. Moreover, he knows who he is; he does not have to prove it to anyone. He replies, "You shall not tempt the Lord your God."

The temptations ask him to be less than who he is. They ask him to rely on his own gifts, to use the things of the world to maintain his own identity, and to use God to affirm himself. The temptations attempt to deny or distort his relationship with the one who has just called him his "beloved." In rejecting the temptations, Jesus shows himself content to wait on God to feed him, affirm him and save him. It is a waiting that he learned in his hidden life, and will manifest itself again when he is on the cross.

To enter into a contemplation of Christ's temptations in the desert is to discover how our energies, now being woven together with Christ's energies, enter into temptation. We find, as we found in the Two Standards, that we are tempted by riches, honour and pride. We want to rely on ourselves, to seek the approval of the world, and to set ourselves up as the centre of our universe. But if we journey with Jesus, we find that we can overcome those temptations because our relationship with the Father, like Jesus', is stronger than our selfishness. We discover that, like Jesus, we are nourished and affirmed, and we find ourselves in that relationship. This manifests our call as companions of the Christ.

Questions for prayer and reflection

1. What happens when you read and contemplate the Temptations of Christ in the desert?

2. What are your deserts? In our work? Your family? Your relationships? Society? The world?

3. Is there a pattern to the way you are tempted?

4. How does the prayer affect the way you encounter temptation and deal with it?

5. What have been the consequences in your life of falling in love with God and allowing God to express his love for you?

6. What have been the consequences of not falling in love with God and of ignoring his relationship with you?

7. How does your intimacy with God express itself in your daily life?

8. How do you distinguish between being pious and being spiritual in your life?

The Movie
The Insider

Director: Michael Mann (1999 – 157 mins.)
Starring: Al Pacino, Russell Crowe, Christopher Plummer, Colm Feore, Michael Gambon

1. Summary

The Insider is based on true parallel stories. Jeffrey Wigand, a research biologist for Brown & Williamson, was arguably the most significant anti-smoking source and one of the keys to a $246-billion settlement against the tobacco industry, and Lowell Bergman, a *60 Minutes* producer, fought to get the story on air despite the objections of Westinghouse, the parent company of CBS.

2. Questions about the Movie

1. "At its core, however, *The Insider* is a story of, as someone says, 'ordinary people under extraordinary pressure.' It shows how difficult and torturous it can be to do the right thing on an individual level and, most important, what bravery actually means and how little the faces and personalities of heroes fit our often simplistic preconceptions." (Kenneth Turan, *The Los Angeles Times*, November 5, 1999) What kind of bravery is called for by Wigand? Bergman? Mike Wallace? What is the result of their acts of bravery?

2. For over two and a half hours we watch the process of newsgathering around a major story. The movie wants us to believe that the structure of the news media centres not around journalistic integrity but around money. The fourth key concept of media literacy points out that all media messages have commercial implications. How does that concept apply here? Do you believe that the news media in the US is as imperiled as is shown here? Why? Why not? Consider the reporting of the major events surrounding 9/11 and the Iraq War.

3. The first and second key concepts of media literacy tell us that all media construct aspects of reality. Mike Wallace is furious about the way the movie represents him. In an interview with *The New York Times*, Wallace said: "If this is entertainment, why does he use my name and have words come out of my mouth that I never would have said? There was never any doubt in anyone's mind at CBS on where I stood on this. And to be portrayed as having lost my moral compass, caved in. To whom? For what? This is important to me...." ("When Newsbroadcasters Become the News," Peter Applebome, *The New York Times*, August 13, 1999) Wallace is involved with the media. Why do you think he is upset that the movie does what he might be called on to do in *60 Minutes* – i.e., construct an aspect of

reality? Could the movie's presentation of him as part showman, part opportunist, have something to do with this?

3. The Relationship of the Movie to the Theme of the Exercise

1. The Exercise tells us that when we believe we have confirmed our identity and are ready to deal with the world, the world fights back to make life unbearable. Jeffrey Wigand believes he is doing the right thing when he testifies at the trial and so is able to work with *60 Minutes* without violating his confidentiality agreement. What makes Wigand so vulnerable? How does the world treat him?

2. In many ways, each of the three main characters – Wigand, Wallace and Bergman – has his own desert experience, complete with temptations. What riches, honour and pride is each of them tempted to accept?

3. Mike Wallace is presented in the movie as being what the Exercise calls the centre of his own universe. He knows what he wants to do with this story and is furious when he doesn't get his way. What does he do to ensure that the show will eventually air? How does this reflect on the way we tend to think the news media operates?

4. The Relationship of the Movie to One's Self in the Exercise

1. Wigand is tempted to be less than who he is. He is tempted to reject his personal integrity. His refusal to give into temptation causes him to lose his family, his career and his good name. What temptation do you face regarding your personal integrity? How do you work to overcome this temptation?

2. God is never mentioned in the movie, yet some religious writers have seen Wigand as a Christ figure. The Exercise tell us that Jesus overcame the temptations because his relationship with the Father is stronger than his selfishness. What in this Exercise gives you hope that you can overcome the temptations to riches, honour and pride that are being offered to you?

3. Wallace and Bergman are presented as strong, successful figures who tend to rely on themselves rather than work with others. What happens to them as a result? Where, in your life, do you see yourself tempted to go it alone, to rely on your own gifts and not seek God's help and love?

13th Exercise
The Call

The Spirit of the Lord is upon me,
Because he has anointed me to preach good news to the
poor.
He as sent me to proclaim release to the captives
And recovery of sight to the blind,
To set at liberty those who are oppressed,
To proclaim the acceptable year of the Lord.

(Luke 4:18-19)

If a devout soul wishes to do something ... that may be
for the glory of God our Lord, there may come a thought
or temptation from without not to say or do it. Apparent
reasons may be adduced for this, such that it is motivat-
ed by vainglory or some such other imperfect intention,
etc. ... He should act against the temptation. According
to St. Bernard, we must answer the tempter, "I did not
undertake this because of you, and I am not going to
relinquish it because of you".

(Sp. Ex. #351)

Grace: This is to ask for what I desire. Here it will be to
ask for an intimate knowledge of our Lord, who has
become man for me, that I may love Him more and fol-
low Him more closely.

(Sp. Ex. 104)

The Nature of a Call

In the temptations in the wilderness Jesus discerns how to behave in the world and returns with that knowledge. He knows he is in the community of the Father and has the support of his family and friends. He knows he is not alone. But he realizes that if he is to share the mercy of the Father with the world, he needs others who are like him – who have seen the misery of this world and encountered the traps and illusions the world uses to ensnare people, and who seek to do something, however small, to relieve that burden of mindless suffering, to enlighten the deceived, and to celebrate the life that comes from knowing one is rooted in love. First he calls people he trusts. Interestingly enough, he does not approach religious figures but ordinary people, like you and me.

Each of us is, at the root of our being, a manifestation of love. It is our identity and we only experience a sense of it when we are in loving relationships. But, as we all know, there are levels to loving. There is the love that is not expressed, and there is the love that is expressed. After that there is the loved expressed and received. Then there is the love shared, and finally there is the love that is the expression and work of that shared love. Our call emerges when the love that is given to us is received and lived out and acted upon. Every call contains the forces of attraction, response, engagement and commitment.

If we look at what we do with our life, we will see we live this way because of a call. Our behaviour is a response to that call. It may be a basic call to survival. It may be hard or monotonous, but we endure it because we care about our family, or a particular cause, or a particular talent. Every call shows itself in what we value, because what we value is where we put our lives.

The call of Jesus to his disciples, and to each of us, asks us to put our lives beyond ourselves in trusting in a relationship with him. When we enter into that relationship, we are given a deeper access to the Father's mercy. But like every relationship, it contains an element of risk. We give up our security to achieve our authenticity.

An Authentic Call

There is a story of an acrobat in a small circus whose single act was to walk a tightrope without a safety net. Above the middle of the high wire was suspended a ring made of rope, soaked in gasoline and set alight. At times he would climb the ladder to the roll of the drums and start his walk, only to turn back. The crowds would jeer. At other times he would leap through the flaming circle. He said he was always scared, and the times he turned back were when his fear got the better of him. But when asked why he would attempt it in the first place, his answer was simple. He would say, "I know my life is on the other side."

When we follow our call we give up our security because our life is on the other side, in the living out of that call. But how do we know we are called? In fact, we are called by many things, so the question is knowing what is the right call. A true call engages us fully, carries us beyond ourselves, connects us, on a whole range of levels, with a reality that is both inviting and mysterious, compassionate and uncompromising. It is profoundly personal. It brings out the best in us and gives us a new and more realistic understanding of ourselves. But in answering a call we also face our demons, as Christ did in the desert: we learn our limitations. We start to appreciate what is given to us on our path and to be grateful for that path and for the companions and adventures we have along that way.

So how can we distinguish a true call? By the fidelity of the one who calls us. That one is true to our relationship in good times and in bad; does not judge us as anything less than lovable and capable of loving; respects our individuality; celebrates with us what is good in life; works along with us in transforming what is damaging in our world; gives us the strength and the courage to hold what is suffering or damaged; lets us experience our freedom to be creative. The one who calls us truly shares with us all that he has and is. When we are called by Christ, he shares with us the life and spirit he has with the compassionate and creative mystery he calls "Abba"..."Father."

Questions for prayer and reflection

1. When have you felt called to do something that you saw as significant? What were the stages of that experience? Looking back, what affirmed you? How did that happen? What forces worked against you? How did they manifest themselves? How did you overcome them?

2. Do the same exercise for two or three other significant life-changing experiences. Can you see a common pattern in the way you are called and the way you respond?

3. Read the call of apostles in the gospels (John ch. 1; Mark ch. 1; Luke ch. 5; Matthew ch. 4). Enter prayerfully and imaginatively into one of those scenes, giving the characters and yourself the freedom to say and do as they wish. What was significant in that scene for you?

4. Who in your world lives out a calling within a family (such as a parent), a job (such as an artist), the community (such as an advocate for human rights), the international scene (such as a world leader), or a religious tradition (such as a saint, the Buddha, Rumi)? Have a conversation with that person about what moves you and what moved them to lead the life they do.

5. Are you experiencing a call now? What form does it take? What are you doing about it?

6. In what ways are you a witness to life for others?

7. Not all of us are asked to be religious but we are all by nature spiritual. In what ways does your intimacy with the spiritual manifest itself?

The Movie
The Full Monty

Director: Peter Cattaneo (1997 – 95 mins.)
Starring: Robert Caryle, Tom Wilkinson, Mark Addy

1. Summary

Six unemployed British steel workers, inspired by the Chippendale dancers, decide they can make a lot of money putting on their own male striptease show. What they plan to do that will make them different from other such shows is to go for "the full monty" – to strip totally.

2. Questions about the Movie

1. "The particular magic of the film is the way in which it draws credible characters in a recognizable setting but elevates them and their story into crowd-pleasing fare without losing sight of the big social picture." (Derek Elley, *Variety*, April 11-17, 1997). How does the movie "elevate" the characters and their story? What techniques are used to do this? What is the "big social picture" of which the critic speaks?

2. "Watching these six men get their act together, literally, is great fun. Each one is an individual with different motives and concerns, and the dynamics among them are entertaining. Of course, they also learn lessons about self-worth, dignity and relationships, but these are subtle and sincere and involved some surprisingly tender moments, as well as some hilarious and unexpected ones." (Judy Gerstel, *Toronto Star*, September 19, 1997) Look at the individual men – Gaz, Gerald, Dave, Horse, Lomper and Guy – and note the lessons each of them learn. Tender moments are not usual for this type of comedy. Choose one such moment that affected you. Why did it work so well for you?

3. "As *The Full Monty*, which takes its title from a slang phrase for total nudity, guides these men toward their own form of flashdancing, it displays tenderness and respect on a par with its great good humor. The film understands that joblessness is a humiliation well beyond nakedness, but it also revels in the sight of downtrodden ex-workers learning to enjoy their new freedom." (Janet Maslin, *The New York Times*, August 13, 1997) How does the movie use humour to portray unemployment? What does it say about the effect of unemployment on a group of men who – for the most part – are being supported by their wives' incomes?

4. "A thick vein of despair runs through the center of *The Full Monty*, and the movie taps into it frequently without quite dyeing the comedy black." (Laura Miller, *Salon.com*, September 5, 1997)

What are some examples of this despair? What is an example of a "black comedy"? What are some of the things that make it "black" – and how does it differ from what we see here?

3. The Relationship of the Movie to the Theme of the Exercise

1. The Exercise lists a number of elements of a true call. How do each of these apply to the call of the six men in this movie?

    • a call that engages us fully
    • a call that carries us beyond ourselves
    • a call that connects us on a whole range of levels with a reality that is both inviting and mysterious, compassionate and uncompromising
    • a call that is profoundly personal
    • a call that brings out the best in us
    • a call that gives us a new and more realistic self-understanding.

2. A true call also brings out the demons in our lives, and these have to be faced. What are some of the "demons" that the men in the movie must overcome?

3. Gaz is the one who calls the others to something. Certain factors, listed below, will lead us to believe in the one who calls us. How does the fidelity of Gaz' call measure up to each factor?

    • he is true to the relationship in good times and bad
    • he does not judge us as anything less than lovable and capable of loving

• he respects our individuality
• he celebrates with us what is good in life
• he works with us in transforming what is damaging in our world
• he lets us experience the freedom to be creative
• he shares with us all that he has and is.

4. The Relationship of the Movie to One's Self in the Exercise

1. At the end of the movie, Dave overcomes his own demon and becomes the one urging the group on. It is Gaz who is unable to act, unsure of what will happen if he goes on. How does the love of his son, Nathan, enable him to overcome his fear and to answer the call?

2. Every call shows itself in what we value, as the Exercise tells us, because what we value is where we put our lives. We see quite clearly what men like Gaz and Dave and Lompar value. What value is shown in what you are called to? How do you react to this call?

3. We can see at work in the movie the norms that the Exercise gives us when it says that for every call there are forces of attraction, response, engagement and commitment. Choose one example of each of these forces from the movie and apply it in your own life in the way you respond to the calls you have received. How would you react differently after making the Exercise and seeing this movie?

14th Exercise
The Cost of Discipleship

If anyone would come after me, let him deny himself and take up his cross and follow me. For whoever would save his life will lose it; and whoever loses his life for my sake and the gospel's sake will save it. For what does it profit a man, to gain the whole world and forfeit his life.

(Mark 8:34-36)

They will strive to conduct themselves as if every attachment ... had been broken. They will make efforts neither to want that, or anything else, unless the service of God our Lord alone moves them to do so.

(Sp. Ex. #155)

Grace: This is to ask for what I desire. Here it will be to ask for an intimate knowledge of our Lord, who has become man for me, that I may love Him more and follow Him more closely.

(Sp. Ex. 104)

The Challenge of Living Authentically

A script we sometimes buy into suggests that implementing decisions is easy. But this is not so. Often the values of the world deride the decisions we make because this world's illusions are fickle and superficial. When we make a radical decision, even though we still live in the world, we do not live as the world proposes we live. For example, to enter into a life commitment flies in the face of overwhelming selfish self-indulgence; to love what is broken transcends the lure of perfectionism; to believe in the power of truth destroys the convenient lie; to live spiritually exposes the shallowness of the materialism that surrounds us.

The Poor in Spirit

A call invites us to a deeper relationship with the divine. As we discovered in the First Week, when we encounter the divine personally and intimately we discover our creaturehood. We experience that we are nothing in ourselves, and exist only because of the relationship God maintains with us, even though we might not be conscious of it most of the time. To exist consciously in that awareness is both liberating and terrifying. It is rather like discovering that the ground we have built our lives on, and our egos, with all of its assumptions and projects, is not solid after all. Until we learn intimately to trust the love that creates, maintains, sustains and delights in us, the familiar is seen to be the product of habit and blindness. But as we learn to trust that relationship with God, we discover that we are not destroyed by our sense of our nothingness. In fact, we become more joyful and free in learning that we are cared for by a Love that is bigger than we can ever imagine.

Walking Through Our Deaths

That perspective is the basis of our discipleship. As we enter the journey to closer union with God, we meet forces that prevent us from fully experiencing that love. To reach the life we desire we must acknowledge and mourn the many deaths that keep us prisoner: the loss of innocence; loss of loving relationships; destruction of our ideals and hopes; despair that goes with accepting as reality that "things cannot change"; cynicism that is suspicious of any form of good; and so on. We have to find ways not to submit to these deaths. How do we do this? First, by acknowledging them for what they are: that takes power away from them. Second, by articulating how they affect us. Third, by entering consciously into those deaths in prayer and ritual, and by offering them up to that transforming power of love that is found in resurrection and in the love that seeks us just as we seek it. To be a disciple is to offer the deaths we experience and to witness to our relationship with the sacred.

Daily Gifts

In so doing, we discover humility. We experience our powerlessness in the face of the powers of this world, of our own disorders, and of the forms of almost malign absurdity that seem to control even the common and simple good. But we also become increasingly attentive to what is given to us daily and to the quiet and often small good that can be found and shared and celebrated in our lives. Often we discover that this is enough for the day and for our needs.

Hungering for Life

But we long for a just world, a good and meaningful life. Because we are honest with ourselves, we wish we could see and know and love the world and ourselves the way the Father sees and knows and loves us. This "more" that we hunger for, that we enter into as we grow into discipleship, becomes the consuming passion that God the lover has for us the beloved. This passion shows itself in mercy.

A Compassionate Mercy

In our world, we strive to be merciful with our slender means as the Father is merciful to us. We give with ourselves what has been given to us. To be sure, we do it out of compassion, because we know what it is to be lost and lonely and unloved, but we also do it because the one who loves us behaves that way, and we desire to be one with the beloved even in the ways that the beloved deals with the world. The disciple seeks at first to imitate the God who calls us all, but the journey to love slowly transforms that imitation into identification. The mercy that finds us and that we allow ourselves to be found by slowly becomes our own life. The lover becomes the beloved in the world.

A Practical Love

In sharing the heart of God, we manifest Christ's love for the Father and the Father's love for his Son. This is not a pious sentimentality or an otherworldly relationship of unnatural intensity. It is simple and direct and practical. It sees what must be done and does it. It sees what needs to be done and does what it can. It manifests the quiet, ongoing creativity of God and the constant patient suffering of God. It says, as Paul says, "Now I live, not I but it is the Christ who lives in me."

Reweaving the World

The life of Christ that the disciple witnesses to with his own life creates community on ever-more encompassing levels of relationships: the inner work to unite the separated parts of the self; the work of creating and maintaining bonds within families, communities, society and nations; the broader dimensions of community, including the ecological and even the cosmic. This sense of unity is fostered by right relationships: the work of the disciple is to establish, preserve and support relationships that give life and are rooted in the mystery of God's creativity.

But to live this way requires courage and a conscious rootedness in God's love, for such a life has to loose the bonds of oppression and unmask the lies that trap the human family. It means being willing to speak for those with no voice, to share the life of the little ones in a way that convinces them of their worth and their goodness. Too often, such a life leads to suffering and persecution. The disciple knows that in this intimate following of Christ, he will be treated in this world just as the Christ was treated.

We are asked to live this way and on this path if we are to help transform this world into a place where good can be seen and cherished, truth known and upheld, love become the basis of all action. The call to discipleship is primarily a call to such a deep intimacy with God that our lives manifest that intimacy in all we do and hold. Each of us is offered that call and that path – the path of the Beatitudes (Matthew 5:1-16).

Questions for prayer and reflection

1. This contemplation is a path through the Beatitudes and describes the life of a disciple. The Beatitudes were central to the First Week, to lead us to a spiritual freedom. Here it is to foster a deeper sense of intimacy with the Christ, the grace we are praying for at this time. You might wish to pray your way through the Beatitudes as if Christ is speaking to you. Stay with each one until it moves you to the next.

2. In your journey through this contemplation, where did you find yourself stopping because something moved you, either positively or negatively? List those moments and go back to them one at a time, staying with each moment until you feel ready to move on.

3. Have a conversation with Christ about how your life resembles his. Ask him to show you how this is so.

4. What fears do you have about developing a closer intimacy with God? Where do these fears come from? What do they suggest about what you should do next? How will you deal with them?

5. What do you find attractive when you contemplate a closer intimacy with God? How do you know if this attraction is deceptive or not? How will you find out? What will you do next?

6. At the end of your prayer periods, do you find yourself being consistently called to pray about something? What? How will you pray about it? (Ask God to show you.)

7. At the end of your prayer periods, have a conversation with the Father, or Jesus, or his mother, or one of your favourite saints about what happened in the prayer.

The Movie
The End of the Affair

Director: Neil Jordan (1999 – 101 mins.)
Starring: Ralph Fiennes, Julianne Moore, Stephen Rea

1. Summary

In 1946, novelist Maurice Bendrix meets with civil servant Henry Miles, the husband of his ex-mistress Sarah. In the midst of the 1944 bombing of London, Sarah abruptly ended her affair with Maurice. Maurice still has no idea why the affair ended and now he arranges to have Sarah followed. He wants to rekindle the affair and she agrees to go with him to Brighton.

2. Questions about the Movie

1. *"The End of the Affair* is Greene dancing on the divide between the rules of religion and the lusts of the flesh. His adulterous husbands and sinning priests have to deal not only with built-in guilt but with the rules of the church, which they never believe in more than while breaking them. The novel is a largely interior affair, existing inside Maurice's mind as he ponders again and again how a woman could seem so close and then suddenly be so far away." (Roger Ebert, *Chicago Sun-Times*, December 3, 1999) How "real" is the faith (or lack of it) that the three major characters profess – if not verbally, then in the way they live and love and move and have their being?

2. "A good part of the story, as was frequently the case with the Roman Catholic Greene's more serious works, deals with matters of the spirit, with questions of faith and belief that play an increasingly crucial role as events unfold." (Kenneth Turan, *Los Angeles Times*, December 3, 1999) Greene and Jordan share a Catholic background, both are literary men who were/are involved in movies, and both have interests in combustible relationships and pseudo-historical/political investigations. How are these mutual elements present in the movie? Read Graham Greene's novel and see just how Jordan has changed things to adapt the novel to the movie. To what degree has Jordan succeeded in capturing the essence of the novel?

3. "The story, at least as Greene conceived it, is about religion, seen not as a solace but as an affliction, presided over by a Deity who, for all Greene's Catholicism, has a lot in common with the grim Lutheran God of Ingmar Bergman: the malignant spider on the wall, watching and spinning his web. There's little place for such an implacable being in the comfortable, sunlit church of Jordan's film." (Philip Kemp, *Sight and Sound*, February 2000) It is obvious that a number

of critics did not like Jordan's change in emphasis. It is said that the God of the novel is a God similar to the Hound of Heaven – out to catch Sarah's soul no matter what – a jealous God who will go to any limits to keep Sarah. How is the God portrayed in Jordan's movie different from this?

3. The Relationship of the Movie to the Theme of the Exercise

1. Many symbolic deaths hold us prisoner, as the Exercise tells us, when we try to answer the call to discipleship. We must acknowledge these deaths, which include

    • our loss of innocence
    • the loss of loving relationships
    • the destruction of our hopes and ideals
    • the despair that comes when we accept that "things cannot change"
    • the cynicism that makes us suspicious of any form of good.

    While Sarah must mourn these deaths in her own life, how is Maurice called to do the same? At the end of the movie he "prays" (though unaware that he is praying), "Now, I'm tired of hating you and you are still there…. I've only one prayer left – forget about me and look after her and Henry." How do each of the above "deaths" apply to Maurice? While we can never know (although the book is said to be based on an actual affair that Graham Greene had during the war) if Maurice learns to mourn these deaths, what do you see in his character that makes you think he will or won't accept his discipleship?

2. To be a disciple is to offer the deaths we experience, as the Exercise tells us, and witness to the relationship we hold with the sacred. How does Sarah offer the deaths she experiences? What one act, what one gift, does she offer someone that shows her relationship with God to be a true and deep one?

3. Above all else, the call to discipleship involves such a deep intimacy with God that our lives manifest that intimacy in all we do and hold. Despite Sarah's diary entry where she says she is too weak to keep either of the only two promises she ever made – to marry Henry and to stop seeing Maurice – there is evidence that she has a deep intimacy with God. Where do we see this in what she does and in what she holds?

172

4. The Relationship of the Movie to One's Self in the Exercise

1. In her diary, Sarah writes that she is in the desert now. "You empty me of love," she says to God, "and then fill that emptiness." How has God done this in your life?

2. Sarah tells Maurice that she never loved anyone as she loved him but that when he came through the door, "another kind of love came with you" and she tried to fight it. In what ways have you tried to fight the love God offers you, the love that will make you experience deaths?

3. When Sarah tells Maurice that people go on loving God all their lives without seeing him, he replies that this is not his kind of love. She says simply: "Maybe there is no other kind." Have you seen God in your life? Where? Think of what Sarah says: "God is in the details."

4. Both Sarah and Maurice are – in the eyes of the world – unusual candidates for discipleship. Why do you think they were called? Why do you think God calls you?

Christ Walks on the Water
(Matthew 14:22-33)

All things are possible with God.

(Mark 10:27)

God our Lord knows our nature infinitely better [than we do]… He often grants us the grace to understand what is suitable for us.

(Sp. Ex. #89)

Grace: This is to ask for what I desire. Here it will be to ask for an intimate knowledge of our Lord, who has become man for me, that I may love Him more and follow Him more closely.

(Sp. Ex. #104)

The Impossible Happens

In this gospel sequence, Jesus has just heard about Herod killing his cousin John. He withdraws to a quiet place to reflect on this news, but when the crowds see where he is going they go to look for him. Feeling sorry for them, he heals the sick among them. In the evening, seeing that they have nothing to eat, he feeds them all from the little food they had. Then he goes up into the mountains to pray. Late that stormy night, the disciples in a boat on the lake see him walking on the waters towards them. They are afraid, but Peter says, "If it is you, let me walk on the waters to you." Jesus says, "Come." Peter gets out of the boat and walks on the water, but, when he feels the force of the wind, is afraid and starts to sink. He cries out to be saved. Jesus stretches out his hand and saves him and they get into the boat. When the others see what he has done, they acknowledge that he is truly divine.

When we enter into this contemplation we feel very much like Peter did. In the midst of living out of our call, we are surrounded by alien forces beyond our control and so we forget our relationship with Christ and try to save ourselves. When this happens we become overwhelmed. In desperation we cry out for deliverance. When we do so, we see that help is at hand, which leads us to a deeper realization of that ever-present mercy of God that calls us but also sustains and saves us. Unfortunately, we often have to be in this situation before we can accept that we are looked after. And to be honest, in every new situation when we are surrounded by those destructive forces, we forget the life lessons of being saved and sink again. We sink until we cry out again in desperation to be saved, and we are saved. In following the path of the disciple, the ego never disappears; in situations of vulnerability it tries to rely on itself. It is the fallen human condition to rely on our own abilities in dire circumstances. We lose touch with that more deeply human aspect of ourselves that knows we live only in relationship and are most fully alive only in relationship with God.

Depending on God

But it is also personally transforming to consider Jesus in his humanity and to see what he does in dire

174

circumstances. He had started his public ministry by doing what John was doing, but here he sees what can happen when people witness in that way. The forces of the world destroy them.

He is grieved by the murder of a family member, but he also faces the consequences of the path he walks. He withdraws, as in a retreat, to enter more self-consciously into that relationship with his Father, to be more deeply rooted and to take heart.

His desire for self-renewal is frustrated by the needs of the crowd, and he puts aside his own ego needs in that compassionate imitation of his Father. He heals the sick; he takes the little food they have and, praying to the Father, experiences once again that mercy passing through him into the world. The loaves and fish are multiplied and all are fed. Even in his extreme need he depends on that relationship with the Father to sustain him and his mission. That love, which names him, as it names us, as the beloved, comes through. The people are satisfied.

It is only then that he continues on his own project. He goes off into the mountains to commune with his Father. Like us doing these Exercises, he realizes that he needs that time to maintain his bond with the source of his life. He takes the time and out of that is renewed to continue his mission. He returns to those whom the Father has given him as companions for the journey and he finds them in need. They are surprised at his mode of coming to them (as they will be surprised in the resurrection sequences) and wonder if it is not a figment of their frantic imaginations. Peter asks him to identify himself through his powers; Jesus accepts and calls him. In that personal calling, Peter is given the power to do what Jesus does. He walks on the water. When we accept our call we are given the same power to do as Jesus does, and to live as Jesus lives. We set out, like Peter, with our eyes fixed on the Christ. It is when we are away from our habitual forms of security and totally dependent on Jesus that our faith falters and we become aware of our situation. We turn towards ourselves and break the relationship we have with the one who calls us. We sink.

We are rescued when we turn in desperation once again to God. The first time we turn is for proof; the second time is at a deeper level. We turn because it is our last resort. In those saving acts we recognize that it is not ghosts or illusions that save us, but the Christ.

Many things happen to us in this contemplation. We recognize that the one who loves us is divine, and that this does not take away from his humanity since he, too, suffers. We also learn to distinguish between the illusions that look like God and the real God, since only God can save us. We find out how vital is our relationship with God in living out our call, because we cannot do it on our own. We discover God's constant fidelity in taking the little we have and making it enough for what we have to do. We learn that the Christ works to maintain his relationship with his Father, and that just as Christ responds to our needs, the Father responds to Christ's needs. We enter more deeply into that creative mercy that witnesses to the Father's love for us, and to Christ's love for us, and we live out and share that creative mercy in our lives.

As we enter into this contemplation and open ourselves to being transformed by God's love, we become like the disciples that Christ gathers around him as we are given that intimate knowledge that makes us his continuing presence on earth.

Questions for prayer and reflection

1. Read Matthew 14:22-33. Enter into a contemplation of it. Where were you? Were you an onlooker? One of those fed? A disciple on the boat? Peter? Jesus? What did the contemplation reveal to you about yourself? About your relationship to God?

2. Have you ever been in dire straits and then, through matters beyond your control, triumphed over that situation? When you relive such situations, what does it say about your life and about God's presence in your life?

3. Are you in a desperate situation now? What is happening? What are you doing to emerge from this situation? How is God helping you to emerge?

4. In what ways can you be creative and joyful in your life in the midst of the unsettling times in which we all live?

5. When you read this Exercise, what are the things that strike and move you? Stay with one of these and see how that gift opens. Stay with the others, one at a time, and see what emerges when we give ourselves time to think about them.

6. After reflecting and praying through these questions, how is your relationship to God changed? Deepened? What areas of growth and challenge remain?

7. Are you still willing to walk with God in the midst of your incompleteness and your questions? Why? How?

The Movie
White Oleander

Director: Peter Kosminsky (2002 – 109 mins.)
Starring: Michelle Pfeiffer, Renée Zellweger, Alison Lohman

1. Summary

15-year-old Astrid Magnussen lives a somewhat unusual life with Ingrid, her artist mother. When Ingrid uses the deadly poison of her favourite flower, white oleander, to murder a man who betrays her, she is sent to prison for life. Astrid spends a decade going from foster home to foster home. She keeps in touch with her mother through letters, and each of them supports the other. Ingrid shows Astrid how to survive, and Astrid finally teaches Ingrid how to love.

2. Questions about the Movie

1. *White Oleander* is adapted from a novel by Jane Finch. The novel is full of talk about flowers – flowers whose qualities are used to illuminate various characters. Both mother and daughter are represented by the white oleander of the title. The white oleander – a relative of dogbane – is an evergreen shrub whose flowers are poisonous.

    The foster mothers who take in Astrid are also represented by flowers – such as the rose arches, Chinese elms and red poinsettia that surround Clair's house. Ingrid's mentor, Olivia, a high-class call girl, has a garden filled with jacaranda and lily-of-the-Nile. Even Ingrid's high-priced publicity-seeking lawyer is described as being "a bouquet of oleander and nightshade" – both poisonous plants. What do the flowers and plants chosen say about each of these characters?

2. On an emotional level, the novel and the movie make use of colour –the pale white of the oleander to evoke the Los Angeles landscape, and the blue of Ingrid's clothing. Finch also writes about smells – such as the violent scent of the perfume Ingrid always wears and the sensual perfume that Olivia gives Astrid. What does a filmmaker do with such sensory elements that the novelist uses to evoke character? Unlike the novelist, who must rely solely on the effect of words and our imaginations to render character and setting in our minds, filmmakers have more tools at their disposal. One of them is image-making, as evidenced by the film's floral motif, but the most important is the actor.

3. "In the complementary but uncomplimentary role, Pfeiffer is fabulous as the first true villain she's ever played on screen: cold, manipulative, sanctimonious and egotistical. Even though she's been convicted of murder, she feels she can still make value judgments on people and have her daughter live by them. She is as scary, in her way,

as Hannibal Lecter." (Stephen Hunter, *Washington Post*, October 11, 2002). The publicity for the film included the tag line "oleanders can be poisonous, so can a mother's love." Which scenes show Ingrid being "as scary as Hannibal Lecter"?

4. *White Oleander* is essentially about a mother–daughter relationship and about the daughter's journey towards maturity. It also poses some interesting questions. Are Ingrid and Astrid – the mother and daughter – sources of poison or victims struggling to deal with their own situations? If they are sources of poison, whom are they poisoning? The people around them or themselves?

3. The Relationship of the Movie to the Theme of the Exercise

1. Astrid tries desperately to live out her call and to grow, but she is surrounded by alien forces at each foster home she enters. What are these forces in each setting? How does Astrid overcome them or succumb to them?

2. Astrid tries to be self-reliant in each situation but she knows she is not. In situations of vulnerability – despite the letters to her mother – she tries to become her own person. What happens to her as a result? Is there any awareness of God's presence in the things that happen? Indeed, is God even mentioned in the movie? Or is God just implicitly present? If so, how?

3. Almost all of the main characters in the movie are confronted with love in one form or another. How does each of them react when the opportunity for love is offered to them?

4. The Relationship of the Movie to One's Self in the Exercise

1. Astrid – through her letters – is able to call out to her mother for help whenever she is overwhelmed and desperate. And, in her own way, Ingrid supplies the needed help. To whom do you turn when you are desperate? What kind of help is offered to you?

2. Does Astrid ever "sink" like the disciple Peter does? Do you? What causes you to turn in on yourself and to break the relationship with the one who calls you?

3. Throughout the movie Astrid has to learn, as the Exercise urges us, to distinguish between the illusions that look like God and the real God. What illusions have appeared in your life with the easy answers that you might have thought was God? How did you distinguish between what is real and what is illusion?

178

16th Exercise
Jesus in the Temple
(John 2:13-22)

This people honours me with their lips,
But their heart is far from me;
In vain do they worship me,
Teaching as doctrines the precepts of men.

(Matthew 15:8-9)

Consider how [the enemy of our human nature] summons innumerable demons, and scatters them, some to one city and some to another, throughout the whole world, so that no province, no place, no state of life, no individual is overlooked.

(Sp. Ex. #141)

Grace: This is to ask for what I desire. Here it will be to ask for an intimate knowledge of our Lord, who has become man for me, that I may love Him more and follow Him more closely.

(Sp. Ex. #104)

Facing Hypocrisy

There is something dreadful when elements in religious organizations preach fear, control access to God through exclusivity, and set themselves up as the sole purveyors of salvation. It is even sadder when those same forces distort and restrict the message of God's compassionate mercy into systems of law and theology. But saddest of all is the lack of the spirit of love, and the self-imposed blindness to that lack, when such figures present themselves to the world as authoritative voices for religious belief. Then we have death masquerading as life. The same is true of social and political organizations that claim to maintain justice but create and uphold laws that favour the powerful, or that claim to search for and speak the truth but manipulate image and word for expedient ends. Jesus is fearless in the face of this hypocrisy. He condemns it.

And what about us, who see these things so clearly and are disgusted by them? What do we do? What do we do with ourselves when we find that we are no better than the institutions and structures we condemn?

This is a subtle and pervasive temptation in our time. Seduced by moral disgust, we either despair and do nothing or react in a violent and destructive manner. If the previous Exercise shows us how fear stops us from being intimate with Christ, this Exercise shows us how both clarity and power are enemies of a full relationship with the one who invites us to share his life. With clarity we can see things as they are, but we react in a worldly way to what we see so clearly. With power we become presumptuous, and act out our desire to change what we perceive wrong in a worldly manner. The journey you are now on invites you not only to walk with the Christ, but to live and act as he lives and acts.

Creating a Sacred Space

In this contemplation, Jesus cleanses the temple by driving out those who corrupted that sacred space

179

where one meets God. How are we supposed to act? We act not in slavish imitation of Jesus' actions in his time, but by putting on the mind and heart of Jesus. This crucial distinction points to the importance of a deep and lived personal intimacy with Christ. In that intimacy he reveals to us and shares with us his relationship with the Father, and invites us to be like him in living out of that relationship. So we act not out of our own perceptions and insights and inclinations, even though these may be valid, but rather out of the stance of being one with the source of all creation and creativity. This becomes our principle for discernment and action. Our role in the world when we act out of this stance is to maintain right relationships between everything and God. What Jesus did in the temple was to display the energy of righteousness against those who had made religion a business transaction rather than the expression of mercy.

In fact, all of Jesus' actions in the temple – from his being found there by Mary and Joseph as a child, to his preaching there, to this final act – are manifestations of being about his Father's business. That business is love – not a sentimental or pious love, not an escapist or exclusive love, not a passive or self-indulgent love, but a love that enters the world to bring everything and everyone into loving relationships with each other. This love has a reverence for life; it practises generosity by sharing time, energy, gifts and resources; it sees itself as responsible for all of creation, human and otherwise; and it is full of care in the way it relates to others. In so doing, it acts as the Father acts towards creation. He has lovingly brought this creation into being; he maintains it and desires to transform it into a habitat where the destructive effects of sin are transformed into creativity and life.

Jesus turns his attention to the temple because for him the temple is the meeting place between God and humanity. That meeting place had been turned into a place where transactions were commercial, political and worldly rather than a spiritual, open space where the sufferings of humanity met the compassion of God. And because the mercy of God refuses to be constrained by disorder, the Father creates a new temple to embody that compassionate love.

Christ is that temple, and his call to each of us is to become that sacred place where the world's pain and brokenness can in humility be met by compassionate mercy and held up to healing: to liberate the oppressed and to celebrate community.

The Holiness of Everything

What Christ does in his life is to restore sacredness to the desecrated. Our intimacy with Christ carries us along that same path. When we walk that path, we start to discover that everything that exists is holy, and that everything we meet can be an invitation to encounter God in a deeper way. Evil, no matter how it is disguised as good, even as religious good, effectively tries to stop us encountering God. But when we have travelled a while with the Christ, as we have done in praying though these Exercises, we start seeing through the illusions that pretend to be holiness. In relating to them for what they truly are, we start taking away the power that they have over us and those whom we care for and whom we are now committed to cherish into the fullness of life. Like Christ, we are invited in love to restore a right order to creation.

When Christ cleanses the temple, he acts as a peacemaker. What is the difference between a peace-keeper, a peace lover and a peacemaker? A peace-keeper sacrifices everything to make sure that there is no disturbance in what is accepted as habitual. Fear and co-dependency underlie that position. A peace lover wants peace but is not willing to commit to any actions that would remove or transform the forces that block right relations between different aspects of creation – people, classes, cultures and nations. A peacemaker commits to establishing those right relations, which are found only when we take on the perspective and the work of the Creator. In cleansing the temple Christ acts as a peacemaker because his deepest desire is to do the will of His Father, and the deepest desire of the Father is that everything be seen as it is: holy. We are holy, our deepest identity is to live that holiness, and our mission in this world, no matter what we do, is to allow the holiness of everything to manifest itself in celebrating life.

Questions for prayer and reflection

1. How do you confuse religion with holiness? How does that restrict your deepest desires? How does it stop you from encountering God?

2. Pray through those manifestations of religion in your life that create a false image of God, yourself and others by offering them up to the transforming spirit of the Father. What happens when you do this? How are you liberated?

3. How can you distinguish between your anger and God's transforming energy in the face of the world's oppressive forces?

4. How do you distinguish between self-indulgence and freedom in your life and in the world?

5. How do you feel when you discover that your growing intimacy with Christ asks you to take a stance in the world? In practical terms, what does that stance look like? (Remember that we are not asked to be seduced by our idealisms, our fears. We are just asked to be where Jesus is.) When you ask the Christ in prayer where you are to be with him, what answers do you get?

The Movie
Iron Giant

Director: Brad Bird (1999 – 86 mins.)
Starring: the voices of Jennifer Aniston, Harry Connick Jr., Vin Diesel

1. Summary

Based on a 1968 story by British poet laureate Ted Hughes, *Iron Giant* is a story of an imaginative nine-year-old boy, Hogarth, who befriends a giant metal machine that falls to earth from the sky in 1958. With the help of a beatnik sculptor, Hogarth attempts to hide the Iron Giant from the government, which believes the creature is a communist plot to take over the United States.

2. Questions about the Movie

1. "A cartoon movie about a child befriending a giant robot from outer space is easy bait for all the traps that befall children's animation: syrupy morality, excessive sentimentality, pointless action, horrid music. The Iron Giant has largely avoided all of this by dint of clever writing and gentle wit, and the result is one of those rare films that will hold the attention of children in the 6 to 12 age range without insulting the intelligence of the adults who accompany them." (Doug Saunders, *The Globe and Mail*, August 6, 1999) How does the movie manage to avoid all the above-mentioned pitfalls and become something more than just a kid's animated action movie?

2. *Iron Giant* could be viewed as a simple adventure story for kids. Yet, a little digging beneath the surface reveals a rather substantial thematic underpinning that has a lot to say about America and its world view in the 1950s and even today. Why is it important that the movie be set in the 1950s? What does the movie say about the US today?

3. "There's a wonderful moment, midway through the film, where the giant simply lies on his back in the junkyard, pondering the stars. In endowing him with such poetry, Bird and McCanlies repay the comic books they clearly loved as boys by making visible their true value. Superman is nothing if not a vision, available to all children, of the powers and the goodness locked up within them. The Giant…feels within himself the soul of a superhero, but he discovers this only through careful attention to the playthings of the human imagination. " (F.X. Feeny, *LA Weekly: Film Review*, August 6-12,1999)

Hogarth: I know you feel bad about the deer, but it's not your fault. Things die. That's part of life. It's bad to kill, but it's not bad to die.

The Iron Giant: You die?

Hogarth: Well, yes, someday.

The Iron Giant: I die?

Hogarth: I don't know. You're made of metal, but you have feelings, and you think about things, and that means you have a soul. And souls don't die.

The Iron Giant: Soul?

Hogarth: Mom says it's something inside of all good things, and that it goes on forever and ever. *The Iron Giant*: Souls don't die.

Does the Iron Giant have a soul because it "thinks about things"?

4. In *Sphere*, a computer thinks about things and makes thoughts real. Does it have a soul?

In *The Matrix*, a computer program creates whole cities and the people inside them. Does it have a soul?

In *Bladerunner*, a cyborg begs its maker to allow it to live. Does it have a soul?

In *AI: Artificial Intelligence*, a robot built to love seeks to become a real boy so that he can be loved by the woman who is his adopted mother. Does it have a soul?

If a machine has artificial intelligence, does it have a soul?

(Adapted from Neil Andersen's Study Guide for The Iron Giant, *Scanning the Movies* program, July 1999)

3. The Relationship of the Movie to the Theme of the Exercise

1. Hogarth has an opportunity to affect the very being of a creature, a weapons destroyer, whose sole purpose is one of violence. As the battle between violence as a remedy for fear and the acceptance of differences reaches a critical point in the film, how is Hogarth seen as a peacemaker? What qualities of the peacemaker – as explained in the Exercise – are found in Hogarth?

2. Although Hogarth is just a young boy, he is about his Father's business – and that business is love. Here are some of the characteristics of this love. How do they apply to Hogarth?

   • this love is neither sentimental nor pious
   • this love is not escapist or exclusive
   • this love is not passive or self-indulgent
   • this love aims to bring all things and all people into loving relationships with each other
   • this love has a reverence for life
   • this love practises generosity by sharing whatever it has.

3. The Exercise speaks of groups that claim to maintain justice, claim to search for and speak the truth, but manipulate image and word for their own ends. The movie is set in 1957, in Rockwell, Maine, a blue-collar fishing village living in the shadow of the Cold War between the US and USSR. The values of Rockwell's citizens are the values of 1950s small-town America: down-to-earth, practical, patriotic and fearful of anything or anyone different. The US reaction to the Cold War was to bomb things. (This was just five years before the Cuban missile crisis,

which would bring the world to the brink of nuclear war.) This was a time of fear and hatred between nations, and children were encouraged to accept these values as their own. Why? Review the scene in the diner where Government Agent Kent Mansley explains this point to Hogarth. How does this also apply to the US today?

4. Relationship of the Movie to One's Self in the Exercise

1. It would be easier for Hogarth simply to be a peace lover and not a peacemaker, easier for him simply to conform to the values of his town and the age. But in accepting the values his mother and Dean offer him, he rejects the values of the town and the military and becomes peacemaker. What values in your life will help you to move from peace lover to peacemaker? Name a situation where you have had to make such a decision.

2. Hogarth strives to do as the Exercise says – to act out of the stance of being one with the source of all creation and creativity. While he may have no knowledge that this is what he is doing, he has been influenced strongly by his mother and by Dean to know that there is something more than what the world holds. What strong influence in your life leads you towards the love that is God in all that you do and say? What stops you from following that influence completely?

3. The way the military and the government act in the movie is an example of how power makes us presumptuous and makes us want to change in a worldly fashion what we perceive to be wrong. How is this a danger in your own life? How is this a danger when you come to discern how to act?

The Raising of Lazarus

(John 11:1-45)

God shows his love for us in that while we were yet sinners Christ died for us.

(Romans 5:8)

Reflect how God dwells in creatures: in the elements giving them existence, in the plants giving them life, in the animals conferring upon them sensation, in humans bestowing understanding. So He dwells in me and gives me being, life, sensation, intelligence; and makes a temple of me, since I am created in the likeness and image of the Divine Majesty.

(Sp. Ex. #235)

Grace: This is to ask for what I desire. Here it will be to ask for an intimate knowledge of our Lord, who has become man for me, that I may love Him more and follow Him more closely.

(Sp. Ex. #104)

Waiting on the Father

In the scriptures Jesus raised the widow of Nain's son and Jairus' daughter from the dead. He did not know either of these two people or their families; he simply acts out of compassion. Jesus also raised Lazarus. Lazarus was his friend and Jesus knew the family very well. The odd thing about the raising of Lazarus is that Jesus knew that Lazarus was sick, although he was not far away, yet he did not go and heal him. After Lazarus died, Jesus waited several days before even going to comfort the family, which seems unusual for someone who embodies the compassion of God. Jesus knew that the religious authorities were trying to kill him; was he afraid for his life? From his previous actions, we know that he is not afraid of those authorities and often challenged them to their faces. We also know that his mission was to be compassionate even in the face of bodily destruction. So why did he delay going to Lazarus until it was too late?

In our own lives we see instances of need. Even though we know that God is fully aware of our needs, nothing seems to be done. This is the case in the world, as well. For many people, this is the reason for not believing in God. We, too, at this stage of our spiritual journey through the Exercises, raise the question: If this is the way you treat the person you say you love and have come to share life with, how will you treat us whom you say you love and are asking to journey with you?

The answer lies in Jesus' relationship with the Father. Jesus does nothing apart from the Father's will, and his whole life is a manifestation of that will. He waited to be called at his baptism; he waits now until the Father tells him to go to Lazarus' tomb; he will wait to be raised from the dead. It grieves him to wait to rescue his friend and to comfort the family. In his waiting he manifests that first commandment to "Love the Lord your God with all your heart and with all your soul and with all your mind, and with all your strength" (Mark 12:30).

In our deepening intimacy with the Christ we, too, are asked to wait on the Father's will. It may grieve us to do that, for there are things we know we can do and things we know need to be done. To seem to be doing nothing while others suffer and die, and to claim at the same time to love them, causes the followers of the Christ to be deemed irrelevant, mindless, passive, or alienated from reality.

But Christianity is more than a program of social action. Waiting on the Father is not doing nothing. It is first and foremost a profound witness of our creaturehood. It is also a profound act of faith and hope and love to wait in that relationship knowing that something will be done, that it will be the right thing, and that what and how it will be done will reveal even more God's selfless, constant, caring compassion. To wait like this in love is not apathy. It is leaning passionately into a relationship committed to making us fulfilled, comforted and cared for. We expect it. We live out of it. And it comes.

The Greatest Gift

When Jesus goes to Bethany to Lazarus' home, Martha and then Mary meet him. Both upbraid him for not using his powers to save their brother from death. But Jesus' call is not to manifest his powers, but to live out his relationship with his Father. Jesus can raise Lazarus from the dead, as he raised two others. But like those two others, Lazarus would eventually die again. Jesus' relationship with the Father allows for resurrection. That relationship manifests a love so strong that death cannot overcome it. One enters into death journeying towards a love beyond name and imagining, and that love enters into death to bring the beloved into that new creation called resurrection. That new creation is not the cyclical return of natural rhythms, nor is it the miraculous raising up of the dead back into earthly life. It is something new, and it attests to the transforming creativity of the Father. In the Lazarus story Jesus manifests that greater gift the Father has for us. It is a gift that does not ignore the wretchedness of a disordered world or the ravages of sin and death and their effects on all of us. Instead, it enters into those places of crisis and takes away their power, making them doorways — however painful and powerful — into new life.

The risk the Father takes with Mary and Martha in denying them immediate access to Jesus' power is the risk the Father takes with each of us. If we are indulged with instant gratification because we know God loves us, and we love God, we reduce God to being a magician and ourselves to a narcissism that ignores the world's suffering. This approach overlooks God's mysterious will to enter into that suffering as a human being, and to endure it even to a humiliating and painful death on a cross. It does not admit that we are invited to follow Christ in living out his passion for the Father, or that intimacy with Christ makes us more human, not less — more aware of the destructiveness of evil but also more aware of the depths of God's love.

When Jesus raises Lazarus from the dead, he does it not to manifest his power but to show the dimensions of his relationship with the Father. He says, "Father, I thank you because you have heard me. I know that you hear me always but I have said this on account of the people standing by that they may believe you sent me" (John 11:41). He calls on the Father and the Father answers. Now he can act. In front of that tomb holding a man four days dead, he cries out in a loud voice, "Lazarus! Come out!" The gospel tells us what happens next. "The dead man came out, his hands and feet bound in bandages, and his face wrapped with a cloth." Jesus said to those around him, "Unbind him, and let him go."

Setting the Captured Free

Now we can see our task. It is God who raises up the dead. Our work is the unbinding and the letting go. If we let God be God, we find ourselves co-operating with him. We cannot overcome sin, or its first fruits, death. Only God can do that. But we can do our part of the relationship and allow those who have been set free to live freely. Too often we are unwilling to unbind and set free because we cannot believe that new life is given to a situation or to people. Our lack of faith in the power of God's love stops us from seeing what is right in front of us. But if we accept the power of the relationship that Christ has with the Father, and which he offers to each of us, we can see as he sees, and then do our part. As Jesus says elsewhere in John's gospel, "Receive the Holy Spirit. If you forgive the sins of any, they are forgiven. If you retain the sins of any, they are retained" (John 20:23). It is only when we share in the relationship that Jesus has with the Father – that is, share their Holy Spirit – that we can unbind, and forgive. That is liberation and life.

Questions for prayer and reflection

1. When you entered this contemplation, what happened to you? Where did you find yourself? What was your relationship to Jesus? To Mary and Martha? How did you deal with Lazarus?

2. When have you been in a dire situation beyond your control and had to wait for God to act? How did you wait? How did you relate to God at that time? What happened?

3. Are you in such a situation now? How are you relating to God?

4. When you look at your culture and the world, your family, you partner, your relationships and yourself, where do you find God bringing the dead to life? How do you co-operate with that?

5. Do you ever, like Jesus did, wait on the Father's moment to act, even though you could do something about a situation that needs remedying? How did you discern what to do and when, or not to do it? What was your prayer then?

6. When have you been liberated from a situation you considered hopeless?

7. When have you liberated others from situations they found hopeless?

8. When have you experienced your sins being forgiven so that you felt like a new person?

9. When have you forgiven someone in such a way that that person came "alive" again?

The Movie
American Beauty

Director: Sam Mendes (1999 – 121 mins.)
Starring: Kevin Spacey, Annette Bening, Thora Birch, Wes Bentley, Chris Cooper

1. Summary

Take an apparently perfect marriage and an apparently perfect family in an apparently perfect neighbourhood. Then add the fact that the father, Lester Burnham, is in the midst of a mid-life crisis that deepens as he realizes he is infatuated with one of his teenage daughter's friends. His daughter, Jane, is in love with Ricky, the shy boy next door whose father is a homophobic ex-Marine. Lester's wife is slowly becoming aware that she no longer has any control over the family. Each of these people is in search of that elusive thing known as American beauty in a variety of forms.

2. Questions about the Movie

1. "*American Beauty* is a film that shows the hunger for God in our modern Western cities is by no means dead. It proclaims that God can be found in our post-modern secular lives. It argues that ordinariness by no means signifies the absence of the divine. It challenges us to open our eyes and look for the God who is present to us in spite of and even in the midst of our messiness." (John O'Donnell, SJ, *National Jesuit News*, February/March 2000) What specific examples from the movie would prove – or disprove – this critic's thesis?

2. "As these characters struggle viciously – and hilariously – to escape the middle-class doldrums, the film also evinces a real and ever more stirring compassion. As it detects increasingly vital signs of life behind the absurd surfaces that Mendes presents so beautifully, the film takes on a gravity to match its evil zest." (Janet Maslin, *The New York Times*, September 15, 1999) Would you classify this movie as a comedy or a drama? Or can both elements be present in a movie? If both are present here, how does that effect the movie's impact on the viewer?

3. "The real targets here are a shopworn pair of twin heroes – the American Dream and the American Family, that once-dynamic duo whose health has waxed and waned over the past century." (Rick Groen, *The Globe and Mail*, September 17, 1999) How are these two groups targeted in the movie? How does the director make these two groups – partly seen in the character of Lester – so pathetically comic and yet so profoundly tragic?

188

3. The Relationship of the Movie to the Theme of the Exercise

1. In his first words of narration, Lester introduces himself and tells us that in less than a year he will be dead. And then he says: "Of course I don't know that yet, and in a way I am dead already." Lester's year to come is a resurrection – he sets himself free and lives freely. What scenes show us how Lester has been set free?

2. As the Exercise tells us, God's gift does not ignore the wretchedness of a disordered world or the ravages of sin and death. It enters into those places and makes them doorways – painful ones – into new life. How does this apply to Lester? To Carolyn? To Ricky? To Jane? What "doors" are opened for them?

3. All of the characters in the movie are waiting for something to happen, for something that will give them new life. But they are looking in the wrong place – they are looking in the world. How do you think their awareness of the presence and love of God in their lives would make a difference to what each of them does at the end of the movie?

4. The Relationship of the Movie to One's Self in the Exercise

1. Consider Lester's last narrative note to the viewer: if you don't share the film's piercing vision of what really matters, someday you will. It took death for Lester to realize this. Do you have to face death before you realize that you ought to "feel gratitude for every single moment of my stupid little life," and that "it's hard to stay mad when there's so much beauty in the world"? What does opening yourself to God's love do to bring forward the understanding of what Lester is saying? What will cause your own resurrection in life?

2. It is often in the very ordinary that we find God, that we see the joys of new life that God gives us. For Ricky this occurred in two places: his video of a floating plastic bag, and the look in the eyes of a dead homeless woman in which he saw God. Where do you find God in the ordinary parts of your life?

3. Our lack of faith in the power of God's love makes us unable to see what is in front of us. Lester may be the only one who has any inkling of what else is out there, but even he sees through a glass darkly. Try as he might, Ricky cannot appear to see an image of God reflected in Lester's eyes at the end of the movie. What is lacking in your faith that stops you from seeing God's love in your life?

18th Exercise
Palm Sunday
(Matthew 21:1-17)

The true light that enlightens everyone was coming into the world; he was in the world, and the world was made through him, yet the world knew him not. He came to his own home and his own people received him not.

(John 1:9-11)

We must carefully observe the whole course of our thoughts. If the beginning and middle and end of the course of thoughts are wholly good and directed to what is entirely right, it is a sign that they are from the good spirit But the course of thoughts suggested to us may terminate in something evil, or distracting, or less good than the soul had formerly proposed to do. Again it may end in what weakens the soul, or disquiets it; or by destroying the peace, tranquillity, and quiet which it had before, it may cause disturbance to the soul. These things are a clear sign that the thoughts are proceeding from the evil spirit, the enemy of our progress and eternal salvation.

(Sp. Ex. #333)

Grace: This is to ask for what I desire. Here it will be to ask for an intimate knowledge of our Lord, who has become man for me, that I may love Him more and follow Him more closely.

(Sp. Ex. #104)

A Servant King

Who do you look for when you look for God? What do you see when you look at death? This final exercise of the Second Week asks both of these questions. Underlying the contemplation of Christ entering Jerusalem and being treated by the people as a king and a secular saviour is the difference between what the world thinks of as redemption and what God offers. The Second Week of the Exercises starts off with a meditation on "The Kingdom." There we are asked to reflect on a king, chosen by God, who invites us to be under his standard. By the time we have journeyed through this Second Week, we discover what that means for us. It is to be poor with Christ in his poverty, humble with Christ in his total dependence on the Father, labouring with Christ as he labours to build a community of life and love.

But what the crowd wants when it gathers palms and celebrates Christ's entry into Jerusalem is a hero who will right their every wrong, a liberator who will overthrow the tyranny of the Roman imperial power and its brutalities, a magician who will cure their every ill, and a religious preacher who will offer a way of life free of stultifying legalism and hypocrisy. When, in their dreadful need, they see Jesus — who raised the dead, cured the sick, challenged the religious leaders, consorted with the poor and the dispossessed and the outcast, fed a multitude from the little they could offer — and when they heard his

190

preaching and his claims to be the chosen one of God, they see this son of Mary as the answer to their dream of a messiah. A new just world order, so long promised by prophets and so long the passionate and desperate dream of humankind, was to be fulfilled in their time and in their world.

They take off their cloaks, strip the palms of their leaves and celebrate the entrance of Christ into Jerusalem, the holy city, so long despoiled by corruption at every level. Now is to be the time of transformation. And it does become a time of transformation. The Christ is the Messiah, the warrior saviour of God – but as God sees it and enacts it, not as the crowd desires it.

Even here, even now, we need constantly to ask ourselves: Who is God for me? How does God act in our world? Is that God the one we want? Is the God of our needs, the same as the God who reveals himself in our prayer and in our lives? Which God do we commit ourselves to follow and to be intimate with?

A New Human

When we look at the scriptures, we see an interesting development in the way Christ presents himself. In the beginning he heals the sick, cures ills, raises the dead, transforms water into wine, feeds the multitudes with almost no food, performs miracles, preaches with power. But when Peter acknowledges him to be more than a miracle worker, and more than one of the earlier prophets come back from the dead – when Peter declares him to be the Messiah, the Special One of God – he begins to present himself differently and to talk about his suffering and death. Peter tells him that that is not how a god behaves; he rebukes Peter, saying he speaks as humans speak who know nothing of how the true God acts. But after Peter's declaration, Jesus performs fewer miracles and when he raises Lazarus, he does it in a way that informs those present that the significant point of his ministry is to reveal who the Father is and how the Father operates. His kingship, though it is in this world, and is firmly concerned with the way the world operates, is not of this world. He does not act as the world wants him to act. His behaviour always manifests his relationship with the Father. So, even though he enters Jerusalem with all the ritual allusions of a worldly liberator, he sees those signs differently. He is entering the contest where the powers of the world are overthrown: he becomes the prototype for the new human who can be so intimate with God, and who can allow God to be so intimate with us, that the values of this world are no longer the most important.

Facing Death

The world's values revolve around coping with death. Death ultimately devalues the world. On the one hand, people flee from death by maintaining the ego and subscribing to forms of ambition. The world is given an importance it cannot maintain. They become over-involved. On the other hand, people despair about the world in the face of death, which radically limits the scope of the world. They refuse to become involved. Even if we accept the reality of death and the absurdity it brings to the human project from a purely natural perspective, we are left with a hollow stoicism or the angst of existential absurdity. The non-spiritual death provides the outer limit of the human condition.

Jesus entering Jerusalem faces his death. He realizes that it will be horrible, shameful and painful, and he wonders if he will break under it. The test for him, as it was in the temptations in the desert, is to see if he will abandon his relationship with the Father and his trust in that relationship. But as he enters Jerusalem, he sees that death as a door through which he must go to meet the Father. For him, death is not an ending – it is a step on the path of his return to the Father. He will enter into death. He will wait for his Father to rescue him in whatever way the Father sees best.

We, too, will die. In fact, each of us is dying at this moment. We can try to avoid thinking about it by hurling ourselves into the world; or we can become so obsessed by it that we are useless in this world. But we have another choice. We can see it as Jesus sees it. We do not know the circumstances of our end, but we know that we can face that end, not as an end in itself, but as a new beginning. How we live shapes how we die, for we die as we live. Like Jesus, we can live in relationship with the Father; like Jesus, we can die maintaining that relationship.

Questions for prayer and reflection

1. Out of what self-image do you live? How is this manifest in what you do each day?

2. Do you feel confident enough of your relationship with the Father to trust your life with him? How could this be a foolish question? Why is this not a foolish question?

3. How does the Father trust you? How do you know this? Is this any different from any other relationship of trust you have?

4. What do you need to do to grow in trust?

5. In a conversation with the Father, ask what he needs to grow in trust of you. What does he say?

6. How do you face your death? How does this shape the way you live?

7. How have we dealt with the imminent death of someone close to us?

8. In your prayer, how do you deal with what Christ is doing? Where are you in relation to Christ in this?

The Movie
Life as a House

Director: Irwin Winkler (2001 – 109 mins.)
Starring: Kevin Kline, Kristin Scott Thomas, Hayden Christensen

1. Summary

In one day, architect George Monroe's life is changed. He loses his job, is diagnosed with a terminal illness – cancer – and told he has only four months to live. He decides to spend his last summer trying to rebuild his relationship with his ex-wife and troubled teenage son and to turn his rundown home into a dream house.

2. Questions about the Movie

1. "You have to approach *Life as a House* knowing that it has no interest in life as it is really lived or people as they really are, and offers lovable characters whose personality traits dictate their behavior, just like on television. What is remarkable is how Kline and Thomas, in particular, are able to deepen their characters by sheer skill and depth of technique, so that we like them and care what happens to them. (Whether it is George and Robin we like, or Kline and Thomas, is beside the point – the characters and actors amount to the same thing.)" (Roger Ebert, *Chicago Sun-Times*, October 26, 2001) This review makes an important point – one that is emphasized in the second of the key concepts of media literacy: media construct a version of reality.

How do you think the main characters in the movie are not "real"? What is the "version" of reality that is chosen? Why did the filmmakers not present us with "real" people?

2. Film critic Philip French says that one of the fastest-growing movie genres today is what he calls "the cinema of redundancy," which he defines as movies that "are fuelled by anger and resentment which cover the protagonists' doubts about their own self-worth, and they involve a reappraisal – comic or agonising – of the meaning of life itself." He also states holds that "In its working-class form, the best example is the gritty *The Full Monty*; the most celebrated middle-class manifestation is the slick *American Beauty*." (Philip French, *The Observer*, March 17, 2002) How is this movie an example of the "cinema of redundancy"? Does it work – in the same way *The Full Monty* or *American Beauty* works? Why? Why not?

3. "Mark Andrus, an Oscar nominee for co-writing *As Good as It Gets*, realizes that it's predictable that George will eventually win over Sam and therefore uses the arc of their relationship to frame a number of other developing relationships that reveal an array of values that have special reso-

nance in this post–Sept. 11 world: the importance of family and community, of love between father and son, of forgiveness and the passage from self-absorption to self-sacrifice." (Kevin Thomas, *Los Angeles Times*, October 26, 2001) It would be so easy to take this type of material over the top into the realm of pure sentimentality. What does the director do to attempt to avoid this – to present sentiment without sentimentality? Would this movie have worked in a world where 9/11 hadn't happened?

3. The Relationship of the Movie to the Theme of the Exercise

1. For the world, as the Exercise says, death leaves either a hollow stoicism or the angst of existential absurdity. At the end of the movie, what are the main characters left with in the face of death?

2. In the face of death, George makes a decision to rebuild his house. Is there any sign of religious hope in what he does in rebuilding the house, or is it just a way to avoid thinking about his death? What does this rebuilding mean to him?

3. We know that how we live shapes how we die. How did George's death reflect his life? How is what Sam does after George's death appropriate to the "new" George? How would George's death have been shaped if he had died at the point where the movie begins?

4. The Relationship of the Movie to One's Self in the Exercise

1. Death always affects us. This movie is not about the deaths of some thousands of people. It is about the death of one man. As the preface for the Requiem Mass reminds us, life is changed, not ended, and so death is a new beginning. This is easy to say. Do you find it easy to believe when someone you love dies? Why? Why not?

2. The ways in which anniversaries of acts of horrific violence – the murder of the 14 women engineering students in Montreal, the bombings in Bali, the destruction of Hiroshima – are marked can make a tremendous impact. Watching the children of the victims of 9/11 gather on September 11, 2002, to read out the names of their dead was a highly emotional experience. This reading of names was one way the United States as a nation coped with these deaths. It had more impact than any homily or speech or poem. Yet there was a finality there – as there is in this movie – that seemed without hope. What gives you hope about people you know who have died? What gives you hope when you consider your own death?

3. In some way, George's way of dealing with his coming death is to bury all thought of it in the house he is building. He tries to avoid what is to come by becoming "busy" with his house. Consider now that you, like all of us, are dying right now, right this moment. How do you deal with this thought?

19th Exercise
Overview of the Second Week

Set me as a seal on your heart,
As a seal on your arm;
For stern as death is love,
Relentless as the nether world is devotion;
Its flames are a blazing fire.
Deep waters cannot quench love,
Nor floods sweep it away.
Were one to offer all one owns to purchase love,
Such a person would be roundly mocked

(Song of Songs 8:6-7)

Let him desire and seek nothing except the greater praise and glory of God our Lord as the aim of all he does. For everyone must keep in mind that in all that concerns the spiritual life his progress will be in proportion to his surrender of his self-love and of his own will and interests.

(Sp. Ex. #189)

Grace: This is to ask for what I desire. Here it will be to ask for an intimate knowledge of our Lord, who has become man for me, that I may love Him more and follow Him more closely.

(Sp. Ex. #104)

The Journey So Far

If the First Week of the Exercises is falling in love, the Second Week is the engagement period. What distinguishes this Week is the growing familiarity between God and us as lovers. The grace we ask for is "an intimate knowledge of our Lord who has become human for me, that I may love Him more and follow Him more closely." In this intimacy, God reveals himself through the Christ and the Christ reveals his secret self, his relationship with the Father. He invites us to share that relationship; through that union we discover what it means to love him and to follow him out of love for him.

The First Week of the Exercises starts off within a fallen creation ruined by the malice of evil, but as we journey through it we discover a path to love that allows us to live in this world in a liberated way. The Second Week invites us deeper into that love, to put on the perspective of God and to see the world as capable of redemption. It further invites us to unite ourselves with God in working for that redemption. In this we not only enter God's world, but we allow God to enter into our world, for it is in our world that this redemption takes place.

To work concretely towards that redemption we need to know ourselves, as well as Jesus; we need to know how Jesus comes to us as well as how the enemies of our human nature lure us away. The easiest way of reflecting on this is to see how we react when we are vulnerable.

With Christ we can accept our vulnerability and the social shame that comes along with living in such an exposed way. This leads to the humility we identify with in Christ. Living from this stance creates community. Or we can flee from our vulnerability into forms of social approval that reinforce the walls around our ego. Then we remained trapped in nar-

195

cissism. To live freely in our vulnerability, we need the humility to ask God not only for help to recognize the pattern of our disorders and to resist them, but also for the grace to love and follow Jesus intimately in our daily life.

To do this we contemplate the life of Christ and the way that Christ's life operates in the world. We see what it is to have love enter our world in a vulnerable way and watch it grow to be mature and responsible. We see that this life lives not out of self-interest but out of authenticity, which constantly calls it beyond itself to risk in the world, trusting God's mercy to protect and sustain it in its needs and relationships. We see this love building relationships and trust; we see it challenging the forces of disorder that tend to deny or subvert the witness of God's love. As this Second Week draws to a close, we see this love, of which we are now a part, walking steadfastly into the face of a death arranged by those forces of disorder, its eyes and heart fixed firmly on the love of the Father, whom it trusts to redeem it from death.

When you reflect on this Second Week, review the way you have journeyed to the place you are at now. Look over your journal and see what has happened.

Walking to the Beloved

See how the freedom you felt at the beginning of this Week became focused and mature and grounded in your life. See if the decisions you have made to follow Christ more concretely in this world really allow you to do that. You can answer that by asking yourself if, as you continue to pray and reflect on Christ's life, you are closer to him or farther away. Whether you are making a decision or not, you can

reflect to see if you are more rooted in a life that allows you to face uncertainty more calmly and creatively. Check if you are enjoying life more and celebrating what is good, and facing responsibly the things you find destructive or debilitating.

If you find yourself rooted in the Father's love, you can continue your journey with Christ and be with him in his suffering, passion and death. This is the time of the naked and intimate embrace of God and the world. It is a time of God embracing us and us embracing God, as Jesus stretches out his hands to embrace both us and his Father.

The Embrace

Imagine someone running to God with arms full of gifts to give him, and God running to that person with arms full of the gifts he wants to give. They meet but they cannot embrace because both of their arms are full. If God puts down his gifts to embrace the beloved, God is seen as naked and vulnerable. This is not a God of power and might, but empty, humble, despised by the world. Often this is not the God we want to follow or get close to or even recognize. We turn away.

Instead of God putting down his gifts, imagine putting down our gifts to embrace God. Then we see ourselves in our abject nakedness, with our deceptions and fears, our selfishness and our disordered passions, and we turn away, ashamed, from that embrace.

The embrace can only happen if God puts down his gifts and we put down our gifts. The embrace can only happen if both have empty arms. In that emptiness is the intimacy of the lover with the beloved. The embrace is possible only if we experience deeply the commitment the Father has for us, and we trust and lean into what is offered in love. In the Third Week we will enter that loving embrace.

Questions for prayer and reflection

1. As you review this whole phase, what was your most life-giving moment? As you reflect on it, what does it mean in your life path?

2. What was your most desolate moment? What does it signify to you?

3. How does the pattern of riches, leading to honour and then pride, operate in your life?

4. How does the pattern of poverty, leading to social dismissal and then to humility, operate in your life?

5. What things would you like to do with your life, if you were free to do them? Would those things make you a better person and this world a better place to live in? What would be the cost of doing those things?

6. How do you share life with those you care about? How do you let them share life with you?

7. How do you deal with death in your life, in your world? How do you deal with the forces of death around you?

8. How do you celebrate life in the midst of a busy and chaotic world?

9. How do you find your rootedness? How do you maintain your relationship to that rootedness so it can support you in your daily life?

The Movie
Shrek

Director: Andrew Adamson et al. (2001 – 90 mins.)
Starring: the voices of Mike Myers, Eddie Murphy, Cameron Diaz, John Lithgow

1. Summary

This animated tale is set in the land of Duloc, in whose woods lives an ogre named Shrek who is feared by all. The heartless ruler of Duloc, Lord Farquaad, banishes all fairytale people from his lands into Shrek's woods. The only way Shrek can get his land back – and some peace and quiet – is to go on a quest to find the beautiful princess Fiona and bring her back to be marry Lord Farquaad, who will then become king. Accompanied by an irritating donkey, Shrek sets out to bring back Fiona, only to discover when he finds her that she is not quite the typical fairytale princess.

2. Questions about the Movie

1. "There is a moment in *Shrek* when the despicable Lord Farquaad has the Gingerbread Man tortured by dipping him into milk. This prepares us for another moment when Princess Fiona's singing voice is so piercing it causes jolly little bluebirds to explode; making the best of a bad situation, she fries their eggs. This is not your average family cartoon. Shrek is jolly and wicked, filled with sly in-jokes and yet somehow possessing a heart." (Roger Ebert, *Chicago Sun-Times*, May 18, 2001) We tend to think of ani- mated movies as something for children to watch, something we take them to or put on the DVD or video machine to keep them enter- tained. What makes *Shrek* an animated movie that works for adults in a different way than it works for children?

2. "But the technological innovations aren't what make this feisty movie entertainment so refresh- ing. Nor is it the story specifics themselves, which occasionally bobble and flag, particularly when Donkey is such an ass. Rather, Shrek lives happily ever after because it's such a feisty but good natured embrace of the inner ogre in every- one, and such an irreverent smackdown of the Establishment in all its "heigh ho" tyranny." (Lisa Schwarzbaum, *Entertainment Weekly*, May 16, 2001) What are some examples of the "inner ogre" in people around you, in people in the news, in yourself? What part of the establish- ment is *Shrek* going after with a "smackdown"?

3. "Funny, irreverent and moving, the unconven- tional *Shrek* may mock fairy tales, but in the process, creates its own. Without giving too much away, the picture questions notions of beauty, asking, just what is beautiful?" (Kim Morgan, *The Oregonian*, May 18, 2001) How does

the movie take conventional notions of the beautiful and turn them upside down? After seeing the movie, how would you answer the question "Just what is beautiful?"

3. The Relationship of the Movie to the Theme of the Exercise

1. Though Shrek is feared as something terrible, we see that he is a very lonely person. No one is allowed to come within his encircled property, and he has no friends. Perhaps this is his way of reinforcing the wall around his ego, of hiding from his vulnerability. How does Donkey break through all his defences? Why does Shrek allow Donkey to do that? What is the result?

2. The Exercise tells us that accepting our vulnerability will lead to humility, and that this will lead to community. Using examples from a number of scenes, trace Shrek's progress from his lack of true self-knowledge to his acceptance of his vulnerability. What community results from this for Shrek?

3. Here is a list of some of the ways that the divine love that the Exercises of the Second Week have called us to enter the world. What are the parallels to Shrek's quest for human love?

   • love enters in a vulnerable way and grows to be mature and responsible

   • love builds relationships and trusts

   • love challenges the forces of disorder in the world

4. The Relationship of the Movie to One's Self in the Exercise

1. What are the "riches, honour and pride" that Shrek has put together for himself before he is forced to leave his home? How similar are these to your own pattern of "riches, honour and pride"? How does Shrek deal with them? How do you plan to deal with yours?

2. Shrek is a very vulnerable creature – partly because of what he is (an ogre) and partly because of the way he has come to see himself. He has to learn to accept this and deal with it (consider his reaction to what he overhears between the princess and the donkey late one night towards the end of the journey). The humility he comes to is hard won. What in your life makes you vulnerable? What allows you to accept this vulnerability? What happens when you do accept it?

3. On his journey, Shrek takes time to reflect on himself in many different ways. The journey becomes for him a voyage of self-discovery. This Exercise is an overview of the Second Week – a voyage of discovery for you. Looking back on this week – and on what you have written in your journal – what has been the most significant thing that you have discovered about yourself in your relationship with God?

Part 3

The Third Week – A Passionate Love

1st Exercise
Preparation for the Third Week

O Lord my God in you do I take refuge;
Save me from all my pursuers, and deliver me,
Lest like a lion they rend me,
Dragging me away with none to rescue.

(Psalm 7:1-2)

Consider how the divinity hides itself; for example, it could destroy its enemies and does not do so, but leaves the most sacred humanity to suffer so cruelly.

(Sp. Ex. #196)

Grace: This is to ask for what I desire. Here it will be to ask for sorrow, compassion, and shame because the Lord is going to His suffering for my sins.

(Sp. Ex.#193)

Sharing the Beloved's Pain

In the Third Week we follow Christ from the Last Supper to his entombment. The grace we pray for is to be as present as possible to him as he journeys through loneliness, pain, humiliation and death to the Father. It is a huge grace to be simply present to another's suffering without running away, falling back into ourselves or trying to remedy the situation. The Christ has chosen to walk to the Father. The circumstances of his life and times have conspired to make this part of his journey as destructive as humanly possible. Yet, in the face of that horror, he does not turn away. We ask for the grace to be with him as we would be with someone we love who is betrayed by friends, wrongfully accused by the religious and political authorities, mocked and tortured by their underlings, and then shamefully left to die on a cross. In being present to him as he endures all of this we share his pain and sorrow.

It is not our pain and sorrow we hold, but his. This phase is not about us – it is about going out of ourselves in compassion to embrace the beloved in his time of greatest need.

What is awe-ful about the drama of the Third Week is the destruction of human good and, in fact, what is best about human nature – by sin, as manifested in personal, social and cultural relationships. Sin moves to make life meaningless; we need to walk through those deserts of meaninglessness to discover that there is an indestructible base to human nature: God's love for each of us. This is the most difficult human journey we can make, but we know it is possible because Jesus has made it, as a human being. In making this journey he breaks the tyranny that the fear of death holds over us, and he breaks that fatal human illusion that insists we are determined fully by our social conditions and even by the stories we tell ourselves. He shows that even when everything is stripped away and we are left as naked desire, even beyond emotion, that desire leans into the Love that created and sustained it and now redeems it. This love does not ignore any of the brutal realities of sin or reduce its consequences. Rather, it shows a love that is stronger than any evil, a light that refuses to be put out by any darkness, a compassion that will not turn aside from any horror.

Entering Mystery

When we enter into situations that reflect this constant reality, we are carried beyond ourselves into silence and stillness. Here we enter a mystery that is so personal and so beyond our own imagining that we feel we have entered a sacred space. We sense our unworthiness and finitude, which manifests in the graces that Ignatius asks us to pray for at this time of shame and confusion. This is not breast-beating or a guilt trip that subtly affirms the ego, it is simply the mode of felt experience of finitude in the presence of the holy.

For St. Ignatius, spirituality is very practical. He asks what we ought to do and suffer for Christ now that we have become intimates with him. We are invited to share in the work and the path of the beloved in the concrete circumstances of our lives. This is not a form of masochism or some contract of repayment. Here we might want to consider how Moses, after encountering God in the burning bush (Exodus 3:1-12), is invited to share in God's work of liberation. We can only respond to that invitation if we ourselves are free, for we cannot give others what we do not have ourselves. Intimacy with the divine makes us free; it is that freedom we see when we follow Jesus as he freely chooses to hand himself over to the Father's will, even as the powers of this world capture and torture him. In these prayer periods we can exercise our freedom by being as present as we can to that witness of freedom. It leads to resurrection, a life that encompasses and goes beyond the powers of this world.

Questions for prayer and reflection

1. Have you ever been present to the dying of someone you loved? How did you feel? What stages of being present did you go through?

2. How was God present to you at that time? How were the people who are close to you present? How were you present to yourself?

3. How did you survive that experience? How has it shaped the rest of your life?

4. When you consider the significant people of your time, or in your life, who have struggled for justice, freedom, human rights, or for a more human and loving life, how does your spirit react? Stay with that feeling and see what it brings to you.

5. How do you enter the quiet heroism of daily living, and the quiet martyrdoms it calls forth?

6. When have you had an experience when your circumstances caused you to behave in ways that took you out of yourself? As you re-enter that experience, now in a more self-conscious and prayerful manner, what does it tell you about yourself? What does it tell you about the forces around you? What does it tell you about your God?

7. Sit with this reflection. What parts move you particularly? Go back to each of these moments and stay with them. What else can you find there? What is revealed to you?

The Movie
Dancer in the Dark

Director: Lars Von Trier (2000 – 140 mins.)
Starring: Bjork, Catherine Deneuve, David Morse, Joel Grey

1. Summary

A single mother, Selma, has emigrated with her son, Gene, to America from eastern Europe in 1964. Because of a genetic defect, Selma will inevitably go blind. To prevent the same thing from happening to her son, Selma struggles to make money working in a factory – not only to make ends meet but also to save money for an operation for Gene. Her life is made bearable by her ability to pretend that she is living in the wonderful world of Hollywood musicals, but when she is fired from her job, her life changes.

2. Questions about the Movie

1. "Since it is impossible to take the plot seriously on any literal level, it must be approached, I think, as a deliberate exercise in soap opera. It is valid to dislike it, but not fair to criticize it on the grounds of plausibility, because the movie has made a deliberate decision to be implausible: The plot is not a mistake but a choice.... *Dancer in the Dark* is a brave throwback to the fundamentals of the cinema—to heroines and villains, noble sacrifices and dastardly betrayals. The relatively crude visual look underlines the movie's abandonment of slick modernism." (Roger Ebert,

Chicago Sun-Times, October 20, 2000) What an unusual movie this is! People either like it or hate it. But either way, it is a movie with something to say, and it says it with a certain style. What do you think the director was attempting to say with this movie?

2. "There are undeniable pleasures to be gained from submitting to luxuriant emotions you suspect are fake.... *Dancer* recalls such weepies as *Stella Dallas* (1937) or *Camille* (1936) – pictures where misunderstood women suffered and performed acts of saintly masochism. But those classic melodramas were motivated by a belief in the beauty of distilled pathos. Here, von Trier appears to be up to something more duplicitous. Indeed, the main difficulty presented by the movie is determining how far it can be taken straight." (Peter Matthews, *Sight and Sound*, October 2000) In trying to decide whether to accept the critic's point of view, think about the closing scenes of the movie. Are they "obscene"? Are they devastating? Why? Why not?

3. "Over the course of more than two hours the viewer is thrown from moments of harrowing realism – scenes whose jumpy rhythm and raw immediacy make you feel as if you're peeking

205

through the window at a moment of private misery – to flights of fantastic absurdity. The one constant presence, and the single force that keeps the movie from collapsing under its contradictory ambitions, is Selma." (A.O. Scott, *The New York Times*, September 22, 2000). What attracts us to Selma? How is the fact that Selma is "mentally challenged" – as is her friend Jeff – handled in the movie? This is the first time that Bjork, a singer, has acted. What is it about her person, her performance, that keeps our attention?

4. "The musical numbers, which grow organically out of the near-blind Selma's detection of music and rhythm in the pounding thrum of factory noise, are affirmations of the magic in the ordinary – railway workers may swing hammers like canes and kick like Kelly, but they remain railway workers. And when people sing, they sing of the flight-giving wonder of singing itself: 'We'll always be there to catch you,' goes one particularly apt lyric… This is fantasy firmly grounded in the soil of the everyday, and fully aware of its populist power of denial." (Geoff Pevere, *Toronto Star*, September 22, 2000) There is no way to avoid talking about the use of musical numbers in the movie. How are the musical numbers integral to the movie? What, for example, is Selma saying to us about herself in "I've Seen It All"?

3. The Relationship of the Movie to the Theme of the Exercise

1. As we prepare through the Exercise to enter into the Third Week and to be with Christ in his passion, how does the movie correspond to the passion of Christ? Consider Selma's love for her son and what she does for him; consider her betrayal, her capture, her trial, her sentence, and – finally – the horror of her death. Then ask yourself how ready you are to follow Christ in his journey.

2. In the Third Week you will exercise your freedom by being present as you can to Christ. How are Selma's two friends – Cathy and Jeff – present to her during her passion and death?

3. The horror and brutality of the act of crucifixion is mirrored in the horrific and realistic portrayal of the hanging that ends the movie. We know why we are moved by the death of Christ, but why are we moved by the death of Selma?

4. The Relationship of the Movie to One's Self in the Exercise

1. During the Third Week you will follow Christ through the terror and horror of his Passion and death. In this movie, you will probably turn away from the horror of Selma's death. If the death of a woman in a movie can have such an impact on you, where will you find the strength to follow Christ and be there for him in his passion and death during this Third Week? This is not a movie but reality. Will you be able to face this reality?

2. Selma was betrayed and left alone by those she considered her friends. Christ was also betrayed, and though he was left alone by his friends, he was not alone. God was with him on this terrible journey. In your life, have you had to go through a "passion" such as the loss of a loved one? Who was there for you at that time?

3. Selma's love for her son, Gene, is one that is, as we read in this Exercise, a love that is stronger than any evil, a light that refuses to be put out by any darkness, a compassion that will not turn aside from any horror. She gives her life for her son. Where in your life do you find such a love?

2nd Exercise
The Last Supper
(Matthew 26:20-30; John 13:1-30)

While we were still helpless, at the right time Christ died for the ungodly. Why, one will hardly die for a righteous person — though perhaps for a good person one will dare even to die. But God shows his love for us in that while we were yet sinners Christ died for us.

(Romans 5:6-8)

Consider what Christ our Lord suffers in His human nature.

(Sp. Ex. #195)

Grace: This is to ask for what I desire. Here it will be to ask for sorrow, compassion, and shame because the Lord is going to His suffering for my sins.

(Sp. Ex. #193)

Celebrating Freedom

In Western culture, our ideas of the Last Supper are strongly coloured by religious paintings of the event and by the piety that surrounds the eucharistic liturgies that derive from it. From these we have received such a formal notion of that meal that we have lost sight of its profoundly passionate celebration of life. The meal celebrates Passover, when the Israelite people gained their freedom from their oppressors, the Egyptians, and started their long journey through the desert to form a religious identity. At that meal, families and friends gather to remember and retell that story, to celebrate God's particular and practical concern for them. That gathering celebrates who they are, God's chosen, and celebrates their intimate relationship with God, which is manifest in what that God has done for them.

In the Passover meal that Christ shared with his friends, he celebrates what it means to be God's chosen: to bear witness to God's mercy, to hope even when there is no cause for optimism, to serve even the self-interested, to give over one's very life to make sure that others receive life. In living this way Christ takes up the meaning of the Jewish Passover and transforms it into something that reveals more of God's intimacy with us. In doing so he reveals to us at a deeper level who we really are and what we are capable of.

Jesus does not deny the past. As a Jewish man, and a rabbi, he has a profound sense of his religious history. But he does not understand himself totally in terms of the past and the texts of the past. He understands himself most fully in terms of his relationship with his Father. He has a personal relationship with God. The Lord becomes Abba, and Jesus is willing to share that relationship with us. The God who saves the Israelites becomes the one who saves each one of us, and all of us.

What Jesus does at the Passover meal is what every one of us does at our family celebrations. We remember the past with the ones who share life with us, and each year we bring something new to that gathering. We bring what has happened to each of us, and we tend to discuss those happenings in that ritual context so that they become part of that occasion.

The ritual gathering on that particular evening becomes more than the celebration of surviving another year under Roman occupation, more than the revival of the hope of yet another liberation from foreign oppression. For Christ, it allows the entry into a new dispensation that allows us freedom in the world, but not the freedom of worldly standards and methods. With the meal he offers, he gives the way of being united with God in more than just memory and ritual. In making the bread and wine he blesses real manifestations of himself, he ensures that his essence remains with those with whom he shares his life and mission. We become what we eat. And what we become is partakers of the same relationship that he has with the Father. It gives a peace the world cannot give, and a rootedness that transcends this world's limitations.

In that rootedness lies freedom and focus. When we love someone, we open ourselves to that person. We give our very selves over to the beloved. We become the beloved, and the beloved, in accepting our gift, becomes us. In Jesus' founding of this new ritual using the elements of the Passover meal, our unity with God is established in a way that is as real and as physical as our own bodies.

The Gift of Mercy

Christ accomplishes this under the most trying circumstances. The people he had gathered around him, had worked with and trained, had celebrated life with and to whom he had revealed all that was given to him to reveal, had not been converted. One would betray him; the rest would abandon him in his hard times. Yet he sees past who they are to what they are capable of. He sees, knows and loves them in ways they do not yet see and know and love themselves. So what he offers to them he offers in hope: hope that what he is doing will make them aware of their deepest identity as able to witness with their lives to God's love for the world. He knows that even after being with him for three years they are riddled with self-interest and ambition. They do not yet understand that love is attentive and disinterested service to the world.

So he serves them. At that Last Supper he washes their feet. Normally this was the role of a servant for guests who had just arrived with dusty feet, or a sign of hospitality for a dignitary. This is humble service, and was never done by the master of the house. While Christ is humbling himself, the disciples are concerned with prestige and with who will be the first in that new kingdom Christ was establishing. They do not see this kingdom in terms of loving service to the Father and to each other. They do not even understand that Christ's whole life was one of service, of returning a fallen and dismayed world to its true identity. So, even with his heart breaking and with the awareness of what was coming next, he performs an act that shows them how to act: he washes their feet. This is not the posturing of honour and pride, nor is it the abjection that comes from a corrupt self-image and false humility. It is the response to a question: How do we celebrate who our neighbour is?

Offered to All

How do we act in this world to bring it life, and to share that life? What do we do to create and maintain the common good? Jesus' answer is humble service. Peter cannot understand or accept this humility.

He refuses to have his feet washed until Jesus replies that unless he allows his feet to be washed he cannot know who it is whom he follows, and thus cannot be one with him. It takes humility to offer a gift; but it also takes humility to receive a gift, accept it, open it and live it. It is this gift of transforming life that Jesus offers and Peter finally accepts. This is the gift that the mercy of God offers to all.

But in the story of the Last Supper, one person refuses that gift and that mercy. Judas leaves that community Christ is establishing and goes to betray him. The gospels tell us that Judas Iscariot kept the community's money and stole from it. In Ignatian terms, from the Two Standards, he chose riches rather than poverty. Scholars have suggested that the relationship between Jesus and Judas fractured because of Judas' ideology. He may have been a zealot who wanted Jesus to use his powers to overturn the political oppression and social corruption of the day. He understood the Messianic rule in secular terms. He was unwilling to follow Jesus' trust in the Father to bring about that new creation. He preferred Jesus to follow him. When it became clear to Judas that Jesus' way was not what Judas wanted, his bitter disappointment led to his rejection of Jesus. We may wonder why Jesus tolerated Judas in the first place. We may wonder about his skills of discerning his disciples. We may even wonder about that today. But Jesus' position is that no one is to be lost. He offers himself to all without reserve. When we look at the other apostles we discover that they are equally venal and self-serving. We may even find ourselves among them.

What Christ offers to his companions at the Last Supper, he also offers to us. We may wonder at his choice. But he knows us better than we know ourselves. He knows how fickle we are; but he also knows that we are capable of being one with him, following him, and sharing his life, joyfully and simply. He knows we are capable of love.

Questions for prayer and reflection

1. What are your moments of deepest meaning when you reflect on the Last Supper in one of the Gospels (e.g. John 13:1-30)? Why do those moments touch you in this way? How do they reflect on your life's journey?

2. Think of an incident where someone you know (e.g., a family member) gave his or her life so that others might have a better life. How did that affect your life?

3. When has someone hoped in you even when you did not hope in yourself? How do you think that changed your life?

4. When you contemplate the Last Supper, where are you in the action?

5. Have you ever been offered a gift you could not pay back? How do you deal with gratitude?

6. Think of some times when your humility brought you a great deal of freedom. What happened?

7. Think of a situation when things stopped going according to what you had planned or hoped. How did you discern what to do next?

8. Think of a time when you betrayed yourself or someone else. How did you find forgiveness?

9. What happens if you do not find forgiveness? Can you allow yourself to be held in God's mercy even then?

The Movie
The Quiet American

Director: Phillip Noyce (2002 – 101 mins.)
Starring: Michael Caine, Brendan Fraser, Do Thi Hai Yen

1. Summary

Based on Graham Greene's novel of love, betrayal and murder and set in 1952 Saigon, *The Quiet American* is the story of a triangle – romantic and political. The three are Thomas Fowler, a jaded British journalist; Alden Pyle, an idealistic American aid worker; and Thomas' young Vietnamese mistress, Phoung.

2. Questions about the Movie

1. "Though it is set in Vietnam before the U.S. got involved on an earthshaking scale, Greene's novel is extremely discerning about what it is in the American character – the messianic zeal, the sureness of being right – that made what came later inevitable. Its message (characterized by the novel's opening Byron quote about an 'age of new inventions / For killing bodies, and for saving souls / All propagated with the best intentions') couldn't be more relevant as we get ready to storm into yet another troubled country very far away." (Kenneth Turan, *Los Angeles Times*, November 22, 2002). There was discussion of either delaying or limiting the release of the film following 9/11. Michael Caine personally campaigned for its release. Why would the studio be reluctant to distribute widely and promote this movie? What is it in the movie that might reflect badly on the US?

2. "Phillip Noyce's movie pares away the novel's meditations on the futility of war and the importance of religion. It retains the book's thoughtful blending of psychological and moral issues, however, and shows how well-meaning people can bring disaster through blind faith in the virtuousness of their ideas." (David Sterritt, *Christian Science Monitor*, November 22, 2002) Almost the only mention of religion in the movie deals with Fowler's wife refusing to grant a divorce on the grounds that she is Catholic. Where do you think the movie removed references to religion? Why did they do this?

3. "Greene said that only a sense of humour allowed him to believe in God; the same thing applies to believing in Michael Caine. He's as stately as a galleon as he pads about the bars and streets of Saigon. But when he has a sharp comment, a witty remark, a passionate insult, his performance flashes with energy. He groans at being called home by the paper, and his assistant says: "I thought you liked London?" "I like it fine. I like it just where it is," he snaps. For a second he's

transformed; Fowler is human." (Peter Bradshaw, *The Guardian*, November 29, 2002) What is it about Caine's acting that makes you believe in him? How does Caine show the humanity of Fowler, the love Fowler has for Phoung? What use does Caine make of silences?

4. *"The Quiet American...*couldn't be more timely with its critique of the arrogance of a nation that sets out to be a moral policeman for the world. In the end, violence touches more than the innocent civilians who die in the blast. Perhaps the best quotation for this riveting film is from the Protestant theologian Reinhold Neibuhr: 'The self-righteous are guilty of history's greatest cruelties. Most evil is done by good people who do not know that they are good." (Frederic and Mary Ann Brussat, *Spirituality and Health*, November 22, 2002) How does Neibuhr's comment apply to the movie? To the characters of Fowler and Pyle?

3. The Relationship of the Movie to the Theme of the Exercise

1. Jesus washes the feet of his apostles to show them that his life is one of service to the world – as theirs and ours must be. This is Christ's response to three questions:

    • How do we celebrate who our neighbour is?
    • How do we act in this world to bring it life?
    • How do we create and maintain the common good?

    How do Fowler and Pyle respond to these questions in the movie?

2. When we love someone, as we learn from the Exercise,

    • we open ourselves to that person
    • we give ourselves over to the beloved
    • we become the beloved, and the beloved, in accepting us, becomes us.

    Fowler tells Pyle that "to lose her would be the beginning of death." Considering these points, do you think that either Fowler or Pyle truly loves Phoung?

3. Within Christ's own disciples was the one who would betray him – one who chose riches over poverty. How are the main characters in the movie – each in their own way – betrayers? What are the "riches" each of them chooses over "poverty"? Whose is the greatest betrayal? Why?

4. The Relationship of the Movie to One's Self in the Exercise

1. As the Exercise tells us, we see that the apostles are venal and self-serving much as Alden Pyle was. What characteristics of yourself do you see in Pyle? In the apostles?

2. When Fowler and Pyle go north and see the dead villagers, Pyle says that "it's not easy to remain uninvolved." Fowler wonders what that does to Pyle's zeal and to his own detachment. As you contemplate the Last Supper, what might stop you from becoming "involved" in it? What would that do to your "zeal" and your "detachment"?

3. In the movie we hear: "Sooner or later one has to take sides – to remain human," and "Maybe people aren't who we think they are." "Who of us is?"

    When have you taken sides? On what issue? In doing this do you put on a face – as Pyle does – for the faces that you meet? What is the main obstacle to being who people think you are?

3rd Exercise
The Agony in the Garden
(Matthew 26:30-46; Mark 14:32-44)

Abba, Father, all things are possible to you; remove this cup from me; yet not what I will but what you will.

(Mark 14:36)

Take, Lord, and receive all my liberty, my memory, my understanding, and my entire will, all that I have and possess. You have given all to me. To You, O Lord, I return it. All is Yours, dispose of it wholly according to Your will. Give me Your love and Your grace, for this is sufficient for me.

(Sp. Ex. #234)

Grace: This is to ask for what I desire. Here it will be to ask for sorrow, compassion, and shame because the Lord is going to His suffering for my sins.

(Sp. Ex. #193)

Freedom and Liberty

There is a difference between freedom and liberty. When we are free, we can make choices that affect our lives, even though we might not be at liberty. This is because we are connected to the source of our life. On the other hand, we might have liberty but not be free: even though we are able to move around, we might be trapped in compulsions and oppressive systems. When Christ leaves with his remaining companions after the Last Supper and goes to the Mount of Olives, he experiences his last moments of liberty and the agonizing tension between freedom and liberty.

If he keeps his liberty he must give up his freedom, his union with the Father, which allows him to be indifferent to the things of this world. If he keeps his liberty he could escape those coming to capture and kill him but then he would no longer be true to his deepest sense of identity. If he keeps his freedom, on the other hand, he will be captured and killed. The tension is agony for him; he prays for the strength to be true to himself and to the God he loves. The choice is between security and identity: he has reached the intensely emotional stage where he has to make an existential choice. In handing over his life to the Father he knows that he is handing his body over to torture and death.

Struck by Terror

We, too, are faced with moments of radical choice in which we are asked to abandon familiar and established ways of doing things and to strike out on our own. Like Christ, we find that our friends and companions are not with us. They might like us and be generally sympathetic to us, but ultimately we are alone. Even when we turn to God in prayer we find emptiness and an absence of consolation. We are struck by terror.

This terror undermines our courage, our connectedness with ourselves and with others; it erodes our self-confidence; and we find ourselves in a no-man's land where our very sense of identity erodes. What are we to do in that situation? Like Christ, we must

213

abandon ourselves to divine providence. We wait. We pray desperately in that darkness. We hand over our lives to the forces beyond our control. We act with the integrity of being kind when we can and being patient when we must. We accept that suffering as it is received, be it through the indifference of our friends or through the realization that we have fallen through the bombed out constructions of the world and its illusions of security. There is no comfort there. We go through the motions of living. As the psalmist says, "O my God, I cry by day, but you do not answer and by night, but find no rest" (Ps 22:3).

Christ enters this intensely human and dark space at Gethsemane. All through Jerusalem, families and friends are celebrating Passover; he has finished his. Oppressed by what awaits him, he goes to one of his favourite places to pray with his close friends. The place offers no comfort; his friends get tired and fall asleep. Even Peter, who promises to remain with him and who vows never to betray him, cannot stay awake. Jesus is alone. He prays to his Father, in the intimacy of that relationship, for the upcoming trial to be taken from him, but affirms that all he wants to do is the will of that mysterious one he calls "Abba." As he prays, he comes to the understanding that if redemption is to be achieved, then he must go through with what lies ahead.

Leaning into the Darkness

He embraces his Father's will, and in this embrace his prayer moves from seeking an escape from suffering to accepting that suffering. In that acceptance he moves from being resigned to divine providence to actively participating in that providence. Within this movement we do not see the Father's presence. Christ receives no assurances that things will turn out right. Throughout his life, Christ has always actively participated in the workings of the divine providence of the Father. To reach that level of co-operation he has learned to wait on the Father, and his waiting here is not hopeless. He leans into the darkness, painful though it is, to say yes to what will happen, because he trusts the Father. His "yes" is more than passively hearing. It says, "I will maintain that integrity that has been my life path." That integrity has been manifested in his three years of public ministry. It has been a constant and loving dependence on the Father's mercy. It will be maintained now even in the face of God's silence.

Jesus arrives at this hard-earned moment and returns to his companions to find that Judas and a band of soldiers have come to arrest him. The public drama of his passion is about to begin. His liberty is taken away and he is prey to the whole range of human evil, from malicious brutality to the cowardice of political authority. In the presence of all these he maintains his freedom, his relationship to the Father.

Questions for prayer and reflection

1. When you read and prayed the scripture passages, were you able to stay with Jesus? What kind of resistances came up? What do they suggest to you?

2. When you spent time with the above reflection on Christ in the garden, what aspects struck you? Did they cause any aspect of your life to rise to your awareness? What was significant about those aspects? How do you deal with them? Can you bring them now to God and stay with those moments? What happens when you do that?

3. How do you live your freedom? What would you consider to be areas of freedom in your life? What would be areas of unfreedom? How do they manifest themselves in terms of this prayer exercise?

4. Recall times when you risked your life in some moment of self-transcendence even though you knew that it would be painful? Is there a common pattern to those moments? What does that pattern tell you about your relationship to God?

5. What areas of your life or your world do you despair over? Does that despair make you frozen or resigned? How can you start to move within that despair? Can you move from resignation, to passive acceptance, to active acceptance? Can you imagine that movement? What does it do to your sense of rootedness?

6. When have you been present to others as they made critical decisions about their lives? How did you find them? How did you find yourselves with them?

7. After reflecting on and praying through these questions, what sense do you have of yourself? Can you accept that sense of self?

The Movie
Igby Goes Down

Director: Burr Steers (2002 – 97 mins.)
Starring: Kieran Culkin, Clare Danes, Jeff Goldblum, Ryan Phillippe, Susan Sarandon

1. Summary

Igby Slocumb, age 17, has a few problems: a schizophrenic father; a self-absorbed, distant and dying mother; a Young Republican big brother; a bored sometime lover; a scheming godfather (complete with druggie mistress). Having flunked out of most of the prep schools on the East coast, Igby tries to hide in New York's underworld. His goal – to stop himself from "going down."

2. Questions about the Movie

1. "Movies like this depend above all on the texture of the performances, and it is easy to imagine *Igby Goes Down* as a sitcom in which the characters don't quite seem to understand the witty things they're saying. All of the actors here have flair and presence, and get the joke, and because they all affect a kind of neo-Wildean irony toward everything, they belong in the same world. It is refreshing to hear Igby refer to his 'Razor's Edge experience' without the movie feeling it is necessary to have him explain what he is talking about." (Roger Ebert, *Chicago Sun-Times*, September 20, 2002) How similar/dissimilar is this movie to a sit-com? What characteristics are typical of a sit-com? How does this movie fit/not fit them?

2. "Igby is, in fact, so irritating that people periodically feel impelled to lash out and hit him out of sheer frustration at the smugness of his baby rebellion." (Kenneth Turan, *Los Angeles Times*, September 13, 2002) Igby's brother tells him: "I think if Gandhi had to spend a prolonged amount of time with you, he'd end up beating the crap out of you too." What is it about Igby that makes people want to hit him, to punish him? At the same time as you might want to hit him, what makes you want to reach out to him?

3. "Sarcasm is Igby's best weapon against emotional battering, even as he slides into drug dealing after Sookie leaves him for Oliver (a rare plot misstep), and he endures a final face-off with his mother on her deathbed. Sarandon expertly mines the scene's gallows humor. But Culkin touches a raw nerve, letting it all bleed as Igby finally drops a lifetime of defenses. You don't expect grit and grace notes in a movie built for laughs like *Igby Goes Down*." (Peter Travers, *Rolling Stone*, October 3, 2002) What do the scenes at the end of the film – the death of Igby's mother, his reaction, and what follows – say about Igby's

character? What kind of growth has he undergone since the opening scenes of the movie?

4. "This film and Salinger's novel [*The Catcher in the Rye*] differ greatly in the details of narrative and character. Yet, there's no mistaking the similarity in tone and sensibility and, particularly, in the capacity to split an audience into warring camps fighting on shared ground. That is, Igby-revilers and Igby-lovers will base their conclusion on precisely the same evidence: The kid's a lying little bastard; he's troubled, self-involved, affects a smug superiority to the many phonies around him, and makes repeated claims on our sympathies he doesn't fully deserve. Yes, Igby, like Holden and all those other alienated youths from Hamlet the Dane to Benjamin the Graduate, is quite a box of parts." (Rick Groen, *The Globe and Mail*, September 27, 2002) How closely would you agree with Groen's assessment of Igby?

3. The Relationship of the Movie to the Theme of the Exercise

1. The Exercise tells us that in our lives we face moments of radical choice. What radical choice does Igby face at the end of the movie? What does his mother do for him just before she dies that both affirms and attacks him, causing him to be confirmed in his need to make this radical choice?

2. This radical choice requires us to abandon familiar things and strike out on our own. Even our friends are not with us. How alone is Igby at the end of the movie as he makes his decision? What

support does he have from his brother? His girlfriend? His godfather?

3. This radical choice eventually causes us to turn and abandon ourselves to Divine Providence. What does Igby turn to in the movie that might be a symbol of Divine Providence? Igby appears to be from a Catholic family: what is the role of religion in his life?

4. The Relationship of the Movie to One's Self in the Exercise

1. The Exercise helps us to see the difference between freedom and liberty. Look back to review the difference between the two. Does Igby have freedom or liberty? Or neither? What is one moment of radical choice in your life? How did you approach it? In liberty? In freedom?

2. One of Igby's moments of radical choice happens at the very end of the movie. How did he react? At one of your own moments of radical choice, when you felt alone and without any self-confidence, what did you do? Did you consider abandoning yourself to Divine Providence? If you did, what happened?

3. Towards the end of the movie it appears that Ollie, Igby's brother, will make a move to comfort and support Igby, to help him as he makes his radical choice. It even seems as if his mother will offer Igby some support. But in neither case is this to be. When have you watched a friend or lover make a "radical choice"? What did you do to support that person?

4th Exercise

The Betrayal

(Matthew 26:47-58; Luke 22:47-57; Mark 14:44-54, 66-68)

If we say we have no sin we deceive ourselves and the truth is not in us. If we confess our sins, [God] is faithful and just, and will forgive our sins, and cleanse us from all unrighteousness.

(1 John 1:8-9)

We must carefully observe the whole course of our thoughts. If the beginning and middle and end of the course of thoughts are wholly good and directed to what is entirely right, it is a sign that they are from the good angel. But the course of thoughts suggested to us may terminate in something evil, or distracting, or less good than the soul had formally proposed to do. Again, it may end in what weakens the soul, or disquiets it; or by destroying the peace, tranquillity, and quiet which it had before, it may cause disturbance to the soul. These things are a clear sign that the thoughts are proceeding from the evil spirit, the enemy of our progress and eternal salvation.

(Sp. Ex. #333)

Grace: This is to ask for what I desire. Here it will be to ask for sorrow, compassion, and shame because the Lord is going to His suffering for my sins.

(Sp. Ex. #193)

Intimate Acts of Violence

After the intense inner journey to freedom in the Garden, Jesus is taken captive by the temple guards. When Judas identifies him with a kiss, Jesus is seized. Someone tries to defend him by striking out at the high priest's servant. In the ensuing conflict, a young man runs off naked. The guards bring Jesus to the courtyard of the high priest where, as he waits, he hears Peter deny him three times. The sequence revolves around the shame of betrayal and of Jesus' response to that betrayal.

Betrayal is an intimate act of violence. The integrity of the person betrayed is shattered: the betrayer has entered a personal space through trust and has violated it. Betrayal destroys the bonds of human relationships and undermines those connections that make us who we are. The betrayals Jesus endures here eat away at his confidence in human nature to maintain the sense of community he strove to witness to. He sees clearly, as the prophet Jeremiah does, that there is nothing so devious and desperately corrupt as the human heart (Jer 17:9). But even here he holds onto what the Father sees of the human heart, rather than what he is experiencing.

The Father sees that heart as lovable and loving, and it is out of that same heart that Jesus sees and lives.

It is this Jesus whom Judas identifies with a kiss to the crowd coming with clubs and swords to seize him. Judas' despair has turned to malice, and his kiss reveals the opposite of what it is symbolizes. It is a lie. Lies destroy relationships – it is no wonder that Satan is called the prince of lies. He stands for the destruction of community, as the Christ stands for the creation of community. Judas' kiss betrays the

218

spirit of community, the creation of which is Christ's mission on earth. Yet Jesus does not react by rejecting Judas. He still calls him "Friend." What Jesus sees in Judas, Judas cannot see in himself. It is because he is caught in his self-image that he later destroys himself; he cannot live with what he has done. God's mercy asks us to live out of God's image of us. It says that no matter what we have done, we are forgiven. We need to learn to accept that forgiveness. Here we can do that by being as present as we can to Christ as he manifests the extent of that forgiveness. His fidelity to the Father and to us, even in his suffering and death, shows that we will not be abandoned. We are asked to dare to believe that and to live out of that belief. It is the path to liberation.

Often we think, and often it is true, that we need to fight for what is right. and that those acts of resistance bring liberation. But here, when the person defends Jesus by cutting off the servant's ear, he is using violence in reaction to violence. Jesus has accepted his path; the violence enacted here tries to stop Jesus from walking his path.

As Ecclesiastes says, there is "a time for war and a time for peace" (Ecc 3:8). How can we know the right thing to do at a particular time? That knowledge comes from doing as Christ does, from putting on the mind and heart of Christ. Here, at his arrest, Jesus does not resist his capture. The one who tries to defend him is not one with Jesus. This is another type of betrayal, no less significant than Judas'. It says, like Judas, I know the best way for God to act. Once again, self-will displaces obedience to God's will.

It is important if you are making a discernment at this time, to examine yourself to see if the choice you make allows you to be present to Jesus as he is, rather than attempt to conscript him to your cause. If it is

the latter, either self-righteousness is leading the way or you will be exposed the way the young man in the story is exposed.

Naked to My Enemies

Mark's Gospel tells us that story: "A young man followed him, with nothing but a linen cloth about his body; and they seized him, but he left the linen cloth and ran away naked" (Mark 14:51-52). Had the young man allowed himself to be seized, he would not have been thus exposed, but he chose his own security and his own shame rather than accompany Jesus. It may be a little story, but it contains the same dynamics as that of Cardinal Wolsey, who sacrificed his integrity and his vocation to serve his king, Henry the Eighth (1485–1547), a contemporary of Ignatius and the early Jesuits. When Wolsey had served Henry's worldly purposes, Henry had him deposed for high treason. Wolsey is reported to have said, "Had I served my God with half the zeal I had served my king, He would not have left me thus naked to mine enemies." This betrayal occurred, Wolsey realized, because the values he held did not arise from a living, passionate and intimate relationship with God.

The Long Last Night

When Jesus is taken, he is carried to the high priest. There, many false witnesses come and testify against him, but since they do not agree among themselves, the high priest asks Jesus directly if he is equal to God. Saying yes meant he was guilty of blasphemy under Jewish law, since no one was the equal of God. The punishment for such blasphemy was death. Even knowing the law, Jesus refuses to betray his relationship with the Father. He is true to

219

that intimacy even though he is humiliated by being spat upon and beaten up by those in the high priest's house.

Outside in the courtyard, though, is one who had followed him so far: Peter, with whom Jesus had an especially close relationship. It is Peter whom he had appointed as his right-hand man; Peter who first recognized him as the Messiah; Peter who saw his transfiguration, who was rescued at the walking on the water. That same Peter had said he would never betray Jesus no matter what. Yet when those in the courtyard ask whether he is a follower of Jesus, he denies this relationship three times. At the third time, when a cock crowed twice, Peter remembered that Jesus had said to him, "Before the cock crows twice, you will deny me three times" (Mark 14:72). He breaks down and weeps. He realizes that despite his special intimacy with the Christ, he is no different from all those others who betrayed the ones they love. He betrays himself in his denial of Christ. His self-image cannot withstand the pressures of the social situation. It isn't that he doesn't know and love Jesus. He does. But here he is a coward. To this point, Peter is brash, impetuous, charismatic. But he lacks courage, a heart bonded to Jesus' heart.

It was sundown when the Passover meal was celebrated. Morning has not yet broken. Jesus waits. He has waited for the betrayer to arrive; he waits for the trial and the verdict of the high priest; he waits for his Father. He waits for the next move. In the midst of this waiting he is focused, not knowing exactly what will come next, but knowing that, when all is being taken away from him and his mission is in ruins, he is still committed to the Father.

Questions for prayer and reflection

1. As you prayed the scripture passages, which part of the contemplation struck you the most? Where were you in the action? What does this suggest to you?

2. When you read the above reflection, what moved you the most? How does that aspect connect to your life and your path? Does it bring back memories? If you go back to those memories with Christ as your companion, what happens?

3. When have you felt betrayed? How did you cope with it? How do you cope with it now?

4. When have you betrayed another person, an ideal, or the way you saw yourself? How did you experience forgiveness? How do you live with those areas where you have not experienced forgiveness? What can you do now about those situations?

5. Do you experience tension in your life between your religion and your spirituality? If so, how does it express itself?

6. How are you rooted in these prayer periods? How does it feel?

7. How are you unrooted in these prayer periods? How can you dispose yourself to be rooted?

8. Sometimes the temptation these days is to try to persuade Jesus not to walk the path he has accepted. Have you experienced this temptation? How does it manifest itself in your life?

9. What happens to you when you stay, simply, with Christ?

10. What are your conversations with Mary, Jesus, or the Father like at the end of these prayer periods?

The Movie
The Butcher Boy

Director: Neil Jordan (1997 – 111 mins.)
Starring: Stephen Rea, Fiona Shaw, Eamonn Owens

1. Summary

The Butcher Boy is an unusual movie, and not an easy one to watch. It is a horrific, yet darkly comic, examination of a disturbed mind, of childhood and of loss. Set in rural Ireland in the early 1960s, the movie follows 12-year-old Francie as he deals with a violent alcoholic father and a manic-depressive suicidal mother. The pressures on Francie are immense as he faces the deaths of both his parents, a session in a boarding school (at which he has visions of the Blessed Virgin), and the tragic outcome of a hatred for his neighbours, whom he holds responsible for his parents' deaths.

2. Questions about the Movie

1. Neil Jordan also directed *The End of the Affair*, which was one of the movies chosen for the Second Week of the Exercises. Here, as in most of Jordan's movies, moral ambiguity prevails. Unlike *A Clockwork Orange*, to which it has been compared, *The Butcher Boy* "refuses to judge its characters or to take sides on the controversial issues of mental illness, violent crimes and society's approach to these problems." (Emanuel Levy, *Variety*, July 21-27, 1997) What is your initial reaction to Francie? How does this change by the end of the movie? Is he the betrayer or the betrayed? Why?

2. Francie's behaviour changes during the movie. "Slowly, almost casually, as he becomes more emotionally untethered, as his family falls apart, as friends and religion fail him, Francie's own mental health slips the surly bonds of sanity, leaving comedy behind…he descends into grotesque violence." (Lisa Schwarzbaum, *Entertainment Weekly*, April 17, 1998) The movie has been called the blackest of black comedy. What is meant by the term "black comedy"? How does it apply here? What one scene would most exemplify the movie as a black comedy?

3. "Jordan is remarkable in his ability to reveal people's inner lives and the interaction between everyday life and an individual's imagination and driving passions. Never has this been more evident than in his unique and uniquely challenging film of Patrick McCabe's celebrated coming-of-age novel, which has been compared to The *Catcher in the Rye* and *Huckleberry Finn*." (Kevin Thomas, *Los Angeles Times*, April 2, 1998) The movie basically looks at everything through the eyes of Francie Brady. But who is Francie Brady for you? Someone to be pitied? Someone to

hate? Someone you are unable to understand? Someone you shy away from watching? Someone who is betrayed? Someone who betrays? Someone whose imagination reminds you of how you are asked to use your imagination in making the Spiritual Exercises? How would you sum up your opinion of Francie in one sentence?

4. "[T]o emphasise the violence distorts the feel of this film: it is endlessly surprising, as what looks at first to be an Irish art movie…jerkily transmutes into something else entirely, something not nearly so easy to categorise: a great film." (Leslie Dick, *Sight and Sound*, #3, 1998) What makes a film great for you? Is this, then, a "great film"? Why? Why not?

3. The Relationship of the Movie to the Theme of the Exercise

1. This movie contains the theme of betrayal of the world, expressed in the television and radio coverage of events such as the Cuban missile crisis. We hear Kennedy say, "The cost of freedom is always high and Americans have always paid it." The movie was made years before 9/11. What sort of political statement do you think that director Jordan was making?

2. Francie is both the betrayer and the betrayed. Choose one of the following characters or groups and show how they also are betrayer and betrayed:

   • his parents
   • the Church
   • the townspeople
   • Joe

   • Mrs. Nugent
   • Our Lady

3. The Exercise says that often we think, and often it is true, that we need to fight for what is right. How does Francie believe he is doing the right thing by his final act of violence, which comes while the townspeople wait for the Virgin Mary to appear?

4. The priest in the village says, "We are here to pray for the redemption of Francie Brady for his terrible crimes." During Francie's final vision, the Blessed Virgin tells him, "God has a very special place in his heart for you." How can there be any redemption for what he has done? For his betrayal?

4. The Relationship of the Movie to One's Self in the Exercise

1. Joe's betrayal of Francie is the final blow. Their friendship was special. Francie always thought that Joe would come to save him. At St. Vincent's, Joe denies their friendship. Have you ever betrayed a friend? Or have you ever come close to doing so? What happened? Did you ever try to repair the break? How?

2. The only consolation religion seems to offer Francie is the visions he has of the Blessed Virgin. But even here he feels betrayed by her, as he seems to indicate at the end of movie. Has your religion – your church – ever betrayed you? What did you do about it? Have you ever betrayed your religion, your church? What have you done about that?

3. With what character in the movie do you most identify when you consider the points made in the Exercise? Why?

5th Exercise
Jesus Before Pilate

[Pilate said to Jesus] "Do you not know that I have the power to release you, and power to crucify you?" Jesus answered, "You have no power over me unless it had been given to you from above."

(John 19:10-11)

Consider all blessings and gifts as descending from above. Thus, my limited power comes from the supreme and infinite power above.

(Sp. Ex. #237)

Grace: This is to ask for what I desire. Here it will be to ask for sorrow, compassion, and shame because the Lord is going to His suffering for my sins.

(Sp. Ex. #193)

Politics and Religion

In the previous contemplations, we saw Jesus betrayed by his companions and by the corruption of some religious authorities. The destructiveness found in venal religious figures is one of the shocking realities of human history. It has set people against people, thrown countries into civil war, divided families, alienated individuals from their deepest selves, been used to justify the pillaging of the earth, and even separated people from the merciful love of God. Yet religious institutions have not disappeared from the face of the earth. We are created spiritual, but we need religion to incarnate that spirit. And so we struggle with the institutionalization of the spirit, which gives it expression but which at times seeks to repress it for institutional reasons. That spirit is not to be denied; it blows where it will. Jesus embodies that spirit as the manifestation of God in the world. It led him to a profound appreciation of the law, which he does not deny but transcends in his person and in the living community to whom he gives it. For him the fullness of the law is summed up in two basic principles: the total, shameless, passionate love of God, and the love of one's neighbour as oneself. We belong to each other; in that belonging we are the community of the Christ longing for the Father.

The political world embodies the rules for belonging, just as the religious world embodies the rules for the spirit. The religious leaders turn Jesus over to the political powers not because they respect them, but because they do not have the authority to put anyone to death. Because Jesus has shown with his life their lack of spirit, they claim he does not belong and is to be treated like an outcast. But their malice goes even further than a tribal or cultic expulsion of a heretic. He is to be eradicated in such a way that will leave no doubt in people's minds that a spirit like his will never be tolerated: by the public humiliation and torture of dying on a cross. For this they needed the collusion of the Roman authority, who alone had the right then to execute criminals.

Jesus is taken to Pilate, the Roman governor of the province. The religious authorities must decide how to use the Roman law to accomplish their goal.

The charge they bring before Pilate is this: "We have found this man perverting our nation and forbidding us to give tribute to Caesar, and saying that he himself is Christ a king" (Luke 23:2). Under Roman law there was one emperor, Caesar. All the lands under Caesar paid taxes or tribute. The accusation against Jesus, then, is that of treason; the penalty for treason is death by crucifixion. Jesus does not reply to the charges.

It is the way of a soiled world to rationalize its needs. Against those forces, innocence and truth are crushed. Perhaps it is naive to expect more than the politically expedient in corrupt and duplicitous social systems. Pilate chooses pragmatically. Even though he can find no fault with Jesus from the charges brought against him, and even though he judges that "nothing deserving death has been done by him" (Luke 23:9), he is trapped by the insistent demands of the chief priests and the rulers and the people, and hands Jesus over to his death. The horror of what he has done is compounded by the fact that instead of releasing Jesus, he is forced to release Barabbas, a man "who had been thrown into prison for murder and insurrection" (Luke 23:25). It may be a scriptural irony that the name "Barabbas" translates as "son of the Father." Jesus also calls himself the "Son of the Father," yet his world will accept only a murderer and a rebel by that name.

Victim and Oppressor

In our own world, we have seen the innocent brutalized and crushed by political and religious forces that seek only their own ends and do not care who is destroyed in the process. Many starve in a world that can feed all; many have no voice or power in their own country; many commit violence after being swayed by the lies of their leaders; many have souls that are deformed by generations of hate; many disappear, unnoticed. This is the fate of the victim. But every single one of these is a member of the human family, a community that extends through time and place. Each one has been uniquely named a child and the beloved of God, just as Christ was. In Christ, each has an identity. Even though the world has denied or ignored or subverted this identity, in the suffering of Christ each is carried to the Father. Our own lives and identities are carried there, too. What Christ suffers, we suffer; what anyone suffers, we suffer, too. We are all one.

We are all one with the oppressor, also, for that oppressor is a victim, too. In denying part of his or her humanity to maintain a position of privilege, the oppressor lives a crippled, wounded life. In fact, it is because of one's hurts that one hurts others. The malice of the chief priests of Christ's day, the self-destructive hate of the Roman soldiers, the animal passions of the crowd, the confusion of Pilate, the circus curiosity of Herod, the self-absorption of Judas – these are all forms of hell. Christ walks through those hells without losing his integrity, even though he is battered and scarred by these encounters. He does not engage those powers at the level on which they think they operate. He maintains his silence in the face of lies and his humanity in the face of inhumanity. He keeps his focus on the Father even as he is treated as an object.

It is often hard for us to see how we damage ourselves and others – such awareness is usually too painful to bear. When we hurt others, we tend to rationalize our actions so we can live with ourselves. When we are present to Jesus in his suffering, we face the suffering of the world as both victim and oppressor. But we are also liberated from the passivity of the victim and the aggression of the perpetrator. We start seeing things as they are. We see with the integrity of Christ a world in pain needing to be redeemed. We also see that the work of that redemption is in embracing that suffering with a love that comes from the Father and returns to the Father.

Questions for prayer and reflection

1. As you contemplate Christ's journey from the house of Annas to the House of Caiaphas, and from there to Pilate, then to Herod and back to Pilate, what strikes you as most compelling? As you stay with those moments, what is revealed to you?

2. What stops you from being seduced by moral disgust? How does that affect your relationship with modern religious institutions? How does that affect your understanding and involvement in the political world around you?

3. Where do you find the face and the person of Christ in the world today? How does that presence engage you?

4. In what ways are you a victim? In what ways does the role of victim rob you of your integrity? How do you cope with that? What happens when you pray about your sense of being a victim?

5. In what ways do you identify with the powers of the world? How does this manifest itself in your daily life, in the choices you make, in the values you adopt? How do you justify that perspective? How do you feel moved when you realize your depth of complicity in that world?

6. How do you find your integrity? How do you maintain it? What are the costs? What is its value?

7. In your prayer, what emerges in your conversations with the Father and with Jesus?

8. Who, in the world today, is Jesus for you? How?

9. Who, in the world today, are you Jesus for? How?

The Movie
Far from Heaven

Director: Todd Haynes (2002 – 107 mins.)
Starring: Julianne Moore, Dennis Quaid, Dennis Haysbert

1. Summary

It is the 1950s, and Cathy lives what she believes to be the perfect 1950s life – great kids, successful husband, social status. When she discovers that her husband, Frank, is gay, her world spins out of control. With no one else to turn to, Cathy speaks out to her African-American gardener, Raymond, and begins a relationship with him that would never have been condoned in 1950s America.

2. Questions about the Movie

1. "Maybe you do need to experience and savour its knife-edge of absurdity, and your own initial incredulity, to appreciate the movie's Wildean connoisseurship of the seriousness in small things. It beats me how some look down on this film as just one big, camp joke. *Far from Heaven* is much more than camp or pastiche. It is an incredible cinematic séance or even a secular High Mass, at which the real presence of the past is quite unexpectedly summoned up and made to live, spectrally, all about you." (Peter Bradshaw, *The Guardian*, March 7, 2003) What was your initial reaction to this movie during the first 10 to 15 minutes? Did your opinion change as the movie went on? Why? Why not?

2. "These Universal films, starring Rock Hudson, Dorothy Malone, Robert Stack, Jane Wyman and Lana Turner, used the conventions of the women's picture to probe the anxieties simmering beneath the surface of a decade notable for its conformity. Though they were immensely popular, it took some years for Sirk to win critical acclaim for his acute social observation and his expressive use of colour, decor and music." (Phillip French, *The Observer*, March 9, 2003) What is director Haynes trying to tell us – by imitating Sirk's style of colour, music and slightly larger-than-life acting – about issues of racism and sexuality?

3. "But by observing – and even, to some extent, exaggerating – the decorum of the era, Mr. Haynes gives *Far from Heaven* an emotional impact that could not have been achieved by conventionally realistic means. The most casual moments are suffused with a feeling of emotional extremity; the air is as charged and threatening as it might be in a horror film. Everyone in this world seems terribly alone – Cathy increasingly so – and at the same time under constant surveillance, spied upon and gossiped about, an instant away from betrayal or ostracism." (A.O.

Scott, *The New York Times*, November 8, 2002). Select one scene that exemplifies the critic's point. Why does it (or why doesn't it) present you with "emotional extremity"?

4. "Their imitation of life from half a century ago holds up a cracked mirror to the here and now. Fears about race, sexuality, feminism – craftily coded in packaging that sells religion, flag and family – are hardly alien to George W.'s America. Haynes makes you drunk on movies again, on raw emotion delivered without the cushion of irony. There are bigger, splashier films this year, but none cuts a straighter path to the heart." (Peter Travers, *Rolling Stone*, October 31, 2002) Would this movie work better if there were irony throughout? How can the director portray "raw emotion" here without cushioning everything with some irony? Does this work for you? Why? Why not?

3. The Relationship of the Movie to the Theme of the Exercise

1. The Exercise reminds us that there are those whose souls are deformed by generations of hate. How do the people in the movie react to those who show love and compassion for persecuted minorities?

2. Cathy is a victim, but she is also part of the community that extends through time and space, a child and beloved of God. While the movie has all sorts of insights that are relevant to us, it presents these insights in the form of a bleak picture of a cold and lonely existence. Where does Cathy go for help when she sees what is hap-

pening? Who are her real friends? Where is God in this movie?

3. How appropriate is the movie's title to the theme of this Exercise, where we are reminded that "here is not heaven"?

4. In our world, as the Exercise tells us, we see the innocent brutalized and crushed by political and religious forces. Cathy asks Raymond: "Do we ever see beyond the surface of things?" Who in the movie is capable of seeing the grace shining through? What happens to them?

4. The Relationship of the Movie to One's Self in the Exercise

1. As the Exercise says, when we hurt others we tend to rationalize our actions so we can live with ourselves. What is Frank's rationalization? What is society's rationalization for the way it treats Cathy? What rationalization did you use when you hurt someone you cared for?

2. When Jesus showed with his life that he was different from the ruling priests, they claimed that he did not belong and was to be treated as an outcast. Something similar happens here in the community's reaction to Cathy. When have you had to choose between acting as society does and acting as Christ asks?

3. There is something of the oppressor in all of us – we hurt others because we have been hurt. The movie contains many examples of this – Frank is one, of course, but there are others. Who are they? How often have you been the oppressor? What have you done to correct the wrongs you did to others?

6th Exercise

Jesus Tortured

(Matthew 27:24-31; Mark 15:15-20)

Jesus said to his disciples, "I say to you that listen. Love your enemies, do good to those who hate you, bless those who curse you, pray for those who abuse you. If anyone strikes you on the cheek, offer the other also; and from anyone who takes away your coat, do not withhold even your shirt. Give to everyone who begs from you; and if anyone takes away your goods, do not ask for them again. Do to others as you would have them do to you."

(Luke 6:27-31)

How much more worthy of consideration is Christ our Lord, the Eternal King, before whom is assembled the whole world. To all His summons goes forth, and to each one in particular He addresses the words: "It is my will to conquer the whole world and all my enemies, and thus to enter into the glory of my Father. Therefore, those who wish to join me in this enterprise must be willing to labour with me, that by following me in suffering, they may follow me in glory.

(Sp. Ex. #95)

Grace: This is to ask for what I desire. Here it will be to ask for sorrow, compassion, and shame because the Lord is going to His suffering for my sins.

(Sp. Ex. #193)

Denying the Human Bond

After Pilate has declared Jesus innocent, he gives into the demands of the mob, which has been incited by the priests. He orders Jesus to be scourged and crucified, but absolves himself of any responsibility. Scourging so weakens a man that he dies more quickly when crucified. It says something about the horror of the world when its compassion must manifest itself in such brutal ways.

In our world, the free gift of our bodies to another is an act of love. The taking of our unwilling bodies by another is an act of constraint. Our liberty is significantly compromised and we are subject to another. Torture goes even further. It radically denies the person any right as a human being or human animal. Its power is in removing those rights in as painful a manner as possible. It says to that person, "You are not equal to other human beings; you have no control over your life, your body or your mind. You are nothing except what the torture creates you to be. You are nothing except in how the torture chooses to humiliate and destroy you." Torture radically denies the bond that connects human to human. For the tortured, isolation intensifies awareness onto the violent and brutal pain over which that person has no control and which becomes the centre of the person's identity.

The Violence of Power

Scourging in Roman times involved stripping the victim naked and lashing the body with a whip made of leather thongs, the tips of which were dipped in lead. Its range covered the whole body. It could remove skin from muscle and muscle from bone,

228

desex the person, smash nerve endings, separate tendons, and even cause toxic shock and death. This was the Roman act of "kindness" to those condemned to be crucified. Jesus received this treatment by the Roman soldiers. Scripture is discreet and succinct on this subject, saying merely that Pilate, "having scourged Jesus, delivered him to be crucified" (Matthew 27:26). When we contemplate this sequence, we are not asked to be voyeurs to this spectacle. Rather, we ask for the grace to be present to Jesus in his agony and to the pain, shame and confusion we experience as we bear witness to the cruelty of the world and to Christ's love for the world. He loves the world and endures its testing of that love.

That testing includes the gratuitous humiliations the Roman soldiers inflict upon him after the scourging. The Romans regarded everyone else as inferior, and so many of the soldiers sent to the provinces to guard the borders, maintain Roman law and peace, be the symbol of Roman power and might, were arrogant and dismissive of those they subjugated. For them, Jesus was just another non-entity from a treacherous mass of tribal conflicts. After he is scourged, the whole battalion of some 500 men gather. They show him what they think of the Jews and of the one who was said to be the king of the Jews. Instead of an honourable crown of laurel leaves, a wreath of thorns was woven and jammed onto his head; instead of the sceptre of royalty he is given a reed; he is stripped and a scarlet robe, signifying nobility, is draped over him. "And kneeling before him they mocked him, saying, 'Hail, King of the Jews!' And they spat upon him and took the reed and struck him on the head" (Matthew 27:29-30). Here is someone without power, innocent, woefully accused and sentenced to death. Now, just after being badly beaten, he is treated as an object of derision and contempt. What are we to make of this act? We may think of the way power abuses the powerless; we may consider how vulnerability brings out the aggression of the insecure; we may even be horrified at humanity's inhumanity to other humans. We could even consider how such things happen today, in foreign places and close to home. We may be filled with a sense of moral disgust and a sense of helplessness. We grieve.

The Mystery of Evil and Suffering

But we are asked to be present to Jesus at a deeper level. He does not curse his tormentors. He does not fall back into a self-enclosed world. He remains open to the mystery as it unfolds — even in the grimmest horror and existential darkness. For him, and as for us now, there is the mystery of suffering and evil; the mystery of the Father's presence in that suffering and evil; the mystery of Divine Providence; the mystery of our own path. Finally, there is the mystery of ourselves as we walk that path and ask: Who am I? Why is this happening to me? How can I endure it?

Christ endures it by taking it one moment at a time; we can endure it by being there for him and with him as he journeys to the cross and moves through the darkness to meet his Father.

Questions for prayer and reflection

1. How are you doing in these contemplations? Can you stay with Jesus? What temptations take you away from being present to him?

2. Where do you find Christ suffering and tortured in the world today? How does that affect you?

3. How are you present to the world of suffering and duplicity that you see in the newspapers and on television?

4. What happens when you become numb to the pain of the world? How does this affect your daily life?

5. How can you be attentive to the world's pain and your own without being destroyed by it?

6. In the above reflection, what points moved you most? What does that say to you? What happens when you go back to those points and remain quietly and prayerfully with them?

7. Where does that prayer carry you?

8. What happens in your conversations with the Father, with Jesus or with Mary at the end of your prayer? What questions arise? How are they answered? Do any of them ask you any questions? What do you say?

The Movie
Three Kings

Director: David O. Russell (1999 – 115 mins.)
Starring: George Clooney, Mark Whalberg, Ice Cube

1. Summary

At the end of the Gulf War, three US soldiers come across a map that shows where Iraq has hidden a huge cache of gold. When they arrive at the site, they find an Iraqi army bent on torturing and killing civilians. These are the people that the US government encouraged to rise up against Saddam and now refuse to help. The three soldiers are faced with a challenge and with a decision that will radically change their lives.

2. Questions about the Movie

1. "Ultimately, I think Three Kings tries to be too many movies at once. It wants to combine the idealism of *Casablanca*, the cynicism of *Treasure of the Sierra Madre* and the antiwar outrage of *Full Metal Jacket*, all while being a heroic American-guy film and a critique of consumer culture.... But even when *Three Kings* loses its focus and shape, its irresistible brio will keep you watching, and wondering what in hell will happen next." (Andrew Ohehir, *Salon.com*, October 1, 1999)

How is the movie idealistic? How is it cynical? How is it a movie about US heroes? How does it critique American consumer culture?

2. "Underlying it all, however, are sentiments that may go over the heads of general audiences, those concerning the amorality and lack of consistent principles in American foreign policy. No Hollywood film in memory has addressed such an issue; but the sobering final impression here is that, unless the world's most powerful country defines what it stands for, it will stand for nothing other than the threat of brute force and economic coercion." (Todd McCarthy, *Variety*, September 27–October 3, 1999). How visible is this message beneath all the black comedy that makes up much of the movie? Although this movie was made in 1999, how does its view of US foreign policy still hold true today? Has there been any change in US foreign policy with regards to Iraq?

3. "*Three Kings* is a movie about people who, by inadvertently pricking the bubble of accepted reality, realize that they're actually living in it." (Geoff Pevere, *Toronto Star*, October 1, 1999) What events lead up to "pricking the bubble"? Does this change the basic characters of the

three kings? How? If not, why does it take an incident like this to bring out their real characters? What price must the three kings pay for what they accomplish?

3. The Relationship of the Movie to the Theme of the Exercise

1. Troy is captured and tortured by a man whose son was killed in the allied bombings. The pain of the scene is not only physical, but also ironic, as the torturer calls Troy "bro" and "my man" and wants to talk about Michael Jackson. How does this scene exemplify what the exercise defines as torture – radically denying the person any rights as a human being or human animal?

2. The Exercise offers us points about torture to consider:

   • the way power abuses the powerless
   • the way vulnerability brings out the aggression in the insecure
   • the way we feel horror at humanity's inhumanity to other humans
   • the way we wonder how such things can happen today, at home and abroad
   • the way such acts fill us with a sense of moral disgust and helplessness

   Troy is not the only one tortured in this movie – both physically and emotionally. How do these points about torture apply to the Iraqi people, whom the US encouraged to revolt against Saddam and then deserted? What scenes of torture show us these points?

3. What begins as a treasure hunt for gold becomes something different. Consider what the Exercise tells us about the shame and confusion we experience as we bear witness to the world's cruelty. What changes the three men from mercenaries to what they become? How gradual or how rapid is the change? What precipitates their final commitment to the Iraqis? What role does religion play in this change?

4. The Relationship of the Movie to One's Self in the Exercise

1. Torture is a terrible thing. In the movie we see through Troy's eyes something of what that pain must be like. The acting in this scene is excellent; something powerful there is passed on to us. How would you react in Troy's situation?

2. Could the treatment of the captured Iraqi soldiers at the start of the movie be considered torture? Why? Why not? Have you ever tortured anyone, physically or psychologically? What drove you to do that? Have you ever thought about wanting to torture people who have wronged you? What stops you from doing it?

3. Torture removes rights as painfully as possible. Has anyone ever removed your rights from you? What were the circumstances? How did this affect you? How did it affect the person who tortured you?

7th Exercise

The Path to the Cross

(Luke 23:26-31; Mark 15:21)

"Do not ask me to abandon or forsake you! For wherever you go I will go, wherever you lodge I will lodge, your people shall be my people, and your God my God. Wherever you die I will die, and there be buried".

(Ruth 1:15-17)

I will beg God our Lord for grace that all my intentions, actions, and operations may be directed purely to the praise and service of His Divine Majesty.

(Sp. Ex. #46)

Grace: This is to ask for what I desire. Here it will be to ask for sorrow, compassion, and shame because the Lord is going to His suffering for my sins.

(Sp. Ex. #193)

Crushed by Suffering

The distance from where the Roman soldiers mocked and spat upon Jesus to where he would be crucified is a little less than a kilometre. He is too weak from the beatings to walk that distance carrying the crossbeam to which his hands would be nailed. The Roman soldiers force a man from the crowd to carry the wooden post. (Roman law allowed any Roman soldier in the line of duty to conscript a bystander to carry his gear for a mile.) Stumbling to his Calvary, Jesus meets the pious women of Jerusalem who would weep and lament for the prisoners going to their death along this route. He tells them not to grieve for him but rather for what the Romans will do to them and their children when those same Roman armies destroy Jerusalem in the not too distant future. As Simon of Cyrene, the conscripted bystander, reaches out to help him in his suffering, Jesus reaches out in that same suffering to comfort the grieving women.

It would be comforting for us to see Jesus in this state as a strong, heroic figure, but he is not. He is a man so crushed by suffering that he arouses pity in those who see him. In his dire poverty he accepts help from others, but he still gives something to the women grieving him. There is a bleak simplicity and an abject nakedness in this pilgrim figure stripped of almost all humanity on his way to his death. We can see this figure in the dispossessed of the world: the starving mother crossing the drought plains of Ethiopia holding a pot-bellied baby too weak to brush the flies from its eyes; the silent stare of a street person in a prosperous Western city looking in what seems like madness beyond the forms of this world; and, if we are honest, we see here our own poverty of spirit, the figure of the pilgrim beggar that finds in every act of human outrage an echo of its own suffering. But whether we can see this or not, we all journey through a life we cannot control towards a death over which we have no control. We are powerless. We take what we have been given, and we offer what we have. Jesus, on his way to his death, does only this.

Transformed by the Encounter with Suffering

He accepts Simon of Cyrene's carrying his cross. Simon, a Jew, had come to Jerusalem to celebrate the Passover and the Feast of the Unleavened Bread, as was required by law for all Judean males. He would have had no desire to carry the cross of a criminal because in doing so he would have become ceremonially unclean and so unfit to eat the Passover meal. To be drafted to do this by Roman force was, for him, not only demeaning, it broke the ethical taboos of his religion. Although his act is not one of gratuitous kindness, it has interesting results. Simon's family is mentioned later in the Scriptures as being Christian and helping Paul in his works. The power of his act of humiliation changes the path of his life. It carries him beyond the safe established confines of his religion to an encounter with a broken man. But instead of being destroyed by that encounter, Simon is transformed. He becomes part of the living force of redemption.

When people go to impoverished countries to help out for awhile, their values are often radically transformed. They encounter the poor in all their misery and ingenuity, and they discover, oddly enough, that that encounter gives their own lives meaning and direction. The same thing happens when we deal with another's poverty and handicap. We might initially experience feelings of distaste and revulsion, but our perceptions change when we discover a common humanity and admit that we do not need to live the life of indifference we had lived before. We may go even further and discover through another's poverty and suffering our own poverty and suffering. In touching that intimate and delicate place in ourselves, we become more attuned to the world's pain and suffering and begin to speak in a language of the heart that is compassion and simple, practical love. If in our contemplation we enter into Simon of Cyrene's world and life, we unearth the transformation occurring in ourselves.

Witness as an Act of Resistance

As such, we can reach out to others in our suffering as Christ reaches out to the grieving women on his path that day. In grief, we can be trapped by the pain of our lives. Those women are not there as paid mourners. They are there because, like marginalized women anywhere, they see the cruel fate brutally meted out to their sons and daughters, their husbands and families. Their act of resistance is to witness and to mourn. They line the route and offer what comfort they can. In response, Jesus offers what he can. He tells them the truth of their lives, saying, "Weep for yourselves and for your children.... For if they do this when the wood is green what will happen when the wood is dry?" (Luke 23:28-31). If the living presence of Divine Mercy in the world is treated this way, what will happen after it is killed? Historically, before the century was over, Jerusalem was sacked and the Jews were driven from the city. But Jesus' lament cuts across time and place. He is the fullest manifestation of the Father's love, and the world in its malice and blindness treats him like a despised criminal. How will the world treat those who come after as his representatives? How will the world treat itself and any who fall under its dominion?

We who live in these times know the answer. But in the face of that death we, like Jesus, can attest with our lives to the love that is beyond death. We live in this world, but we do not have to live by the values of this world. The mystery that calls Jesus beyond death calls us also.

Questions for prayer and reflection

1. In the prayer, what moved you most? How? Return to that moment and stay there to see if there is anything else there for you. When you speak to God about this moment, what is revealed to you?

2. In the prayer, what repelled you the most? Where did you feel the driest, or the most alienated, or the least like praying? Why? Return to that moment and stay there for some time to see if there is something there for you. When you speak to God about this moment, what comes to you?

3. Have you ever been compelled to do something for someone else that changed your life for the better? What aspects of your life are like Simon of Cyrene's?

4. In our world today, we are called to witness to violence and the destruction of innocence without turning away from that destruction. How do we witness to that in ways that maintain our integrity?

5. In your conversations with God, or with Mary, what strikes you?

6. In the contemplations where do you find yourself – as an onlooker, a participant in the action, or one of the main figures? What does this say to you?

7. Do the prayer or your reflections trigger memories in you? What is the relationship between the prayer and those memories?

The Movie
The Sweet Hereafter

Director: Atom Egoyan (1997 – 112 mins.)
Starring: Ian Holm, Sarah Polley, Bruce Greenwood

1. Summary

A small community is torn apart by a tragic schoolbus accident that kills most of the town's children. Mitchell Stephens, an opportunistic lawyer, descends on the town determined to profit from the tragedy by having the parents launch a class-action lawsuit. There he discovers deep secrets in the town, secrets that mirror his own. A young girl who was crippled by the accident helps lead people from loss to grief to the sweet hereafter.

Note: Russell Banks' novel tells the story through four characters. Screenwriter Egoyan chose to follow one point of view and to break up the narrative through the use of multiple time frames. The movie moves back and forth between the accident, the time before it, and the time afterward. Be patient – it will all come together.

2. Questions about the Movie

1. "Egoyan is a director whose films coil through time and double back to take a second look at the lives of their characters. It is typical of his approach that *The Sweet Hereafter* neither begins nor ends with the bus falling through the ice of a frozen lake, and is not really about how the accident happened, or who was to blame. The accident is like the snow clouds, always there, cutting off the characters from the sun, a vast fact nobody can change." (Roger Ebert, *Chicago-Sun Times*, October 10, 1997) This is a challenging film to follow. Was it worth the effort? What appealed to you about this way of telling a story in a movie? Do you think the movie would have had the same impact if a straightforward narrative had been used – as it was in the novel? Why? Why not?

2. "One was lame and could not dance the whole of the way." During a series of flashbacks, Nicole, the survivor, reads The Pied Piper of Hamelin to two of the children who are to die. Egoyan has said that the poem clarified the central theme of the movie for him. How is this story a metaphor for the town's failure to protect the children? Who is the piper? The bus driver? The lawyer? Nicole's father? Or Nicole herself – whose lie leads the townspeople to the safety of the "sweet hereafter"?

3. Partway through the movie, there is an image of the school bus skidding off the road and sinking into a frozen lake. How does this image become the basis for the moral inquiry about the value of community and the nature of the bonds between

parents and children that form the basis for this movie? How does life go on for the townspeople? What hope is there for them at the end of the movie?

4. "There are heroes and heroines in this film, imperfect people, but who at the end change and are changed, who go ahead, one foot in front of the other, who do not give up. There are threads of lies and truth. And ultimately there is love, love that gives rather than takes." (Rose Pacatte, FSP, from a paper presented at World Congress Unda/OCIC, August 6, 1998) Where is the love that gives rather than takes? Which of the people in the film are heroes/heroines? Who are the most imperfect people? How are their lives changed?

3. The Relationship of the Movie to the Theme of the Exercise

1. Throughout the movie, Stephens speaks with his daughter, Zoe. He encounters the poor in all their misery in the person of Zoe. Remember the first time we see him talking with her, when he says, "I have to know whom I am talking to." How do these encounters change him, give his life meaning and direction? Or do they?

2. Throughout the movie, Mitchell encounters people who in their grief are trapped by the pain of their lives. How does he deal with their pain? Recall the scene with Wanda and Hartley, the parents of Bear. What comfort does Mitchell offer these people? Who is changed in these encounters – Mitchell or the townspeople? How? Does Mitchell represent the "world"? If so, what do the townspeople represent?

3. We are called to live in the world but not live by the world's values. There are many examples – as we are often reminded – of people in the movie who live in the world with the values of the world. There is at least one exception. Would you say that Nicole represents someone who lives in the world but does not accept the world's values? If not, Nicole, then who? Anyone? No one? Is there no hope for any of the townspeople?

4. The Relationship of the Movie to One's Self in the Exercise

1. The movie contains examples of people whose acts of kindness, like Simon of Cyrene's, are not gratuitous. Have you ever been "forced" into an act of kindness? How did it change you? Or did it?

2. The women who line the route to the cross are there because their witness and mourning are acts of resistance, as the Exercise tells us. The townspeople have seen the fate brutally meted out to their children, and they witness and mourn. Where is your act of resistance to the poverty and oppression you see around you every day?

3. Nicole alone is able to help the townspeople work towards the "sweet hereafter." She reaches out to the pain and suffering of her world to help them change. How she does it is morally questionable. Or is it? What – or who – helps you to reach out towards the "sweet hereafter" in your life?

237

8th Exercise

The Crucifixion of Jesus

(Mark 15:22-40; Matthew 27:33-55; Luke 23:32-49; John 19:17-37)

We know that all of creation groans and is in agony even until now; and not only creation but we ourselves, who have the first fruits of the Spirit, groan inwardly as we await the redemption of our bodies. For in this hope we are saved. But hope is not hope if its object is seen; how is it possible to hope for what one sees? And hoping for what we cannot see means awaiting it with patient endurance. The Spirit too helps us in our weakness for we do not know how to pray as we ought; but the Spirit himself intercedes for us with groanings too deep for words.

(Romans 8:22-26)

We must make ourselves indifferent to all created things, as far as we are allowed free choice and are not under any prohibition. Consequently, as far as we are concerned, we should not prefer health to sickness, riches to poverty, honour to dishonour, a long life to a short life. The same holds for all other things.

(Sp. Ex. #23)

Grace: This is to ask for what I desire. Here it will be to ask for sorrow, compassion, and shame because the Lord is going to His suffering for my sins.

(Sp. Ex. #193)

Witnessing a Death

In a crucifixion, the arms and feet are nailed in such a way that when the body is upright, the shoulders become dislocated. The result is agony, as those limbs are asked to bear the weight of the body. If one relaxes, one suffocates, and so one thrusts against the cross for breath. But this pushes against the nails and that pain becomes unbearable. The gospel writers are aware of the medical effects of such a torture, which was commonplace in their time. Their accounts contain the discretion of the lover who is aware of, but unwilling to depict, the beloved's final anguish. What they hold in their hearts of an experience that goes beyond words, we too can hold in our hearts as we contemplate those final hours of Christ on the day before the Jewish sabbath began.

Yet we are given something in the scriptural descriptions of Christ's dying on the cross. For Mark, the crucifixion plunges us into the profoundest depths of human misery and abandonment; Matthew gives us Jesus as the new Moses, whose suffering allows us to become intimates with the Father without the intermediary of temple religion; Luke presents the Messiah who remains as a healer and reconciler even in the midst of his anguish; John shows us a Christ who even on the cross is in full command of his destiny. The central questions for us, though, are these: How are we present to Christ on the cross? What Christ is given to us in our contemplation at this time?

Throughout the Exercises, St. Ignatius presents us with a Christ who enters his poverty to be completely disposed to the Father's will. He witnesses with his life to his trust in the Father's compassionate

238

mercy for all, even in the face of his suffering and death. The Exercises present an encounter with Jesus that is in accordance with the different facets of the crucified Christ of the gospels. We are asked to be present as fully as possible to that Christ.

Those passages leave out many painful things, even though the gospels are written from the perspective of the resurrection. None describe the actual crucifixion and, like the contemplation of the hidden life, we depend on what we need from it to be given in prayer. But we do know that Jesus' scourged and bleeding body was stripped naked and nailed to the cross, which was then lifted and fixed in a hole in the ground. Medical evidence says that a crucified person would slowly drown as the exhausted body slumped and the lungs filled with water. And so the victim dies.

Living Our Own Deaths

But we are here not just to witness to a death, although there is a death. We are here to be present to the way Jesus lives his dying, trusting in a life beyond death. He is stripped and his blood-stained clothes are gambled for. As he hangs there, struggling between the pain of dislocated joints and shattered nerve endings pushing against the nails, trying to breathe, he remains faithful to the Father. He prays for those who crucified him; he pardons the thief; he gives his mother a home; with his dying breath he hands his spirit over to the Father. All this occurs amidst his growing pain and exhaustion.

It is not as if he forgets himself. He thirsts, and he acknowledges his sense of abandonment. He is besieged by temptation and cries out in the words of the Psalmist: "My God, my God why have you forsaken me?" (Ps 69:21). Even though he feels forsaken by the Father, he dies as he has lived, faithful to that relationship. On the cross, Christ waits on the Father as he has waited on him all his life. In that waiting he is stripped of any sense of his relationship with the Father.

We contemplate this dying knowing how the story continues. We know that at his death there are signs that he does indeed witness to the Father's love for the world. The unbelieving Roman centurion who is stationed at the cross acknowledges, "Truly this man is the Son of God" (Mark 15:39). Death is seen to be overthrown, for as Matthew tells us, "Tombs were opened, and many bodies of the saints who had fallen asleep were raised, and coming out of the tombs after his resurrection they went into the holy city and appeared to many" (Matthew 27:52-3).

But Christ, in his humanity, does not – cannot – live his resurrection before his death. He can only live his death until, at the Father's dispensation, he is raised. He endures the fullness of his death, just as each of us must live out our death – we cannot avoid it. We can know and believe the Father's mercy for each one of us, for we experienced it as we did the Exercises of the First Week. But we do not know, until we experience it, the Father's mercy for us in our dying. Like Christ, we lean into that mercy and that mystery. Doing so allows us to put death in perspective, but it does not allow us to dismiss death. We all must die.

In contemplating Christ's death, we are not asked to die his death, or to take him down from the cross. We are asked only to be as fully present as possible to his dying, and to our own dying, as he was to his. We can do both because his dying reveals to us something that we, even now, find it almost impossible to believe: that God manifests his love by enduring, without cursing or damning us, a shameful and

239

agonizing death for us even as we reject him and his mercy. This is not to make us feel guilty or duty bound to follow him. On the contrary, it is to assure us that we are free and that we can live that freedom in the face of the trials, illusions and punishments of this world. When we contemplate the death of Christ, we can live the deaths of our own lives and of our world to the hope of the resurrection.

Questions for prayer and reflection

Note: When we contemplate Christ's crucifixion, anything can happen. We must be careful not to manipulate ourselves to feel or experience one thing or another. All we are asked to do is to be present. Sometimes our emotions go deeper than our feelings, and we feel nothing. Sometimes we are carried by our prayer into moments of deep feeling. We need only to be truthful to what happens in the prayer.

1. How did the prayer go? What stood out for you as you entered the scene of the crucifixion?

2. Where were you in the action of the contemplation? Why is this significant?

3. How do you live your life in the face of your own oncoming death? How would you like to live your life when you face that fact?

4. How does God's mercy shape the way you live with yourself and with others?

5. As Christ continually suffers in every act of injustice, every broken relationship, every illusion maintained, any beauty despoiled, every act of violence, how is the mercy of the Father brought to that situation for you?

6. What do you do when the Father does not seem to care?

7. How do you pray in the face of pain and suffering?

8. Call to mind times when you were in situations that were destructive of the life you needed. How did you maintain your integrity at those times? How were you rescued?

9. What does the cross of Christ truly mean in your life?

10. How is that cross misrepresented and misused in this world? How does that trap people?

The Movie
The Mission

Director: Roland Joffe (1986 – 126 mins.)
Starring: Robert DeNiro, Jeremy Irons, Ray McAnally
1986: Palm D'Or – best film at the Cannes Film Festival

1. Summary

In a 1750 Treaty, the Spaniards gave a portion of Latin America to the Portuguese. As part of the treaty, the Jesuits were ordered to leave the missions they had founded so that the Portuguese could use the Indians as slaves. The Jesuit Fr. Gabriel, who built a mission to convert the Indians, wants the Europeans to learn to live in peace with the Indians. Mendoza, an ex-slaver become Jesuit, organizes the natives to resist the attempted takeover. Watching over all this is Cardinal Altamirano, sent by the Vatican to solve a political dilemma. If the Jesuits remain as defenders of the natives, then the Vatican might be at odds with Spain and Portugal and lose political power.

2. Questions about the Movie

1. "The focus of *The Mission* is the story of the crises of conscience faced by two very different Jesuits when, at last, the Pope's envoy decides against the local priests. Will they take up arms against the crown to protect the Indians, who trust them and to whom they've brought God's love? In addition, will audiences understand the parallels between the 18th century and the late 20th, when many priests in Latin America have also found themselves at odds with Rome?" (Vincent Canby, *The New York Times*, November 14, 1986) What parallels is the critic speaking about?

2. The striking opening scenes of the martyrdom of the Jesuits is only the first of many scenes that use water as a symbol. Water has, of course, a religious significance – the sacrament of Baptism. The image of water has been used throughout film history. Federico Fellini ended all of his films by bringing his main characters to water to symbolize their rebirth and change. How is water used in *The Mission*? What does it symbolize?

3. The music composed by Ennio Morricone has become well known on its own. It was written to provide mood and atmosphere, but here it does much more. What does the music in the movie serve as a symbol for? How does it do this?

4. "It is left to the brilliant Irish actor Ray McAnally to find the deepest, most fascinating contradictions in the movie. As the churchman Altamirano, McAnally encompasses a very good man, forced to make a very bad decision. At the end of *The Mission*, Joffe holds on a close-up of Altamirano staring into the camera. There is the guilt and despair of centuries in that look. It sends a cold shudder down the spine." (Ron Base,

Toronto Star, November 14, 1986) How did you feel at the end of the movie? With which character did you identify most? Why?

3. The Relationship of the Movie to the Theme of the Exercise

1. Christ was brutally tortured and cruelly murdered in the name of politics and religion – evil set out to destroy good. The movie shows the genocide of the Guarani natives by Portuguese soldiers. This bloody spectacle is one of evil obliterating good, all in the name of politics and religion. What other parallels are there between the death of Christ and the death of the Jesuits and the Guarani?

2. The Exercise tell us that the Messiah Luke presents remains a healer and reconciler even in the midst of his anguish, while in John we have a Christ who even on the cross is in full command of his destiny. As Christ figures, which of these two descriptions fit Gabriel and Mendoza best? Why? How is this shown?

3. The crucifixion and death of Christ speak strongly to us about many things. How did God speak to people through this movie? What does the movie teach us about discipleship in our own time and what it might cost us?

4. The Relationship of the Movie to One's Self in the Exercise

1. Christ died so that love might have a place in this world, triumphing over the "might" that would destroy that love. Towards the end of the movie, Father Gabriel, faced with obeying a command that he knows is morally wrong, says, "If might makes right, love has no place in the world. It may be so; I had no strength to live in a world like that." How do you reconcile this statement with what we believe Christ died for?

2. The forgiveness scene is one we can all respond to. We have all either forgiven or been forgiven. Mendoza reacts in a certain way to this forgiveness. When do you recall both forgiving and being forgiven? How did you react to this?

3. Mendoza's climb up the waterfall is his own way of the cross – and it is his old self that dies. Anyone in search of integrity must also begin by climbing up a metaphorical waterfall. It has been said that such a task is a life project without guarantees. What is your own way of the cross – your own waterfall – that you must face? Will you have the courage to climb up your falls? To face your enemy? To love them, no matter what the cost?

Christ is Laid in the Tomb

(Matthew 27:55-61; Mark 15:42-47; Luke 23:50-56; John 19:38- 42)

Wretch that I am! Who will deliver me from this body under the power of death? All praise to God through Jesus Christ our Lord....

(Romans 7:24-25)

Death no longer has dominion over him.

(Romans 6:9)

The more the soul is in solitude and seclusion, the more fit it renders itself to approach and be united with its Creator and Lord; and the more closely it is united with Him, the more it disposes itself to receive graces and gifts from the infinite goodness of its God.

(Sp. Ex. #20)

Grace: This is to ask for what I desire. Here it will be to ask for sorrow, compassion, and shame because the Lord is going to His suffering for my sins.

(Sp. Ex. #193)

The Ruins of a Life

We are told that some of those who followed Jesus witnessed his death. After he died, one of his disciples asked Pilate for the body, and it was taken down. His followers wrapped it with spices and laid in a nearby tomb. In this contemplation we are asked to be present to this sequence of events.

When we see someone suffering in agony, it comes as a relief to us when that person dies. We think, well, at least now it is over and we can get to the business of the funeral. This gives us something to do, which means we get a break from that dreadful burden of waiting, knowing our limited abilities to control our own or anyone else's living and dying.

In their waiting by the cross, those who followed Jesus – as family, friend, and disciple – enter into their anguish and grief. Since our lives are all woven together in a common fabric of relationships, the cruelty inflicted on someone who is part of our life traumatizes us. We enter into a sense of disbelief that eats away at what has become familiar, and we enter a new world where we are forced to chart a course through the unknown. We may struggle against the strangeness that envelops us, and enter into a profound desolation for what is lost. We become strangers to ourselves. As we wait with those waiting by the cross, we mourn the loss of hopes, ideals and dreams. We had cherished the possibility that God's mercy would touch human hearts, and that the works of the one we followed would bring about that intimate sense of belonging and community where all could find a home.

Instead we wait for a tortured man to die, someone who has touched our hearts and imaginations and our lives, someone with whom we were willing to risk our lives. He dies calling out to the Father. In our pain as his lovers, we cannot even begin to imagine the pain of the one who called him "Son" and "Beloved." What can we do now? The big schemes of a transformed world are in ruins. The ache in our hearts, which we finally acknowledged because it seemed something could now be done about it, is again rawly exposed to the absurdity of the world.

An Act of Mercy

The pain and the outrage and the despair made Joseph of Arimathea bold: he goes and asks Pilate for the body. Once Pilate had ascertained that the Christ was dead, he gave it to him. Maybe this is the work of good people in the world, to bury the dead so that they may not be further desecrated. It is a small and manageable good, and may be all that is possible today. The charitable act of burying the dead is a profoundly human concern that echoes through the ages and stories of diverse cultures. We find it in the biblical story of Tobias' father and in the Greek drama *Antigone*, where a young girl follows her heart and attempts to bury her dishonoured brother even though that ritual act has been forbidden on pain of death. Sophocles shows the malice possible in the human heart that would regard even such a work of mercy as a crime. We find it in stories of indignities suffered by the dead as a show of their persecutor's power, and in Christ's mockery on the cross in the crucifixion. What Joseph of Arimathea does restores some dignity to Christ's body.

It is an act of love and relief, though bitter anguish, to touch the corpse of someone we love. It is the body and yet it is not the body. And in the case of Jesus, it is a body transformed. Cold, bloody, broken, the smell of terror and human waste. In the gathering dark, one can do only the bare necessities. No time to prepare the body properly. It is bound with the linen cloth and the spices and laid in the tomb.

Keeping Vigil

In our contemplation, we are asked to keep vigil by that tomb. We are asked to continue to be present as fully as possible. And so we wait. We do not know what will happen or how it will happen for us. We cannot create resurrection for ourselves. It is a gift, and it depends on the dispensation of the Father. We cannot will Christ's resurrection. We can fantasize how it might be and imagine it happening, but such stories come from ourselves. The resurrection, when it happens, comes from beyond ourselves.

As you wait, reflect on how you first got to know Jesus in this retreat. Reflect on how you and Jesus became intimates. Remember the good times and the bad times together. Ponder on things that happened that did not make sense at the time.

Even if you think you have run out of things to think about, this does not mean that the prayer is finished. You need to wait in that empty space when first your mind goes blank, and then your heart settles into the silence of the pain and sinks deeper and deeper – past feeling, even past emotion – into that presence that holds us and all things into being.

Questions for prayer and reflection

1. What happened to you as you waited for Christ to die?

2. How did you deal with his death?

3. Were you able to be merciful to the body? To the others around you?

4. How did you wait at the tomb in prayer? In silence? Just waiting? What came up during those times? What happened when you brought those things to your conversation with God, the Christ, or Mary?

5. How do you behave at the funerals of those you have known? How was the prayer the same as, or different from, those times?

6. When has something or someone precious been taken from you? How did you cope? If you re-enter those moments now in your prayer, can you see in them the death of Christ for you? What happens when you do so?

7. What are the dead in your life now that you keep watch over? Can you allow yourself reverently to bury them? To offer them back to the mystery Jesus calls "Father"? What happens when you allow yourself to do this?

8. If in a separate prayer period you were to go over the events of this Third Week – from the Last Supper to the Waiting at the Tomb, as you have experienced them in prayer. What strikes you as most significant? Why? How does that affect you?

9. Is there any unfinished business to this Week, or to your prayer at this time, or to your life as you see it now, that you would like to pray about?

10. Can you speak to the mystery called "Father" about those things? What happens when you do?

The Movie
About Schmidt

Director: Alexander Payne (2002 – 126 mins.)
Starring: Jack Nicholson, Hope David, Kathy Bates, Len Cariou

1. Summary

Warren Schmidt faces an ambiguous future when he retires. His wife of 42 years dies suddenly; his daughter is about to marry a man he does not like and she does not want him to attend her wedding; and he sponsors an orphan in Tanzania. Coming to terms with all of this makes him look at the failure he believes his life was and is.

2. Questions about the Movie

1. "What is extraordinary about Payne's film is the way it combines the most deliciously extreme and nihilist black comedy with forthright sentimentality – and somehow makes the combination work…. Opinions will vary about the final two minutes of this movie…. It took nerve for Payne to declaim such a big emotional finish, but I submitted wholeheartedly to its trumpet-blast of defiant non-irony, in which those deep old-man wrinkles around Schmidt's eyes, which he told Ndugu he hated so much, become the tracks of his tears. A little rich for many palates, yes. But for me it was a gloriously satisfying, resounding major chord. Alexander Payne has created a tender, acrid, comic masterpiece." (Peter Bradshaw, *The Guardian*, January 24, 2003) What are some instances of black comedy in the movie? How did you react to the ending of the movie? Why do you agree or disagree with Bradshaw's comment that it all ends on a "resounding major chord"?

2. "Schmidt is a man with an unhappy inner self, but no supportive inner life other than that provided by the conventions and values of middle-class middle America." (Philip French, *The Observer*, January 26, 2003) What are some of the conventions and values of middle-class middle America shown in the movie? Which of them are acceptable to you? With which do you disagree?

3. "What makes this exquisitely observed slice of American screen realism transcend itself is finally its moral sensibility. The movie's quest to discover how one ordinary person can make more of a difference turns out to be as serious as its title character. The common-sense answer it comes up with, is as simple and modest as it is profoundly moving." (Stephen Holden, *The New York Times*, September 27, 2002) What kind of moral sensibility did you find in the movie? Is the common-sense answer realistic, or is it a Hollywood ending designed to please audiences? Why? Why not? How does Schmidt

come to know that he can make a difference? How does he react to this realization?

4. "Payne employs a novel voice-over technique. Schmidt tells his interior monologue in the form of a series of letters to a six-year-old Tanzanian child named Ndugu, whom Schmidt impetuously decides to sponsor.... He pours out his heart to Ndugu, revealing intimacies most would only tell closest adult friends, and the device is as touching as is strange: He really wants the poor, starving child to have a happy life. Schmidt envies the tot's innocence: 'Life is short, Ndugu,' Schmidt smugly advises, and even as we laugh, we have to look more closely at the defeated man on the poster. Could that be our own worn face staring back at us?" (Peter Howell, *Toronto Star*, December 20, 2002) What are the main things about himself that Schmidt tells Ndugu? Why do you think he is capable of saying such things only in a letter to a boy he does not know and will never meet? What do you make of the response that is sent to Schmidt by the nun who writes for Ndugu?

3. The Relationship of the Movie to the Theme of the Exercise

1. The Exercise talks about our entering into a sense of disbelief that eats away at what has become familiar. Following his wife's death and his retirement, Schmidt finds himself in such a situation. What are some examples from the movie that show the falling apart of the familiar for Schmidt?

2. At this time we also enter a world where we are forced to chart a course through the unknown. Schmidt undertakes a voyage in his motor home into the unknown. What are some of the adventures that he has to chart his way through? What does he learn from each of these?

3. At this time, we enter into a profound desolation for what is lost. We become strangers to ourselves. How is this true of Schmidt? Consider what he has lost and what he finds when he looks at himself. What makes his desolation lift? How is Schmidt at the end of the movie different from at the beginning?

4. The Relationship of the Movie to One's Self in the Exercise

1. Almost all of us have suffered through the death of someone close to us – perhaps we were even there while that person went through agony and suffering. Schmidt faces the death of his wife in shock and then in anger when he finds out about the affair she had with his best friend. How did you react to the death of someone you loved? How would you face up to learning something about that person that presents him or her in a different light?

2. It is not until the final images of the movie that we see that there has been a real acceptance and change in Schmidt. In the Exercise we move from suffering with Christ in his death to waiting for what is to come. How have you accepted what Christ's death means to you in your own life?

3. The Exercise tells us that our lives are all woven together in a common fabric of relationships. Schmidt's relationships are fragile and the fabric is easily torn – look at his relationships with his friend, his daughter, the people he meets on his trip. How are your relationships with the people around you? What holds these relationships together? What tries to tear them apart?

10th Exercise

The Descent into Hell:
The interlude between the burial and the resurrection

Now the Lord is the Spirit, and where the Spirit of the Lord is, there is freedom.

(2 Corinthians 3:17)

It will be very profitable for the one who is to go through the Exercises to enter upon them with magnanimity and generosity toward his Creator and Lord, and to offer Him his entire will and liberty, that His Divine Majesty may dispose of him and all he possesses according to His most holy will.

(Sp. Ex. #5)

Grace: This is to ask for what I desire. Here it will be to ask for sorrow, compassion, and shame because the Lord is going to His suffering for my sins.

(Sp. Ex. #193)

Intimate Healing

In the next stage on our spiritual journey, we will move onto Christ's resurrection. In the first contemplation to the Fourth Week, which deals with the resurrection and living that resurrection in our daily lives, St. Ignatius makes this interesting observation: "This is the history. Here it is how after Christ expired on the cross His body remained separated from the soul, but always united with the divinity. His soul, likewise united with the divinity, descended into hell. There he sets free the souls of the just" (#219).

The work of the Christ extends through all states of being. In Ignatius' iconography, that work extends to those who, through no fault of their own, are trapped in situations where they cannot express or receive love. What they experience is very similar to what Christ experienced on the cross: a sense of innocence violated and forsaken, of peace frustrated, of goodness tormented, of wholeness broken, of longing unfulfilled, of blessedness misinterpreted. What they experience is their radical helplessness. All they can do is wait, as Christ waited on the cross.

We experience much the same thing today, and during our vigil outside Jesus' tomb. But the divine mission of God is not constrained by bodily limitations. That spirit of compassionate love desires to liberate all from whatever limits their freedom to live fully. It enters our places of imprisonment to bring us to a spiritual freedom from oppression. When we are present at the tomb in a state of unknowing, something is happening to us at levels below our bodily consciousness. We are being liberated.

248

Radical Transformation

Just as the Father reaches into death and brings the Son to resurrection, so the Son reaches into the most broken and desolate places of existence to witness with his spirit the depth of the compassionate mercy of his Father. That transformation is one of spirit, of heart, of imagination, of desire, of perception. The spirit is transformed because we experience in the midst of our despair a hope that refuses to give us up. It encourages us to believe that we are redeemable and that, even as we wait by the tombs of our lives and hopes, we are in the process of being redeemed. When we finally dare to allow ourselves to accept that gift, offered freely and simply, we discover our hearts expanding to accept our own suffering and the suffering of others. We find that we can hold the world without despair or depression but with a sense of wonder. That wonder transforms our imagination. It realizes that the world and life does not have to be the way it is depicted, and that we do not have to accept the world given in its distortions.

In fact, we discover our heart's desire: that unbroken intimacy with the Father, through Christ, is to re-create the world into a home for all. We can do this because we now perceive the possibilities for life inherent in the situations we are living through. We are no longer trapped. We see a path through the gloom; we find the energy to follow it, and we walk that path with hope and commitment and in union with everyone who lives the same felt relationship with the source of life.

The Liberation of the Most Alienated

Christ's descent into the dead and into hell brings to life, in our own lives, what he finds there. What rises from the depths, deeper than original sin, is original grace. As that grace emerges into our daily lives, it brings with it the deaths it transforms as it passes through them. We discover that we come from God, we return to God, and the path to God is God. This is not to say that there is no suffering on the path. In fact, we constantly leap into the furnaces of affliction, and are transformed there, on this journey. In doing so we do what the Christ did in bringing us to freedom. The creativity of God transforms evil into good, suffering into joy, isolation into community, imprisonment into freedom, death into resurrection.

In death, Jesus waits on the Father for deliverance. He waits in a love that does not deny death and suffering but accepts it on the path back to the Father. That waiting is active, not passive; in fact, Christ is most creative when he is on the cross. That dying and death and entombment draws out into the open all the pain and malice of a betrayed creation. There it encounters the constant love of God, who does not shrink from this horror. In that embrace Jesus dies; in that embrace creation is renewed. In the patience of Christ on the cross we discover the patience of the Father, whose gift is time and the open door in every moment of time to the fullness of life. Christ's descent into hell is a manifestation of that gift. It is the Father's desire that nothing and no one, in no moment of creation, be lost – not even what seems irredeemable, not even what is trapped in hell.

When we enter into this contemplation and spend time in it, we aid in that redemption and we uncover its effects in our lives.

Questions for prayer and reflection

1. What were the most moving moments in this contemplation? Return to them, one at a time, and wait for their significance to be expanded in your prayer.

2. Is there a pattern to those moments? What do they tell you? How do you respond to that pattern?

3. Can you, in your prayer, bring Christ to those places in your life and in the world where you experience hell? What happens when you do that?

4. When have you been in situations that were sheer hell for you? How were you liberated? How do you account for that liberation? Return to those moments prayerfully and see how the Christ was present at those times. (You might want to ask at the beginning of that prayer for the presence of Christ to identify itself to you.)

5. What was the most desolate moment in this contemplation? Why do you think this moment stands out? Return to that moment in prayer, stay there and see what happens.

6. How does this prayer, and its repetitions, help you see what has been going on during the Exercises of this Week?

7. In what ways are you creative? In what ways are you now asked to be creative? Pray for the answers to these questions to be revealed to you.

8. How do your conversations with the Father, the Christ or Mary on these prayers illuminate your life and your path?

The Movie
Chicago

Director: Rob Marshall (2002 – 113 mins.)
Starring: Catherine Zeta-Jones, Renée Zellweger, Richard Gere, Queen Latifah

1. Summary

Based on the Kander and Ebb stage musical, the movie takes the dark tale of two murderers – Roxie Hart, who killed her lover, and Velma Kelly, who killed her husband – and turns it into an imaginative descent into the hell of the Roaring '20s, where we meet not only Roxie and Velma but their lawyer, Billy Flynn, and a prison matron with a heart of gold.

2. Questions about the Movie

1. Billy Flynn says: "This trial…the whole world…it's all…show business!" *Chicago* was a critical and popular success, winning many awards along the way. Why are we often drawn to shady characters in movies? How is it that some of our favourite movies ask us to love bad guys and villains, and we go along with this even though chances are that most of what they do is way beyond what we find to be acceptable behaviour? Should filmmakers make movies that look at topics such as pornography (e.g., *Boogie Nights*)? Should entertainment be used to debate hot social issues such as corporate ethics (e.g., *The Insider* or *Erin Brokowich*), racism (e.g., *Malcolm X*, *The Pianist, Far from Heaven*)? How is it that an Oscar winner for Best Picture can take us through a world of gangsters, betrayal, corruption and murder and see us humming and tapping our toes all the way to Chicago? Why do our daily moral codes seem to be so easily suspended in the dark? Or is it all just entertainment?

2. Roxie says: "I love my audience. And they love me. And I love them for loving me. And they love me for loving them. And we love each other. And that's because we didn't get enough love in our childhoods." One of the themes of the movie is our desire for fame and the dangers that come from wanting it, getting it and losing it. Is this a sufficiently "heavy" idea on which to hang a two-hour movie? How is the director able to do this? With characters? With the musical numbers? Or does he not do it and we end up with a pleasant but flawed movie?

3. *Chicago* "merrily jabs at the celebrity-lust of our own era. In the strong and most biting number, Roxie perches on Billy's lap like a dummy…and chants the melodies that he, the ventriloquist, feeds into her mouth. Behind the ladies and gentlemen of the press jerk on wires, yanked from on high by a second Billy, and compete to do his bidding. As a musical demonstration of spin, it couldn't be meaner." (Anthony Lane, *The New*

Yorker, January 6, 2003) What are some examples, in our time, of this sort of spin that we have come to recognize? What are some examples of celebrity-lust in our time? Why are people so besotted with celebrities?

4. *Chicago* "puts the cynicism up front where it can titillate, horrify and instruct us. The movie cheerfully displays the backstabbing and lies – the desperation to be No. 1 and have everyone else be zero – that go into making the tabloid and celluloid shams that beguile us." (Richard Corliss, *Time,* December 16, 2002) What are some examples of cynicism in the movie? How do they "titillate, horrify and instruct" you?

4. "*Chicago,* in its caustic high-spirited way, presents us with a vision of women on the cusp of feminism who will do anything to break free of the conventionality imposed by men. They'll sing and dance in sleazy nightclubs, kill their boring and ruthless spouses, and become infamous to escape punishment for their crimes. Bravado is all – far more vital than morality – and *Chicago,* freshly transplanted from the stage, is a thrilling ode to the intertwined glories of sex, showmanship, and lying: what the film calls 'the old razzle-dazzle.'" (Owen Gleiberman, *Entertainment Weekly,* January 3, 2003) How are women portrayed in the movie? How are men portrayed? How accurate a portrayal do you think these presentations are of the role of men and women in the Chicago of the 1920s?

3. The Relationship of the Movie to the Theme of the Exercise

1. Sartre wrote that hell is other people. Roxie and Velma exemplify this – each trying to one up the other. Velma says [about Roxie]: "First she steals my publicity. Then she steals my lawyer, my trial date. And now she steals my goddamn garter!" The world of Chicago is one of despair and depression. Unlike the Exercise, the characters hold this world without a sense of wonder and in a state of despair and depression. What are some examples of the loss of wonder, of the despair and depression in the movie?

2. The Exercise tells us that God transforms
    • evil into good
    • suffering into joy
    • isolation into community
    • imprisonment into freedom
    • death into resurrection.

    Chicago, the musical, is about a world with no true moral framework. How does the movie deal with each of the above themes?

3. The work of Christ extends to all – they have only to accept it. In *Chicago,* where do we find examples of
    • innocence violated and forsaken
    • wholeness broken
    • longing unfulfilled
    • blessedness misinterpreted.

4. The Relationship of the Movie to One's Self in the Exercise

1. The Exercise tells us that along our journey we are constantly leaping into the furnaces of affliction. In *Chicago,* the characters are in real affliction, yet they are not transformed by it. What are some of the afflictions you have faced? How have you been transformed by them?

2. Through their own fault, Roxie and Velma are trapped in situations where they cannot express or receive real love. What situations have you been in – through your own fault or not – where you have felt trapped and unable to love or receive love?

3. When Christ descends into hell, he brings back – as the Exercise tells us – a bringing to life in our own lives. The characters in *Chicago* never really return from hell and so bring nothing back. What is the hell into which you have descended in your life? What have you have brought back from it?

Part 4

The Fourth Week – A Transforming Life

1st Exercise
Preparation for the Fourth Week

I am about to create new heavens and a new earth;
The things of the past shall not be remembered
Or come to mind.
Instead there shall always be rejoicing and happiness in
which I create;
For I create Jerusalem to be a joy
And its people to be a delight;
I will rejoice in Jerusalem and exult in my people.
No longer shall the sound of weeping be heard there,
Nor the sound of crying.

(Isaiah 65:17-19)

Consider the divinity, which seemed to hide itself during the passion, now appearing and manifesting itself so miraculously in the most holy Resurrection in its true and most sacred effects.

(Sp. Ex. #223)

Grace: Here it will be to ask for the grace to be glad and rejoice intensely because of the great joy and the glory of Christ Our Lord.

(Sp. Ex. #221)

The True Meaning of Joy

This final set of Exercises moves through a sequence that ranges from experiencing the resurrection of Christ to living the spirit of that resurrection in the world. The grace we ask for at the beginning of every prayer period is "To be glad and rejoice intensely because of the great joy and

glory of Christ our Lord" (#221). Two things should be noted of this grace. First, the focus is on the great joy and glory of Christ. That joy gives us our own – not vice versa. Imagine seeing a young child playing and feeling happy because that child is having fun. Our first experience of the resurrection is like that. That first state of joy carries us out of ourselves; we pray to be happy because we experience Christ's joy and can enter into that joy.

Ignatius also recommends that we ask for that grace to be intensely glad and to rejoice intensely. Not only do we need to ask for that grace and expect it, we also need to live as if we have received it. At this time we avoid all those things that may cause us to lose that grace and seek those things that contribute to that state of being.

Joy is often equated with loud celebrations. True joy is not like that. Joy is the felt sense of being rooted in God's love. It is calm and focused and deep. The enemy of our human nature does not want us to be joyful, and so lures us away from it. Unless we counteract that temptation, we start moving from being joyful to being happy, from being happy to being excited, and from being excited to being in a state of pleasure. From there it is easy to slip into giddiness and then to desolation. Pleasure is a delight in the things that stimulate the senses. I can have pleasure in a good meal or in an ice-cream cone on a hot day. Excitement is an intensification of that pleasure, to the extent that it blocks out a sense of calm and of control. Happiness is when my desires coincide with

257

the energies around me and I am affirmed in myself. Joy is acknowledging in a self-conscious manner my rootedness in a love and a life that is larger than me and that I know cares for me. In joy I can appropriate my self-transcendence; in pleasure I experience my selfhood solely in a physical way. Joy lies at one end of the continuum of delight; pleasure lies at the other end.

In this Week, as we enter more and more deeply into the resurrection, we want to remain recollected so that we do not lose all the gifts we have been moving towards during our retreat, like people who earn a small fortune working long, hard hours in remote areas, only to lose it in a frenzy of mindless self-indulgence when they return to the world they left behind.

Remaining Recollected

As we remain recollected, we become more in union with God. We find that we share the same spirit and the same focus, work and joy as the continuing presence of the resurrected Christ in the world. A path leads through this Week of our growing union into the mind and heart of God. We left the previous Week in a state of waiting. That waiting empties us. In that emptiness we get glimpses of the risen Christ. As we reflect on the glimpses, learning to believe and accept what we are being given, we enter a state of quiet, focused awareness of the joy present in every moment and in everything. We celebrate that awareness by sharing with whomever we meet what has been given to us. This is the work that is resurrection in the world. It is not to proselytize or to be graciously condescending from a spiritually superior position. Rather, we live out of the sense that we are related to everything and everyone, real-izing that dimensions of that relationship are still oppressed or living with illusion. As we strive to repair those relationships we find ourselves back in the world of the First Week, but at a deeper and more comprehensive level. Thus the journey starts over again. It is a spiral, a never-ending journey into the unfathomable depths of God's love. In this we are like Mary, the mother of Jesus. She brings Christ into the world. She shares Christ with the world. She suffers with Christ in the world. She experiences his resurrection, and becomes part of the community that is his resurrected presence in the world.

A Meeting with a Mother

And so we start with Mary. Ignatius presents Jesus appearing to Mary as the First Contemplation on the Resurrection of Christ. He writes, "He appeared to the Virgin Mary. Though this is not mentioned explicitly in the Scriptures it must be considered as stated when Scripture says that He appeared to many others" (#299). For Ignatius, the relationship between Jesus and his mother is very special. Without her free and generous consent at the Annunciation, his whole mission as a human would have been frustrated. Ignatius has included her in the conversations he invites those making the Exercises to conduct at the end of their prayer periods. Here he suggests that she is the first person Jesus appears to after he is raised from the dead.

He is, after all, flesh of her flesh, for it is through her that he has become incarnate. Beyond the bonds of parent and child, of Jewish mother and son, lies the deeper connection of resurrected body to its closest kin. She is the closest human being to him and so, for Ignatius, it is only in the nature of love that he should appear to her first.

We are invited, as we are at every contemplation, to be present at that meeting in all of its quiet, deeply personal intimacy when grief and resignation turn to incredulous wonder, mutual concern and affirmation. What had been told to her before – that he was to suffer, die and then rise from the dead – and what she had pondered on and held in faith now is seen and felt, is fact and true. In these moments of acceptance between Jesus and his mother, and between them and us in prayer, is only the simple, open conversation of heart to heart.

We have all heard stories of things, relationships or people lost, and of a life spent dealing with the emptiness, only to have what was believed gone forever returned forever. Such things happen in real life, too. Soldiers lost in battle are held for dead, mourned for, and then turn up again. Families are separated by war or other circumstances and reunite years later. Reunion is part of the human story.

Here Jesus and Mary experience something similar, except she saw her son tortured and killed. We live with Mary's grief: just as her son's life was held to be of no worth, her sacrifices to bring him into the world and to protect him with Joseph become worthless. Two lives wasted. One was devoted to the other, and that other was forsaken and crucified. We have to sit with that welling sense of emotion that comes from places too deep to be named as love comforts love, and claims love. We have to sit with Mary's embrace of Jesus and Jesus' embrace of Mary. We also have to sit, quietly and passionately, with our embrace of both. We, too, are included in that love.

Questions for prayer and reflection

1. Have you ever lost anything and then, against all odds, found it again? Enter into that state of simple joy again. What other memories or incidents does it raise for you? What do you experience as you savour those memories?

2. Where are you in the contemplation when the resurrected Jesus comes to his mother? How did that feel? What were the most moving moments? Why? What did they bring back to life for you? How did they transform the destructiveness of the previous Week?

3. What was your conversation after the prayer with Mary, Jesus, the Father? Where does that conversation lead you to next?

4. What do you do to stay in that quiet joy? What do you have to do to stay there?

5. What are the forces that try to move you away from that quiet focused rootedness? Can you acknowledge them without being driven by them?

6. As you sit in that quiet joy, what arises as gift for you?

7. What happens as you stay with that gift? As your staying quietly in that simple space opens that gift, you too are being opened by that gift. How does that feel?

8. Do you experience the gift of being able both to give and to receive as gratitude? Do you have a sense of how gratitude can be a way of life?

The Movie
Billy Elliot

Director: Stephen Daldry (2000 – 107 mins.)
Starring: Jamie Bell, Julie Walter, Gary Lewis

1. Summary

It is 1984 and, in a northern England mining town, a group of miners are on strike. Eleven-year-old Billy Elliot, whose father and brother are on strike, does not like the boxing lessons he is taking at school and decides to join the girls' ballet class. Billy's talent is encouraged by the ballet teacher, Mrs. Wilkinson, who manages to arrange an audition for Billy to the Royal Ballet School. Now Billy must face his family.

2. Questions about the Movie

1. *Billy Elliot* begins with a miners' strike. "[A]nd as you watch the police beat back the strikers with shield and truncheon, you see the crude ballet of social grievance to which Jamie's answer is a ballet of a far more liberating kind." (Alexander Walker, *The Evening Standard*, September 28, 2000) How do these two types of "dance" illustrate the tragedy that underlies the movie – the narrow-mindedness, the resistance to change, the bigotry and violence?

2. "Daldry isn't afraid of going for the emotional jugular, but he deftly sidesteps the mawkish. Yes. Billy Elliot follows a well-trod formula, and it hits one or two false notes…. But in the face of a movie so artfully made, so deeply charming, so heartfelt, it's not only pointless to resist, it's damn near impossible." (David Ansen, *Newsweek*, October 16, 2000) This is a major point – were you able to resist the movie? Was it indeed so artful, so charming, so heartfelt, that you could not help but become involved? Why? Why not? What does it take to involve you in a movie – make you feel with the characters – to make you possibly even shed a tear at the end?

3. "The achievement here, thanks largely to cinematographer Brian Tufano (*Trainspotting*), is that the film says the obvious through the innocence of a childhood perspective. Yes, unemployment and repression are everywhere here, but joy, the movie suggests, is just about keeping your feet tapping." (Liam Lacey, *The Globe and Mail*, October 13, 2000) How does the movie use the child's perspective – especially Billy's? Is the theme of the movie as simple as Lacey suggests? Why? Why not? How would you sum up the theme of the movie in one sentence?

4. "Where this really scores and tugs the emotions, though, is in the dance sequences themselves, set largely to a medley of '80s hits and comprising unorthodox moves guaranteed to blow away the

stereotypes of ballet – with one particularly glorious set-piece guaranteed to have even the most stoic of viewer complaining of something in their eye. Bell is as accomplished a dancer as he is an actor, carrying the movie with astonishing aplomb." (Caroline Westbrook, *Empire On Line*, Issue 136, October 2000) Which of the dance pieces in the movie worked best for you? What most caught your attention in that scene?

3. The Relationship of the Movie to the Theme of the Exercise

1. After the tumultuous Third Week of the Exercises, we enter into this Fourth Week – a time of joy. We need to experience this joy. Why is this movie possibly one of the best movies for this point in the Exercises?

2. Billy experiences in his dancing a sort of disappearing from himself; he feels a change in his body, as if electricity is coursing through him. Review the definitions of the following terms in the Exercise. Which best suits Billy at the end of the movie? Why?

   • pleasure
   • excitement
   • happiness
   • joy

3. Billy's father comes to discover, as the Exercise tells us, that we are related to everything and everyone. His eyes are opened to another way of life, which causes hardships in almost every aspect of his life. But it also brings him happiness. How does this change come about?

4. The Relationship of the Movie to One's Self in the Exercise

1. The grand leap with which Billy propels himself on stage at the end of the movie is an expression of all he has worked for and expresses the great gifts he has been given. We hope that he will not lose these gifts as he goes on in his career. You have been moving towards gifts during the Exercises. How will you express these gifts even more as you move into the Fourth Week? What will you do to try and ensure that you do not waste them as you return to the world?

2. Billy finds his talent and then almost loses the chance to develop it as he misses the first audition. Things change and the lost chance is regained. In your life, which lost chances have most affected you? What did you do to regain them? Or did you give up and move on? If so, what did you leave behind?

3. Billy's relationship with his mother was a very deep one – recall his visit to her grave and the time he believes he sees her as he goes to drink milk from the bottle. So much is left unsaid but understood in these scenes. Think about the letter Billy shows Mrs. Wilkinson that his mother wrote him before she died. When Mrs. Wilkinson says that his mother must have been very special, Billy replies, "Nah, she was just me mam." For Ignatius, as we read in the Exercise, the relationship between Jesus and his mother is very special and his appearance to her after his resurrection is a time of great joy for them both. Think about your relationship with your mother/ What times of shared pleasure and joy can you recall?

Christ Appears to Mary Magdalene

(John 20:1-18)

Jesus said, " I will not leave you desolate; I will come to you."

(John 14:18)

Consider the office of consoler that Christ our Lord exercises and compare it with the way in which friends are wont to console each other.

(Sp. Ex. #224)

Grace: Here it will be to ask for the grace to be glad and rejoice intensely because of the great joy and the glory of Christ Our Lord.

(Sp. Ex. #221)

Waiting in Emptiness

It would be wonderful if we could discern a pattern to the resurrection appearances of Christ, but we cannot. They move beyond the limits of our imagination. When we enter the stories themselves, in a contemplative way, we discover that they stretch our imagination by constantly surprising us and by inviting us to deeper and unsuspected intimacies with God.

One such story is the first resurrection account in John's Gospel. A woman who had been exorcised by Jesus and had become one of his close followers comes to the tomb. Seeing that the stone has been taken away from the entrance, she runs and tells Peter and John. They go to the tomb, see that what she has said is true, and return home. She, however, stays there weeping and looking into the empty tomb. As she turns from the tomb she sees someone she mistakes for the gardener and asks him where the body has gone. The stranger says her name, "Mary," and she recognizes him as the Christ. She then holds onto him so hard that he says: Don't hold onto me so hard, but go to the others and tell them, "I am ascending to my Father and to your Father, to my God and your God." She goes back to the disciples, tells them what had happened and repeats his words to her.

Being Found by What We Lost

In this poignant scene of seeking and finding the beloved, of embrace and mission, we find a sequence of events that transforms our own experience of intimacy with Jesus. He has attracted our attention, he has rescued us, we follow him and become part of his life as he becomes part of our life. Then that relationship is destroyed as he is betrayed and killed. In our sorrow we wait by the tomb, but in itself it does not give life. As we linger there, things come to us – images and feelings of consolation – but we cannot name them properly because we are still caught up in the world of death. It is only when those things strike our sense of identity, which lies deeper than our grief, that we discover what has greeted us. It is the Christ! It is hard to believe – the one we loved and lost returns to us transformed. We fall into the arms of the beloved. But the story does not end there. For that love to be fulfilled, both of us must return to the source of our loving. The path seems to diverge again.

Jesus needs to return to the Father, and we need to create the community that bears his name in its return to the Father. The love we share does not disappear so soon after being found again. There will be a new way of loving – not between individuals and God, but rather in community. The community called Church is the embodied presence of that shared presence of love. All this might sound like science fiction, as we struggle to understand it. But it really isn't. It is just the nature of love becoming more and more manifest. If we can stay with that state of consolation of being loved, the path to community will unfold.

It is the nature of love not to abandon anyone, and so Jesus in his resurrected state comes back to those he loves. It is significant to note that in the scripture stories, Jesus does not show himself in his resurrected state to any but those whom he loves and who love him. Those who do not love cannot see love. They always read it as something else. But to those who love and who seek love, love comes. One of the gifts of the resurrection is that it can open us to dimensions of love that we did not think possible. Here, in Mary's loving, we experience someone who had thought she had reached the limits of love. She came to grieve the end of that love by going to the tomb. To her surprise she finds it open and empty. On our spiritual journey to love, we come to the stage of emptiness and are asked, as in the final contemplation of the Third Week, to wait in that emptiness. When Mary waits, the Christ comes to her.

Waiting in the emptiness, as Christ experienced on the cross, removes all our pre-conceptions of how love can present itself. So when the Christ appears to Mary, she does not recognize him. She supposes he is a gardener. Christ does not appear in the drama of worldly power with pomp and circumstance and special effects. He does not seek to impress or to terror-ize. He appears in a simple, ordinary way. For resurrection comes in simple, ordinary ways. When someone is moving through mourning, we notice that signs of new life come in the person's ability to appreciate, perhaps even without knowing it, simple, everyday things. As you journey through the day with this contemplation, try to be conscious of the effect in your life of the little things that give you joy.

Named by God

But Jesus goes even further with his friend Mary. He calls her by name. In grief we often lose a sense of who we are; we have entered a new territory where everything is strange and we have even become strangers to ourselves. But when we are found by love we are brought back to ourselves, and to a new sense of ourselves and of life. This is the gift Jesus gives Mary when he acknowledges her and calls her by name. She responds by recognizing him. This is what the gift of love does – it enables us to recognize others for who they really are. To be called by God in love gives us our identity. To respond to that love changes our perspective and our hearts. We see with the eyes of love, and we see God in the commonplace. What before seemed insignificant now becomes worthy of notice and contemplation. When we enter into that state of contemplation, which is not just reserved for prayer periods, we start discovering God in all things. Here Mary discovers Jesus and embraces him.

We need to remain in that embrace and to allow that healing touch to transform us. When lovers embrace, they open their spirits to each other in mutual vulnerability. That openness has the effect of giving us courage and a sense of connection that remain even when we are physically separated from the beloved. We see this in little children who are loved. They are not fearful and insecure, but are filled with a sense of wonder and creativity. The same thing happens when people fall in love, and when we are touched by resurrection. We fall in love with God again in a whole new way. Like Mary Magdalene, we are tempted to hold onto that love in ways that are appropriate only to a past life. The new life that love calls us to fills us with a sense of our true identity, of wonder and of creativity. We find ourselves responding to that love as Mary did, by wanting to share it with whomever she encounters. That love does not turn us in on ourselves, it turns us to the world and to those who need to know the good news that love is stronger than death, that the gift of forgiveness is more powerful than any alienation, and that life is more creative than evil. It is this message that Mary carries back to the disciples when she tells them that she has seen and touched the risen Christ.

Always Going Home

Christ's journey, however, is not over. In sharing his resurrected life he begins his return to the Father when, in him, all things will be restored to the Father. His risen body becomes us, on our own spiritual journey to the fullness of life. Christ himself returns to the Father. Love responds to love, is attracted to love and becomes united to love. He goes before us to assure us of where we, too, are going. He does not just show us that death is not the end of life, he also desires us to know that life leads to more and fuller life. Death is just a door that opens to the fullness of life. In this contemplation, we are given not only an experience, but a direction and a gift that opens to broader and deeper dimensions of love. We need to sit and allow that gift to come to us and open us so that we may open it.

Questions for prayer and reflection

1. What gift was given to you in this contemplation? How do you feel about that gift? How does it change the way you see yourself, others or the world?

2. How do the prayer periods in this contemplation stretch and liberate your imagination?

3. Have you ever mistaken love for something else? How did you find out what it really was?

4. What happens these days when you find a quiet place and dare to let your deepest longings for love rise in prayer? How are they answered?

5. When you look back over your life, what happens to you when you dare to love?

6. Do you feel that sense of daring now? For what?

7. Where does your creativity come from?

8. What causes you to wonder in delight? Do you think of these as manifestations of resurrection? Do you allow yourself the time to savour these moments? What happens when you do?

9. If you were to examine your life, or even the past few days, looking for those moments of wonder, what do you find? What do those moments tell you?

10. In your conversations after the prayer with the Father, Jesus or Mary – or all three – what comes across or stays with you?

The Movie
The Royal Tenenbaums

Director: Wes Andersen (2001 – 110 mins.)
Starring: Danny Glover, Gene Hackman, Anjelica Houston, Bill Murray, Gwyneth Paltrow, Ben Stiller,
Luke Wilson, Owen Wilson

1. Summary

After two decades of failure, betrayal and disaster, three child prodigies, now grown up and, along with their mother, return to the family home. Their father, Royal, who had left them long ago, comes back with the announcement that he has a terminal illness and wishes to make things right again with his family.

2. Questions about the Movie

1. "By the final stretch, the ache these characters feel – about their unfulfilled potential and their unrealized relationships with those closest to them – should be palpable, not to mention deeply moving. It's a story of a desperate attempt to repair missed connections, one inevitably doomed to failure but not without dividends." (Todd McCarthy, *Variety*, October 8-14, 2001). The critics were sharply divided about this movie – they either hated it or loved it. When you read the above review excerpt, you can almost feel that the next sentence McCarthy writes will begin with "but." What is your feeling about the movie? How would you write the next sentence of this review based on your thoughts and feelings?

2. A very interesting use is made of music in the movie, such as the way the movie mixes snippets from Ravel's F Major String Quartet and Vince Guaraldi's "Christmas Time Is Here," which was composed for a Peanuts Christmas television special. What is the role of music in this movie? How is "Hey, Jude" used to set up the children's failures? What does "Down by the Schoolyard" add to Royal's day out with his grandsons? Think of two other scenes where music is used for a specific purpose. Does the music work for you in those scenes?

3. "Many of us will love this movie, this troubled clan, in the same way that many of us love our own families – despite ourselves, counterintuitively yet warmly, and for reasons that have little do with reason itself." (Rick Groen, *The Globe and Mail*, December 21, 2001). Which members of the family do you come to care for most? Why? What is it about these completely unhinged people that causes you to care about them at all?

4. "Andersen has given his audience just enough to get by. If you blink, you may miss a gesture or a line or a detail that alludes to a critical aspect of his characters' emotional lives, the core dilemma they've been hiding for fear of being exposed

and embarrassed before the world." (Kent Jones, liner notes for the DVD version of *The Royal Tenenbaums*) What are some examples of details in this movie that the audience has to grasp?

3. The Relationship of the Movie to the Theme of the Exercise

1. The Exercise tells us that it is the nature of love not to abandon anyone. "I want this family to love me," declares Royal. First he tells his wife, Ethel, that he came back because he is ashamed of himself. But then he tells her that he did what he did so that he could win his family back and get rid of Henry, and because he was broke.

    Royal is a complicated person. Are all these statements contradictory? Does he really love his family? How does he "return" to each of them?

2. The gift of love enables us to recognize others for who they really are. How does this statement hold true – or does it – for the following examples of love we see in the movie?

    • Royal for his wife and children
    • Ethel and Henry
    • Chas and his children
    • Margot and Eli
    • Ritchie and Margot
    • Raleigh and Margot

3. When little children are loved, as the Exercise says, they are not fearful or insecure. How well loved by their parents were Chas, Ritchie and Margot? How much of what happens to them grew out of their fear and insecurity? What about Chas' two sons – are they loved? How does their father's love for them differ from Royal's love for

them? What impact does this difference have on their lives?

4. The Relationship of the Movie to One's Self in the Exercise

1. Love responds to love, is attracted to love and becomes united to love. Royal's real love for his children brings them all together so that at Royal's funeral it can be said that he would have found the event satisfactory. Where is there such love in your own life? To whom have you offered love? What has been the result?

2. The Exercise tells us that when lovers embrace, they open their spirits to each other in mutual vulnerability. There are many example of this in the movie – think of the love between Ritchie and Margot. How does love in your life make you vulnerable? To what are you vulnerable? What happens as a result of that vulnerability? How does that vulnerability make you feel connected even when we are physically separated from the one you love?

3. To those who love and to those who seek love, love comes. Love is something we all seek in our lives. Each of the main characters in the movie is in search of a real love – some desperately, some calmly. By the end of the movie we sense that some of them have found it. How often have you sought love? The love of another person? The love of God? Where do you seek such love? When that love – of another person, of God – comes into your life, what difference does it make? As Ignatius would ask: What have you done to seek such love? What are you doing to seek such love? What will you do to seek such love?

3rd Exercise
Doubting Thomas
(John 20:19-31)

They said to him, "What must we do, to be doing the works of God?" Jesus answered them, "This is the work of God, that you believe in the one whom he has sent."

(John 6:28-29)

Recall to mind the blessing of creation and redemption, and the special favours I have received.

(Sp. Ex. #234)

Grace: Here it will be to ask for the grace to be glad and rejoice intensely because of the great joy and the glory of Christ Our Lord.

(Sp. Ex. #221)

Fear and Joy

Before the disciples experience the resurrection, they are filled with fear and huddle behind closed doors. In this story Jesus enters that closed room, wishes them peace and shows them his pierced hands and side as proof of who he is. Their fear is transformed into joy. In this joy he breathes the Holy Spirit onto them and missions them to forgive sins. One of the disciples, Thomas, was not there when this happened and refuses to believe it took place. Eight days later, as they are all gathered again, Jesus reappears. He shows his hands and his side to Thomas, exhorting him to believe. Thomas, transformed by that empirical evidence, believes.

This story opens with Jesus repeating in dramatic fashion the mystery of the Incarnation. In both mysteries he enters our human world, which is self-enclosed out of fear, and his presence transforms that world. In this resurrection narrative the disciples are afraid they will be treated as Jesus was by the authorities and the mob. The resurrected Christ does not abandon them in their fear but enters their little world and wishes them peace. Inasmuch as we become manifestations of the resurrected Christ we, too, are asked to enter the worlds of fear and self-enclosure and bring a peace that comes from rootedness in the Father's love. That relationship casts out fear. Interestingly, when we do this, we are tested as Christ was tested. We need to show signs that we live out of our relationship with the Father before others will believe us. The most effective sign of that is if, in our suffering, we remain faithful and loving.

When the disciples see the risen Christ, he shows them signs that it is truly he. In our prayer these days, when we might find it difficult to believe the resurrection can be present in our lives, we need to ask for that grace of having the risen Christ come and identify himself to us in ways that we can believe. We might wish in our ill-conceived pride that we do not need this, but in our experienced poverty we know that we do. This is the shameless asking of the beloved that is known as praying for a particular grace. As in any love relationship, we cannot demand that the one we love does what we seek, but we can ask and we can dispose ourselves to receive what we ask for. The same is true of God. He does not demand that we behave as he wishes, but he can ask and dispose himself to receive what we are willing to offer in love.

The Gift of the Spirit

Christ asks that when we accept the proof that he has risen from the dead, we live as he lived and love as he loved. As he says, "As the Father has sent me, even so do I send you" (John 20:21). But to do that we need to have the same spirit as the Christ: a spirit of loving reverence for all, of courage and creativity, of joy and compassion. It is the spirit that embodies Christ's relationship with the Father. Christ gives the disciples that relationship and that spirit when "he breathed on them and said to them, 'Receive the Holy Spirit'" (John 20:22).

This action echoes the creation of humans in the book of Genesis. There "the Lord God formed man of dust from the ground and breathed in to his nostrils the breath of life; and man became a living being" (Genesis 2:7). In the scriptures a human is not body and soul – that is a Greek distinction – but dust animated by the Lord God's breath or spirit. This makes humans living beings. When Christ breathes on the disciples he is creating a new being out of the chaos of their creation. When we enter this contemplation we dispose ourselves for God to breathe on us and make a us a new creation. We become transformed. We move from fear to love, from self-doubt to self-acceptance, from confusion to creativity. That new creation makes us more like Christ, and we find ourselves filled with his spirit and doing what he has been doing in the world: forgiving sins. In the passage from John we are contemplating, Jesus says, "Receive the Holy Spirit. If you forgive the sins of any they are forgiven; if you retain the sins of any they are retained" (John 20:22-23).

Forgiving Sin

But what does it mean to forgive sins? Maybe it would help if we looked at what sin does. It causes division by setting people against each other and even against themselves. It promotes self-hate and spreads illusions that deceive us about our true nature. It is destructive and does not delight in joy or in celebrating life. It oppresses. To forgive sins, therefore, is to create community and self-acceptance. It is to seek the truth and maintain it. It is to cherish creativity and to celebrate life wherever it may be found. It is to transform chaos into relationships that foster healing and peace. It liberates the imagination and the spirit. It grounds us in that constant and compassionate presence of the mystery we call Father. We see that this is what Christ's coming into our world has done for us: when we experience resurrection, we find our new and transformed selves doing the same thing for the world, and in concrete ways for those we meet.

Until we experience the risen Christ in our lives, we cannot see how this is possible: all we have to inspire us is the exhausted, pragmatic politics of the world and the tragedies that result. We consider it escapist fantasy to believe otherwise, and we think spiritual maturity means accepting the world as it is and of accommodating it. We refuse to believe that we can experience the risen Christ in our prayer. We refuse to open ourselves to believe – lest we get hurt or disappointed – that the Christ desires to come to those who, in their own small ways, love God.

Personal Proof Beyond Disbelief

This is Thomas' problem. He was not with the original eleven when Christ appeared to them in the closed room. He does not think that what they have told him is possible. Yet, in his mercy, Christ appears to Thomas and to the others once again that very next week in that very same place. He tells Thomas, "Put your finger here, and see my hands; put out your hand and place it in my side; do not be so faithless, but believe" (John 20:21). Jesus does not say, Well, if Thomas does not believe, that is his problem. The Thomas he knows and loves is the Thomas he chose to be his companion. It is this same Thomas who said, when the plots were strong against Jesus, "Let us go up to Jerusalem and die with him." Jesus knows Thomas loves him in his own way. He also knows that Thomas really cannot believe that the Father's love can raise Jesus from the dead, or that Jesus, after all he had been through, including being abandoned by his disciples, would care to return to them if he had indeed been raised from the dead. But Jesus did both things, and here he does one extra thing. He comes back just for Thomas. He gives Thomas the proof he needs to commit himself to that love Jesus offers. And Thomas, in a passionate response, does commit himself, crying out, "My Lord and my God!" (John 20:28).

Thomas is like us. When we have been loved beyond our disbelief, then we can acknowledge personally and intimately what love is. In this contemplation we ask for that grace to experience this personal love that God has for each of us in ways that move us beyond our disbelief into a new way of seeing and being that makes us creative, compassionate and joyful.

Questions for prayer and reflection

1. When you entered this contemplation, what were the elements of personal surprise? How did they manifest themselves? How did you respond?

2. How did you experience the risen Christ in this contemplation?

3. What is the relationship between your fear and your lack of belief? Can you see in your history where that fear shaped the way you believe?

4. Where did that fear come from? Can you invite the risen Christ to enter into that fear, or those areas and sources of fear? What happens when you do this in prayer?

5. How do you respond to the experience of the risen Christ in your prayer?

6. What difficulties do you have in forgiving yourself, others and the world?

7. What happens when you ask that the breath of Christ be blown on those areas? How do you experience that breath?

8. In what ways are you like Thomas? What happens when you contemplate the Thomas incident in these prayer periods? What happens to the Thomas aspects of yourself?

9. In your conversations with God, Jesus, or Mary – or all three – after the prayer, what surfaces that is significant?

10. What is the next step in your growth to spiritual freedom after these prayer periods? What will you do, concretely and practically, to facilitate that next step?

269

The Movie
Monsoon Wedding

Director: Mira Nair (2001 – 115 mins.)
Starring: Naseeruddin Shah, Lillete Dubey, Shefali Shetty

1. Summary

In modern India, Western ways collide with age-old traditions in *Monsoon Wedding*. An arranged wedding between Aditi, who is rebounding from an affair with a TV host, and Hermant, the groom from Texas, sees the coming together in New Delhi of relatives from both sides of the family who are spread out all over the world. Through four days, we watch the preparations for the wedding and the search for love.

2. Questions about the Movie

1. "The setting is upper-middle-class New Delhi and an extended family of well-off professionals who speak more English than Hindi…. On the surface, they're confident and secure, but underneath they're snobbish, status-conscious, ill at ease, and the mood of the family is reflected in the monsoon season – hot, uncomfortably humid, about to erupt in torrential rain. The family belongs to the Indian diaspora, its children scattered to the four corners of the earth…and they are torn between their traditional culture and the Western world in which they thrive." (Philip French, *The Observer*, December 30, 2001) How westernized are the members of the family? How have they managed to mix their own traditions with the Western culture that seeks to impose itself on them?

2. "The acting and interacting of the ensemble cast is exemplary, although, because Nair forgoes easy exposition, it takes us time to sort out the various relationships, a difficulty that the disoriented groom confesses to sharing. But from the start, we're fascinated by this world and its contradictions." (Philip French, *The Observer*, December 30, 2001) What is it about this world that fascinates us? The closeness of family? The music used to express emotions so openly?

3. "The penny finally drops in a riveting sequence at the film's climax…. The scene is static, virtually silent, and the father, now in possession of the secret, is forced to make an impossible choice between duelling loyalties: on one side, the past and deep-rooted tradition; on the other, the present and unvarnished truth. For once, these two strains will not meld. Choose he cannot, but choose he must, aware that great sorrow lies down either path. But not just sorrow. The climax ends and the denouement follows, when the monsoon brings its cathartic rains." (Rick Groen, *The Globe and Mail*, March 1, 2002) Water is often used as a symbol of cleansing, of rebirth. How is this evident at the end of the movie?

3. The Relationship of the Movie to the Theme of the Exercise

1. Sin fragments and causes division by setting people against each other and even against themselves, as the Exercise tells us. How is this true in the movie? What is the "sin" here?

2. The sin in the world is destructive and does not delight in joy or in celebrating life. It oppresses in every aspect of our lives. How does sin oppress the people involved in the wedding? Consider these people:

   • Aditi, the bride
   • Lalit, her father
   • Hermant, the groom
   • Uncle Tej
   • Ria
   • Dubey, the wedding planner

3. As the Exercise says, to forgive sin is to create community and self-acceptance. How is this evident at the end of this movie? For Aditi and Hermant? For her parents? For Dubey? For Alice, the maid? For Ria?

4. The Relationship of the Movie to One's Self in the Exercise

1. Sin promotes self-hate and spreads illusions that deceive us about our true nature. It is clear how this works in the lives of the family. Where does this take place in your life? What can you do to change this – to become what God calls you to be?

2. Aditi makes her decision: "I don't want to start something new based on lies and deceit." We see how Hermant reacts. Where have you been faced in your life with a choice on making a fresh start that could have involved "lies and deceit"? What has happened as a result?

3. As we enter this Exercise, we enter the process of being transformed. We have seen in the movie how many of the main characters move from fear to love, from self-doubt to self-acceptance, from confusion to creativity. How is this taking place in your life at this point in the Exercises?

4th Exercise
The Road to Emmaus
(Luke 24)

Make me know your ways, O Lord;
Teach me your paths.
Lead me in your truth and teach me,
For you are the God of my salvation;
For you I wait all day long.
Be mindful of your mercy, O Lord,
and of your steadfast love,
For they have been of old.
According to your steadfast love remember me,
For your goodness' sake, O Lord.

(Psalm 24:4-7)

This is a cry of wonder accompanied by surging emotion as I pass in review all creatures. How is it that they have permitted me to live and have sustained me in life!

(Sp. Ex. #60)

Grace: Here it will be to ask for the grace to be glad and rejoice intensely because of the great joy and the glory of Christ Our Lord.

(Sp. Ex. #221)

Moving Beyond Our Fantasies

As we continue to contemplate the resurrection, we find that our joy becomes more integrated into our sense of self. That transformation allows us to become even more open to the mystery that is the journey of our life. We tend to understand that mystery by the story we tell ourselves about our life. Resurrection changes that story. We cannot change that story ourselves. In fact, when we try to do that we end up with fantasy. There are many kinds of fantasy: simple escapist fantasy, untouched by existential reality, where we can daydream about perpetual youth and riches, or of utopian societies where all are politically equal; modified forms of fantasy, such as a perfect, anxiety-free existence fuelled by the narcotics of drugs, ambition or social conditioning; or ideological and religious fantasies. In fact, we feed on fantasy. Sometimes we think we are converted, but all we have done is substituted one fantasy for another.

There comes a time when we discover that the fantasies we have lived out of are unable to bear the burden of brute reality. The large systems we might have trusted in and even devoted our lives to maintaining break down. We find ourselves slipping between the gaps of their supposedly impermeable surfaces. We are hurled back into chaos and uncertainty. We suffer from anxiety and a sense of meaninglessness. We hold onto lesser things, knowing their inadequacy, just for the sake of holding onto something. We sometimes guard those things – hobbies, jobs, political affiliations, ethnic partisanship – fiercely and blindly, knowing that without them we would be lost. We even claim that such commitment gives us access to God. One of the fantasies we have is about God and how God operates and is present in the world. When bad things happen, we ask: How can God allow this? Unless we find a suitable answer

272

to that question, we abandon God. That is not a bad thing, surprisingly, because what we are abandoning is not God but a fantasy of God. Our spiritual drive to the true God – our deepest desire – takes over and we begin a spiritual journey that moves beyond our fantasies. We encounter that God who is always coming towards us and walking with us in our pain.

The two disciples of Jesus walking to Emmaus, about 20 kilometres outside Jerusalem, after the celebration of Passover and the Sabbath had held onto such fantasies about Jesus. "We had hoped he was the one to redeem Israel" (Luke 24:21). Instead of the political hero they wanted, they got a crucified prophet. In their disillusionment, even when they heard the reports of Jesus' resurrection, they could not grasp its import. For them it is just anecdotal data. It makes no sense in terms of the way they view the world.

But something happens to them. On their way back to Emmaus, they encounter the risen Jesus but do not recognize him because they can see only out of their fantasy. What Jesus does is unravel the material of their fantasy – in their case, the Scriptures – and reinterpret it in light of his relationship to the Father. This allows him to show the path of the Messiah as depicted in their sacred writings. He explains that the Christ was destined to suffer and then enter into his glory. When they hear these things, their deepest desire is felt and held, given expression and answered. They move from being despondent to being inflamed in the spirit. As they reflect, "Did not our hearts burn within us while he talked to us on the road, while he opened to us the scriptures?" (Luke 24:32).

Reimagining God

Even though we are in a resurrection context, we too need to look at our mistaken expectations of how God should behave. Such expectations cause us to miss the resurrection experience that is present to us even at this moment. We need to ask to have the scriptures of our lives and of our religion opened to us so we may see who Christ is for us here and now. To help us in this process we might, in this prayerful contemplation, imagine walking with Jesus on the road to Emmaus and bring to him all the areas in the world and in our lives where we do not see the merciful presence of God. We need him to open our hearts, our minds and our eyes to him.

Journeying with God

In this gospel story this is exactly what Christ does. The two disciples so share his spirit that when they arrive at their little town as evening falls and he appears to be going further on, they ask him to spend the night with them. As he blesses and breaks the bread at supper, they recognize him and he disappears from their midst. The journey they have made with him changes them – they now share his same spirit. They have become community, which is manifest in their desire to share their home and their meal with him. Through this sharing, they recognize him in the breaking of the bread – the same act of community that he had enacted at the Last Supper, saying that what they shared then was his body. The two disciples thus become the continuing body of Christ on earth.

In their transformation they do exactly what Christ has done to them. Even though it is night and they are tired, they set out at once for Jerusalem to tell the others what had happened. While they are gathered as community, Christ appears to all of them, "and while they still disbelieved for joy, and wondered, he said to them, "Have you anything here to eat? They gave him a piece of broiled fish and he took it and ate before them" (Luke 24:41-43).

The joy the two disciples felt on the road to Emmaus increases as they share their experiences, and in that community Christ comes. His reappearance increases their joy so much, they cannot believe such a thing is possible. To prove it is he and not a ghost, the Christ eats a piece of fish. When they accept that it is truly him, he missions them to continue his work of reconciling all to each other in the building up of community.

The Path of Joy

As we enter more and more deeply into this contemplation, we discover that the joy we experience opens up to more and deeper joy, and that this deepening joy comes about by the creation of community. In the gospel story the two disciples encounter the risen Christ and become joyful. To share that joy they return to the other disciples with the good news. The larger community is missioned to share that joy. That path of joy goes from those two to the rest of the apostles and through these, in mission, to the whole world. That path becomes possible when the disciples accept the reality of a Christ who, through journeying into suffering and death, has risen. He witnesses, with his very life, the reality of a love that is not fantasy but the compassionate mercy of God that embraces each and every one of us, a mercy that is almost too much to bear. If we undertake that journey to Emmaus with our own broken illusions, we experience that growing joy that transforms us and, through us, the whole world.

Questions for Prayers and Reflection

1. What fantasies did you have about God? How did they shape your life and your expectations of life? How does this contemplation and its repetitions move you beyond those fantasies?

2. What were the most significant moments for you in this contemplation? Why?

3. As you walked with the risen Christ through the path of your life, what was explained to you that is helpful for you now?

4. Think of the community of people who are important to you. How do you share life with them? In what way is that a manifestation of the risen Christ?

5. How does this contemplation address the suffering in your life?

6. The contemplations of the Fourth Week invite you to enter into a relationship with the risen Christ and to experience how that intimacy opens up your life. As you reflect on these contemplations, how is your life being opened up?

7. How can you distinguish between fantasy and experiences of the resurrected Christ? How do suffering, forgiveness, community, and an ongoing relationship with the compassionate mystery of the Father help you learn to make that distinction? What happens when you ask the Christ to help you make the distinction? What response do you get?

8. What arose from the conversation you had at the end of the prayer periods with the Father, Jesus or Mary?

The Movie
Matchstick Men

Director: Ridley Scott (2003 – 116 mins.)
Starring: Nicholas Cage, Sam Rockwell, Alison Lohman

1. Summary

Roy and Frank specialize in small scams that have resulted in a lucrative partnership. Roy's private life, however, is not so successful. He's an obsessive compulsive agoraphobe (he's got problems leaving the house), and his problems mount when he learns one day that he has a 14-year-old daughter, Angela. After meeting him, Angela develops a fascination for this stranger who happens to be her father. This man who should be the moral compass for her own values instead intrigues her with the deftness and success of his cheating and stealing.

2. Questions about the Movie

1. "When you look back on this film (and it's one of those that compels you to), there are puzzling but not insurmountable questions about the way events unfolded. Maybe it would help to see it again. Maybe that's the con." (Chris Knight, *The National Post*, September 12, 2003) What do you think the con was? Was there more than the one found at the end of the movie? The novel does not contain the final two scenes of the movie – in the rug showroom and in Roy's home. What would you think if the movie ended just after Roy visits his ex-wife?

2. "Music is used very purposefully in this movie. Sometimes recognizable songs provide comment on dialogue and/or actions. Sometimes effective soundtrack music contributes to the mood of a scene. Most of the songs are not just recognizable tunes, but are performed by their original artists, some from the '60s or '70s and some from the recent past.

• We hear "Good Life," by Frank Sinatra, behind Roy looking anxiously out the window at his swimming pool.

• We hear "This Town Is a Lonely Town," by Frank Sinatra, behind Roy eating tuna from a can.

• We hear "Summer Wind," by Frank Sinatra, during Roy's phone calls.

• Angela's entrance into Roy's house is accompanied by music heavy with woodwinds and percussion.

• We hear "Beyond the Sea," by Bobby Darin, behind Roy buying ice cream for Angela.

• We hear Herb Alpert and the Tijuana Brass playing "Tijuana Taxi" during Angela's discovery of Roy's conning gear intercut with dance bar music while Roy and Frank con Chuck at the Spearmint Rhino.

- We hear a pop song when Roy receives the pizza.
- We hear "I'm Leaning on the Lamp," by George Formby, behind Roy trying to find Angela outside her summer school.
- We hear "Danke Shoen," by Wayne Newton, when Roy tells Frank that he is quitting the confidence business.
- We hear "Summer Wind" for the second time when Roy goes home to Kathy, which continues into the credits.

Consider these uses of music and how they might influence the way that viewers feel or interpret the scenes in which they occur. If they are recognizable artists, consider how the authenticity of the song might add to its effect on the viewers." (Neil Andersen, Study Guide for *Matchstick Men*, *Scanning the Movies*, September 2003)

3. In *Matchstick Men*, our witnessing of Angela as she learns the truth about her father is a chance to experience ethical and unethical actions and weigh in with our own moral stance. By being media literate we can consider the ethics, characterizations, ideological positions and other issues in a "safe" environment. A movie is such a "safe" place. There we can talk about difficult topics, keeping their ideologies at arm's-length, rather than having to admit to holding one position or another. It's a great means of prompting debate easily because people don't have to own or defend opinions, just examine them. Then we can decide where we might wish to take a moral stand in our own world – the real world – and ideally make our own decisions about the various moral codes we encounter in books, television, music and movies. What difference does looking at this movie through the eyes of media literacy make to you in how you react to it?

3. The Relationship of the Movie to the Theme of the Exercise

1. When the movie opens, Roy already suffers from what the Exercise calls anxiety and a sense of meaninglessness. What has brought him to that point? How is this manifested in his life? What changes his situation?

2. As we enter more deeply into this contemplation, it is clear, as the Exercise notes, that this deepening joy comes about through the creation of community. What community did Roy try to build as a result of the joy he experienced with Angela's arrival in his life? Does it work? Why? Why not?

3. Towards the end of the movie – with the revelation of the large con – Roy finds himself back in the chaos and uncertainty that the Exercise talks about. He breaks down totally in front of his ex-wife when he realizes what has really happened. At this point he can either go back or go on to face reality. Which does he choose? What impact does it have on his life? Why do you think he made the choice he did?

4. The Relationship of the Movie to One's Self in the Exercise

1. The Exercise reminds us that sometimes we think we are converted but all we have done is substituted one fantasy for another. Towards the end of the movie, it is clear that this has happened to Roy in a very stunning way. Where have you either been tempted to do this or actually done it? What happened as a result?

2. In his journey, Roy finds that Angela – the daughter he never knew he had – becomes an anchor for him, opening new paths into life, helping him overcome the demons that haunted him. Who is the "Angela" in your life helping you on your spiritual journey to God? What has "Angela" done to help you along in this journey? Have you always been open to "Angela"? If not, what stopped you?

3. At the end of the movie, Roy has at last abandoned his fantasies and found his way towards his deepest desire. While this is – explicitly – not expressed as being God, it is a place where he can find peace of mind. What fantasy do you have to abandon before you can reach your deepest desire – God?

5th Exercise
Feed My Sheep
(John 21)

For God alone my soul waits in silence;
For my hope is from him.
He only is my rock and my salvation,
My fortress; I shall not be shaken.
On God rests my deliverance and my honour;
My mighty rock, my refuge is God.

(Psalm 62:5-7)

I will ponder with great affection how much God our Lord has done for me, and how much He has given me of what He possesses.

(Sp. Ex. #234)

Grace: Here it will be to ask for the grace to be glad and rejoice intensely because of the great joy and the glory of Christ Our Lord.

(Sp. Ex. #221)

The Mission

Even though Jesus' companions now know that he is risen and is present to them, they do not know when and how he will appear to them. This seemingly haphazard way of relating disconcerts them. In retrospect we can see that he has breathed on them and given them his mission and spirit: now they need to learn to live out of that mission and spirit. If he remains with them, they will depend on him and not on the spirit, which is his intimate relationship with the Father.

In the last chapter of John's Gospel, Peter and the others wait for Jesus. He does not appear. Finally, during the night Peter decides to go fishing, and the rest go along. When morning breaks they see someone on the shore. He asks them affectionately if they have caught anything; they say no. He suggests casting the net on the other side of the boat: when they do so, they catch an incredible number of fish. John, realizing it is the Lord on the shore, tells Peter, who jumps overboard and swims to the beach. When the rest arrive, they find that Jesus has prepared fish and bread for them on a charcoal fire.

Like the disciples, we cannot predict how and when the risen Christ will appear to us. These days we realize that Jesus has risen from the dead and that, in some profound way, he is with us, even though we do not experience him all the time. We cannot compel him to remain with us. Like Mary Magdalene, we want to cling to him, but he says, "Do not cling to me." We are not yet ready, we feel, to strike out on our own, to trust ourselves as he obviously trusts us. But we know we can't just mope. Life must go on. We pick up our lives and our jobs and continue. When we do that, conscious of how inadequate it all is, he comes and offers us within our daily lives even more than we can imagine. With this we are fed for the next step.

Beyond Friendship to Love

In that next step, Peter and Jesus go walking. Jesus asks Peter, "Do you love me?" He uses the

Greek word *agape* (a-ga-pay), which means a self-sacrificing love that gives all of life meaning. Peter replies, "Yes, Lord, you know I love you." But the word John uses for Peter's answer is *philia*, meaning friendship. Jesus responds, "Feed my lambs." Again Jesus asks Peter the same question using the same words, and again Peter replies using the same words. Jesus says, "Tend my sheep." The third time Jesus asks the question "Do you love me?" he uses the word Peter uses: *philia*. It is as if he is saying, are we really friends, then, if not intimates? Peter cries because he knows what he is capable of, and what he is not capable of. He says, yes, they are friends, and Jesus says, "Feed my sheep." There is a movement in Jesus' questions in terms of Peter's capabilities. The difference between feeding lambs and tending sheep is that lambs are born in enclosures, which protect them; sheep are left out in the open. Easily excitable and somewhat stupid, these animals can forage for themselves but need to be protected from thieves and beasts of prey. That third mission Jesus gives Peter is to be not only shepherd but also nourisher of Jesus' flock. In accepting and living out this mission, Peter moves from fisherman to shepherd, from being Jesus' friend to sharing his spirit, from *philia* to *agape*. This is his baptism, and it changes his life. In that journey to love, he discovers a love that carries him to a death similar to the Christ's.

In our journey through the resurrection, we are also called to move from being friends of Christ to sharers in his spirit and mission. In this journey we discover what it means to die to ourselves, to take up our cross daily, and to follow Jesus' path. Opening the gift of the resurrection does not necessarily make our lives easier, and we may be tempted to stop at any part of the journey. But if we walk that journey, even as we grow in freedom, we find that our liberty is constrained. We become committed to a way of life that demands a practical and spiritual asceticism. We ask ourselves if the things and patterns in our daily lives bring us closer to God or not. This examination calls us to adopt the things that bring life and to avoid those that lead to despair. We realize that we are not at liberty to do and act as we please: even though our lives are more our own, they are at the same time less and less so.

Sinking into Selflessness

This rootedness that allows self-transcendence is common in the different traditions of the spiritual path we are on. In Buddhism, for instance, Dogen writes, "To study the Way is to study the self, to study the self is to forget the self, to forget the self is to awaken into the ten thousand things." The asceticism of living the resurrection calls for a deep entry into ourselves, to the point where we realize our basic emptiness. Through that emptiness, at its own time, the energies of the resurrection arise. Their rising carries us beyond ourselves into the work of redeeming creation. That work also requires asceticism – the asceticism of self-forgetfulness that promotes joy and community. As the medieval Christian mystic Meister Eckhart points out, "The more deeply we are our true selves, the less self is in us." That is why, on the morning walk with Jesus after Peter commits himself and is given his mission, Jesus says to him, "Truly, truly, I say to you, when you were young you girded yourself and walked where you would; but when you are old, you will stretch out your hands and another will gird you and carry you where you do not wish to go" (John 21:18). Accepting and opening the gift of the risen Christ in our lives, carries us beyond ourselves into the world of affliction that cries out to be saved. The cost is no less than everything – even our very lives, as we may imagine them.

Why do it, then? Because heaven is sharing the vision and the work and the ministry of the Father. It is a way of seeing and labouring and being, here in the world, that unites us through space and time with all those forces that build up, without ceasing, a new creation. In this new creation, God is all in all, and everything and everyone has been healed and transformed by love and celebrates that love in every moment of their lives. There is hard work, yes, and there is the suffering of a creation being transformed, but there is also profound and abiding delight that comes from being rooted in love and being creative through that loving.

If we are honest with ourselves, we can see how much we are like Peter in our relationship with Jesus. We would love to be better companions of Christ, but we are aware of our weakness in the face of suffering. We can only offer friendship. Still, Christ sees what we need and knows what we can do when we are given what we need. He knows we need the Spirit, and that when we are given that Spirit we become his continuing resurrected presence on earth. For now, that is enough.

Questions for prayer and reflection

1. How are you living these days with the prayer experiences you have been having?

2. How do they shape each other?

3. This contemplation has three parts: the frustrating evening of fishing; the breakfast with Jesus; the missioning of Peter. Which part engaged your attention most? What does that suggest to you? Return to that moment and let it engage you again. What happens?

4. How does this contemplation adjust the way you might have thought about living the resurrection? What questions does it raise for you? How will you deal with those questions?

5. In what ways is the resurrection changing your life? What do you need to live those changes in wholesome ways?

6. How do you experience the difference between being a friend of Jesus and a lover of Jesus? What do you need to ask him to do to help you be one with his spirit?

7. The gospel story contains other elements not touched upon here. Do any of them lead you to a closer understanding of yourself and a closer identification with the risen Christ? What does that tell you about yourself and about the way God sees you?

8. Do you think Peter feels guilty during his conversation with Jesus? Do you think Jesus is trying to make him feel guilty? Why is guilt not helpful in loving someone? In what ways does your perception of God make you feel guilty? Do you use guilt to distance yourself from God? How does God respond to you when you are in that state?

9. How does God ask you to feed his lambs and his sheep?

10. How do you feel about being asked to share God's creativity and love?

11. In your conversations at the end of the prayer with the Father, Jesus or Mary, what do you discuss? What do you hear?

12. Can you stay in the moments of gratitude this contemplation, and its repetitions, create in you? How?

The Movie
Lost in Translation

Director: Sophia Coppola (2003 – 105 mins.)
Starring: Bill Murray, Scarlett Johansson

1. Summary

Bob Harris, a movie star, is in Tokyo to film a whiskey commercial. A man in mid-life crisis, he is having marriage problems. Charlotte is a young American in Tokyo with her photographer husband. Unable to sleep, Bob and Charlotte cross paths one night in the hotel bar. From this chance meeting grows a very special friendship as they set out together to discover something of the people and culture of Japan.

2. Questions about the Movie

1. This is a very difficult movie to categorize. Is it a comedy? A romance? A travelogue? It could be any of these things or all of them. Is it comic to deal with melancholy? Is it romantic when there is no consummation? Is it a travelogue when we mostly see Japan through windows? What was this movie for you?

2. The critics and the public raved about the movie. Some thought it the best film of the year. It was the hit of the 2003 Toronto International Film Festival. One critic wrote: "You won't find a subtler, funnier or more poignant performance [Bill Murray's] this year than this quietly astonishing turn." (Richard Corliss, *Time*, September 22, 2003) Do you agree with Corliss? How is the film both "quiet" and "astonishing"? Does a movie have to "yell" at you to reach you?

3. Bill Murray emerges "as a complete character – honourable and venal, fallible and funny, adding vulnerability to the panache. It's easy to understand why a young woman in her 20s might fall for him or why a young woman director would want to explore that appeal." (Liam Lacey, *The Globe and Mail*, September 19, 2003) Charlie Chaplin had the same sort of appeal in the silent film era. Take one scene where Bob is front and centre. How does Bill Murray manage to pull all of this off – through his looks, his words, the way he speaks and moves, the way he listens?

4. Many believe that movies are just escapist entertainment, designed to get us away for a few hours from the problems of our lives. And they do that – no question. Yet they can do much more. "How instinctively we react – and connect – when a film captures a feeling that is all too common and all too real…. Shall I go forward? Shall I go back? Shall I try again? Should I just give up? Such questions strike at any stage in life and they settle in like a persistent dream" in this movie.

(Peter Howell, *Toronto Star*, September 19, 2003) Are these questions ever answered for Bob and Charlotte? Can you think of one or two other movies that have struck you in the same way? What do these types of movies have in common?

5. Before Bob and Charlotte part on the streets of Tokyo as Bob leaves for the airport, they whisper something to each other that – on purpose – the audience cannot hear. What do you think they said to each other?

3. The Relationship of the Movie to the Theme of the Exercise

1. Bob and Charlotte are each committed to a way of life that is difficult, and they have no reason to believe it will become easier in the near future. Yet they continue on their journey, stronger as a result of the friendship they have developed, a relationship that grows roots that go deeper than sex. In the Exercises we learn that even though our lives are more our own, they are also less and less so. How is this true in the lives of Bob and Charlotte at the end of the movie?

2. There is a profound and abiding delight, we read in this Exercise, at being rooted in love and being creative through that loving. The Japan that was such a difficult and disorienting place for Bob and Charlotte in their loneliness comes alive and becomes a delight as their love grows. What are some examples in the movie where we see such a change take place?

3. Both Charlotte and Bob know that they must go on with their own lives – that they cannot (as the Exercise puts it) just mope around. Life must go on. What will each take with them from the other that will give them what they need to pick up their lives and their jobs?

4. The Relationship of the Movie to One's Self in the Exercise

1. As the Exercise points out, Peter can offer only friendship to Christ. By the end of the movie, it is clear that this is all Bob can offer Charlotte – and vice versa. What can you offer to Christ? What has he asked of you? What is your response?

2. Bob and Charlotte's friendship is an amazing one in which each gives the other something that will help the other grow. They both are in really bad shape (Charlotte: "I don't know what I'm supposed to be." Bob – "I'm completely lost.") What they share makes a difference and they are able to go on. What can Christ's friendship offer to you?

3. While Bob and Charlotte are called only to be friends, Christ calls you to share in his spirit and in his mission. How does he call you to share in his spirit? In his mission? What is your response?

6th Exercise

The Ascension

(Luke 24:44-52; Acts 1:1-11)

Jesus: "I do not pray for these only, but also for those who believe in me through their word, that they may all be one; even as you, Father, are in me, and I in you, that they may also be in us".

(John 17:20-1)

Reflect how God dwells in creatures.

(Sp. Ex. #235)

Grace: Here it will be to ask for the grace to be glad and rejoice intensely because of the great joy and the glory of Christ Our Lord.

(Sp. Ex. #221)

Our Mystical Life

We come from God and we return to God. We know this is true, but we do not know exactly how it happens. We live day by day, we have projects and long-term plans, we have a general direction to our lives. Depending on the decisions we make, we can either aid or hinder the community of God's people. Underneath this sense of identity is the larger dynamics of our clan, our society, our culture. These also have projects and orientations, and play themselves out more or less unconsciously in our lives. But pervading all these, rooting and transcending them, are the creating energies of God present in and working in everything and everyone to bring us to ever fuller and more joyful dimensions of being with God. That will not cease until all becomes all in God.

We start this journey even before we are born, and we continue it even after our bodies have died. In this journey we imitate the one made by Christ, the Second Person of the Trinity, who became human, died, rose from the dead, and returned to the Father. When we contemplate Christ's return to his Father as we pray on the Ascension, we enter into the dynamics of a mutual love relationship that reaches through death to achieve a union of intimacy and creativity big enough to encompass the whole of creation. This is our entry into a life of mysticism that is our true nature. But how do we enter into that mysticism and experience it in our own prayer? First, we participate in the story of the Ascension.

In the story in Acts, Jesus leads his disciples to Mount Olivet after proving that he has risen in his body from death and promising to send them the Holy Spirit. On that mountain he was lifted from their sight. As they were gazing into the sky, they noticed with them two men in white who informed them that the Christ would return the same way he left in glory.

Claiming Our Deepest Desire

Entering the contemplation, we can experience the joy of the resurrected Christ's return to the Father and the joy of the Father's reception of his Son. This is the moment when Jesus' deepest desire is answered.

Resurrection allows us to admit our deepest desire in all of its raw urgency, because we see in the Father's raising Christ from the dead that that desire is answered. The joy of the resurrection is what we experience when we let ourselves admit that our deepest desire can and will be answered. What does that desire look like? We desire life – life in all its fullness. We desire that all our hurts be healed and all our joys celebrated in ways that even now we cannot imagine. We desire that the terrors of the world be transformed into ecstasy. We desire that broken relationships be healed, that whatever is oppressed be liberated, and that all see and know and love themselves and all others the way the Father sees and knows and loves all. We desire that we become like God, for we are made in God's image and likeness.

In the contemplation of the Ascension, we experience in prayer Jesus' deepest desire being answered, and we enter into the intimacy of that answering. This is where the totality of human love embraces and is embraced by divine love. That totality of human love includes our deepest nature, as well as all the manifestations of love that we have been offered or have desired. As we enter into this contemplation, we can allow ourselves to experience the love we need to be fulfilled. We can allow ourselves to be immersed and embraced by its delight and its joy of finding its beloved. We can experience something of what the Father and the Son experience at that moment.

Leaning into Love

We can also experience, as in any human parting, the sadness that Jesus' companions felt when they saw him leave. This is not the sadness of a broken relationship – their desire is held by the promise of that further gift of the Spirit that Jesus shares with the Father, and by the promise of Jesus' eventual return. We, too, can experience the gift of desire and of anticipation. This is rather like the feelings of a child on Christmas Eve waiting to celebrate Christmas, to receive presents and to enjoy the gathering of family and friends at Christmas dinner. We can sit with the sense of Jesus' promise, knowing that even as we have already received more than we expected, what is to be given is more than we can imagine. In that spirit of passionate waiting we lean into a love that transforms us – body, spirit and soul. Our bodies in resurrection become as Christ's body did, and so the divine love that embraces us not only liberates our spirit and purifies and redeems our soul, it also reveals to us that our bodies will also be glorified, not subject to illness, time, decay and the laws of nature as we now understand them. The energies of the Ascension show us that the body is not left out of our relationship with the Father. What happens to our body is a symbol of the commitment of that love. The love of the Father that calls Christ back to him in his body also calls us back in our body to the same glory that Christ shows.

In our contemplation here we can experience in our body something of that glory. We know that matter is compressed energy. In resurrection, the matter of the body becomes liberated. In the ascension that liberated energy becomes a manifestation of love. As we pray this contemplation on the Ascension, we can pray to experience our bodies as energized into a love liberated for intimacy with the Father and for creative service in the world.

Questions for prayer and reflection

1. What were the significant moments of this contemplation for you? How did you experience them? Why were they significant?

2. What does this contemplation reveal to you about the Father's love for you?

3. How does it reveal you to yourself?

4. What does it reveal to you about what your body is capable of being? How does this change your self-image?

5. How do you find yourself leaning into the love that desires you?

6. When you reflect on the journey that is your life, what can you chart as the significant moments that made you more aware that you are loved and capable of loving?

7. What stops you from loving?

8. What do you need to transform those blocks into creativity? What happens when you pray out of that need?

9. In your conversations at the end of the prayer with the Father and with Jesus, what has been given to you?

The Movie
A Knight's Tale

Director: Brian Helgeland (2001– 132 mins.)
Starring: Heath Ledger, Mark Addy, Rufus Sewell

1. Summary

Inspired by *The Canterbury Tales*, this is the story of William Thatcher, a young squire, who breaks all the rules when he passes himself off as a nobleman and shows that he has a gift for jousting. On the journey to become the jousting champion of the country, he meets the then-unknown writer Geoffrey Chaucer. William convinces Chaucer to forge genealogy documents that will pass him off as a knight. With these in hand, William goes on to face his fiercest rival and to find romance.

2. Questions about the Movie

1. "This is a deeply silly film. It deserves a special Silly Oscar of its own. It has the silliest lines, the silliest setpieces, the silliest performances of anything I can ever remember seeing. And yet I came out of the cinema with a great big grin on my face. It's somehow very entertaining, and its bizarre, in-your-face anachronisms are carried off with such insouciance, such cheerful effrontery, that you can't help indulging them." (Peter Bradshaw, *The Guardian*, August 31, 2001) Movies affect different people from different cultures in different ways. This critic is British. How much do you agree with this critic? Why do you think that even a "silly" movie – which this may or may not be – can pertain to the Exercise? Is there room for "humour" in spiritual matters?

2. "Was there any other musical era more prone to mock-heroic medievalist posturing than the one that produced both progressive rock and heavy metal? If jousting called for a musical soundtrack, certainly it wasn't lyres." (Geoff Pevere, *Toronto Star*, May 11, 2001). Music plays an important part in this movie, as it did in some of the others you have looked at in the Exercises. This time, the movie uses contemporary pop music, inserting the pulse of the present into the long ago past (consider the opening joust, where the crowd sings Queen's "We Will Rock You." What does the use of this type of music – in that and other scenes – do to the mood and tone of the movie? What other type of music would you have used: Gregorian chant? Medieval lute and lyre? Classical? Why? Why does the movie use other types of music (e.g., the final joust and end of the movie)?

3. Consider the way the jousting matches take place – and without any computer animation or camera tricks. "Such pure action conjures up another past – the childhood pleasures of a

Saturday matinee, where the thinness of the movie did nothing to dilute the magic in the air. At best, this picture recycles that magic for the evening of our lives – quite simply, *A Knight's Tale* is a night's entertainment." (Rick Groen, *The Globe and Mail*, May 11, 2001) What is the purpose of a night out at the movies? Is it just to entertain? We watch as a man "changes his star." We are amused, of course. But perhaps there is just a touch of magic in the air. What causes the magic? Does everyone who sees the movie find the magic? Ought we to go to movies looking for "messages" or just to be thrilled by the magic in the air? Why do you go to movies? Why else might you want to go to movies?

4. Writer/director Brian Helgeland: "I wanted to make the Middle Ages feel as alive as they were to the people who inhabited them. These people weren't living in an archaic time. They were in the present. For the movie to work, the audience has to be invited in. They can get pushed away or overwhelmed by period costumes, obscure speech and antique music. There must be relatable elements. Our goal was to create a seamless bridge between then and now." (Liner notes for DVD version of *A Knight's Tale*) What are the "relatable elements" of which Helgeland speaks? Do they work to the extent that you felt "invited in" to this world? Why? Why not?

3. The Relationship of the Movie to the Theme of the Exercise

1. The Exercise tells us that our decisions can aid or hinder the building up of the community of God's people. Underlying our own identity is – among others – our culture. Will's era had at least two cultures – the noble class and the lower class. How can Will move from one culture to the other? How does this build up the community of God's people? Why don't Will's friends try to do the same? What drives Will that his friends don't have – that makes them content to be where they are?

2. Pervading all that we do are the creative energies of God present in everything and working in everything and everyone. How are these "creative energies" shown to be present in the various characters in the movie?

3. Christ's resurrection allows us to admit our deepest desires. How are the desires expressed in the Exercise found in the movie?

    • the desire for life in all its fullness
    • the desire that our hurts be healed
    • the desire that broken relationships be reforged
    • the desire that whatever is oppressed be liberated

4. The Relationship of the Movie to One's Self in the Exercise

1. Prince Edward rewards Will, saying that he knows that both he and Will try to hide who they are and are unable to do so. "Your men love you. If I knew nothing else about you that would be enough. You tilt when you should draw and that is knightly, too." The society and culture of which the Exercise speaks comes to accept Will for who he really is – despite his outward appearance. When have you tried to hide who you are, for whatever reason? Has this aided or hindered the building of the community of God's people? How? What did you do about it?

2. In his love for Jocelyn, Will finds what the Exercise calls the love he needs to be fulfilled. This is a symbol of the love of God that we need to be fulfilled. As you strive to accept God's love, where have you found a love that helps you in your quest?

3. Will's father puts him in the service of a knight to save Will from a life of poverty. There is a sadness of parting there. Unlike the disciples' parting with Jesus in the Ascension, there is no joy for Will, for he does not know if he will ever see his father again. What partings in your life resemble Will's parting from his father? The disciples' parting from Jesus?

7th Exercise
The Gift of the Spirit
(Acts 2)

The fruit of the Spirit is love, joy, peace, patience, kindness, goodness, faithfulness, gentleness, self-control.

(Galatians 5:22-23)

We call Spiritual Exercises every way of preparing and disposing the soul to rid itself of all inordinate attachments, and, after their removal, of seeking and finding the will of God in the disposition of our life for the salvation of our soul.

(Sp. Ex. #1)

Grace: Here it will be to ask for the grace to be glad and rejoice intensely because of the great joy and the glory of Christ Our Lord.

(Sp. Ex. #221)

Finding Who We Are

Living fully and willingly in the world, without being seduced by its illusions, carries us farther along our spiritual journey than fleeing that world because of its brokenness. We are not to deny this life and this path in favour of some other-worldly paradise, or stoically defy death by pursuing pleasure. Rather, we are to live fully, with all our pains and problems and with the continuing wretched situation of the world. This is possible when we live in relationship with the Father and share the gift of the intimacy between Father and Son.

That intimacy is fulfilled in the Ascension of the risen Jesus back to his Father. The fruit of that coming together for us is Pentecost, the gift of their Spirit to us. We may think of this as a wedding in which we are invited guests sharing in the joy of the union. In sharing this joy, we become part of that union while living in this world. This joy transforms the world and gives us the energy, courage, vision and love to be personal embodiments of God's Spirit in the world. This is what happened to the disciples in the upper room in Jerusalem after the Ascension.

They were gathered together there when "suddenly a sound came from heaven like the rush of a mighty wind and it filled all the house where they were sitting. And there appeared to them tongues as of fire, distributed and resting on each one of them. And they were all filled with the Holy Spirit and began to speak in other tongues as the Spirit gave utterance" (Acts 2:3-4).

We need to know that the word for "wind" and the word for "spirit" are the same in Hebrew. We also need to see that the giving of the Spirit in tongues "as of fire" manifests itself in the speaking in "tongues," which enflamed the spirits of those who heard them and led them to become disciples (Acts 2:41-42). At Pentecost, that first year in Jerusalem, God's very own Spirit is given to Jesus' companions, who share it with the world. It is the nature of love not to be withheld: in that sharing, love becomes more and more present in the world and community is created.

Receiving the Gift

When we enter this contemplation we ask to be given God's Spirit. We enter the scene as one of the ones chosen by Christ gathered in prayer, and open ourselves to receiving that Spirit. We allow that gift to descend through our bodies, feeling the Spirit's descent into every aspect of ourselves so that we are intimately connected to both heaven and earth. We feel the rootedness that grounds us, body and soul, arise until in that descent and arising we know that we are the presence of love in the world. We stay in this state of consolation, calmly breathing in love to our depths and breathing out love to the world. We stay in this state as long as we can and return to it, during all the repetitions of this contemplation.

What we are given in this state of intimacy allows our vocation, whatever it is, to become manifest in the world. The word "vocation" and the word "voice" have the same Indo-European root – uek(s), to speak. When we find our vocation, we find our voice. Finding our vocation means expressing our deepest desire in our life and with our life. A vocation is an expression of life that gives life and shares life and celebrates life. A vocation to priesthood or religious life is only one of countless forms of vocation. What the disciples received at Pentecost was such a vocation. Through it they finally found their voice.

Sharing the Gift

After the gift of the Spirit in tongues of fire, the disciples spoke in tongues so that all who heard them, even though they were of different nationalities and spoke different languages, understood. This gift allowed them to enter into other people's worlds, to touch their lives and transform them. This is the pattern of God's mercy we have contemplated before. In the Incarnation, God became a vulnerable human and was born a baby in Bethlehem. In the passion and death of Christ, that same God entered into the world's pain and suffering. Through his death, he entered the hellish confines of human existence where whatever is good but separated is offered life.

Now, at Pentecost, we see that mercy fearlessly and compassionately entering the lives of those who had not experienced God's compassion. We experienced this in the first three Weeks of the Exercises. In the First Week we encountered that love coming to us to heal and liberate us from sin. In the Second Week we were invited to journey with Christ into our own poverty and the world's. In the Third Week, as companions of Christ, we journeyed with him into the depths of evil to embrace that evil and thereby offer it up to the transforming mercy of the Father. Now, in the Fourth Week, we are offered, for ourselves, the same Spirit that was given at Pentecost, so that we can live in the world creatively, joyfully and fully alive.

That creativity and joy is the grace we pray to receive in this contemplation – it is not just for ourselves but for others. It desires to be shared with anyone who has experienced that profound and ceaseless yearning, common to all, for life, love, freedom, joy and a community where one feels always and deeply at home. There everyone speaks and understands the language of the heart.

Questions for prayer and reflection

1. What happened of significance when you prayed for the gift of the Spirit? How did you feel? In what ways were you energized?

2. What struck you most deeply as you entered the contemplation as one of Christ's disciples?

3. Where else in your life do you feel creative and alive? How do you express this?

4. Where do you see the need for creativity and a fuller sense of life? Is there a link between your creativity and the areas of need in the world?

5. Do you have or feel connected to a community of creative people? How do you celebrate life together?

6. Who has helped you on your journey to being creative, free and loving?

7. Whom are you helping to live life more joyfully, creatively, simply, hopefully? What is your relationship with that person or group?

8. What happens when you explore your spirit links with significant people in your life – living or dead, near or far, throughout the ages or in different religious traditions? How have these people made you who you are? How do they encourage you or confirm you in your spiritual journey?

9. Where is the Spirit leading you now?

10. In your conversation at the end of the prayer with the Father, with Jesus or with one of your spiritual mentors, what comes to you that is significant?

11. When you prayed through the above reflection, what aspects struck you the most? What happened when you used those as an entry into prayer?

The Movie
The Truman Show

Director: Peter Weir (1998, 105 mins.)
Starring: Jim Carrey, Ed Harris, Laura Linney

1. Summary

Truman Burbank is unaware that he is the star of a non-stop television show filmed by 5,000 cameras. His quaint hometown is a giant studio set run by Christof, a visionary producer/director/creator. All the folks who live and work in Seahaven are actors – including his wife. One day a huge stage light falls from the "sky" in front of Truman, and Truman gradually begins to see his life and his world for what they are.

2. Questions about the Movie

1. "It's a film whose conceit, however ingenious, doesn't bear too much scrutiny, or the logic breaks down. There's a preciousness to this picture, a certain delicacy, that doubles as an overriding strength and a faintly troubling weakness. Watching *The Truman Show* is the cerebral equivalent of cradling a Fabergé egg: You love to turn it around in your mind, marvelling at the intricacy and proud of yourself for deciphering the inscription. Yet, somehow, you can't help but harbour the real fear that this exquisite fake will break into pieces, and you'll be forced to solve another conundrum – was it truly compelling art or just flimsy whimsy?" (Rick Groen, *The Globe and Mail*, June 5, 1998) What is your response to Groen's question? What make a film "compelling art" rather than just "flimsy whimsy"?

2. "[I]f you find yourself wondering what happens to Truman after he escapes into the 'real world,' it ain't because…the movie wants you to. On the contrary, all that high-five cheering at the end is a sure sign the movie desperately wants you to believe that everything for Truman is going to be just fine. Yet, you can't, because the issues it raises, not to mention the way it implicates us as voyeuristic viewers, are simply too unsettling to be neatly contained by the movie." (Geoff Pevere, *Toronto Star*, June 20, 1998) Which issues are so important that we can't just leave them once the movie is over? What is your reaction to the ending of the movie? Were you satisfied? Was there something missing?

3. "Weir shows a mastery of tone as he shifts the film from acute social satire to an often penetrating meditation on the forces that control our existence." (Peter Travers, *Rolling Stone*, June 25, 1998) What areas of society does the movie satirize? What forces does the movie say are controlling our existence?

4. The key concepts of media education remind us that all media construct aspects of reality. Christof

is – in many ways – the ultimate exemplar of this and the other key concepts. He decides the point of view, the ideology, the value messages – even the commercial implications, which are covered through product placements. Look at the outline of these key concepts on page 26. Think of particular scenes in this movie that exemplify each of the concepts. Consider the scene on the bridge when Truman meets his father: the way it is staged, the directions from Christof, the camera angles, the music, even the viewers' response. Why is it important for everyone to be media literate – to know how to watch carefully and think critically about the mass media?

3. The Relationship of the Movie to the Theme of the Exercise

1. As Truman begins to walk out the stage door, Christof says: "There is no more truth out there than in the world I created for you…but in my world you have nothing to fear. You can't leave. You belong here with me." Moments earlier, Christof responded to the plea from a TV executive that "We can't let him die in front of a live audience" by saying, "He was born in front of a live audience." What does Christof represent? What does Truman have to fear in Christof's world? What would allow Truman to live fully and joyfully in Christof's world?

2. When the movie ends, Truman has conquered his fear of being on the water and is about to go through a door into a world he cannot hope to understand but that he feels offers him freedom. He does these things in response to a voice within him that tells him that this is the right thing to do. The Exercise tells us that to live fully with all

of our pains and problems and with the continuing wretched situation of the world is possible in relationship with the Father. Truman has no visible personal religious beliefs. Why does he listen to this voice within?

3. When we accept the Spirit, we feel intimately connected to both heaven and earth. At what point in the movie does Truman reach this moment of intimacy? What steps must he take to reach this point? How does the Spirit guide him? Through whom? His "father"? Sylvia? Christof?

4. The Relationship of the Movie to One's Self in the Exercise

1. Within all of us, the Exercise notes, is a profound and ceaseless yearning for life, love, freedom, joy and a community where we feel always and deeply at home. Truman believed – for some 30 years – that he had fulfilled such a yearning. His life changes drastically when he finds this is not true. Where in your own life have you realized that you have not fulfilled your own yearnings? What are you doing about it?

2. Christof tells the interviewer: "We accept the reality of the world with which we are presented. It's that simple." Is it? Is Truman a prisoner or a performer? Does he – as Christof says – "prefer his cell"? Does he live freely and willingly in his world? What about you?

3. At the end of the movie, as Truman reaches out to go through the stage door, he believes that whatever comes next will eventually enable him to live joyfully and fully alive, although he cannot be sure of that. When have you done something similar? What did you find on the other side of your "stage door"?

8th Exercise
Contemplation to Advance in Love (I)

Therefore I tell you, do not be anxious about your life, what you shall eat or what you shall drink, nor about your body, what you shall put on. Is not life more than food, and the body more than clothing? Look at the birds of the air; they neither sow nor reap nor gather into barns, and yet your heavenly Father feeds them. Are you not of more value than they?

(Matthew 6:25-27)

Consider all gifts and blessings as descending from above.

(Sp. Ex. #237)

Grace: This is to ask for what I desire. Here it will be to ask for an intimate knowledge of the many blessings received, that filled with gratitude for all, I may in all things love and serve the Divine Majesty.

(Sp. Ex. #233)

The Spiritual Journey

Our spiritual journey is like a spiral – we seem to return to the places, situations or projects we left behind. But we re-enter that world not as prisoners, trapped by its seductions, illusions and temporary stays of relief, but free. We see it in all its incompleteness and brokenness. We realize that we are invited to work towards bringing it to wholeness, so that it is part of the community of all creation and an ongoing manifestation of God's endless creativity.

And so we are inspired – by the love that calls us to life and then to more life – to share that life with those who reach out for love, and we gratefully accept the love that is offered to us by those who travel on the same path to the fullness of life. We give and we receive in love. In this contemplation St. Ignatius has some insightful observations about the nature of love, knowing full well that it is one of the most misused and misunderstood words in any language. He says first that "love ought to manifest itself in deeds rather than in words" (#230). What we do reveals who we are; what we do with who we are reveals what we value. We experienced this when we contemplated God's relationship to creation. In these contemplations we experience a God who is totally involved in creation, and who never stops sustaining, maintaining and transforming it.

Moreover, we encounter there a God who enters that creation to heal it and redeem it from the perversions that evil has inflicted on it. We encounter a God who is willing to transform evil into good by embracing the forces of evil and death and, through that embrace, allowing the compassionate mercy of the Father to bring them to resurrection. We have met in our prayer a God who became human as we are human, who walked the path of being human in all of its joy and its terror, and who shows us that the path leads back to the one he calls, intimately and simply, "Abba." This is a God whose word is incarnate, whose relationship with us is found in what he has done for us. When we enter that relationship – as we have done in the contemplations in the Exercises – we discover a God who works with us and for us, a God who invites us to work with him and with all those forces of creation that have committed themselves in him to loving.

Creating Community

Such a love is communal and mutual. We do not love alone, or in a vacuum. Always – before us and behind us, above us and below us, surrounding us and embracing us – is the love of the Father and the Son. We experienced that love in the outpouring of the Spirit on us at Pentecost. That outpouring never ceases: in it we live and move and have our being. In prayer we come to deeper and more conscious realizations of that abiding presence, which is a pure, simple unconditional gift. St. Ignatius says in setting up this contemplation that love consists in the mutual sharing of what is good. "For example, the lover gives and shares with the beloved what he possesses, or something of that which he has or is able to give; and vice versa, the beloved shares with the lover" (#231).

Narcissism is the opposite of love. Narcissists demand love and see themselves as the sole object of love. Narcissists cannot return love; what they claim to offer as love usually benefits only themselves. Narcissism destroys community. Love, on the other hand, works to create community. Such a community is manifest in a mutual giving and receiving; it roots itself in the generosity of God that extends itself everywhere and to everyone. Narcissism is closed by a selfishness that can be personal or ghetto-like, ethnic or racial, social or national. Community, however, is open to the intimate, the integrated, the grounded in an identity that is realized in the personal, the social, the national and the cultural, but knows that these in themselves cannot bring us all to the fullness of life, which is found only in the mystery we call God. In themselves, these are incomplete and transitory manifestations of the divine creativity in time. Evil emerges when these incomplete manifestations hold themselves as fixed and whole and complete in themselves. The work of loving is first, to see everything and everyone as incomplete, and second, to realize that the incomplete is not a curse but a blessing that allows us to reach out, without illusions, for that fullness of life offered by the beloved, who is divine, to us and to all.

In that reaching out we share what has been given to us.

An All-Embracing Love

To experience this grace more fully, as we begin this prayer we become aware that we are always in the presence of God and the saints, always surrounded by the love of those who love us and by the forces of all that is good in creation. We recognized that all of these work for our good by protecting, interceding, encouraging and celebrating our lives and our paths. The prayer reminds us that we are never alone, and that the energies of our lives are woven together in a community of love that extends through time and space. This community works to heal our disorders, enlighten our ignorance, transform our alienations and unblock our creativity. As we become aware of this community, which is always present to us, even here, even now, we can see it at work in our lives and in our prayer, which participates in this unceasing activity. Prayer and work, sleep and play, eating and voiding – all of these activities operate from the same stance of being one with God's spirit and energies in the world.

In this and the following contemplations, all of which are designed to make us more and more aware of this all-embracing love, St. Ignatius suggests that we ask for what we desire. "Here it will be to ask for an intimate knowledge of the many blessings received, that filled with gratitude for all, I may in all things love and serve the Divine Majesty" (#233). It is a grace to see our lives as they are; it is a great grace to see in all the aspects of our lives, the abiding presence of love holding and transforming us even in the dark times. We will know we have received this grace when we discover that our prayer is filled with gratitude and when, out of that gratitude and that gratitude only, we are moved to enter into the work of building up the community of love that offers life to all.

Questions for prayer and reflection

1. In this contemplation, what moves you the most? Why?

2. How does this contemplation put your life in context?

3. What things in your life are, or have been, a blessing for you? What happens when you take time out to be grateful for them? How does that gratitude shape the way your feel about your life now?

4. How do you feel called to live a loving life now?

5. What areas in your world do you feel need transforming? What part can you play in transforming the world?

6. Make a list of the people, past and present, who form your community of love. What happens when you have a prayerful conversation with them as part of this contemplation?

7. In the course of these Exercises, what has been given to you as pure gift?

8. What, in your loving, do you offer to your beloved? What do you offer to God?

9. How does your life reveal to you and to others what you really value?

10. In your conversations with the Father or with Jesus, what is given to you that is significant for your life?

The Movie
Bend It Like Beckham

Director: Gurinder Chadha (2002 – 112 mins.)
Starring: Parminder K. Nagra, Keira Knightley, Jonathan Rhys-Meyers

1. Summary

An 18-year-old East Indian girl, Jess, is torn between following her family traditions – getting married and raising a family – and achieving superstardom on the soccer field.

2. Questions about the Movie

1. *"Beckham's* story…is a fantasy of solvable problems and resolvable difficulties that appeals to our better selves if it's done with genuine heart and insight, which is very much the case here. For there is all the difference in the world between recognizing the humor in individuals while still treating them with respect and cheapening characters by turning them into sitcom caricatures. There is a reality underneath *Beckham's* easy humor, an impeccable sense of milieu that is the result of knowing the culture intimately enough to poke fun at it while understanding its underlying integrity." (Kenneth Turan, *Los Angeles Times*, March 12, 2003). How does the movie make the characters "real" – fully developed – rather than caricatures?

2. "[I]t's a culturally cross-wired sports comedy that's infused with what might be called the greater global vibe of Title IX – that is, the spirit of sports equality as experienced by the first generation of women who grew up taking that equality for granted. Made with a craftsmanship and pizzazz that restores your appreciation for honest commercial moviemaking, *Bend It Like Beckham* puts a new definition of femininity on screen, casual and cool and in your face." (Owen Gleiberman, *Entertainment Weekly*, March 21, 2003) How "really" are women "represented" in this movie?

3. "The movie also puts a wry, inclusive spin on Jess' little parable of feminist achievement – though she and her friends face gender bias in their quest to play a man's game, they find their biggest advocates to be the men in their lives. They also discover the only place to fully pursue their dreams is the United States, and *Beckham* becomes that rare – and getting rarer – case of a foreign film that makes you proud to be an American." (Gary Thompson, *Philadelphia Daily News*, April 4, 2003) Why would the critic feel he has to make two such statements about this movie?

3. The Relationship of the Movie to the Theme of the Exercise

1. Ignatius tells us that love is shown in deeds rather than in words. The Exercise expands on this when it says that what we do reveals who we are, and what we do with who we are reveals what we value. How does this apply to Jess? To her father? To Joe?

2. Sin fragments and causes division by setting people against each other and even against themselves. Narcissism is closed by a selfishness that can be ethical or racial. Community, the Exercise tells us, opens us to integration. Consider these moments in the movie, when Jess' father says:

   "What bigger honour is there than respecting your parents?"

   Joe, the coach, says, "Your parents don't always know what's best for you, Jess."

   Jess tells Tony: "It's OK with me!" [when he tells her his secret].

   Jess tells Joe: "She called me Paki — you wouldn't understand."

   Joe replies: "I'm Irish, of course I understand what that feels like."

   How do these moments exemplify these two positions?

3. At this point in the Exercises, we realize that we are called to share the love and life we have been given with those who reach out for love and, at the same time, to accept love from others. How does Jess try to reach out to the people around her to give them love even though she may not understand exactly what she is doing? From whom does Jess accept love?

4. The Relationship of the Movie to One's Self in the Exercise

1. The love God has given us allows us to reach out and share this gift; you have watched this unfold in the movie. What have you been given? How will you share it with your community?

2. The movie cuts back and forth from the final football (soccer) game and the wedding. The music cuts from the traditional music of India to Western opera – "Nessun Dorma." This use of music adds great emotion to both moments – it is an example of the new way of seeing, of being creative, compassionate and joyful that the Exercise speaks of. Where in your life has music played such a role?

3. As we enter this Exercise, we are brought back to the world from which we set off sometime ago. But now we see it as it is – broken and incomplete – and are invited to work towards making it whole. In the movie we see how Jess comes to understand this and the difference it makes in her life. How is this taking place in your life at this point in the Exercises? How are you planning for it to take place in your life as you finish the Exercises?

Contemplation to Advance in Love (2)

Blessed be the God and Father of Our Lord Jesus Christ, who has blessed us in Christ with every spiritual blessing in the heavenly places, even as he chose us in him before the foundation of the world, that we should be holy and blameless before him. He destined us in love to be his own through Jesus Christ.

(Ephesians 1:3-5)

I must be convinced that in Christ our Lord, the bridegroom, and in His spouse the Church, only one Spirit holds sway, which governs and rules for the salvation of souls.

(Sp. Ex. #365)

Grace: This is to ask for what I desire. Here it will be to ask for an intimate knowledge of the many blessings received, that filled with gratitude for all, I may in all things love and serve the Divine Majesty

(Sp. Ex. #233)

All Creation Is Charged with God's Energies

What have we received from God? Rather than thinking about it, let us allow the love that shapes us to reveal it to us. We are creatures, and a part of God's constant creativity. We do not have the power of our existence within ourselves; in fact, should God remove his loving attention from us, we will simply cease to exist. The very basis of our existence is radical dependence upon God.

At our most material level, the elements that make up physical existence were formed at that first physical moment of creation. The very matter that was formed in the Big Bang billions of years ago when energy became physical and exploded outwards – in the creation of universes and galaxies and solar systems that are still expanding into nebulae, burning up into supernova, and imploding into Black Holes – is the same matter that makes up our bodies. Our physical bodies contain the memory of the cosmos from its very beginning, and each of our bodies is a symbol of that cosmos. Our relationship to that cosmos is basic and eternal. We do not know all the properties of the matter of which we are made, but we do know that it makes us one with all of creation. Let us stay for a while in the mystery of our oneness with the elements of creation. In them and in us is the gift of God's indwelling.

Creation is made up of levels of existence. Biological life emerges from the swirl of proteins and carbon; we share that higher level of existence with the myriad plant forms that grace our planet. Grasses and seaweeds, giant trees and orchids, wheat and lichen are all related to our biological bodies. If we open our awareness to our ecological interconnectedness, we discover a mutuality in which we shape, and are shaped by, our relationships to plant life. We cultivate certain crops and modify the DNA of others. We depend on the pharmaceutical properties of some of these to maintain our lives or enhance our awareness of the mysteries that surround us. The mystery of God's indwelling is in them and in us. Let us ask for the grace to experience the wonder of that unity we share with the biosphere, and to experience God's indwelling there.

Beyond that level is our animal existence. We have heightened sensation and possess innate skills to gather food, reproduce, care for our young, create a clan structure and explore our environment. Within our symbiotic relationship to the animal world are the totemic forces of our spiritual nature that are given animal energies, characteristics and structures. Our human body is more than an animal body, to be sure, but our bodies belong firmly and irreducibly to the animal kingdom. In this prayer of thanksgiving let us be aware of the gift of the body, the delight of the senses, our rootedness in the physical, which allows us to connect and communicate with others to form community and express intimacy. Let us allow ourselves to be open to the mystery and to the delight of God's indwelling in it.

Sacred Spaces

Encompassing all of these is Christ incarnate. Christ became human because the human has the possibility of becoming divine. The incarnate God shares with us the gifts of memory, understanding, will, imagination, creativity and the freedom to choose life. He shares with us as a member of the human family, offering us the gifts that the Father has given to him: the gift of resurrection and the gift of union with the Father in the life of the Trinity. That gift allows us, even in our earthly pilgrimage, to become sacred spaces wherein the divine may dwell and embody the divine compassion on earth. When we open ourselves to that gift and experience it, we become the image and likeness of God on earth. Let us open ourselves to celebrating that gift of the fullness of life offered to us freely and joyfully now.

All of this enormous sweep of God's love from the beginning of time through the cosmos, through evolutionary history and through the community of human history leads up to the Incarnation and the resurrection of the Father's Son. It continues through the traditions of love that he offered to all, which comes, at this very moment, to our own life and loving. Let us take some time to enter into this history contemplatively, allowing the love that creates us and redeems us and loves us into journeying back to the Father to carry us to that intimacy of passionate union with him. There we may savour with our senses, physical and spiritual, the delight he has in us.

We have been given our own path, with our own blessed history, our own personal encounter with salvation, our own personal entry into God's particular love for us, and our own intimate sense of being the beloved of Jesus and of the Father. Let us enter into that blessed history that has been revealed to us in this journey, and let us open and savour the gift that allows us to know deeply and intimately and truly that we are the beloved and intimate of God.

In order to appreciate what we have been given, St. Ignatius, in the Exercises here, offers a prayer we can pray out of the deep affection we feel for God:

Take, Lord, and receive all my liberty, my memory, my understanding, and my entire will, all I have and possess. You have given all to me. To you, O Lord, I return it. All is yours, dispose of it wholly according to your will. Give me Your love and Your grace, for this is sufficient for me (#234).

In this context of love, the lover gives his life for the beloved, and here the beloved offers the beloved's very identity to the lover. All the beloved asks for is the lover's love and the gift of the spirit. It is enough, for that love creates, sustains, protects and transforms the beloved. That love lives out of the intimate knowledge that all is gift.

Questions for prayer and reflection

1. How do you relate to the community that is creation? How do you live out of those deep connections that extend through time and space and all of human history?

2. What are you grateful for? How do you show this gratitude?

3. What do you take for granted? How do you deal with those things?

4. How do you experience your rootedness in God and in creation? How does this manifest itself in your prayer and in your daily life?

5. What in this prayer moved you? What moved you the most?

6. How does this prayer shape your relationship with God?

7. If you were to write the "Take, Lord, receive" prayer of St. Ignatius in your own words, what would it look like?

8. What offering can you make out of love to the source of all loving? What occurs to you as you pray this question?

9. Where is the place of evil and human suffering in this dynamic of loving?

10. Where do you fit into it?

The Movie
Moulin Rouge

Director: Baz Luhrmann (2001 – 128 mins.)
Starring: Nicole Kidman, Ewan McGregor, John Leguizamo, Jim Broadbent

1. Summary

Living in 1899 Paris, Christian, a destitute writer, falls in with a diverse group of people who inhabit the world of the Montmartre district and the legendary Moulin Rouge club. There he falls in love with Satine, the Moulin Rouge's highest paid star and one of Paris' most famous courtesans.

2. Questions about the Movie

1. "The musical is the most delicate of movie genres and seems, in its very vulnerability, closer to live theatre than any other form of cinema. That is, when the fragile magic works, the experience is transporting, and we feel alive in the dark; but when it doesn't, the effect is deadening, and we somehow feel complicit in the failure. With Baz Luhrmann drawing upon every directorial trick in his formidable arsenal, *Moulin Rouge* goes to awfully impressive lengths to reinvigorate, almost to reinvent, the movie musical." (Rick Groen, *The Globe and Mail*, June 1, 2001) How well do you think Luhrmann succeeds in this?

2. "Each of these characters is seen in terms of their own fantasies about themselves. Toulouse-Lautrec, for example, is flamboyant and roman-tic; Christian is lonely and lovelorn; Satine has a good heart and only seems to be a bad girl; Zidler pretends to be all business but is a softy, and the Duke can be so easily duped because being duped is the essence of his role in life. Those who think they can buy affection are suckers; a wise man is content to rent it." (Roger Ebert, *Chicago Sun-Times*, June 1, 2001) How does the fact that these are archetypal characters appeal to you?

3. "It's good to be able to craft energetic, entertaining musical numbers, but there's the danger to end up with a futile, purposeless costume revue. This never happens here because, as familiar and melodramatic as the story can be, it still involves us completely…. When we see Satine for the first time, we fall in love with her along with Christian, and we root for him, for them, through the rest of the film. The delightfully twisted musical numbers that punctuate their tale aren't gratuitous but integral to the drama. Most every important declaration is made through song, be it Christian belting out Elton John's 'Your Song' or Satine serenading him with 'Come What May.'" (Kevin LaForest, *Montreal Film Journal*, June 2001) How did the director attempt

to make the songs integral to the movie? To the development of the characters?

4. "With its Orphean plot molded in the likeness of a tragic 19th-century novel, *Moulin Rouge* is set in a heightened interpretation of end-of-century Paris. The whole stylistic premise has been to decode what the Moulin Rouge was to the audiences of 1899 and express that same thrill and excitement in a way to which contemporary movie-goers can relate." (Baz Luhrmann, the director, in the liner notes for the DVD version) How well were you able to relate to what was on the screen? Did it thrill and excite you?

3. The Relationship of the Movie to the Theme of the Exercise

1. Through the movie we often hear, "The greatest thing you'll ever learn is to love and be loved in return." And at the end of the movie, Christian says: "Above all a story about love, a love that will never end." This Exercise is also about love – and a love that will never end. What is the difference between the two loves?

2. As we give thanks for the gift of the body and how it allows us to connect and communicate with others to form community, consider how this is shown to us throughout the movie. What is one scene in the movie where this was particularly true for you?

3. The Exercise talks of the use of the imagination and the awareness of the delight of the senses that we need to find. Think of the use of music and of pop culture references in the movie. How are these used to express the imagination and the delight of the senses in the "Love Medley" that Christian and Satine sing in the Elephant?

4. The Relationship of the Movie to One's Self in the Exercise

1. The Exercise asks us to consider what we have been given and reminds us that we have been given our own path, our own blessed history, our own personal encounter with salvation, our own knowledge of being loved by God. In many ways the movie shows us how Christian and Satine were also given much – they gave love and were loved in return. What about you? What gifts have you been given that the Exercises have made clear to you? How different might they be from the gifts you thought you had before doing the Exercises?

2. We know what return Christian and Satine made for what they had been given. What return can you make for what you have been given? Christian and Satine made real the oft-repeated phrase "The greatest thing you'll ever learn is to love and be loved in return." How will you take the prayer of Ignatius found in this Exercise and make it into something real in your life?

Contemplation to Advance in Love (3)

I give thanks to God always for you because of the grace of God which was given you in Christ Jesus, that in every way you were enriched in him with all speech and all knowledge — even as the testimony to Christ was confirmed among you — so that you are not lacking in any spiritual gift, as you wait for the revealing of our Lord Jesus Christ; who will sustain you to the end, guiltless in the day of our Lord Jesus Christ. God is faithful, by whom you were called into the fellowship of his Son, Jesus Christ our Lord.

(1 Corinthians 1:4-9)

Soul of Christ, sanctify me
Body of Christ, save me
Blood of Christ, inebriate me
Water from the side of Christ, wash me
Passion of Christ, strengthen me
O Good Jesus, hear me
Within your wounds, hide me
Permit me not to be separated from You
From the wicked foe defend me
At the hour of my death call me
And bid me come to you
That with Your saints I may praise You
For ever and ever. Amen.

(Prayer of St. Ignatius)

Grace: This is to ask for what I desire. Here it will be to ask for an intimate knowledge of the many blessings received, that filled with gratitude for all, I may in all things love and serve the Divine Majesty.

(Sp. Ex. #233)

The Gift of Life

There are levels to revealing a gift. First the gift must be offered; then it must be received and accepted. Next it must be opened and used. Finally, it must be shared. That sharing is a celebration not only of the gift, but of the giver, the receiver and the community that gift creates.

No matter who we are or what state we are in, we have all been given a gift: the gift of life. That gift goes beyond mere survival of ourselves as wounded individuals. That gift of life asks us to see and know and love ourselves the way God sees and knows and loves us. Often our own pain, or the lies of the world, stops us from seeing that gift. Instead we see life as harsh, nasty and brutal, and view living a vicious struggle for survival. And so the very idea of life as a gift of love for love seems, at best, naive and sentimental and simply untrue. Many of us refuse to receive the gift, and see the gift-giver as demanding and judgmental, powerful and capricious, cruel and terrifying. We might say that since we did not ask to be born we are condemned to live, and even if we receive the gift we do not accept it. But there is in every one of us a dreadful hunger for love and truth, justice and community, beauty and joy, security and acceptance. Even if we do not accept the gift of life, the longing for life never leaves us. It haunts our every waking moment, and all we say and do; it haunts our dreams and all our fumbling attempts at relationships.

But imagine one day that we say to ourselves, "There must be more to life than what I have been enduring." We set out in our own quiet and secret way to see what that "more" can be. When we do that, we start opening the gift of life. This is a difficult task, a lifelong task, for we must become aware of the lies in our life that give us a false image of ourselves, an image that we are unlovable and unloving, that we are alienated individuals, and that God is a tyrant. Our lives are multi-layered; at every layer, the lies and deceptions need to be unmasked and the work of restoring begun. As we enter this work we discover more and more the joy of living and we discover the God who labours constantly to bring us to that joy.

Sharing Life

Indeed, in this contemplation to experience love St. Ignatius asks us "to consider how God works and labours for me" (#236). As we labour to bring a fuller life into our world, we labour with a God whose delight is to bring that life into our world. In that labouring we discover a God who has invited us to be co-creators of his community of love and others extending through time and space who also work at this one project of community. At this level we find out how interrelated we are with the saints and martyrs and mystics, the holy ones of every spiritual path and tradition. We learn that their works of love, as diverse as their identities, all share the one work of love – the work of a God whose compassionate care and mercy manifests itself in that unceasing activity of creating.

When we join in that creating, we see and love the world as God sees and loves the world. We see its beauty and its brokenness and join with the holy ones of all time in the sacred work of redemption. Then every simple act of kindness, every moment of humble service, every work of unnoticed devotion, every silent prayer, every quiet gesture of forgiveness, every act of celebration, is an expression of that sacred work. That shared life is the opening of the gift and the celebration of the gift.

Celebrating Life

While all of this comes from deep within us and pours itself out in our daily lives, it reveals to us that the gift of life that we offer to all we meet has first been offered to us. We humbly share it, knowing that when we act as the face and hands and heart of God in the world, we do so in lives that we have handed back to God. We do so knowing that what passes through us into the world, though shaped and coloured by our unique personalities and times, is that unending, compassionate mercy of divine love. The sole delight of that love is that everyone and all things come to the fullness of life, where all evil will be transformed into creativity, all suffering will be healed into joy, all oppression will be rewoven into community, all death will be lifted up to resurrection. This is the journey to the fullness of life. We are invited to this journey in order to participate and co-create. It is the gift. We are able.

When we enter the world with a heart transformed, the world is transformed no matter what we do.

Questions for prayer and reflection

1. Where are you on your journey of life as a gift?

2. What obstacles are you facing on that journey? How do you live with them?

3. What started you off on your journey? How has your life changed since you began it?

4. What image do you have of yourself? How does this shape what you do and how you do it?

5. What image do you have of God? How does this shape your relationship with him/her/the Trinity?

6. What sense do you have of the world and of your being in the world?

7. Where do you find others who openly share your values and your deepest desires? How do you support and encourage each other?

8. How do you celebrate life?

9. What is the next step on your journey?

10. What happens when you ask God and the community of God that question in prayer?

11. In this contemplation, and in your repetitions of it, what moves your spirit most to a deeper intimacy with God?

12. In your conversation with God, or the community of the holy, at the end of your prayer, what emerges as important for you now?

The Movie
Crouching Tiger, Hidden Dragon

Director: Ang Lee (2000 – 120 mins.)
Starring: Chow Yun-Fat, Michelle Yeoh

Note: If possible, watch the subtitled version of the movie. Much of an actor's art lies in the use of voice to express emotion, mood and character. Dubbed movies can never have the full impact of the original.

1. Summary

The movie takes place in feudal China. A magical jade sword disappears and is sought by its owner, Li, a great warrior. At the same time he seeks revenge for his master's death by the evil Jade Fox. On his journey, he is accompanied by Yu, the woman he loves but who will not declare her love for him. It is also the story of Jen, a governor's daughter and her love for the outlaw Lo, the Dark Cloud.

2. Questions about the Movie

1. "Thematically, *Crouching Tiger, Hidden Dragon* has a rich underlying foundation. It ruminates on the true nature of freedom and how everyone, regardless of their circumstances, is a prisoner of one sort or another. Of equal importance is the way it balances the timeless equation of love, honor, and sacrifice. When viewed from any perspective, be it the lofty perch of a jaded critic or the less demanding vantage point of the average movie-goer, *Crouching Tiger, Hidden Dragon* stands out as one of the year's most complete, and exhilarating, motion picture experiences. (James Berardinelli, *ReelViews* – on-line, 2000) From what perspective did you view the movie? What was your first reaction to it?

2. "Mr. Lee brightens the stockpiling by giving the picture a knockabout, screwball comedy bounce. With pairs of lovers expressing their affection through nose-to-nose physicality, it could be "Hit Me, Kate!" Because the women are treated as generously as the men – and are more important to the narrative – *Tiger* is just the film for an audience transfixed by the weekly girl-power cool and soap-opera bloodshed of *Buffy, the Vampire Slayer*.... The picture frees the genre from being part of a man's, man's, man's world." (Elvis Mitchell, *The New York Times*, October 9, 2000) How far would you go in agreeing or disagreeing with Mitchell's comments?

3. "While undeniably exotic to Western eyes, Ang Lee's film is not entirely foreign. The landscapes and costumes speak a universal language, the Taoist acrobatics suggest a refinement of *The Matrix*, and the adventure in the desert conjures up any number of classic westerns." (Brian

D. Johnson, *Maclean's*, February 26, 2001) How does the movie remind you of a classic western?

3. The Relationship of the Movie to the Theme of the Exercise

1. There is in each one of us a dreadful hunger for love and truth, justice and community, beauty and joy, security and acceptance. In each of the four main characters of this movie – Yu Shu Lien, Li Mu Bai, Jen Yu, and Lo – we see this hunger. How does it drive each of them?

2. When Li Mu Bai leaves Wudan, Yu Shu Lien asks him if he was enlightened. He replies: "No. I didn't feel the bliss of enlightenment. Instead…I was surrounded by endless sorrow." The Exercise tells us that one day we will see that there must be more to life than what we have been enduring. And then we set out – in our own quiet way – to see what that more can be. What does Li Mu Bai find that "more" to be?

3. The Exercise tells us that there are layers in our lives; at every layer the lies and deceptions need to be unmasked and the work of restoring begun. How does this apply to Jen Yu? To Yu Shu Lien?

4. The Relationship of the Movie to One's Self in the Exercise

1. This final Exercise reminds us that the lies of the world stop us from seeing the gift of life given to us by God. Li Mu Bai says: "The things we touch have no permanence. My master would say: there is nothing we can hold onto in this world. Only by letting go can we truly possess what is real." What has the Exercises showed you that you must let go of? What is the "real" you hope to possess?

2. The Exercises have shown us our call to set out on a journey to the fullness of life. We are invited on this journey to participate and co-create. It is the gift. Li Mu Bai has set out on such a journey – as has Jen Yu, in her own way. As the Exercise puts it, we are able. Li and Jen were able. You are able. How do you participate and co-create in your journey to the fullness of life?

3. At the close of the Exercises, we read that when we enter the world with a heart transformed, the world is transformed no matter what we do. Jen's last act transformed herself and her world. Now, it is your turn. You are to go back into your world with a heart transformed by these Exercises. What have you done to transform your world? What are you doing now to transform the world? And what will you do to transform your world?

Conclusion
The Eye of the Spirit

The Journey Began

What have we done through the Exercises of St. Ignatius? We have gone on a journey where we have allowed ourselves to be found by God. We have entered into a union with God that manifests itself in our mutual labouring to transform creation into community. The presentation of the Exercises in this book focuses on media. Why? Christ is the medium of the Father. In our living out of the resurrection, we also become God's media. When we use film as contemplation, we recognize that the relation between that media and God's media is intrinsic to both. Films presents us with open, imagined worlds that we enter to complete and to find ourselves by losing ourselves and finding ourselves again. Films do and give what the Father does and gives. Both create and invite us to create along with them. Both concentrate on how we understand ourselves in our world.

The Exercises offer us a way of looking critically and lovingly at ourselves, and offer us choices of how we wish to be present to our world. The illusions we accept to be ourselves are taken away in the First Week. We find our true life in the Second Week. In the Third Week this life stands the test of death. In the Fourth Week we are liberated from the power of death for the service of the Divine Mystery. Our journey calls us always to be moving beyond ourselves and ever deeper into the love of God. In order to do this we are constantly drawn from the worlds we have imagined and into the world as imagined by the mystery of the God we describe as Compassionate Mercy. This journey never ends. As we journey through the Fourth Week, we discover that we are not carried to a mythic paradise. We find ourselves once again in First Week, where we have to discover even more deeply how we are loved. There is no end to God's love, and no end to our journeying ever deeper into that love and to the community created by that love.

The Importance of Reflection

For St. Ignatius, the most important thing in a person's life is to find God. Everything else is secondary. Finding God is more than having encounters with God. It is more than recognizing that we have had those encounters. It is discovering what those experiences mean and what direction they have given to our lives. That direction shows itself in what we do with our lives, and in the values we hold. For Ignatius, then, reflecting on what we do, or have done, is essential; it is the only way of keeping hold of the gift of our lives.

In spiritual direction there is some confusion about this way of proceeding. Some people want the reflection to have the same sense of drama and involvement as the prayer experience. When this does not happen, the reflection process is dismissed or overlooked.

Ignatius carefully sets up the preparation for the prayer. Here it has been those dispositional exercises that you answered before watching the films. For the sake of clarity, these have been written in a certain reflective style to focus your attention in a particular way to watch the film. Watching the film is the contemplative act – another stage of the prayer. After that comes the examination of the experience of watching the film in that particular context.

These three stages are all part of Ignatian prayer, but each has its own style and mode of operating. Each builds on the previous stage, and the final stage completes the prayer experience. Avoiding that stage causes God's communication with us to be incomplete. In this concluding chapter we complete the communication that God has been having with us through the Spiritual Exercises and film. It deliberately uses a style and voice that is different from the rest of this book in order to create the necessary distance that will allow us to see where we have gone and where we are going. We are panning back and out from the close-ups of the individual Exercises and from the medium shots of the reviews of individual Weeks to an overview of what we have experienced since the moment we committed ourselves to the journey of engaging with this book. This overview is a necessary part of the prayer experience, our encounter and communication with God.

If we abandon this stage or try to make it similar to the contemplative moment of prayer we lose the fruit of that contemplative moment. The result is not knowing what the prayer means, or where God is in our lives, or what direction our lives are taking. We fall back into uncertainty and sometimes even question the validity of what we experienced, especially when we encounter hard or painful passages.

We are not doomed to live our lives in uncertainty. The journey we have been on shows us that we are rooted in love and are loved even when we may doubt ourselves or others or the path we walk. That love is present and communicates with us in our daily lives. When we reflect on what we have been and are given, we discover how God communicates with us. This is individual, personal, and intimate. No one else can teach us that language. It is the language of lovers.

It is one thing to love, but it is something else to know we are loved, and how we are loved. For some, that is more than enough. Still, there is always that excess, which is love's nature, to give more and still more of itself. Now it invites us to examine how we have journeyed into that love, and to see the way we experienced each stage of that love as it manifested itself in our lives. The Ignatian tradition breaks this down into the experience of each Week; now it seeks to show how that experience was allowed to develop through the overall structure of the Exercises.

We look back to discover what happened to us and how God speaks to us now, taking unto ourselves more passionately and intimately the experience of the Exercises. Those who have done the Exercises over the years have discovered that they come to insights given to them in their contemplations years before. It was only in the process of living and reflecting that they came to some understanding of what had been given to them.

Basic to the Exercises is the compassionate mercy of God. It runs through every Week, and every Week develops a deeper and more comprehensive awareness of how intimately that compassionate mercy is woven into our very lives on a unique and personal level. That mercy comes to us in the First Week, when we are trapped in sin, to liberate us. That mercy, in human form, invites us to walk a very human journey with him in the Second Week as we both return to the mystery he calls "Abba." That mercy enters into death to conquer the forces of death in the Third Week, and we are asked to endure with him. Finally, that mercy shares with us the Spirit of the resurrection and union in the Father in the Fourth Week.

Our Personal Worlds

That mercy not only enters our human world, it enters each of our unique and personal worlds. We each live in a world that is shaped by our personal experiences, and no two people's experiences are alike. This is not to say that each of us is trapped in our own little world, though sometimes it may feel like that. There are large overlaps, and we can communicate with one another, in spite of the many differences of culture, gender, race and temperament, because we share at a most basic level the same human spirit. But the world each of us is intimate with is a world of feeling and value; that world is personal and real for us. That world is a construct of our imagination. We live in imagined worlds, and the imagined is real. We may share a communal imagination, but each of us has a private imagination that is a unique composite of the diverse elements of the communal world. The way that composite is structured and maintained is individual. From this unique perspective we read ourselves, others, what passes for the world, and God. It is from this personal standpoint that we watch films and create our opinions about them.

To say that we live in these imagined worlds is not to say that we live in imaginary worlds. It is just that the imagined is the real. What we imagine is maintained by the stories we live out of. The imagined is a constructed world of texts. These are narratives that range from the genetic codes that name us

through individual and family stories, to the cultural histories that situate us in the bigger world. Our understandings of ourselves are encoded by these texts. When we engage in an Ignatian retreat, the conversions we experience move us from one way of reading ourselves, others, God, and the world, to another way. This occurs through yet another text that we call the Spiritual Exercises. Here that text has been translated into the films that you have seen and the accompanying commentaries. The Exercises enable us to examine the stories we tell ourselves and others to hold onto our imagined worlds, but they also help us see the lies and deceptions these stories embody. This is not to leave us without any stories. We need stories to live. The Exercises offer us a way of restoring our lives in such a way that the new stories we find free us and our imaginations.

These constructed worlds we live in are real to us. They affect how our energies are manifested or repressed, are known or unknown. We accept as normal, first, the ways our families have formed us and, next, the ways of life our societies and cultures offer us. The way we understand our very being has been informed by these stories, and while these texts allow some expression of who we are, they repress or ignore, subvert or displace those other expressions that could contribute to how we see ourselves. When this happens, the "I" I feel myself to be, and act out of, is not really my identity. Who I think and feel and say I am is not who I really am.

So how we read ourselves, the world and others, including God, is a constructed text that, being distorted, distorts our reading. We might consider that text to be real, but "realism" is not "reality." Furthermore, this "realism" contains theologies. We create a God and believe it to be truly God. But often these theologies are quite different from the ones we find in the stories that write us, in which we are not the author but merely a character. How we see God and ourselves is quite different from the way God sees God's own self and us. God sees us as lovable and capable of even the most self-sacrificing love. This is the story given to us in the sacred texts of human history. The one Ignatius uses is the Bible.

In the dynamics of the Spiritual Exercises, these two stories meet. In the plot of the Exercises, the story changes as we journey through the Weeks. The lies that we have accepted as real and that have shaped our lives are uncovered and their abusive power is broken so we can enter a new story in which we journey with Christ through his birth, life, death, resurrection and return to the Father. In that journey we discover that our story is a contemporary manifestation of the Gospel. Our personal story becomes symbolic of the larger story of salvation. To appreciate fully that almost unbelievable gift of salvation, we have to see what has happened to us in our spiritual journey. We will do this by looking at the experience, the dynamics, and the way the graces we prayed for came to us during the Four Weeks of the Exercises.

The First Week: Discovering God

Understanding Ourselves

Ignatius asks us in the First Exercise of the First Week to meditate on a particular telling of creation history. We may not approve of the way the myth depicts creation history, but it does contain valuable insights into our self-understanding. The myth Ignatius uses moves from the First sin – that of the angels, to that of Adam and Eve "and the enormous corruption it brought to the human race" and, finally, to the effects of one radically significant sin in the life of someone just like us. The first insight this myth contains is that the stories that shape our particular being participate in that history of corruption, however it may be understood. The stories of our selves extend through time and space and spirit. Whether we like it or not, we are part of that larger story.

But it is the nature of the ego to deny or ignore that larger history of which we are just a tiny part, and to seek to establish itself as the centre of the cosmos. In the First Exercise, the presentation of that history, in mythic form, throws how we normally look at ourselves into a more realistic mode. Even before we were born, the creation we enter has been corrupted, and to such an extent that often and unwittingly we participate in that corruption. In the presentation of the Exercises, the question arises whether it is "useful" to give this meditation in its literal state. There is the claim that the language of the "sin of the angels" and that of "Adam and Eve" is not relevant to contemporary culture. However pertinent that may be, there is a deeper resistance to be overcome in seeing that our very selves, and our very self-understanding, is caught up in the denial of that larger context. The quest for relevance often subverts the more difficult question of transcendence.

Exploring Our Blindness

Only when we see how trapped we are by forces that are larger than us and beyond our control can we begin to realize that we have not been destroyed by the malignant agencies in creation. We have been protected by a love that is even larger than cosmic and human evil. The larger context of disorder is contained within the absolute context of the "Infinite Goodness" of God. When we ignore either of these contexts, or both, we operate out of a false notion of ourselves. This false perspective distorts everything we see and do. Even our understanding of God becomes falsified, and our theology becomes a form of self-justifying ideology. "Infinite Goodness" is then read as a kind of God who justifies the self people see themselves to be and find support for in the rituals and cultic practices of their belief system. We misread not only from our own personal bias but also from the deeper social and cultic bias that gives us the communal systems of understanding ourselves. The First Exercise exposes our blindness

The knowledge we gain from the First Exercise helps us see our own sins. This is what happens in the Second Exercise. There we look at the ways in which we have personally been seduced and trapped by evil and even participated in doing evil. The Second Exercise forcefully brings to our limited understanding the awareness that, even amidst ignorance and denial, we find the actions of a willful self that destroys love.

Against this growing self-awareness is the awareness of the self held by God. Ignatius facilitates the journey from the first to the second through questioning (#53) and comparison. "What am I compared with all of humanity?... What are they when compared with all the angels and saints in paradise?... What is all of creation when compared to God?" (#58). In this intense, prayerful questioning, our image of ourselves breaks down. This does not happen in a vacuum. It occurs within the mercy of a God who desires that we know ourselves truly as being loved even though we are sinners. Ignatius asks those making the Exercises to have a conversation with Christ on the cross, before whom they place themselves (#53). For Ignatius, Christ on the cross represents a God who is willing to endure even a painful and humiliating death so that nothing and no one will be lost. It is a manifestation of love that goes beyond the limits of the human imagination. In this encounter with such a love, the bonds that limit the human imagination are broken. Energies of the self are liberated or integrated or renewed in such an encounter. But this is not an easy thing for those making the retreat. They endure the struggle of the self to hold onto fixed and cherished ways of seeing and behaving that have become second nature. Here those on retreat experience a dying to the false self, a liberation of energy and a sense of wonder and amazement that there is such a love and that such a love cares for each one of us in such an intimate and personal way.

The energies that make up our spirit are not just an amorphous collection of power. That power has been trained to express itself and understand itself in ways that have been shaped by society and the significant units of society, such as family, education and religion. Even our basic desires have been socialized; what we feel we truly desire is not what we really need. One of the gifts of the First Week is to discover what we truly need; we do this when we discover who we truly are. This discovery energizes us in much the same way prisoners or addicts might feel when they are set free from what holds them captive. Here, the liberation from the distortions of such a socialization is not anarchy but rather the response to being loved as we are. The wonder and surging emotion we experience in the First Week comes because our lives have changed. That change makes us understand our lives differently. Rather than dwelling in the obsessive enclosure of narcissism, we discover that we are invited to live out of the open myth that incarnates God's mercy. We do not have to be trapped by a single and reductive understanding

313

of ourselves. This allows us to hold at the same time the many different and diverse stories that make up each of our lives. We can admit that we are blind, and that we sin in our blindness, but we also discover, simultaneously, that we are cared for even as we sin and live in sinful situations. The tunnel vision that has dominated our lives and the way we understand them opens up into a fuller context of accepting God's mercy. As a result, we open to wonder and to the surging emotion of other possibilities for our lives. We discover in our stories ourselves as loved and as sinners.

Love Offered and Accepted

The dynamics of the First Week deconstruct the story of self and the illusions of that false self. Those illusions consist of the way we see ourselves, others, the world, creation and God. The deconstructions work by bringing to light what has previously been ignored or taken for granted in the false story. They bring to light the larger story of God's love and show how that love has always been present in time and in our own personal histories.

The larger story of creation is shown to affect the narrow world of immediate needs that we often live out of. In the Ignatian Exercises, that larger story moves from the fall of angels, through Adam and Eve (one radically destructive act), to our own sins, and then to hell. Additional exercises can include "death and other punishments of sin, on judgement" (#71). We are enclosed in a reality that goes beyond the immediate borders of our everyday concerns. We find ourselves in a "controlled" setting in which God's creativity is not apparent. The effect is a sense of entrapment beyond our power to escape. The "escape" provided comes neither from the world, from creation, nor from the sense of self we seek to maintain. It comes from Christ on the cross – a figure of the wholly absurd to the worldly self. That manifestation of God's love makes no sense to any form of selfishness. To be prayerfully present to that self-sacrificing love draws out all the poisons that blind us from recognizing our truest selves. What emerges from this encounter is a history of sin and of involvement in sin.

This does not foster a complacency with the self and its constructed self-serving stories. The ego's self-assurance is undermined. Moreover, the graces of shame and confusion (#48), sorrow (#55) and abhorrence (#63) that the person doing the Exercises prays for in the First Week also work to erode the pride of the false self. I feel "shame" when "I" admit "I" am accountable for my sinful actions, and I experience confusion when the "order" of the ego is experienced as disorder. Sorrow emerges from an awareness that we have created chaos when we thought we were doing only good. We experience ourselves embroiled in a lack of order from which we are helpless to extract ourselves despite our best efforts. Then, we abhor the evil we have done and we abhor the nature of our world, which debases our humanity by encouraging and promoting those forms of disorder that trap us, sometimes using even our most noble desires.

But with the deflation of the ego, we discover in the First Week that we are not destroyed. We discover a God working to find us through creation and to sustain our humanity even as we sin, and in our helplessness and deceptions. The focus of the First Week is not to destroy us. The grace we are given is that we are loved with a love that seeks and knows us as we really are and does not turn aside from loving us even when we turn aside from whom we really are.

That awareness of being so loved opens us up and directs us to live lives of greater integrity. It moves us to restore the world: the human contexts we live out of, our histories, our relationship with God, our story of who God is.

The love we have been offered and have accepted in the First Week of St. Ignatius' Spiritual Exercises is just the beginning of the journey to love ourselves properly: to express our deepest desire, to incarnate what we truly value, and to manifest our true relationship with God. By the end of the First Week, the story has changed. We are given an entry into reality. We now need to learn how to live that reality without falling back into selfishness.

The Second Week: Discovering Ourselves

Looking at the World God's Way

In the First Week, God enters our story; in the Second Week, we enter into God's story and into God's way of telling stories, which is always through humankind. This interweaving of our story and God's is done through contemplation on gospel texts. When we contemplate, we bring our life energies into dialogue with the life energies of God, as expressed in the incidents of scripture. In this weaving together of our energies and the divine energies, we become gospel – living texts of God in our world. An incarnation that is personal and unique to each one of us occurs. In the First Week, we operated out of a limited context of fallen creation; in the Second Week, the story broadens. The movement is from the world perceived in worldly terms to that same world perceived from heaven, from the narcissistic projections of the ego to the humble service of one called to be an intimate companion of Christ.

In the Second Week we are invited to look at the world with the eyes and heart of God. We enter our first contemplation from the perspective of the Trinity, above time looking into time. With this contemplation on the Incarnation, our imaginations enter the space and the concerns of the three Persons of God. If the secular postmodernism of the world today, with its emphasis on image and sign, holds that we become what we perceive, the Exercises offer us a spiritual postmodernism that carries us to become what we imagine, energized by God's love.

The Second Week dares us to imagine. Our imaginations can do this because First Week graces erase the repressive structures and dynamics of an imagination limited by sin, allowing for something new, a personal dialogue with God that transforms the world, to emerge. This is peculiarly postmodern. We become signs of God's presence in today's world. Previously, modernism controlled the imagination by secular systems – think of the prevalence of Freud or Marx or fascism in the 20th century. Those systems even created the ways we were to understand God: Freud with an emphasis on interiority; Marx with a focus on social justice; fascism with the submission of the individual to the institutional. Postmodernism liberates the imagination from such control. The power of film is to provide accessible and alternative modes of examining reality. We see in the contemporary world the horror created by those whose imaginations are frozen in modernist ideologies: genocide, ethnic cleansing, ecological disasters, blatant political agencies of misinformation, and wars waged in the name of religion or the good but whose effects cannot be contained or transformed by those religions or that particular good. The scope of these defy imagination, structured by modernist narratives.

Following God More Closely

Despite the present climate of atrocity, the unimaginable is at work: God cares. God cares enough to find a way to save us. Even harder to imagine is that we can become God-like in our caring and in our doing. That is the grace of the Second Week: "To follow and imitate more closely our Lord who has just become man for me" (#109).

The Ignatian text defines for us – in story form – how God operates in the world. This is a God of humility, born "in extreme poverty, and…after many labours, after hunger, thirst, heat and cold, after insults and outrages, [that] He might die on the cross, and all this for me" (#116). When we enter God's story through Ignatian contemplation, we imitate God's way of being in the world. We start to become the continuing presence of Christ in the world. We give up the self-aggrandizement of our ego for a path of humble service desiring only what God desires. We do this because we desire to be one with the love that has liberated us, a love that manifests itself in the emptying out described in Philippians 2:1-11.   Thus, in the Nativity contemplation, which follows the Exercise on the Incarnation, the Ignatian text suggests to the one making the Exercises: "I will make myself a poor, little, unworthy slave…and serve…with all possible homage and reverence" (#114), Joseph and Mary in this time of need. Here the abstraction of the first line of the Principle and Foundation – "Humans are created to praise, reverence, and serve God" (#23) – is picked up and made human. We serve God in whatever way is helpful.

The emerging story of those who engage in the Ignatian Exercises is one of service done out of such an intimacy with Christ that it overflows in acts of a contemplative love. Their actions in the world are read in the manifestations of the Divine Will. They embody in their particular ways the creativity of a God labouring in the world. This human labouring is modelled by the scriptural life of Christ.

Choosing a Standard

In the Exercises, the scriptural contemplations on the infancy narratives and the private life of Jesus act as prefaces to the contemplations on the public life of Christ. Linking the two is the significant meditation on "Two Standards." It shows how Satan and Christ operate in the world. But the focus of the Exercise is to discover how the dynamics of Satan and of Christ operate in the very lives of those engaged in the Exercises. Here it is not a matter of choosing between the two. It is refining the ways we examine our lives so that we may better understand how we can be trapped, and how we may better follow Jesus. The Exercise helps us to identify with Christ and with his way of living in our world today, and to become aware of the wiles and strategies of that enemy of our human nature who seeks to stop us from living like Christ in our world. It raises the question of how we discern how to incarnate our deepest desire: union with the Divine. In this meditation we learn how we are tempted and how we are called by God.

When we enter areas of personal vulnerability we find ourselves tugged by conflicting feelings. These Ignatius describes as the Standard of Satan and the Standard of Christ. The Standard of Satan is to covet riches – by using our supposed strengths to overcome that vulnerable situation, the more easily to attain the empty honours of this world, [and so] come to overweening pride (#142). This approach reinforces our narcissism. The Standard of Christ, on the other hand, invites us to accept our poverty in the face of that vulnerability, knowing that such a position means rejecting – and being rejected by – the corrupt values of this world. From this approach springs humility (#146).

Here the Ignatian Exercises present us with a certain reading of the Christ story and a certain way of inserting ourselves into that story. Christ's story is presented as one of evangelical service to the Father through humility. The mission of Christ is to offer to the world the compassionate mercy of the one he calls "Father." He does the Father's will in all things. This is the basis of the Ignatian dictum of "finding God in all things." When we do the Exercises, we are disposed to find God in all things, as Christ did. The process of identification with Christ continues with a contemplation of specific incidents in Christ's life. Indeed, the rest of the Second Week outlines this call to service. The previous contemplations, from the Nativity to the setting out to the Jordan, show a Christ who manifests a radical dependence on God and on God's existential mercy. In that growing relationship with the Father, he manifests a waiting on God to reveal most clearly what is to be done. Jesus waits – from the finding in the Temple when he is about 12 to his baptism at age 30 – for the Father to show him what to do next. In this hidden life Christ does not do nothing. He learns to be patient and to be attentive. He seeks God's will. That gift is given to him at his baptism in the river Jordan. That radical and focussed attentiveness is named in the baptism by the Father as "My beloved Son." As we enter these contemplations we also wait to be named, in our attentiveness, the Beloved of God.

The sequence of contemplations on Christ's earthly ministry from then on promotes the existential engagement and development of discipleship in those doing the Exercises. This culminates in the last contemplation of this Week: that of Christ's entry into Jerusalem as king, which Christians celebrate on Palm (Passion) Sunday. From this sequence we learn what it means to be God in the world – not triumphalism or the despotism of an ego, but focused service in bringing the compassionate mercy of God to the concrete situations of daily life.

The kingdom meditation that introduces the Second Week of the Exercises is re-appropriated in Palm Sunday, where Christ the King enters Jerusalem not as conqueror but as one whose life is so focused on his love for God that he is willing to face the seeming failure of his earthly mission and a painful death on the cross. At this stage of their spiritual journey, those doing the Exercises are likewise disposed to a similar passionate love for God. The Ignatian choice of scripture texts during this week promoting this identification are those of evangelical service: they are not texts of healings, exorcisms, or power, though one may experience any of these in a contemplation. They are texts that witness in a specific, incarnate way to the mercy of God present in the world. We should note the peculiar absence of Mark's gospel in the pre-passion contemplations of the Exercises. Ignatius' Christ is not the existential mystery of Mark; rather, he manifests an identity of service opening to the Father. The person doing these Exercises is invited to walk a similar path.

The Three Classes

This process is reinforced by a self-awareness that emerges from the Two Standards and intensified by a reflection on the Three Classes of People and the Three Degrees of Humility. The latter two Exercises, which follow immediately after the one on the Two Standards, develop the stance of going against selfish desires. They promote a desire for poverty because Christ was poor and, from that identification with Christ, to a similar humble evangelical service in the world

Ignatius sees the person in the Second Week of the Exercises as one who is finally in the company of the creator and redeemed aspects of creation, labouring for a fallen world. For example, in the Three Classes of Persons, the setting of the meditation is "to imagine myself in the presence of God and all his saints" (#151). This is not a privileged moment; we live in that state every second of our lives, even though most of the time we are not aware of it. In that state the person of the Second Week is shown three possibilities of living life: living heedless of God or of oneself; living in the hope that God will approve of all that the person does; or living simply for God.

Ignatius places this Exercise before any contemplations of Christ's public life. It is clear that as Christ lives attentive solely for the Father, Ignatius expects us to make similar choices in our own public life. In Christ's public life, a significant shift occurs in his evangelical service when Peter acknowledges him to be the Son of God. After that, the prophecies of the passion emerge. Jesus says that Peter's awareness comes from the Father. Peter's resonance with the Father allows him to identify Christ as the Father's saviour, the Messiah. Our work in the Second Week is to come to such an intimate knowledge of Christ that we, too, are able to profess that the one we have met in our contemplations is that same Christ. When we do this, we can then move with Jesus towards the second half of his ministry, that of the passion.

Similarly, it is our own resonance with the Father in becoming words of God, and thus intimates of Christ, that allows our own entry into the passion. That passion is the radical acknowledgment of ourselves for God. This is the grace of the meditations on both the Three Classes of Persons and the Three Degrees of Humility. If a person enters into the Spiritual Exercises with the desire to make a concrete decision about something, that decision is made during this Second Week as a concrete manifestation of God's will. The grace of the Second Week is a bonded intimacy with Christ that leads us to desire to be with him, whatever he does, and to share with him whatever the Father decrees. Any decision made here is the active identification with Christ's incarnate servant poverty in works of evangelical service. Active entry into that servant poverty that the scripture depicts as the passion of Christ happens in the Third Week.

The Third Week: Walking with God

The Ignatian Magis

In the Third Week we imagine the torture and death of the physical body of Christ, and enter into some kind of identification with him through our contemplation of the scripture texts that deal with his trials and death. Those texts, which are presented from the perspective of the resurrection, depict the passion and death of Christ by the powers of the world as his abandonment of his self-identity to the mystery of his Father, for whom he is the Beloved.

Inasmuch as we have identified with Christ in the Second Week, in our contemplations on his sufferings we now share, on a spiritual and imaginative level, his fate.

The imagined world we constructed with the Christ during the Second Week, and the sense of intimacy we sought and found with him, are all offered up to the all-consuming mystery of the Father. In that vulnerability, the world and that relationship are attacked by the powers of evil, to which we are still prey. That evil moves to render meaningless the things and relationships we hold dear. We experience this abandonment in our prayer. We experience no more than Christ did, and no more than his disciples did when he died. That the meaning of Christ's life to his disciples has been destroyed by his death is shown by the two disciples on the road to Emmaus: "We had hoped he was the one to redeem Israel" (Luke 24:21). Christ's death destroys the world that his intimates had constructed around him. But what remains is not nothing. It finally becomes possible to see the divine play of the Father. It is only through death that resurrection can happen. It is only through the destruction of the worldly, explicate order of things that the divine, implicate order is revealed. Matthew's gospel depicts this as the rending of the temple veil (27:51).

Inasmuch as we can enter into the action of the Third Week our world – the imaginative system we live out of – is exposed to the same dynamics that Christ and his companions encountered. This is different from the destruction that is a necessary part of the liberating process of the First Week. There the systems of illusion and deception are unmasked and devalued. In the Third Week it is the highest possible good on the human level, the Word made Flesh, that is undone. In the Ignatian magis, the human best is displaced by the divine better. Thus scripture can have Jesus in his agony say to his Author, "Not my will but yours be done."

The Ignatian magis permits the transformation of human effort into modes of resurrection. Then, there is the "surrender" of self-love and of personal will and interests to that of the Divine Creativity. Because we are human, our egos never disappear; but the ego's meaning, and its activities, are once again brought into question. Hence the question Ignatius offers for reflection to the person contemplating Christ's passion in the presence of the creative mystery of God's love: What ought I to do? (#197).

What are we to do? How are we to describe the response of the those in the Third Week? Think of what happens to you when you are present at the dying of someone you love. After awhile there are no words, no story, even no feeling. Emotion does not necessarily have to express itself in feeling. Instead there is numbness, blankness, a growing sense of meaninglessness of what might be considered socially appropriate at that time. There is an erasure of all forms of human comfort and connection. There is simply the waiting in mystery. What remains is a radical simplicity oriented to the one Jesus calls "Abba."

This simplicity is also manifest in the Ignatian texts of that Third Week, the only Week in which there are no meditations or contemplations constructed by Ignatius. For those praying through that Week there is the simple division of the passion into sections, if those divisions are helpful, and limited instruction. The self-understanding created by the constructs and dynamics of the self, as depicted in the Exercises and mediated by personal history, is reduced to its basic orientation: towards God. Here the focus of the decision made in the Exercises is tested against its ability to be maintained without the support of our giftedness, or society's approval, or the impetus of narcissistic behaviour, without "riches," "honour" or "pride." If the decision is a manifestation of these latter three, its impetus is destroyed in the entry into Christ's passion.

Those who enter the Third Week become mysterious to themselves, even in the decision they might have made. That mystery connects intimately with the mystery we call "Father."

What mediates between these two mysteries are the texts of scripture and the text of Ignatius. The scriptural texts contain a minimal narrative of what is happening inside Jesus and a minimal sense of what is happening outside of him and around him. Both are characterized by huge gaps. For example, the act of crucifixion is not described, as in Matthew's gospel (ch. 27, between verses 35 and 36). Moreover, in that paragraph (verses 32-44), five of its nine sentences begin with the metonymic conjunction "and." Metonymy indicates the fragmentation of perspective where moments are not joined by the unifying context of metaphor. What holds the texts together is beyond earthly powers.

Shame and Confusion

A similar erasure of human meaning occurs through the graces to be prayed for at this time. Those involved in the Third Week are instructed to beg for "shame and confusion," which we experience when the self dissolves into mystery. This is not the shame and confusion that come in the First Week with a true awareness of ourselves as sinners. This is the shame and confusion that come when we move to an unawareness of self after having found a sense of identity that fills us with life and purpose.

How, then, are we to understand this shame and confusion that is the grace of that Third Week? It emerges from the sense of horror and the abjection of self we experience in the presence of the sublime, the sense of defilement (as when Moses takes off his shoes in the presence of the burning bush, because the place is holy) that we sense as we "intrude" on a sacred space and moment. The shame and confusion occur because we are breaking taboo (hence the need for the rules against scruples that Ignatius gives in the Exercises [#345-351] – for scruples presuppose that one can contract the holy). When Christ broke taboos, the social texts of belonging – by not washing, breaking the Sabbath, consorting with the impure, calling himself the Son of God, cleansing the Temple – he is doing it in response to a higher value: his calling as the Beloved of the Father. But while this higher value radically relativizes the norms of the social and religious order and displaces their claim to legislate the Absolute, the "lower" powers assert their authority in destroying him physically.

Similarly, when we break taboos within our own socialized ways of acceptable behaviour, both patriarchal and matriarchal, we too are destroyed. We experience this as the "nothingness" we encounter in the Third Week. When we break these taboos within lived awareness of God's mercy, we are resurrected.

From Death to Life

The Third Week, then, is the passage through the death of self. In that passage the understanding of death is inverted so that the implicate order becomes explicate. Death is revealed to be not the end of life but a transition to that mystery beyond its power that absorbs and transforms its meaning. Thus, the meaning of "sacrifice" we encounter here is both "to kill by offering up" and "to make holy" at the same time. What in the faith context is mystery, in the secular context is chaos. Sacrifice changes the fragmentation of the closed myths of life by death to the open myth of resurrection. In sacrifice, what constructs and maintains the social world, the symbolic order, is rent. The temple veil is split and the dead rise and roam about the streets. To the Jewish sensibility of Jesus' time, crucifixion was an abomination. It was the manifestation of a radical impurity incompatible with temple order and ritual. Their symbolic order could not countenance the order of "Abba" where a shameful death introduces the unimaginable Other into the world. As Peter points out to the rulers of that symbolic order after the resurrection, "This is the stone which was rejected by you builders but which has become the cornerstone" (Acts 4:11).

In God's merciful love for all of humanity, what has been laid waste by the powers of the world survives beyond that world. It becomes the resurrected body, the food of life, the Body of Christ in Christian liturgy. The same mystery that feeds those enduring the annihilations present in the Third Week is the same mystery to whom Christ turns in the first temptation in the desert after his baptism. It is not food, but rather the relationship with God, that gives life. It is significant that Ignatius puts within the Third Week Exercises the "Rules with Regard to Eating." There the emphasis is on the control of the appetite and on the disordered appetite by a focusing on more spiritual things (#214, 215). Those spiritual things give value to the appetite. The physical gets its full meaning only in the spiritual.

In the Third Week, and at those times when social norms and constructs lose their authority, it is very easy to fall into the more primitive mode of basic gratifications. Ignatius prevents this return to the First Week temptations and to the sensual body as the basis of satisfactions by asking us to share, or at least bear witness to, what "Christ Our Lord suffers in his human nature" (#195). The Third Week asks, "What I ought to do and suffer for Him?" (#197). Within the mysterious freedom of God's mercy, for whom anything is possible, the Third Week indicates a process of salvation in which love is not a cure, or a return to some stable and established mode of existence, but rather a radical irruption of the divine into human suffering, carrying it to resurrection.

In that human passion we enter a love that risks death. The Son enters death in a passionate love for the mystery he calls Father. The Father, in his passionate love for his Son, the "Beloved," reaches into death and brings the Christ to resurrection. Resurrection belongs to a significantly different order of existence than rebirth, the cycle of nature, or a return from the dead, as happened to Lazarus and to Jairus' daughter. Resurrection creates an openness to the miraculous, to what is possible but beyond the powers of creation. It comes as pure gift from God.

The Fourth Week: Celebrating Life

A New Way of Being

Resurrection is not something we can journey to; it is something that comes to us. We can choose the way we live, and thus create the way we approach death, but death defines the limits of human endeavour. It is only the power of God that transforms the meaning of death for us, and only the power of God that controls what happens after death. So resurrection remains a mystery. All we can do is reflect prayerfully on the stories of resurrection given to us. In doing so, we open ourselves to the power those stories point to and describe. That power breaks into our world to transform the way we imagine ourselves, others and God.

This new way of being is one of openness. In that space we submit to being recreated by the Father; it is he, not history, that defines us. This is apparent in the First Contemplation (#218) in the Fourth Week of Ignatius' Exercises. There he has Our Lord appearing to Our Lady. This is not mentioned in scripture, but Ignatius says, "It must be considered as stated when Scripture says that He appeared to many others" (#299). When we are gifted with the graces of the Fourth Week, we become an open text, sacred scripture, written by the Father. Our brokenness does not disappear; it is given new meanings. We are still broken people in ways the world sees and understands, but that brokenness becomes the script with which God writes a new story. As St. Paul says, in his understanding of this gift, "I will boast all the more gladly of my weakness, so that the power of Christ may dwell in me. Therefore I am content with weakness, insults, hardships, persecutions and calamities for the sake of Christ; for whenever I am weak, then I am strong" (2 Cor 12:9-10).

Sin, the powers of the world and our personal bias all tend to limit the meaning of things. Sin tells us that we are unlovable and incapable of loving. The world defines who we are in terms of nationality, ethnicity and gender. We choose how we will present ourselves to others, and who we think we are. Resurrection breaks down the power of these limitations. We discover that we are loved radically and unconditionally. We discover that we can love others in a self-sacrificing way for their good. We discover that we can be human in ways that are not conscripted by borders. We start seeing ourselves as mystery, participating in the Mystery we so inade-quately call "God." We are possessed by a sense of wonder and creativity as we behold our world.

We start to see in our own lives the dynamics of salvation history. We come from God; we return to God; the path of being lost and then found, which is described in Scripture, echoes not only our individual journeys, but the journey of the human race and all of creation. Because of the inter-connectedness of all of creation, what we do and value affects everything else. We see ourselves as committed to a loving relationship with all of creation, we see our lives as symbols of that commitment.

This awareness of mutuality is present even in the texts of the Exercises themselves. Thus, the riches and honour that Satan uses to tempt humans (#142) in the Second Week are now gifts shared between lover and beloved (#231) in the Fourth Week. Similarly, creation is not seen as going to hell (#106) but, from this new perspective, is an instrument of the sanctifying process (#236) of a God who works and labours in all things for our salvation. This is a God who gave us the Christ. When we bond with that Christ in the Exercises, journey with him back to the Father and receive the gift of their mutual Spirit, we become signs of the continuing presence of the resurrected Christ on earth. We witness to Jesus' resurrection, not to our own. We live beyond ourselves into the self that we will become. Hence, in the Fourth Week, we were invited to "ask for the grace to be glad and rejoice intensely because of the great joy and glory of Christ our Lord" (#221). That joy and glory are not our own. They occur because of what has happened to Christ and been manifested through his body. That resurrected body shows what is possible for every body. It manifests the gift of the Father offered to each of us.

For those living in the graces of the Fourth Week, that commitment is manifest in what we do. Ignatius points out that "love ought to manifest itself in deeds rather than words" (#230). Christ's resurrected body does different things than he did before his death. The risen Christ does no healing; he does not fight worldly or religious authority, but the disciples do so after they receive his risen Spirit. His appearing transforms the way those close to him see and act. Resurrection becomes a site of new meaning. Thus, for Mary Magdalene, the "gardener" becomes "Christ" (John 20:15); for the disciples in the upper room before Pentecost "fear" becomes "gladness" (John 20:19-21); for the disciples who are catching no fish, a lack becomes abundance (John 21:3, 11). Jesus' resurrected body manifests the Divine love.

Renewing Creation

As we participate in the gifts of the Fourth Week by accepting the gift Christ shares with us, we become resurrection sites for others. We experience the power of God moving through our brokenness to create Incarnation in our lived world. This emptiness is the necessary condition for the power of resurrection to become manifest through us. Awareness of our emptiness never goes away; it shows us that the grace in action of the Fourth Week is pure gift, a manifestation of God's mercy and not our intrinsic right. We remain broken, even in our joy, just as the Christ, in his resurrection, still bears the scars of his passion. Through that emptiness God's mercy enters the world, and draws up, and out, the pain and misery of fallen creation. In that emptiness the world's misery meets the Father's mercy. The Buddhist concept of shunyata can be translated as "emptiness/the fullness of being" at the same time. In resurrection we experience shunyata: simultaneous emptiness and the fullness of Being.

We do not disappear in that emptiness. Our identity is not found in ourselves but in the relationship God has with us. Now we understand "self" as emptied to embody mystery. As such, it is not, in its freedom, limited by worldly norms of acting and self-understanding and presentation. It is flexible – it is all things to all people (1 Cor 9:22) – and indifferent, which allows it to be so passionate for the Father that we become "a fool for Christ" (#167), the sign of contradiction in the world that displaces closed myths with mystery.

The destruction of the power of closed myths, especially death, produces the creative and joyful quality of the Fourth Week. Particular ideologies with single and restrictive readings of reality are devalued, and the diversity of what is given through God's abundance is celebrated:

> All things counter, original, spare, strange;
> Whatever is fickle, freckled (who knows how?)
> With swift, slow; sweet, sour; adazzle, dim;
> He fathers-forth whose beauty is past change...
> (Gerard Manley Hopkins, "Pied Beauty")

In the same way, we are accessible multiple readings, so that we become, like St. Paul, "all things to all people" (1 Cor 9:22). This delight in difference is the manifestation of joy, which is a grace of the Fourth Week. As a eucharistic preface for Easter tells us, it is "the joy of the resurrection [that] renews the whole world."

The entry into joy is not for spiritual self-gratification but for the renewal of creation, where we labour with the Beloved as together we do the Father's will. Ignatius does not impose what we have to do. He leaves it up to each of us to discern what we can do lovingly. He merely points out in the contemplation "Leaning into Love" that after considering what God does for each of us, and shares with each of us, "I will reflect upon myself, and consider…what I ought to offer the Divine Majesty, that is, all I possess and myself with it" (#234). How we do this depends on our situation and abilities. As we share in the life and the gifts of the divine, we also share in a care for creation. All this arises from our loving response to the mercy of God. As we take up this care, we discover that we are interconnected with all levels of creation and connected with the Creator. We live our lives only in the context of this connectedness, and not from some intrinsic nature, since at this level of commitment, the self is "empty," or at best a trace, or gesture of the Divine Mercy to the world.

This work we do in the spirit of gratitude and joyful service, and the dialogue with the world, becomes possible from this perspective. As the Spiritual Exercises of St. Ignatius show, when we accept and live out the orientation to love – our basic desire – this creates open spaces, possibilities and transformations through which the Word becomes flesh in our time and in our bodies.

Appendix A: List of 52 Films Used

About Schmidt
The Adventures of Priscilla, Queen of the Desert
A.I.: Artifical Intelligence
Almost Famous
American Beauty
Bend it Like Beckham
Big Fish
Billy Elliot
Bowling for Columbine
The Butcher Boy
Chicago
Crouching Tiger, Hidden Dragon
Dancer in the Dark
The End of the Affair
Far from Heaven
The Full Monty
Gossip
Harry Potter and the Chamber of Secrets
Hearts in Atlantis
The Hours
Igby Goes Down
The Insider
Insomnia
Iron Giant
A Knight's Tale
Koyaanisqatsi

L.A. Confidential
Life as a House
The Lord of the Rings
Lost in Translation
Magnolia
Matchstick Men
The Matrix
The Mission
Monsoon Wedding
Moulin Rouge
Mystic River
O Brother, Where Art Thou?
Pleasantville
Punch-Drunk Love
The Quiet American
Requiem for a Dream
The Royal Tenenbaums
Romeo + Juliet
Shrek
Stand by Me
The Sweet Hereafter
The Thin Red Line
Three Kings
The Truman Show
2001: A Space Odyssey
White Oleander

Appendix B: Adapting the Exercises for Shorter Periods of Time

While this book presents a way of doing the Spiritual Exercises over an extended period of time — a wonderful way to integrate spiritual growth into daily life — the authors realize that some individuals or groups may wish to use some of the material in a shorter period of time. There are many ways to do so; the following are just a few suggested ways using both the retreat format and the theme format.

1: A Day of Recollection – Becoming Aware that We Are Loved

The Second Week: 18th Exercise – *Life as a House* (pp. 190–194); and

The Fourth Week: 1st Exercise – *Billy Elliot* (pp. 257–261).

2: A Weekend Retreat

The First Week: 2nd Exercise – *Stand by Me* (pp. 49–53);

The First Week: 8th Exercise – *Adventures of Priscilla, Queen of the Desert* (pp. 88–91); and

The First Week: 6th Exercise – *The Thin Red Line* (pp. 80–83).

3: A Five-day Retreat

The Fourth Week: 6th Exercise – *A Knight's Tale* (pp. 283–288);

The First Week: 3rd Exercise – *Magnolia* (pp. 54–68);

The Second Week: 9th Exercise – *Punch-Drunk Love* (pp. 144–148);

The Second Week: 5th Exercise – *The Hours* (pp. 122–126); and

The Fourth Week: 7th Exercise – *The Truman Show* (pp. 289–303).

4: An Eight-day Retreat

The First Week: 7th Exercise – *Big Fish* (pp. 84–87);

The First Week: Theme – 2001: *A Space Odyssey* (pp. 32–35);

The Second Week: 7th Exercise – *Harry Potter and the Chamber of Secrets* (pp. 132–139);

The Second Week: 14th Exercise – *The End of the Affair* (pp. 168–173);

The Third Week: 2nd Exercise – *The Quiet American* (pp. 208–212);

The Third Week: 9th Exercise – *About Schmidt* (pp. 243–247);

The Fourth Week: 8th Exercise – *Bend It Like Beckham* (pp. 294–298); and

The Fourth Week: 10th Exercise – *Crouching Tiger, Hidden Dragon* (pp. 304–308)

AGMV Marquis

MEMBRE DE SCABRINI MEDIA

Québec, Canada
2004